THE TRUE AND INVISIBLE ROSICRUCIAN ORDER

TREE OF LIFE DIAGRAM

THE TRUE AND INVISIBLE ROSICRUCIAN ORDER

An Interpretation
of the
Rosicrucian Allegory

and

An Explanation
of the
Ten Rosicrucian Grades

Paul Foster Case

SAMUEL WEISER, INC.

York Beach, Maine

First published in 1985 by
Samuel Weiser, Inc.
Box 612
York Beach, Maine 03910-0612

First paper edition, 1989

99 98 97 96 95 94
10 9 8 7 6 5 4 3

Library of Congress Cataloging-in-Publication Data
Case, Paul Foster
      The true and invisible Rosicrucian Order.
      Includes index.
      1. Rosicrucians.   I. Title.
BF1623.R7C3   1985   135'.43   85-3185

ISBN 0-87728-709-0
MV

Printed in the United States of America

The paper used in this publication meets the minimum requirements of the American National Standard for Permanence of
Paper for Printed Library Materials Z39.48-1984.

TABLE OF CONTENTS

LIST OF ILLUSTRATIONS

LIST OF ILLUSTRATIONS

A NOTE TO THE READER

This work by Dr. Paul Foster Case (1884-1954) is completely self-revealing as to its source and its intention. We who are the Stewards of the Order that he founded according to the instructions of his teacher ask only that you listen to its message with your hearts as well as your minds.

In a lifetime of service and teaching, the original manuscript for *The True and Invisible Rosicrucian Order* was expanded and revised several times. The present work represents the full maturation of his understanding of the subject.

If, at the completion of this volume, you should be desirous of pursuing further the mysteries and disciplines of the Tarot and the Tree of Life, you may contact:

Builders of the Adytum, Ltd.
Dept. TIRO
5101 North Figueroa Street
Los Angeles, CA 90042

Also by Paul Foster Case

Dr. Case's linkage with the Mystery School tradition is also indicated by several of his other works, which include:

THE TAROT, A KEY TO THE WISDOM OF THE AGES
THE MAGICAL LANGUAGE
THE BOOK OF TOKENS
THE GREAT SEAL OF THE UNITED STATES
THE MASONIC LETTER G
THE NAME OF NAMES

PART ONE

THE ROSICRUCIAN ALLEGORY

THE BEGINNINGS OF ROSICRUCIANISM

OSICRUCIANISM CAME INTO public notice early in the seventeenth century. The initial Rosicrucian manifesto, *Fama Fraternitatis*, was first issued as a manuscript and circulated among German occultists about the year 1610. It elicited several responses prior to the publication of the first printed edition at Cassel in 1614. In 1615 there was another printing, this time at Frankfurt-am-Main, and the same year and place seem to have seen the appearance of the second manifesto, *Confessio Fraternitatis.* Dutch translations of both books came out in 1615, and by 1617 four editions of the German version had been published at Frankfurt. Others followed in the years immediately succeeding.

The *Fama* and the *Confessio* tell the story of the Order and its mysterious Founder and set forth its principles and philosophy. These tiny volumes aroused great interest. Alchemists and Qabalists, magicians and astrologers, kept the German presses busy with letters and essays addressed to the mysterious Brothers. For six or seven years the Rosicrucian question engaged the minds and pens of European occultists.

In 1616 was published another little book, *The Chymical Marriage of Christian Rosenkreutz.* To it may be traced the supposition that the Order was founded by a man named Christian Rosenkreutz or by one who adopted this name as a mystical title. Years later, the authorship of *The Chymical Marriage* was acknowledged by Johann Valentine Andreae, who said it was a revision of an alchemical romance he had written in his youth, long before the publication of the *Fama* and the *Confessio.*

The style of this work is altogether different from that of the two manifestoes. Andreae seems to have revamped *The Chymical Marriage* in the hope of profiting by the excitement stirred up by the two manifestoes. He was interested in schemes for universal reformation and may have planned to establish a secret society of his own. Like many others of that period, he was familiar with the literature of alchemy, and his romance shows that he had more than a smattering of occult learning. Yet the assertion that Andreae founded Rosicrucianism has no support in fact. Arthur Edward Waite has dealt adequately with this question in his *Brotherhood of the Rosy Cross*.[1] We share his conviction that Andreae had no part in the authorship of either the *Fama* or the *Confessio*. Toward the close of his life Andreae ridiculed Rosicrucianism, and he probably never understood its real objectives. His book, however, roused great interest and fixed in the uncritical occult mind the mistaken notion that the Order was founded by a man named Christian Rosenkreutz. Even this name has been transformed by the carelessness that seems to be characteristic of a certain type of professed occultist. So little do some who write glibly about Rosicrucianism know of its origins that one writer tells his Theosophical readers the Founder's name was Christian Rosencrans.

In 1652 Thomas Vaughan edited and published an English translation of the two manifestoes. In his preface, Vaughan declares that the translation is the work of an "unknown hand," and says, "The copy was communicated to me by a gentleman more learned than myself." This version was reprinted by Arthur Edward Waite in his *Real History of the Rosicrucians*, published in 1887. The same version, duly accredited to Waite's history, was printed in a manual issued in 1927 for members of the Societas Rosicruciana in America. By 1937 the Rosicrucian Fellowship at Oceanside, California, made belated acknowledgment of the existence of the manifestoes in a series of magazine articles.

Possibly these manifestoes also may have been included in the miscellany of things Rosicrucian and otherwise printed at Quakertown, Pennsylvania, by Dr. R. Swinburne Clymer. Dr. Clymer offers voluminous documentary evidence that he is Grand Master of the Rosicrucian Order established by Pascal Beverly Randolph in 1856. Such as it is, few will seek to dispute this claim, for Randolph's titles to serious consideration may be judged by his own words. In *Eulis* (edition of 1874, page 47) he writes: "Very nearly all which I have given as Rosicrucian originated in my own soul."

Among various publications of the society designated by the initials AMORC, there was a pamphlet entitled *Fama Fraternitatis*, but it was a strictly modern production, having no connection with the original manifesto apart from the title.

The Rosicrucian name flourishes because few persons who are attracted by the magic name and fame of the Order have any knowledge of the first published utterances of the Fraternity. Thus, it seems wise to reprint the English translation again. The manifestoes are short. Their anonymous authors needed but few words to say their say, but no person properly qualified to understand these little books could have mistaken their true purport. On the other hand, they were so written that, as they put it, they would not "move gross wits." Nor have they, from that day to this.

---

[1] Arthur Edward Waite, *Brotherhood of the Rosy Cross* (London: William Rider & Son, 1924).

Minds duly and truly prepared can grasp what is hidden behind their story of the Order, and to help serious students of occultism to such understanding is the purpose of our work.

Our title is intended to intimate that the *Fama* and the *Confessio* were written by members of an actual fraternity that conceals itself from all who are incompetent to share its aims and participate in its work. This fraternity is not an organized society like the Freemasons. One may not join it by making application for membership, paying entrance fees and dues, and passing through ceremonies. The Rosicrucian Order is like the old definition of the city of Boston: it is a state of mind. One *becomes* a Rosicrucian: one does not *join* the Rosicrucians. The manifestoes make this clear, as will be shown hereafter.

The Order is designated as being invisible by the manifestoes themselves. It does not come in corporate form before the world, because by its very nature it cannot. True Rosicrucians know one another, nevertheless. Their means of recognition cannot be counterfeited nor betrayed, for these tokens are more subtle than the signs and passwords of ordinary secret societies.

Let none suppose that because the Rosicrucian Order is invisible it is composed of discarnate human intelligences. Neither are its members supermen inhabiting a region vaguely designated by the term "higher planes." The Order is invisible because it has no external organization. It is not composed of invisible beings. Its members are men and women incarnate on earth in physical bodies. They are invisible to ordinary eyes because the minds behind those eyes cannot recognize the marks of a true Rosicrucian.

To say this is, of course, to repudiate any and all pretensions of societies claiming to be direct historical successors to the authors of the original Rosicrucian manifestoes. From what is written in the *Fama* and the *Confessio*, the only possible conclusion is that every claim to historical descent, every assertion that this or that association is "the original Order," must be judged invalid.

Probably some of these pretensions are made in good faith. There is reason to believe that societies calling themselves Rosicrucian were organized shortly after the publication of the manifestoes, and it is possible that they have continued in some form to this day.

Here and there in America and Europe are societies working according to the Rosicrucian pattern explained in this book. Their members do not believe the societies, as such, to be the Rosicrucian Order. Having learned from the manifestoes the distinguishing marks of a Rosicrucian, these persons know that insofar as they exhibit these marks they are links in the chain of the invisible Order. They understand also that the membership of even the societies that falsely claim historic connection may include some who are true Rosicrucians, just as there are other persons in various parts of the world who merit this designation even though they may never have heard of the Order. How this can be will, we trust, become evident to the unprejudiced reader who follows carefully the argument of this book.

These conclusions are not offered as unsupported opinions. They are presented as being the inevitable consequences of unequivocal statements in the *Fama* and the *Confessio*. Unless one knows the contents of these initial announcements of the Rosicrucian Order, he can form no clear notion of what Rosicrucianism really is. Thus, the first step in our exposition is to present the manifestoes themselves. We use the translation published by Thomas Vaughan, because careful comparison with early German editions shows the substantial accuracy of this "work of an unknown hand." The spelling has been modernized, but we have made no other alterations.

CHAPTER II

FAMA FRATERNITATIS
OF THE MERITORIOUS ORDER OF THE ROSY CROSS

ADDRESSED TO THE LEARNED IN GENERAL
AND THE GOVERNORS OF EUROPE

EEING THE ONLY WISE AND merciful God in these latter days hath poured out so richly His mercy and goodness to mankind, whereby we do attain more and more to the perfect knowledge of His Son Jesus Christ and of Nature, that justly we may boast of the happy time wherein there is not only discovered unto us the half part of the world, which was hitherto unknown and hidden, but He hath also made manifest unto us many wonderful and never-heretofore seen works and creatures of Nature, and, moreover, hath raised men, indued with great wisdom, which might partly renew and reduce all arts (in this our spotted and imperfect age) to perfection, so that man might thereby understand his own nobleness and worth, and why he is called *Microcosmus*, and how far his knowledge extendeth in Nature.

Although the rude world herewith will be but little pleased, but rather smile and scoff thereat; also the pride and covetousness of the learned is so great, it will not suffer them to agree together; but were they united, they might out of all those things which in our age God doth so richly bestow on us, collect *Librum Naturae*, or, a Perfect Method of all Arts. But such is their opposition that they still keep, and are loath to leave, the old course, esteeming Porphyry, Aristotle, and Galen, yea, and that which hath but a mere show of learning, more than the clear and manifested Light and Truth. Those, if they were now living, with much joy would leave their erroneous doctrines; but, here is too much weakness for such a great work. And although in Theology, Medicine and Mathematics, the truth doth oppose itself, nevertheless, the old Enemy, by his subtlety and craft, doth show himself in hindering every good purpose by his instruments and contentious, wavering people.

To such an intention of a general reformation, the most godly and highly illuminated Father, our Brother, C.R.C., a German, the chief and original of our Fraternity, hath much and long time laboured, who, by reason of his poverty (although descended of noble parents), in the fifth year of his age was placed in a cloister, where he had learned indifferently the Greek and Latin tongues, and (upon his own earnest desire and request), being yet in his growing years, was associated to a Brother, P.A.L., who had determined to go to the Holy Land. Although this Brother died in Cyprus, and so never came to Jerusalem, yet our Brother C.R.C. did not return, but shipped himself over, and went to Damascus, minding from thence to go to Jerusalem. But by reason of the feebleness of his body he remained still there, and by his skill in medicine he obtained much favour with the Turks, and in the meantime he became acquainted with the Wise Men of Damcar in Arabia, and beheld the great wonders they wrought, and how Nature was discovered unto them.

Hereby was that high and noble spirit of Brother C.R.C. so stirred up, that Jerusalem was not so much now in his mind as Damcar; also he could not bridle his desires any longer, but made a bargain with the Arabians that they should carry him for a certain sum of money to Damcar.

He was but of the age of sixteen years when he came thither, yet of strong Dutch constitution. There the Wise Men received him not as a stranger (as he himself witnesseth), but as one whom they had long expected; they called him by his name, and showed him other secrets out of his cloister, whereat he could not but mightily wonder.

He learned there better the Arabian tongue, so that the year following he translated the Book M (Liber Mundi) into good Latin, which he afterwards brought with him. This is the place where he did learn his Medicine and his Mathematics, whereat the world hath much cause to rejoice, if there were more love and less envy.

After three years he returned again with good consent, shipped himself over Sinus Arabicus into Egypt, where he remained not long, but only took better notice there of the plants and creatures. He sailed over the whole Mediterranean Sea for to come unto Fez, where the Arabians had directed him.

It is a great shame unto us that wise men, so far remote the one from the other, should not only be of one opinion, hating all contentious writings, but also be so willing and ready, under the seal of secrecy, to impart their secrets to others. Every year the Arabians and Africans do send to one another, inquiring of one another out of their arts, if haply they had found out some better things, or if experience had weakened their reasons. Yearly there came something to light whereby the Mathematics, Medicine, and Magic (for in those are they of Fez most skillful) were amended. There is nowadays no want of learned men in Germany. Magicians, Cabalists, Physicians and Philosophers were there but more love and kindness among them, or that the most part of them would not keep their secrets close only to themselves.

At Fez he did get acquaintance with those which are commonly called the Elementary inhabitants, who revealed unto him many of their secrets, as we Germans likewise might gather together many things if there were the like unity and desire of searching out secrets amongst us.

Of those at Fez he often did confess, that their Magic was not altogether pure, and also that their Cabala was defiled with their Religion; but, notwithstanding, he knew how to make good use of the same, and found still more better grounds for this faith, altogether agreeable with the harmony of the whole world, and wonderfully impressed in all periods of time. Thence proceedeth that fair Concord, that as in every several kernel is contained a whole good tree and fruit, so likewise is included in the little body of man, the whole great world, whose religion, policy, health, members, nature, language, words, and works, are agreeing, sympathizing, and in equal tune and melody with God, Heaven, and Earth; and that which is disagreeing with them is error, falsehood, and of the devil, who alone is the first, middle, and last cause of strife, blindness, and darkness in the world. Also, might one examine all and several persons upon the earth, he should find that which is good and right is always agreeing within itself, but all the rest is spotted with a thousand erroneous conceits.

After two years Brother R.C. departed the city Fez, and sailed with many costly things into Spain, hoping well, as he himself had so well and profitably spent his time in his travel, that the learned of Europe would highly rejoice with him, and begin to rule and order all their studies according to these sure and sound foundations. He therefore conferred with the learned in Spain, shewing unto them the errors of our arts, and how they might be corrected and from whence they should gather the true *Inditia* of the times to come, and wherein they ought to agree with those things that are past; also how the faults of the Church and the whole *Philosophia Moralis* were to be amended. He shewed them new growths, new fruits, and beasts, which did concord with old philosophy, and prescribed them new *Axiomata*, whereby all things might be fully restored. But it was to them a laughing matter, and being a new thing unto them, they feared that their great name would be lessened if they should now again begin to learn, and acknowledge their many years' errors, to which they were accustomed, and wherewith they had gained them enough. Whoso loveth unquietness, let him be reformed (they said). The same song was also sung to him by other nations, the which moved him the more because it happened to him contrary to his expectation, being then ready bountifully to impart all his arts and secrets to the learned, if they would have but undertaken to write the true and infallible *Axiomata*, out of all the faculties, sciences, and arts, and whole nature, as that which he knew would direct them, like a globe or circle, to the only middle point and *centrum*, and (as it is usual among the

Arabians) it should only serve to the wise and learned for a rule, that also there might be a society in Europe which might have gold, silver, and precious stones, sufficient for to bestow them on kings for their necessary uses and lawful purposes, with which society such as be governors might be brought up for to learn all that which God hath suffered men to know, and thereby be enabled in all times of need to give their counsel unto those that seek it, like the Heathen Oracles.

Verily we must confess that the world in those days was already big with those great commotions, labouring to be delivered of them, and did bring forth painful, worthy men, who brake with all force through darkness and barbarism, and left us who succeeded to follow them. Assuredly they have been the uppermost point in *Trygono igneo*, whose flame should now be more and more brighter, and shall undoubtedly give to the world the last light.

Such a one likewise hath Theophrastus been in vocation and callings, although he was none of our Fraternity, yet, nevertheless hath he diligently read over the Book M, whereby his sharp ingenium was exalted; but this man was also hindered in his course by the multitude of the learned and wise-seeming men, that he was never able peaceably to confer with others of the knowledge and understanding he had of Nature. And therefore in his writings he rather mocked these busybodies, and doth not altogether show them what he was; yet, nevertheless, there is found in him well grounded the aforementioned Harmonia, which without doubt he had imparted to the learned, if he had not found them rather worthy of subtle vexation than to be instructed in greater arts and sciences. He thus with a free and careless life lost his time, and left unto the world their foolish pleasures.

But that we do not forget our loving Father, Brother R.C., he after many painful travels, and his fruitless true instructions, returned again into Germany, which he heartily loved, by reason of the alterations which were shortly to come, and of the strange and dangerous contentions. There, though he could have bragged with his art, but especially of the transmutations of metals, yet did he esteem more Heaven, and men, the citizens thereof, than all vainglory and pomp.

Nevertheless, he built a fitting and neat habitation, in the which he ruminated his voyage and philosophy, and reduced them together in a true memorial. In this house he spent a great time in the mathematics, and made many fine instruments, *ex omnibus hujus artis partibus*, whereof there is but little remaining to us, as hereafter you shall understand.

After five years came again into his mind the wished-for Reformation; and in regard to it he doubted of the aid and help of others, although he himself was painful, lusty, and unwearisome; howsoever he undertook, with some few adjoined with him, to attempt the same. Wherefore he desired to that end to have out of his first cloister (to which he bare a great affection) three of his brethren, Brother G.V., Brother I.A., and Brother

I.O., who had some more knowledge of the arts than at that time many others had. He did bind those three unto himself, to be faithful, diligent, and secret, as also to commit carefully to writing all that which he should direct and instruct them in, to the end that those which were to come, and through especial revelation should be received into this Fraternity, might not be deceived in the least syllable and word.

After this manner began the Fraternity of the Rosy Cross—first by four persons only, and by them was made the magical language and writing, with a large dictionary, which we yet daily use to God's praise and glory, and do find great wisdom therein. They made also the first part of the Book M, but in respect that that labour was too heavy, and the unspeakable concourse of the sick hindered them, and also while his new building (called *Sancti Spiritus*) was now finished, they concluded to draw and receive yet others more into their Fraternity. To this end was chosen Brother R.C., his deceased father's brother's son; Brother B., a skillful painter; G.G.; and P.D., their secretary, all Germans except I.A., so in all they were eight in number, all bachelors and of vowed virginity, by whom was collected a book or volume of all that which man can desire, wish, or hope for.

Although we do now freely confess that the world is much amended within an hundred years, yet we are assured that our *Axiomata* shall immovably remain unto the world's end, and also the world in her highest and last age shall not attain to see anything else; for our Rota takes her beginning from that day when God spake *Fiat* and shall end when He shall speak *Pereat;* yet God's clock striketh every minute, where ours scarce striketh perfect hours. We also steadfastly believe, that if our Brethren and Fathers had lived in this our present and clear light, they would more roughly have handled the Pope, Mahomet, scribes, artists, and sophisters, and showed themselves more helpful, not simply with sighs and wishing of their end and consummation.

When now these eight Brethren had disposed and ordered all things in such manner, as there was not now any need of any great labour, and also that every one was sufficiently instructed and able perfectly to discourse of secret and manifest philosophy, they would not remain any longer together, but, as in the beginning they had agreed, they separated themselves into several countries, because that not only their *Axiomata* might in secret be more profoundly examined by the learned, but that they themselves, if in some country or other they observed anything, or perceived some error, they might inform one another of it.

Their agreement was this:

First, That none of them should profess any other thing than to cure the sick, and that gratis.

Second, None of the posterity should be constrained to wear one certain kind of habit, but therein to follow the custom of the country.

Third, That every year, upon the day C., they should meet together at the house *Sancti Spiritus,* or write the cause of his absence.

Fourth, Every Brother should look about for a worthy person who, after his decease, might succeed him.

Fifth, The word R.C. should be their seal, mark, and character.

Sixth, The Fraternity should remain secret one hundred years.

These six articles they bound themselves one to another to keep; five of the Brethren departed, only the Brethren B. and D. remained with the Father, Brother R.C., a whole year. When these likewise departed, then remained by him his cousin and Brother I.O., so he hath all the days of his life with him two of his Brethren. And although as yet the Church was not cleansed, nevertheless, we know that they did think of her, and what with longing desire they looked for. Every year they assembled together with joy, and made a full resolution of that which they had done. There must certainly have been great pleasure to hear truly and without invention related and rehearsed all the wonders which God hath poured out here and there throughout the world. Every one may hold it out for certain, that such persons as were sent, and joined together by God and the Heavens, and chosen out of the wisest of men as have lived in many ages, did live together above all others in highest unity, greatest secrecy, and most kindness one towards another.

After such a most laudable sort they did spend their lives, but although they were free from all diseases and pain, yet, notwithstanding, they could not live and pass their time appointed by God. The first of this Fraternity which died, and that in England, was I. O., as Brother C. long before had foretold him; he was very expert, and well learned in Cabala, as his Book H witnesseth. In England he is much spoken of, and chiefly because he cured a young Earl of Norfolk of the leprosy. They had concluded, that, as much as possibly could be, their burial place should be kept secret, as at this day it is not known unto us what is become of some of them, yet everyone's place was supplied with a fit successor. But this we will confess publicly by these presents, to the honour of God, that what secret soever we have learned out of the Book M, although before our eyes we behold the image and pattern of all the world, yet are there not shewn unto us our misfortunes, nor hour of death, the which is known only to God Himself, Who thereby would have us keep in continual readiness. But hereof more in our Confession, where we do set down thirty-seven reasons wherefore we now do make known our Fraternity, and proffer such high mysteries freely, without constraint or reward. Also we do promise more gold than both the Indies can bring to the King of Spain, for Europe is with child, and shall bring forth a strong child, who shall stand in need of a great godfather's gift.

After the death of I.O., Brother R.C. rested not, but, as soon as he could, called the rest together, and then, as we suppose, his grave was made, although hitherto we (who were the latest) did not know when our loving

Father R.C. died, and had no more but the bare names of the beginners, and all their successors to us. Yet there came into our memory a secret, which, through dark and hidden words and speeches of the hundred years, Brother A., the successor of D. (who was of the last and second row of succession, and had lived amongst many of us), did impart unto us of the third row and succession; otherwise we must confess, that after the death of the said A., none of us had in any manner known anything of Brother C.R., and of his first fellow-brethren, than that which was extant of them in our philosophical *Bibliotheca*, amongst which our *Axiomata* was held for the chiefest, *Rota Mundi* for the most artificial, and *Protheus* for the most profitable. Likewise, we do not certainly know if these of the second row have been of like wisdom as the first, and if they were admitted to all things.

It shall be declared hereafter to the gentle reader not only what we have heard of the burial of Brother R.C., but also it shall be made manifest publicly, by the foresight, sufferance, and commandment of God, whom we most faithfully obey, that if we shall be answered discreetly and Christian-like, we will not be ashamed to set forth publicly in print our names and surnames, our meetings, or anything else that may be required at our hands.

Now, the true and fundamental relation of the finding out of the high-illuminated man of God, Fra. C.R.C., is this: After that A. in *Gallia Narbonensi* was deceased, there succeeded in his place our loving Brother N.N. This man, after he had repaired unto us to take the solemn oath of fidelity and secrecy, informed us *bona fide*, that A. had comforted him in telling him that this Fraternity should ere long not remain so hidden, but should be to the whole German nation helpful, needful, and commendable, of the which he was not anywise in his estate ashamed. The year following, after he had performed his school right, and was minded now to travel, being for that purpose sufficiently provided with Fortunatus' purse, he thought (he being a good architect) to alter something of his building, and to make it more fit. In such renewing, he lighted upon the Memorial Table, which was cast of brass, and containeth all the names of the Brethren, with some few other things. This he would transfer into a more fitting vault, for where or when our Brother R.C. died, or in what country he was buried, was by our predecessors concealed and unknown to us. In this table stuck a great nail somewhat strong, so that when it was with force drawn out it took with it an indifferent big stone out of the thin wall or plastering of the hidden door, and so, unlooked for, uncovered the door, whereat we did with joy and longing throw down the rest of the wall and cleared the door, upon which was written in great letters

Post CXX Annos Patebo

with the year of the Lord under it. Therefore we gave God thanks, and let it rest that same night, because first we would overlook our *Rota*—but we refer ourselves again to the Confession, for what we here publish is done for the help of those that are worthy, but to the unworthy, God willing, it will be small profit. For like as our door was after so many years wonderfully discovered, also there shall be opened a door to Europe (when the wall is removed), which doth already begin to appear, and with great desire is expected of many.

In the morning following we opened the door, and there appeared to our sight a vault of seven sides and seven corners, every side five foot broad and the height of eight feet. Although the sun never shined in this vault, nevertheless it was enlightened with another sun, which had learned this from the sun, and was situated in the upper part in the center of the ceiling. In the midst, instead of a tombstone, was a round altar, covered with a plate of brass, and thereon this engraven:

A. C. R. C. *Hoc universi compendium unius mihi sepulchrum feci*

Round about the first circle or brim stood,

Jesus mihi omnia.

In the middle were four figures, inclosed in circles, whose circumscription was

        1. *Nequaquam Vacuum.*
        2. *Legis Jugum.*
        3. *Libertas Evangelii.*
        4. *Dei Gloria Intacta.*

This is all clear and bright, as also the seventh side and the two heptagons. So we kneeled down altogether, and gave thanks to the sole wise, sole mighty, and sole eternal God, who hath taught us more than all men's wits could have found out, praised be His Holy Name. This vault we parted into three parts, the upper part or ceiling, the wall or side, the ground or floor. Of the upper part you shall understand no more at this time but that it was divided according to the seven sides in the triangle which was in the bright center; but what therein is contained you (that are desirous of our Society) shall, God willing, behold the same with your own eyes. Every side or wall is parted into ten squares, every one with their several figures and sentences, as they are truly shewn and set forth *concentratum* here in our book. The bottom again is parted in the triangle, but because therein is described the power and rule of the Inferior Governors, we leave to manifest the same, for fear of the abuse by the evil and ungodly world. But those that are provided and stored with the Heavenly Antidote, do without fear or hurt, tread on and bruise the head of the old and evil serpent, which this our age is well fitted for. Every side or wall had a door for a chest, wherein there lay divers things, especially all our books, which otherwise we had, besides the *Vocabulario* of Theophrastus Paracelsus of Hohenheim, and these which daily unfalsifieth we do participate. Herein also we found his *Itinerarium* and *Vita*, whence this relation for the most part is taken. In another chest were looking-glasses of divers virtues, as also in other places were little bells, burning lamps, and chiefly wonderful artificial songs; generally all was done to that end, that if it should happen, after many hundred years, the Fraternity should come to nothing, they might by this only vault be restored again.

Now, as yet we had not seen the dead body of our careful and wise Father, we therefore removed the altar aside; then we lifted up a strong plate of brass, and found a fair and worthy body, whole and unconsumed, as the same is here lively counterfeited, with all the ornaments and attires. In his hand he held a parchment called T, the which next unto the Bible is our greatest treasure, which ought not to be delivered to the censure of the world. At the end of this book standeth this following *Elogium*.

Granum pectori Jesu insitum

C.R.C. ex nobili atque splendida Germaniae R.C. familia oriundus, vir sui seculi divinis revelationibus, subtilissimis imaginationibus, indefessis laboribus ad coelestia atque humana mysteria; arcanave admissus postquam suam (quam Arabico et Africano itineribus collejerat) plus quam regiam, atque imperatoriam Gazam suo seculo nondum convenientem, posteritati eruendam costodivisset et jam suarum Artium, ut et nominis, fides ac conjunctissimos heredes instituisset, mundum minutum omnibus motibus magno illi respondentem fabricasset hocque tandem preteritarum, praesentium, et futurarum, rerum compendio extracto, centenario major, non morbo (quem ipse nunquam corpore expertus erat, nunquam alio infestare sinebat) ullo pellente sed Spiritis Dei evocante, illuminatum animam (inter Fratrum amplexus et ultima oscula) fidelissimo Creatori Deo reddidisset, Pater delicitissimus, Frater suavissimus, praeceptor fidelissimus, amicus integerimus, a suis ad 12 annos hic absconditus est.*

Underneath they had subscribed themselves:

1. *Fra.* I.A. *Fra.* C.H. *electione Fraternitatis caput.*
2. *Fra.* G.V.M.P.C.
3. *Fra.* F.R.C., *Junior haeres S. Spiritus.*
4. *Fra.* F.B.M.P.A., *Pictor et Architectus.*
5. *Fra.* G.G.M.P.I., *Cabalista.*

---

*See page 131 for translation.

Secundi Circuli.

1. *Fra.* P.A. *Successor, Fra.* I.O., *Mathematicus.*
2. *Fra.* A. *Successor, Fra.* P.D.
3. *Fra.* R. *Successor Patris* C.R.C., *cum Christo triumphantis.*

At the end was written;

Ex Deo nascimur, in Jesu morimur, per Spiritum Sanctum reviviscimus.

At that time was already dead Brother I.O. and Brother P.D., but their burial place, where is it to be found? We doubt not but our Fra. Senior hath the same, and some special thing laid in earth, and perhaps hidden, like our Father C. We also hope that this our example will stir up others more diligently to enquire after their names (which we have therefore published), and to search for the place of their burial; the most part of them, by reason of their practice and medicine, are yet known and praised among very old folks; so might perhaps our Gaza be enlarged, or, at least, be better cleared.

Concerning *Minutum Mundum,* we found it kept in another little altar, truly more finer than can be imagined by any understanding man, but we will leave him undescribed until we shall be truly answered upon this our true-hearted *Fama.* So we have covered it again with the plates, and set the altar thereon, shut the door and made it sure with all our seals. Moreover, by instruction, and command of our *Rota,* there are come to sight some books, among which is contained M (which were made instead of household care by the praiseworthy M.P.). Finally, we departed one from the other, and left the natural heirs in possession of our jewels. And so we do expect the answer and judgment of the learned and unlearned.

Howbeit we know after a time there will now be a general reformation, both of divine and human things, according to our desire and the expectation of others; for it is fitting, that before the rising of the Sun there should appear and break forth Aurora, or some clearness, or divine light in the sky. And so, in the meantime, some few, which shall give their names, may join together, thereby to increase the number and respect of our Fraternity, and make a happy and wished for beginning of our *Philosophical Canons,* prescribed to us by our Brother R.C., and be partakers with us of our treasures (which never can fail or be wasted) in all humility and love, to be eased of this world's labours, and not walk so blindly in the knowledge of the wonderful works of God.

But that also every Christian may know of what Religion and belief we are, we confess to have the knowledge of Jesus Christ (as the same now in these last days, and chiefly in Germany, most clear and pure is professed, and is nowadays cleansed and void of all swerving people, heretics, and false prophets), in certain and noted countries maintained, defended, and propagated. Also we use two Sacraments, as they are instituted with all Forms and Ceremonies of the first and renewed Church. In *Politia* we acknowledge the Roman Empire and *Quartam Monarchiam* for our Christian head, albeit we know what alterations be at hand, and would fain impart the same with all our hearts to other godly learned men, notwithstanding our handwriting which is in our hands, no man (except God alone) can make it common, nor any unworthy person is able to bereave us of it. But we shall help with secret aid this, so good a cause, as God shall permit or hinder us. For our God is not blind, as the heathen's Fortuna, but is the Churches' ornament and the honour of the Temple. Our Philosophy also is not a new invention, but as Adam after his fall hath received it, and as Moses and Solomon used it, also it ought not much to be doubted of, or contradicted by other opinions, or meanings; but seeing the truth is peaceable, brief, and always like herself in all things, and especially accorded with by *Jesus in omnia parte* and all members, and as He is the true image of the Father, so is she His image, so it shall not be said, This is true according to Philosophy, but true according to Theology; and wherein Plato, Aristotle, Pythagoras, and others did hit the mark, and wherein Enoch, Abraham, Moses, Solomon, did excel, but especially wherewith that wonderful book the Bible agreeth. All that same concurreth together, and maketh a sphere or globe whose total parts are equidistant from the center, as hereof more at large and more plain shall be spoken in Christianly Conference.

But now concerning, and chiefly in this our age, the ungodly and accursed gold-making, which hath gotten so much the upper hand, whereby under colour of it, many runagates and roguish people do use great villainies, and cozen and abuse the credit which is given them; yea, nowadays men of discretion do hold the transmutation of metals to be the highest point and *fastigium* in philosophy. This is all their intent and desire, and that God would be more esteemed by them and honoured which could make great store of gold, the which with unpremeditate prayers they hope to obtain of the all-knowing God and searcher of all hearts; but we by these presents publicly testify, that the true philosophers are far of another mind, esteeming little the making of gold, which is but a *parergon*, for besides that they have a thousand better things. We say with our loving Father C.R.C., *Phy. aurum nisi quantum aurum,* for unto him the whole nature is detected; he doth not rejoice that he can make gold, and that, as saith Christ, the devils are obedient unto him, but is glad that he seeth the Heavens open, the angels of God ascending and descending, and his name written in the book of life (in den Boecke des Levens).

Also we testify that, under the name of *Chymia*, many books and pictures are set forth in *Contumeliam gloriae Dei*, as we will name them in their due season, and will give to the pure-hearted a catalogue or register of them. We pray all learned men to take heed of this kind of books, for the Enemy never resteth, but soweth his weeds till a stronger one doth root them out.

So, according to the will and meaning of *Fra.* C.R.C., we his brethren request again all the learned in Europe who shall read (sent forth in five languages) this our *Fama* and *Confessio,* that it would please them with good deliberation to ponder this our offer, and to examine most nearly and sharply their arts, and behold the present time with all diligence, and to declare their mind, either *communicatio consilio,* or *singulatim* by print. And although at this time we make no mention either of our names or meetings, yet nevertheless everyone's opinion shall surely come to our hands, in what language so ever it be, nor anybody shall fail, whoso gives but his name, to speak with some of us, either by word of mouth, or else, if there be some let, in writing. And this we say for a truth, that whosoever shall earnestly, and from his heart, bear affection unto us, it shall be beneficial to him in goods, body, and soul; but he that is false-hearted, or only greedy of riches, the same first of all shall not be able in any manner of wise to hurt us, but bring himself to utter ruin and destruction. Also our building, although one hundred thousand people had very near seen and beheld the same, shall forever remain untouched, undestroyed, and hidden to the wicked world.

Sub umbra alarum tuarum, Jehova.

CHAPTER III

THE CONFESSION
OF THE ROSICRUCIAN FRATERNITY

ADDRESSED TO THE LEARNED OF EUROPE

ERE GENTLE READER, YOU shall find incorporated in our Confession thirty-seven reasons of our purpose and intention, the which according to thy pleasure thou mayest seek out and compare together, considering within thyself if they be sufficient to allure thee. Verily, it requires no small pains to induce any one to believe what doth not yet appear, but when it shall be revealed in the full blaze of day, I suppose we should be ashamed of such questionings. And as we do now securely call the Pope Antichrist, which was formerly a capital offence in every place, so we know certainly that what we here keep secret we shall in the future thunder forth with uplifted voice, the which, reader, with us desire with all thy heart that it may happen most speedily.

Fratres R.C.

Confessio Fraternitatis R.C. ad Eruditos Europae.

Chapter I

Whatsoever you have heard, O mortals, concerning our Fraternity by the trumpet sound of the *Fama R.C.*, do not either believe it hastily, or willfully suspect it. It is Jehovah who, seeing how the world is falling to decay, and near its end, doth hasten it again to its beginning, inverting the course of Nature, and so what heretofore hath been sought with great pains and daily labour He doth lay open now to those thinking of no such thing, offering it to the willing and thrusting it upon the reluctant, that it may become to the good that which will smooth the troubles of human life and break the violence of unexpected blows of Fortune, but to the ungodly that which will augment their sins and their punishments.

Although we believe ourselves to have sufficiently unfolded to you in the *Fama* the nature of our Order, wherein we follow the will of our most excellent Father, nor can by any be suspected of heresy, nor of any attempt against the commonwealth, we hereby do condemn the East and the West (meaning the Pope and Mahomet) for their blasphemies against our Lord Jesus Christ, and offer to the chief head of the Roman Empire our prayers, secrets, and great treasures of gold. Yet we have thought good for the sake of the learned to add somewhat more to this, and make a better explanation, if there be anything too deep, hidden, and set down over dark, in the *Fama*, or for certain reasons altogether omitted, whereby we hope the learned will be more addicted unto us, and easier to approve our counsel.

Chapter II

Concerning the amendment of philosophy, we have (as much as at this present is needful) declared that the same is altogether weak and faulty; nay, whilst many (I know not how) allege that she is sound and strong, to us it is certain that she fetches her last breath.

But as commonly even in the same place where there breaketh forth a new disease, nature discovereth a remedy against the same, so amidst so many infirmities of philosophy there do appear the right means, and unto our Fatherland sufficiently offered, whereby she may become sound again, and new or renovated may appear to a renovated world.

No other philosophy have we than that which is the head of all the faculties, sciences and arts, the which (if we behold our age) containeth much of Theology and Medicine, but little of Jurisprudence; which searcheth Heaven and earth with exquisite analysis, or, to speak briefly thereof, which doth sufficiently manifest the Microcosmus man, whereof if some of the more orderly in the number of the learned shall respond to our fraternal invitation, they shall find among us far other and greater wonders than those they heretofore did believe, marvel at, and profess.

Chapter III

Wherefore, to declare briefly our meaning hereof, it becomes us to labour carefully that the surprise of our challenge may be taken from you, to shew plainly that such secrets are not lightly esteemed by us, and not to spread an opinion abroad among the vulgar that the story concerning them is a foolish thing. For it is not absurd to suppose many are overwhelmed with the conflict of thought which is occasioned by our unhoped graciousness, unto whom (as yet) be unknown the wonders of the sixth age, or who, by reason of the course of the world, esteem the things to come like unto the present, and, hindered by the obstacles of their age, live no other wise in the world than as men blind, who, in the light of noon, discern nothing only by feeling.

Chapter IV

Now concerning the first part, we hold that the meditations of our Christian Father on all subjects which from the creation of the world have been invented, brought forth, and propagated by human ingenuity, through God's revelation, or through the service of Angels or spirits, or through the sagacity of understanding, or through the experience of long observation, are so great, that if all books should perish, and by God's almighty sufferance all writings and all learning should be lost, yet posterity will be able thereby to lay a new foundation of sciences, and to erect a new citadel of truth; the which perhaps would not be so hard to do as if one should begin to pull down and destroy the old, ruinous building, then enlarge the forecourt, afterwards bring light into the private chambers, and then change the doors, staples, and other things according to our intention.

Therefore it must not be expected that newcomers shall attain at once all our mighty secrets. They must proceed step by step from the smaller to the greater, and must not be retarded by difficulties.

Wherefore should we not freely acquiesce in the only truth than seek through so many windings and labyrinths, if only it had pleased God to lighten unto us the sixth Candelabrum? Were it not sufficient for us to fear neither hunger, poverty, diseases, nor age? Were it not an excellent thing to live always so as if you had lived from the beginning of the world, and should still live to the end thereof? So to live in one place that neither the people which dwell beyond the Ganges could hide anything, nor those which live in Peru might be able to keep secret their counsels from thee? So to read in one only book as to discern, understand, and remember whatsoever in all other books (which heretofore have been, are now, and hereafter shall come out) hath been, is, and shall be learned out of them? So to sing and play that instead of stony rocks you could draw pearls, instead of wild beasts, spirits, and instead of Pluto you could soften the mighty princes of the world? O mortals, diverse is the counsel of God and your convenience, Who hath decreed at this time to increase and enlarge the number of our Fraternity, the which we with such joy have undertaken, as we have heretofore obtained this great treasure without our merits, yea, without any hope or expectation; the same we purpose with such fidelity to put in practice, that neither compassion nor pity for our own children (which some of us in the Fraternity have) shall move us, since we know that these unhoped for good things cannot be inherited, nor conferred promiscuously.

Chapter V

If there be any body now which on the other side will complain of our discretion, that we offer our treasures so freely and indiscriminately, and do not rather regard more the godly, wise, or princely persons than the common people, with him we are in nowise angry (for the accusation is not without moment), but withal we affirm that we have by no means made common property of our arcana, albeit they resound in five languages within the ears of the vulgar, both because, as we well know, they will not move gross wits, and because the worth of those who shall be accepted into our Fraternity will not be measured by their curiosity, but by the rule and pattern of our revelations. A thousand times the unworthy may clamour, a thousand times present themselves, yet God hath commanded our ears that they should hear none of them, and hath so compassed us about with His clouds that unto us, His servants, no violence can be done; wherefore now no longer are we beheld by human eyes unless they have received strength borrowed from the eagle.

For the rest, it hath been necessary that the *Fama* should be set forth in everyone's mother tongue, lest those should be defrauded of the knowledge thereof, whom (although they be unlearned) God hath not excluded from the happiness of this Fraternity, which is divided into degrees; as those which dwell at Damcar, who have a far different political order from the other Arabians; for there do govern only understanding men, who, by the king's permission, make particular laws, according to which example the government shall also be instituted in Europe (according to the description set down by our Christianly Father), when that shall come to pass which must precede, when our Trumpet shall resound with full voice and with no prevarications of meaning, when, namely, those things of which a few now whisper and darken with enigmas, shall openly fill the earth, even as after many secret chafings of pious people against the pope's tyranny, and after timid reproof, he with great violence and by a great onset was cast down from his seat and abundantly trodden under foot, whose final fall is reserved for an age when he shall be torn to pieces with nails, and a final groan shall end his ass's braying, the which, as we know, is already manifest to many learned men in Germany, as their tokens and secret congratulations bear witness.

Chapter VI

We could here relate and declare what all the time from the year 1378 (when our Christian Father was born) till now hath happened, what alterations in the world he hath seen these one hundred and six years of his life, what he left to be attempted after his happy death by our Fathers and by us, but brevity, which we do observe, will not permit at this present to make rehearsal of it; it is enough for those who do not despise our declaration to have touched upon it, thereby to prepare the way for their more close association and union with us. Truly, to whom it is permitted to behold, read, and thenceforward teach himself those great characters which the Lord God hath inscribed upon the world's mechanism, and which He repeats through the mutations of Empires, such an one is already ours, though as yet unknown to himself; and as we know he will not neglect our invitation, so, in like manner, we abjure all deceit, for we promise that no man's uprightness and hopes shall deceive him who shall make himself known to us under the seal of secrecy and desire our familiarity. But to the false and to impostors, and to those who seek other things than wisdom, we witness by these presents publicly, we cannot be betrayed unto them to our hurt, nor be known to them without the will of God, but they shall certainly be partakers of that terrible commination spoken of in our *Fama*, and their impious designs shall fall back upon their own heads, while our treasures shall remain untouched, till the Lion shall arise and exact them as his right, receive and employ them for the establishment of his kingdom.

Chapter VII

One thing should here, O mortals, be established by us, that God hath decreed to the world before her end, which presently thereupon shall ensue, an influx of truth, light, and grandeur, such as He commanded should accompany Adam from Paradise, and sweeten the misery of man: Wherefore there shall cease all falsehood, darkness, and bondage, which little by little, with the great globe's revolution, hath crept into the arts, works, and governments of men, darkening the greater part of them. Thence hath proceeded that innumerable diversity of persuasions, false-hoods, and heresies, which make choice difficult to the wisest men, seeing on the one part they were hindered by the reputation of philosophers and on the other by the facts of experience, which if (as we trust) it can be once removed, and instead thereof a single and self-same rule be instituted, then there will indeed remain thanks unto them which have taken pains therein, but the sum of so great a work shall be attributed to the blessedness of our age.

As we now confess that many high intelligences by their writings will be a great furtherance unto this Reformation which is to come, so do we by no means arrogate to ourselves this glory, as if such a work were only imposed on us, but we testify with our Saviour Christ, that sooner shall the stones rise up and offer their service, then there shall be any want of executors of God's counsel.

Chapter VIII

God, indeed, hath already sent messengers which should testify His will, to wit, some new stars which have appeared in *Serpentarius* and *Cygnus*, the which powerful signs of a Great Council shew forth how for all things which human ingenuity discovers, God calls upon His hidden knowledge, as likewise the Book of Nature, though it stands open truly before all eyes, can be read or understood by only a very few.

As in the human head there are two organs of hearing, two of sight, and two of smell, but only one of speech, and it were vain to expect speech from the ears, or hearing from the eyes, so there have been ages which have seen, others which have heard, others again that have smelt and tasted. Now, there remains that in a short and swiftly approaching time honour should likewise be given to the tongue, that what formerly saw, heard, and smelt shall finally speak, after the world shall have slept away the intoxication of her poisoned and stupefying chalice, and with an open heart, bare head, and naked feet shall merrily and joyfully go forth to meet the sun rising in the morning.

Chapter IX

These characters and letters, as God hath here and there incorporated them in the Sacred Scriptures, so hath He imprinted them most manifestly on the wonderful work of creation, on the heavens, on the earth, and on all beasts, so that as the mathematician predicts eclipses, so we prognosticate the obscurations of the church, and how long they shall last. From these letters we have borrowed our magic writing, and thence made for ourselves a new language, in which the nature of things is expressed, so that it is no wonder that we are not so eloquent in other tongues, least of all in this Latin, which we know to be by no means in agreement with that of Adam and Enoch, but to have been contaminated by the confusion of Babylon.

Chapter X

But this also must by no means be omitted, that, while there are yet some eagle's feathers in our way, the which do hinder our purpose, we do exhort to the sole, only, assiduous, and continual study of the Sacred Scriptures, for he that taketh all his pleasure therein shall know that he hath prepared for himself an excellent way to come into our Fraternity, for this is the whole sum of our Laws, that as there is not a character in that great miracle of the world which has not a claim on the memory, so those are nearest and likest unto us who do make the Bible the rule of their life, the end of all their studies, and the compendium of the universal world, from whom we require not that it should be continually in their mouth, but that they should appropriately apply its true interpretation to all ages of the world, for it is not our custom so to debase the divine oracle, that while there are innumerable expounders of the same, some adhere to the opinions of their party, some make sport of Scripture as if it were a tablet of wax to be indifferently made use of by theologians, philosophers, doctors, and mathematicians. Be it ours rather to bear witness, that from the beginning of the world there hath not been given to man a more excellent, admirable, and wholesome book than the Holy Bible; Blessed is he who possesseth it, more blessed is he who reads it, most blessed of all is he who truly understandeth it, while he is most like to God who both understands and obeys it.

Chapter XI

Now, whatsoever hath been said in the *Fama*, through hatred of impostors, against the transmutation of metals and the supreme medicine of the world, we desire to be so understood, that this so great gift of God we do in no manner set at naught, but as it bringeth not always with it the knowledge of Nature, while this knowledge bringeth forth both that and an infinite number of other natural miracles, it is right that we be rather earnest to attain to the knowledge of philosophy, nor tempt excellent wits to the tincture of metals sooner than to the observation of Nature. He must needs be insatiable to whom neither poverty, disease, nor danger can any longer reach, who, as one raised above all men, hath rule over that which doth anguish, afflict, and pain others, yet will give himself again to idle things, will build, make wars, and domineer, because he hath gold sufficient, and of silver an inexhaustible fountain. God judgeth far otherwise, who exalteth the lowly, and casteth the proud into obscurity; to the silent he sendeth his angels to hold speech with them, but the babblers he driveth into the wilderness, which is the judgment due to the Roman impostor who now poureth forth his blasphemies with open mouth against Christ, nor yet in the full light, by which Germany hath detected his caves and sub-terranean passages, will abstain from lying, that thereby he may fulfill the measure of his sin, and be found worthy of the axe. Therefore, one day it will come to pass, that the mouth of this viper shall be stopped, and his triple crown shall be brought to naught, of which things more fully when we shall have met together.

Chapter XII

For conclusion of our Confession we must earnestly admonish you, that you cast away, if not all, yet most of the worthless books of pseudo chymists, to whom it is a jest to apply the Most Holy Trinity to vain things, or to deceive men with monstrous symbols and enigmas, or to profit by the curiosity of the credulous; our age doth produce many such, one of the greatest being a stage-player, a man with sufficient ingenuity for imposi-tion; such doth the enemy of human welfare mingle among the good seed, thereby to make the truth more difficult to be believed, which in herself is simple and naked, while falsehood is proud, haughty, and coloured with a lustre of seeming godly and human wisdom. Ye that are wise eschew such books, and have recourse to us, who seek not your moneys, but offer unto you most willingly our great treasures. We hunt not after your goods with invented lying tinctures, but desire to make you partakers of our goods. We do not reject parables, but invite you to the clear and simple explanation of all secrets; we seek not to be received by you, but call you unto our more than kingly houses and palaces, by no motion of our own, but (lest you be ignorant of it) as forced thereto by the Spirit of God, commanded by the testament of our most excellent Father, and impelled by the occasion of this present time.

Chapter XIII

What think you, therefore, O mortals, seeing that we sincerely confess Christ, execrate the pope, addict ourselves to the true philosophy, lead a worthy life, and daily call, intreat, and invite many more unto our Fraternity, unto whom the same Light of God likewise appeareth? Consider you not that, having pondered the gifts which are in you, having measured your understanding in the Word of God, and having weighed the imperfections and inconsistencies of all the arts, you may at length in the future deliberate with us upon their remedy, cooperate in the work of God, and be serviceable to the constitution of your time? On which work these profits will follow, that all those goods which Nature hath disposed in every part of the earth shall at one time and altogether be given to you, *tanquam in centro solis et lunae*. Then shall you be able to expel from the world all those things which darken human knowledge and hinder action, such as the vain (astronomical) epicycles and eccentric circles.

Chapter XIV

You, however, for whom it is enough to be serviceable out of curiosity to any ordinance, or who are dazzled by the glistering of gold, or who, though now upright, might be led away by such unexpected great riches into an effeminate, idle, luxurious, and pompous life, do not disturb our sacred silence by your clamour, but think that although there be a medicine which might fully cure all diseases, yet those whom God wishes to try or chastise shall not be abetted by such an opportunity, so that if we were able to enrich and instruct the whole world, and liberate it from innumerable hardships, yet we shall never be manifested unto any man unless God should favour it, yea, it shall be so far from him who thinks to be a partaker of our riches against the will of God that he shall sooner lose his life in seeking us, than attain happiness by finding us.

Fraternitas R.C.

CHAPTER IV

THE INNER MEANING OF THE MANIFESTOES

BEFORE WE ENDEAVOR TO interpret the *Fama* and the *Confessio*, it may be well to bring forward some evidence that they really have an inner meaning. This evidence is furnished by the plain language of both books. It is abundant and unmistakable.

Chapter V of the *Confessio* says: "We affirm that we have by no means made common property of our arcana, albeit they resound in five languages within the ears of the vulgar, because, as we well know, they will not move gross wits." The same chapter speaks of a time "when our Trumpet shall resound with full voice and with no prevarications of meaning, when, namely, those things of which a few now whisper and darken with enigmas, shall openly fill the earth."

The introductory paragraph to the *Confessio* is equally explicit. "We know certainly that *what we here keep secret* we shall in future thunder forth with uplifted voice" (italics ours). Again, the opening sentence of the first chapter runs: "Whatsoever you have heard, O mortals, concerning our Fraternity by the trumpet sound of the *Fama R.C.*, do not either believe it hastily, or willfully suspect it." This intimates the presence of a hidden meaning behind the surface of the letter. The hint is amplified by these words in Chapter XII of the *Confessio*: "We do not reject parables."

Both the *Fama* and the *Confessio* are addressed to a particular class of persons, the *erudite* of Europe. *Erudite* means literally, "away from rudeness." Some etymologists believe the Latin root has an affinity with a noun signifying "a lump of metal." This would make the word particularly appropriate, because the authors of the manifestoes, as Hermetic philosophers, must have been accustomed to thinking of enlightened men as purified and transmuted metals. Here is also a resemblance to the Masonic symbolism that likens an uninitiated, untrained man to a rough ashlar, or "rude stone," in contrast to a perfected initiate, who is typified by a perfect ashlar, or "dressed stone." Apart from these implications of etymology, *erudite* designates a particular class of persons, those well versed in books, familiar with languages, and acquainted with antiquities.

In the early seventeenth century many Europeans of this class were familiar with a system of occult philosophy that provides keys to the inner meaning of the Rosicrucian allegories. That system was expressed in cryptic language. For more than two centuries it had exerted great influence on European thought, and when the *Fama* and the *Confessio* were published, they reflected that influence. This philosophy was the Secret Wisdom of Israel, the Hebrew Qabalah.

Among notable students of this esoteric doctrine were Raymond Lully (died 1315), John Reuchlin (1455-1522), John Picus de Mirandola (1463-1505), Henry Cornelius Agrippa (1486-1535), Theophrastus Paracelsus (1493-1541), William Postel (1510-1581), Heinrich Khunrath (1560-1601), Robert Fludd (1574-1637), Jacob Boehme (1575-1624), Athanasius Kircher (1601-1680), and Thomas Vaughan (1621-1665). Elias Ashmole, who founded the Ashmolean Museum and was active in the Masonic Fraternity, was also a student of this Hebrew wisdom, and to this day the rituals and lectures of Freemasonry are full of traces of the same secret doctrine.

In his short essay on the Qabalah, C.D. Ginsburg says:

> A system of religious philosophy, or more properly of theosophy, which has not only exercised for hundreds of years an extraordinary influence upon the mental development of so shrewd a people as the Jews, but has captivated the minds of some of the greatest thinkers in Christendom in the sixteenth and seventeenth centuries, claims the greatest attention. These men, after restlessly searching for a scientific system which should disclose to them the "deepest depths" of the Divine nature, and show them the real tie which binds all things together, found the cravings of their minds satisfied by this theosophy.[1]

The *Fama* says the instruction received by Brother C.R. at Fez included Qabalah, and intimates that he was sufficiently versed in Hebrew Wisdom to be able to detect certain errors in the Mohammedan Qabalah, which derives from the Hebrew. The *Fama* speaks also of the Qabalistic attainments of Brother I.O., one of the first four members of the Fraternity, who was "very expert, and well learned in Cabala, as his book called H witnesseth." Again, in the list of names appended to the Latin *Elogium* in the *Fama*, the fifth is that of Fra. G.G., whose initials are followed by his title, *Cabalista*.

Both the *Fama* and the *Confessio* describe Rosicrucian philosophy in precisely the terms Qabalists use in speaking of the history and nature of

---

[1]Christian D. Ginsburg, *The Kabbalah* (London: Routledge & Kegan Paul, Ltd., 1925), 83.

their esoteric doctrine. The *Fama* says: "Our philosophy also is not a new invention, but as Adam after his fall hath received it, and as Moses and Solomon used it, also it ought not much to be doubted of." The same book says this philosophy is that "wherein Enoch, Abraham, Moses, Solomon, did excel, but especially wherewith that wonderful book the Bible agreeth."

The *Confessio* amplifies this by saying: "No other philosophy have we than that which is the head of all the faculties, sciences and arts, the which (if we behold our age) containeth much of Theology and Medicine, but little of Jurisprudence; which searcheth heaven and earth with exquisite analysis, or, to speak briefly thereof, which doth sufficiently manifest the Microcosmus man."

Compare these extracts from the manifestoes with what Qabalists assert concerning their philosophy:

> The Kabbalah was first taught by God Himself to a select company of angels, who formed a theosophic school in Paradise. After the fall the angels most graciously communicated this heavenly doctrine to the disobedient child of earth, to furnish the protoplasts with the means of returning to their pristine nobility and felicity. From Adam it passed over to Noah, and then to Abraham, the friend of God, who emigrated with it to Egypt, where the patriarch allowed a portion of this mysterious doctrine to ooze out. It was in this way that the Egyptians obtained some knowledge of it, and the other Eastern nations could introduce it into their philosophical systems. Moses, who was learned in all the wisdom of Egypt, was first initiated into it in the land of his birth but became most proficient in it during his wanderings in the wilderness, when he not only devoted to it the leisure hours of the whole forty years, but received lessons in it from one of the angels. By the aid of this mysterious science the lawgiver was enabled to solve the difficulties which arose during his management of the Israelites, in spite of the pilgrimages, wars and the frequent miseries of the nation. He covertly laid down the principles of this secret doctrine in the first four books of the Pentateuch, but withheld them from Deuteronomy. This constitutes the former the man, and the latter the woman. Moses also initiated the seventy elders into the secrets of this doctrine, and they again transmitted them from hand to hand. Of all who formed the unbroken line of tradition, David and Solomon were most initiated into the Kabbalah.[2]

---

[2]Ginsburg, *The Kabbalah*, 84-85.

The Qabalah contains many references to alchemy, notably the little treatise entitled *Aesch Metzareph,* or *Purifying Fire.* The tradition that alchemy is an Egyptian art, given to the world by Hermes Trismegistus (identified with Enoch by many alchemical writers), was well known to the erudite of Europe in 1614. Indeed, many alchemists recognized the close relation of their art to the Qabalah, as did the writer of *The Glory of the World,* who says:

> Know, then, that Almighty God first delivered this Art to our Father, Adam, in Paradise. For as soon as He had created him, and set him in the Garden of Eden, He imparted it to him in the following words: "Adam, here are two things: that which is above is volatile, that which is below is fixed. These two things contain the whole mystery. Observe it well, and make not the virtue that slumbers therein known to thy children; for these two things shall serve thee, together with all other created things under heaven, and I will lay at thy feet all the excellence and power of this world, seeing that thou thyself art a small world."[3]

The doctrine of the "small world," or microcosm, comes direct from the Qabalah. Paracelsus appears to have been first to introduce the term *microcosm* into the literature of alchemy, but long before his day others had elaborated on the idea it expresses, namely, that in man cosmic forces and laws are operative in a miniature representation of their work in the great universe, or macrocosm. Hence, it is noteworthy that the Rosicrucians defined their philosophy as one that sums up the meaning of the word *Microcosmus.* In the first paragraph of the *Fama* they announced the purpose of the Fraternity as being to enable man "to understand his own nobleness and worth, and why he is called *Microcosmus,* and how far his knowledge entendeth in Nature."

Alchemical books are written in cryptic language. This language, moreover, is basically the same, whether the book be ancient or modern. We have reason for thinking that the alchemical secret language is not precisely the same as the "magical language" mentioned in the manifestoes, although the latter abounds in alchemical and Qabalistic terms. According to the alchemists themselves, their peculiar terminology has veiled meanings that, they assert, dawn gradually on the understanding of a diligent reader (provided he is aided by Divine inspiration) if he has patience to go over the books again and again. A seeker for light on alchemy must address himself to prolonged study, but God's grace gives the light itself. Even so, the Rosicrucian manifestoes declare their words will not move gross wits, and that persons greedy, lustful, impatient, and desirous of power to domineer

---

[3]Robert Valens Rugl, *The Glory of the World* (York Beach, ME: Samuel Weiser, Inc., 1974), 203.

over others will neither grasp the true import of the books nor make contact with the Fraternity.

Now since the *Fama* and *Confessio* distinctly declare themselves to have been written by alchemists and Qabalists, is it not reasonable to expect them to have been composed in the same cryptic, allegorical style one finds in other books written by such men? May it not be that if we employ the keys of Qabalistic and alchemical interpretation to these manifestoes we shall discover a meaning different from what appears on the surface, a meaning that agrees with the essential doctrines of other Qabalists and alchemists? We may at least make a trial of this method, to find out whether or not the Rosicrucian cipher decodes into an intelligible message when unlocked by these Qabalistic keys.

Among the latter, the most important is the key of Gematria. The word *Gematria* is a late Hebrew noun, probably derived from the Greek *geometria* (geometry). It designates a system of biblical interpretation used by orthodox Hebrew Rabbis, long before the Qabalah was written down. This method of interpretation is foreign to modern ways of thinking, but there can be no question that it was not only known but used daily by most of the erudite of Europe in the seventeenth century.

The basis for Gematria is the fact that neither Greeks nor Hebrews had numeral symbols other than the letters of their respective alphabets. Thus it came about at some remote period of antiquity, when all arithmetical calculation and all expression of numbers employed the letters of the alphabet, that somebody noticed that some numbers made intelligible words. From this primitive discovery it was a short step to spelling words in such a way that the word itself should be an aid to memory, enabling the initiate to recall the mathematical formula corresponding either to the succession of the letters or to their total value. If we bear in mind the fact that the beginnings of all scientific knowledge and of all philosophy were among the priesthoods of India, Egypt, Israel, and Greece, it is not difficult to understand why their sacred literatures contain special spellings and phrasings that throw light on one another because they have the same numeral values.

Fantastic as this may seem to the modern mind, precisely this method was employed in composing some parts of the Hebrew Scriptures, in selecting names and epithets for Christ in the New Testament, and in such writings as those of Philo Judaeus, Plutarch, and Plato and in the books of the Gnostics. Furthermore, the formulas concealed by these words and phrases were often numbers that had to do with the measurement of space, or geometry, sometimes as applied to astronomy, sometimes to music, and especially to the art of architecture.

It must be remembered that geometry was considered to be a science revealing deep mysteries of God. Nor will the reader forget the reverence paid to numbers in the writings of Greek philosophers. Most modern mathematicians scoff at these old conceptions, but the time may

Table 1. Table of Numerical Values

Hebrew Characters	English Equivalents	Number	Greek Characters	English Equivalents	Number	Roman Letters	Number in Qabalah Simplex
א	A	1	A α	a	1	A	1
ב	B	2	B β	b	2	B	2
ג	G	3	Γ γ	g	3	C	3
ד	D	4	Δ δ	d	4	D	4
ה	H	5	E ε	e	5	E	5
ו	V	6	Z ζ	z	7	F	6
ז	Z	7	H η	h	8	G	7
ח	Ch	8	Θ θ	th	9	H	8
ט	T	9	I ι	i	10	I(J)	9
י	I	10	K κ	k	20	L	10
כ	K	20	Λ λ	l	30	M	11
ל	L	30	M μ	m	40	N	12
מ	M	40	N ν	n	50	O	13
נ	N	50	Ξ ξ	ks	60	P	14
ס	S	60	O o	o	70	Q	15
ע	O	70	Π π	p	80	R	16
פ	P	80	P ρ	r	100	S	17
צ	Tz	90	Σ σ ς	s	200	T	18
ק	Q	100	T τ	t	300	V(U)	19
ר	R	200	Υ υ	u	400	X	20
ש	Sh	300	Φ φ	ph	500	Y	21
ת	Th	400	X χ	ch	600	Z	22
ך	K final	500	Ψ ψ	ps	700		
ם	M final	600	Ω ω	O	800		
ן	N final	700					
ף	P final	800					
ץ	Tz final	900					

come when truly enlightened minds may perceive that some of these old notions are not such meaningless superstitions after all.

For our present purpose, the main thing to establish is the fact that in the seventeenth century every member of the special class of persons to whom the *Fama* and the *Confessio* were addressed was familiar with Gematria. Furthermore, they were fully persuaded of the value of biblical interpretations based on this ancient system of combining numbers and letters. They employed it in their endeavors to understand the Scriptures, so as to apply the principles laid down in the sacred oracles to the better direction of their lives. This was true of men who had no particular interest in alchemy and other occult arts. It was even truer for the inner circle that was devoted to such esoteric doctrines. Thus, the principal key to the cryptic writings of seventeenth century occultists is Gematria.

To understand it we must know that every letter of the two biblical alphabets, Hebrew and Greek, has a specific number. In books written during the sixteenth, seventeenth, and eighteenth centuries, a similar system was adapted to the alphabet of the Latin in which the Rosicrucian manifestoes were first written. The accompanying Table 1 on page 34, shows the numeral values of the letters in these three alphabets, together with the system of transliteration we have adopted for giving the original spelling of these words in English characters. This method, as applied to Hebrew and Greek, is not without defects, but as it has been used for many years, especially for the transliteration of Hebrew, we have thought best to adhere to it.

Every Hebrew and Greek word is a number, which is the sum of the values of the separate letters. This rule applies also to many Latin words and phrases used by alchemists and occult philosophers during the seventeenth and eighteenth centuries.

For Qabalists, identity of number between two words or two phrases is a signal that these words and phrases explain one another or have some affinity of meaning. Often, but not always, the single digit that sums up this numeral value may be taken as a clue to the hidden significance. Thus, the Hebrew word AChD, *achad* (unity), is composed of letters whose values are 1, 8, and 4, adding to 13. Another word, AHBH, *ahebah* (love), is composed of letters whose values are 1, 5, 2, and 5, adding also to 13. The reduction of 13 to its "least number" by adding the digits 1 and 3 produces 4, and because 4 is the number of the Hebrew letter Daleth, the various occult meanings of that letter are understood by Qabalists to provide clues to the affinity between *achad* and *ahebah*, unity and love.

By applying Gematria to an analysis of the Rosicrucian manifestoes we expect to bring to light meanings hitherto hidden. This will help us to rend the veil of allegory that hides the true import of the *Fama* and the *Confessio* behind an outer semblance of preposterous fiction. Such an analysis is offered in the chapters following.

It is by no means complete. These two little books contain a profound esoteric instruction, and there remain not a few "gross wits" to whom we should be sorry to impart it. Yet we believe this to be the only explanation of these texts that is based on the canons of interpretation indicated by the manifestoes themselves as being keys to their hidden meaning. It is, moreover, more complete and orderly than the expositions given in earlier versions of this book.

To sum up then, our aim is to set before the reader evidence that the original Rosicrucian pamphlets contain an allegory of initiation that must have been understood perfectly by many Qabalists and alchemists of that period. Michael Maier read the riddle and wrote at length concerning the true purposes of the Fraternity. So did Robert Fludd and Thomas Vaughan. Elias Ashmole incorporated the substance of a whole paragraph from the *Fama* in the introduction to his *Theatrum Chemicum Brittanicum*, a collection of alchemical texts by English adepts.

That many persons were deceived by the literal sense of the *Fama* and the *Confessio* must be conceded. A tremendous excitement was produced by their appearance. Pamphlets attacking and defending them poured from the presses of that period. Persons who believed themselves worthy of admission to the Fraternity published letters in the newspaper or brought out essays advancing their claims to recognition.

It has been asserted that none of these applicants for admission to the Order received an answer. Such an assertion, on the face of it, is one that cannot possibly be proved. One would have to know all the persons who made application to the anonymous authors of the manifestoes. Many were disappointed, and after a few years the Rosicrucian excitement died down.

Yet there is evidence that some, such as Vaughan, Fludd, Ashmole and Maier, felt full assurance that they understood the *Fama* and the *Confessio.* Others might be named, but to do so would be to burden these pages with more than they can conveniently carry. Let me then repeat what was said in the first chapter. The Rosicrucian Order is a reality. He who is duly and truly prepared to enter it will do so no matter where he may live. It is active in the affairs of men today, as it has been since the very beginning of human society, and will continue to be active throughout the future. It has a vital message for us now, and in this transition period of human history, when all values are being questioned and all men of vision are beginning to realize that the establishment of a new world order is imminent, the principles of genuine Rosicrucian philosophy may shed light on and help to solve the grave problems confronting all of us.

CHAPTER V

OUR FATHER AND BROTHER, C.R.C.

 COMMON ERROR IS THE opinion that the Rosicrucian Order was founded by an actual person named Christian Rosenkreutz. The alchemical romance *The Chymical Marriage of Christian Rosenkreutz*, as we have said, is responsible for this mistaken notion. Johann Valentine Andreae wrote the first draft of this story at the age of sixteen, and a remarkable performance it was, considering the age of the author and the nature of the subject. Arthur Edward Waite thinks that when the Rosicrucian controversy was at its height, this juvenile composition was dressed up by Andreae "with a few Rosicrucian tags and tie-ups, to express his detestation of the *Fama,* its claims and all its ways, by making confusion worse confounded in respect of the debate, then raging at its height."[1] Certain it is that the manifestoes were composed by another mind than that which reveals itself in Andreae's alchemical fantasy. Certain also is that the hero of *The Chymical Marriage* must not be confused with the central figure of the Rosicrucian allegory. Christian Rosenkreutz, the child of Andreae's imagination, is not "Our Brother and Father, C.R.C."

No names of persons appear in the manifestoes. Initials only designate the Founder of the Order and his associates. Yet the *Fama* distinctly says it *has* published the names of the Brethren. In the paragraph immediately following the long description of the vault, we read:

> At that time was already dead, Brother I.O. and Brother P.D., but their burial place, where is it to be found? We doubt not but our *Fra. Senior* hath the same, and some special thing laid in earth, and perhaps hidden, like our Father C. We also hope that this our example will stir up others more diligently to inquire after their names

---

[1]Arthur Edward Waite, *The Brotherhood of the Rosy Cross* (London: William Rider & Son, 1924), 209.

(which we have therefore published), and to search for the place of their burial; the most part of them, by reason of their practice and medicine, are yet known and praised among the very old folks; so might perhaps our Gaza be enlarged, or, at least, better cleared.

Here is an excellent example of cryptic writing. On the surface it seems to refer to two deceased members of the Order. Yet a little farther on it becomes evident that more than two are indicated, as we see from the words "the most part of them... are yet known by very old folks." What is meant is that the "names" of the Brethren, which are actually published under the "blind" of initials, are names known to very ancient peoples, because they are actually words, or else suggest words, to be found in Hebrew and in Greek. Like Father C. they are hidden. By diligent inquiry, according to a method known to the same "very old folks," the buried names will be revealed.

This method is the long-established letter-number system of the Qabalah. The learned of Europe at the time of the publication of the manifestoes would have known this system well and used it in seeking clues to the inner secrets of alchemical books, following it over and over in diligent inquiry. What seems to the modern mind a strange procedure and a strange sort of reasoning was their daily habit of thought. It was by this means they sought to enlarge their *Gaza*. *Gaza* is a word in both Greek and Latin meaning "treasure" or "treasury" and is thus used once in the New Testament. To get at the meaning of the Rosicrucian allegory we must adopt the mental approach used by those Qabalists of Europe. Thus, we shall find the Rosicrucian treasure better cleared, and not until it is cleared may we judge whether it is truly a treasure or simply a piece of antique nonsense, quaintly fashioned but of little worth.

The particular numbers we have noticed, 3, 5, and 8, receive special emphasis in the Rosicrucian texts. Three Brethren are called to help the Founder begin the Order. Elsewhere the fraternity of wise men of all ages is compared to a Trigon of Flame. The authors of the manifestoes say they belong to the third row of succession in the Order. The ceiling of the vault is "parted in the triangle," or subdivided according to a scheme of triangles. So is the floor, and a triangle is in the bright center of the ceiling. All this would have reminded Qabalists of the triads emphasized in Hebrew wisdom, and alchemists would have been familiar with the many repetitions of the number 3 in Hermetic literature.

The numbers 5 and 8 are given prominence in the description of the vault, since every side of that structure is said to be five feet broad and eight feet high. Qabalists would recognize these two numbers as being of paramount importance in their special mysteries. So would alchemists, who would remember that the triad of Sulphur, Mercury, and Salt is fundamental in the Great Work, and that the power of this triad is brought to bear on a pentad, or Five, consisting of the four elements and the Quintessence, so that there is a definite ogdoad in alchemy, as in other forms of arcane instruction.

Qabalists would know that the name Messiah, spelled MShICh in Hebrew, adds up to 358, composed of the digits 3, 5, and 8. Readers possessing some knowledge of Gnostic Christianity would know that since the number of Jesus, written in Greek, is 888 and that of Christ, in the same language, is 1480, Jesus is to Christ as 3 is to 5, because 888:1480 as 3:5. Hence, the Greek word for Christ, 1480, is to the combination Jesus Christ, 2368 by Greek numeration, as 5 is to 8, because 1480:2368 as 5:8. Even exoteric Christianity calls 8 the Dominical number or the special number of Christ. Thus, the grouping of the eight initials of the Founder into three *R*s and five *C*s would hardly have escaped the notice of those at whom the manifestoes were directly aimed.

In the German of that period, *C* represented the sound *K*. The word for *cross*, now spelled *Kreutz* in German, was spelled *creutz* in the *Fama*. Thus, if we turn the initials into Hebrew letters, the *C*s will represent the letter Kaph, and the *R*s will stand for the letter Resh. If we take the initials as representing Greek letters, the *C*s will represent the letter Kappa, and the *R*s will stand for the letter Rho.

By Greek numeration, the five *C*s will represent a total of 100, because Kappa is the number 20. Rho is 100; thus, the three *R*s among the initials add to 300. Hence, the total value of the eight initials, by Greek Gematria, is 400. Since the writers of the manifestoes were Christian Qabalists, we have good reason for supposing they would use Greek, Hebrew, and Latin Gematria in composing their cryptogram.

When the eight initials are taken as Hebrew letters, the result is different, for the numeral value of the letter Resh (corresponding to *R*) is different from that of Rho, the Greek equivalent of *R*. Resh is 200, so that the three *R*s in the ogdoad of initials would represent in Hebrew Gematria the number 600, instead of the Greek 300. The value of the five *C*s would be the same as in Greek, because both Kaph and Kappa are numbered 20. Thus, the Hebrew values of the eight initials would be 600 + 100 = 700.

The Greek numeration would have been very suggestive to a Gnostic Christian. The total, 400, is the number of the Greek letter Upsilon, closely resembling in form our letter *Y;* and this letter is the initial of the noun *huios*, meaning "son." In Gnostic Christianity, therefore, it was a familiar symbol of the second Person of the Trinity, God the Son, viz., Jesus Christ. Erudite readers familiar with the Pythagorean doctrines would have been struck by this correspondence, for the Romans called Upsilon the "Letter of Pythagoras," who is said to have taught that it represented by its two horns the two different paths of virtue and vice, the right branch leading to the former, and the left branch to the latter. Thus, this letter was the symbol of the Way of Life, and here we may remind ourselves that God the Son, or Jesus Christ, who is also represented by the letter Upsilon, is reported to have said: "I am the Way." Finally, alchemists also used this letter to designate their great secret. One text says: "This heavenly dew and its power is contained in everything. It is treated by the world with contempt and rejected by it. As it grows, it becomes divided into two branches, white and red, both springing from one root—Y."

The text from which this is quoted shows the Pythagorean Y, or Upsilon, with the alchemical symbol for Sulphur above the left-hand branch of the letter and the symbol for Mercury above the other branch.

By Greek Gematria, furthermore, the number 400 is that of the word *krios*, meaning "ram." Thus, the number of the Pythagorean letter is also the number of the name of the first sign of the zodiac, *Krios*, or Aries, the ram. Every beginner in astrology knows that the conventional astrological symbol for this sign is exactly the same as the letter Upsilon in the Greek alphabet. This correspondence, moreover, leads to much else, because the Ram, or Aries, is the Lamb of Gnostic Christianity; and we shall find later on that the Hebrew interpretation of this ogdoad of initials gives us a plain intimation that the Founder of the Rosicrucian Order is none other than this same Lamb, and is even named "Lamb" by the Hebrew equivalent to one arrangement of his initials. But we must defer developing this point, though we mention it now to prepare you for what is to come.

Finally, 400 is by Greek Gematria the number of the noun *oinos* (wine). William Jennings Bryan and certain Theosophists to the contrary notwithstanding, the New Testament meaning of this word is fermented wine, not unfermented grape juice. All doubt as to this is removed by the passage in Ephesians 5:18, "Be not drunk with wine." In the Greek original, the word is precisely the same as the one used in recording the miracle of changing water into wine. It is the same in meaning as the Hebrew IIN, *yahyin*, derived from a root meaning "to effervesce." In the parable of the new wine in new wineskins, the inner meaning depends on the fact that wine, in the process of fermentation, produces a gas that would burst an old and fragile wineskin.

Thus, the word *oinos*, in its New Testament usage, represents something able to effect a psychological transformation. From India, right down through the ages, various intoxicating substances have been used to symbolize a power that can take man out of the limitations of his ordinary consciousness. Thus, the counterfeit ecstasy of vinous intoxication becomes the symbol of another "wine," which can lift man out of himself into a higher order of knowing and being. In Christian symbolism, there is a direct connection between wine and blood, which the reader will do well to keep in mind as this interpretation unfolds itself. It links up with the meaning of the Christian sacrament of the Eucharist and the saying of Jesus: "I am the true Vine."

A reader of the manifestoes who had studied Qabalah would notice that 400 is the value of the last letter of the Hebrew alphabet, Tav, which was written in ancient Hebrew as a cross of equal arms, sometimes made like the plus sign + and sometimes like the arithmetical symbol of multiplication, ×. Such a reader, reflecting on Christian esoteric doctrine, would have realized that Tav, as the *last* letter of the Hebrew alphabet, might be taken as the *end* of the Old Testament dispensation, and he would scarcely have failed to notice that the Hebrew alphabet ends with the cross.

In Greek, the noun for cross is *stauros,* and its number is the number of *he gnosis* (the wisdom) and of *he kleronomia hagion* (the sacred inheritance). This would have been particularly significant in connection with the fact that the manifestoes were announcing the work of the Order of the Rose Cross, inasmuch as the Greek word for Rose is *rhodon,* and its number, 294, is the number also of *ekklesia* (Church). Rose Cross, therefore, would mean to the initiated "Church of the Gnosis," and the Gnosis is, in very truth, based on knowledge of the true meaning of the *stauros,* or cross, represented in the Hebrew alphabet by the letter Tav.

In confirmation of this, consider the following statement by the English translator of Jacob Boehme's *Signature of All Things:* "There is One Character by which God has characterized both himself, and all the creatures, and shewn that his presence is in all things; yet so that each creature has its wonder, either of the heavenly or of the earthly mystery. This peculiar mark, shape, and figure, that it may appear as peculiar is the Cross in the sphere and mercurial wheel of nature, which goes through all the three principles."[2]

A Qabalist would also have known that 400 is the numeration of the Hebrew phrase, HNNI ISD BTzIVN ABN, "Behold, I lay in Zion for a foundation a Stone." He would have known, if he were an alchemist, that this ABN, *Ehben* (stone) is the Philosophers' Stone, or Stone of the Wise. And as a Qabalist he would have known that the "wise" are those whose mental state is described by the Hebrew noun MShKIL, *maskeel.* In this connection note that *maskeel* is applied in the Qabalah to the ninth Sephirah—*Yesod,* the Foundation—and that it is the Hebrew equivalent of "the erudite," so that it describes the very type of person to whom the manifestoes were addressed. They were aimed at persons who had some knowledge of the "Stone in Zion," which is described in Isaiah 28:16 as being laid for a *Yesod,* or Foundation. And they would have known that the real secret of this Stone is also the real secret of the Cross, which is the end, and so the fulfillment, of that whole dispensation that is represented symbolically by the 22 letters of the Hebrew alphabet.

Readers who interpreted the ogdoad of initials as Hebrew letters would be struck immediately by their total value of 700. For they would have read in the *Zohar* that 700 is a "complete number," symbolizing a profound mystery of male and female. They would have known that this mystery is what was represented by the rod of Aaron, the pot of manna, and the stones of testimony that Moses put in the ark of the covenant.

---

[2]Jacob Boehme, *The Signature of All Things* (Cambridge and London: Thomas Clarke & Co., Ltd., by arrangement with J.M. Dent & Sons, Ltd., 1969).

Such readers would know also that the contents of the ark were hidden by a golden lid or cover, named KPRTh, *kapporeth* (the mercy seat). The number of *kapporeth* is 700, which is also the number of another word, spelled with the same letters in a different order: PRKTh, *paroketh*. The *paroketh* was the veil of the Holy of Holies. Thus, the *paroketh* hid the ark itself, and the *kapporeth* concealed what was in the ark. Hence, both words indicate occultation, secrecy, and mystery.

The four Hebrew letters composing these words are letters corresponding to Jupiter, Mars, the Sun, and Saturn. These planetary names are given in alchemy to four "metals" that are actually four nerve centers in the trunk of the human body, below the throat. The forces working through these four centers are forces of occultation, because their combined activity results in ordinary human consciousness. Thus, they are the forces that hide the sacred mystery from the eyes of the profane. Yet the same forces are employed by initiates to open the higher vision that enables man to comprehend the true meaning of that same mystery, which is the mystery of his own true nature.

Moreover, 700 is the value of the noun MSRTh, *mawsoreth* (a bond, a yoke). Ezekiel used it when he wrote of the "bond of the covenant." It suggests limitation, and the wise reader will do well to remember what the covenant was that Ezekiel wrote about. From the same letters is composed another word, MSThR, *mistawr*, used in Isaiah 45:3 to designate a secret place containing hidden treasure.

Again, 700 is the number of the proper name Seth, the third son of Adam. The *Zohar* says: "The name Seth symbolizes an end, being composed of the last two letters of the alphabet in regular order, Sh Th." As used here, the word *end* signifies consummation, completion, fulfillment. For alchemists, therefore, Seth would represent the consummation of the Great Work. Thus, it is no surprise to find, among the many names alchemists used to indicate what is called the "white stage" of the Stone—the stage wherein the Stone transmutes base metals into silver—this very name Seth.

Furthermore, the *Zohar* says also: "This name symbolized the reincarnation of the spirit which had been lost, being of the same letters as the word *shath* (set) in the sentence 'God hath replaced for me another seed instead of Abel' [Genesis 4:25]."

Seth replaced Abel and was the first of an unbroken line of ancestors traced by St. Luke in his genealogy of Jesus Christ. Even the exoteric interpreters of Christian doctrine held, and do still, that Abel was the antetype of Jesus. When the New Testament came to be written in Greek, the Gnostics who prepared the text were careful to select words that by their numeration would preserve the secrets of the arcane wisdom. So to the central figure of the New Testament they gave names and epithets whose numbers are clues to the inner mystery. Every one of the more important titles and epithets of Jesus Christ is a multiple of 37, the number of the name Abel. Gnostic Christians would have known this in the year 1614, just as we know it today.

Again, one of the commonest devices in Christian symbolism is the monogram of Christ. This is the monogram that Constantine placed on his standard, or labarum. The Church uses this symbol in innumerable ways. It is almost as familiar as the cross, of which indeed it is a variant. This monogram is composed of the first two letters of the Greek noun *Christos.* These letters are Chi and Rho, and their numbers are 600 and 100. Note that in this particular connection the very same numbers are the result of adding the values of the three letters Resh and the five letters Kaph, which are the Hebrew equivalents of the letters *R* and *C.* Thus, the three Hebrew *R*s add up to the number of a letter having a close affinity in sound with the Hebrew Kaph, the Greek letter Chi. The five *C*s add up to the number of a letter that is the same in sound and meaning as the Hebrew letter Resh, although its number is different. It is as if the Greek values were a transposition, or reversal, of the Hebrew. Here we may point out that the fundamental Christian attitude is an exact reversal of exoteric Judaism. Furthermore, the fundamental practial counsel of the esoteric Christian doctrine is all summed up in the one word *Reversal,* of which more presently.

Even a tyro in Qabalah would have known also that 700 is the value sometimes, but not always, assigned to the letter Nun when this letter is placed at the end of a word. Nun is one of five Hebrew letters that always have a different *form* when they come at the end of a word, and often a different numeral value. Thus, the fact that the eight initials used in speaking of the hero of the Rosicrucian allegory have Hebrew values that add to the *final* value of Nun would be a clue not likely to be missed by anyone deserving to be included among erudite Europeans in 1614.

The authors of the *Fama* proclaim themselves in no uncertain terms as having "the knowledge of Jesus Christ." This knowledge is by no means mere exoteric Lutheranism, as Mr. Waite seemed to believe. It is a true Gnosis, having a direct bearing on the welfare of the individual man and woman and on the development of a more perfect social order. The erudite for whom these manifestoes were written were persons whose reading and study had prepared them for initiation into the deeper mysteries of the Gnosis. The members of the Invisible Order were seeking to get in touch with such persons. They even knew that there were some outside the official circle of the instituted mysteries who were nevertheless actually members of the Order, even though unknown to themselves. And there were others who were ripened by their studies to the point where they could pick up the clues given in the *Fama* and the *Confessio,* even though they might not have entered fully into the circle of initiates.

Persons of this latter class would be familiar with the fact that the great symbol of the early Christians was a fish. They would know that by drawing this fish on the ground, where it could be instantly erased, members of the early Christian secret society tested strangers and made themselves known to each other. Nor would such readers be ignorant of the fact that the initials of the Greek sentence meaning "Jesus Christ, Son of God, Savior" spell the Greek noun *Ichthys* (fish), which is the Greek equivalent for the Hebrew letter name NVN, Nun.

Alchemists among these readers might have known that the numeration of *Ichthys* by Greek Gematria is 1219 and that 1219 is also 23 (the number of ChIH, *Chaiah*, the Hebrew name for "life force") multiplied by 53 (the number of ABN, *Ehben*, the Hebrew noun meaning "Stone") used by more than one alchemist to designate the Philosophers' Stone, which was also the Elixir of Immortality. They would have known also that the meaning of the noun *Nun*, taken as a proper name, is "perpetuity, eternality, or everlastingness." And they would have known that the name Jesus is merely a variant of Joshua, the successor of Moses, whose father was named Nun.

The everlastingness represented by the name of the father of Joshua was unquestionably associated by the ancient Hebrews with the power of begetting descendants, that is, with procreative power. Thus, we find the word *Nun* used also as a verb meaning "to sprout, to grow," and it is an open secret that the mystery veiled by the letter of both Testaments in the Bible is a mystery summed up in these words: Generation and Regeneration.

Once their minds were turned by the number 700 to the letter *Nun*, Qabalists would remember the *Book of Formation*'s assertion that *Nun* stands for the zodiacal sign Scorpio, which governs generation because it rules the reproductive functions. They would know that Scorpio is related to the Ogdoad, or 8, because it is the eighth sign of the zodiac.

If they knew Tarot, they would know that Key 13 corresponds to Scorpio and is entitled "Death" because of the connection between Scorpio and the eighth house of the horoscope, termed "the house of death." The eighth house is also the "house of inheritance," and in all its meanings "inheritance" signifies something transmitted by parents to offspring, so that it has a direct correspondence with the verbal meaning of *Nun*, "to sprout." Furthermore, the Greek noun *he kleronomia* (the heritage), which is the number 407, or 11 × 37, was applied by Gnostic Christians to Jesus Christ and to the traditional wisdom transmitted orally that the Hebrews called Qabalah. That this wisdom is related to inheritance is not due to its being passed on from mouth to ear only but also to the fact that its central mystery is a mystery of sex. For a development of this theme, the reader will do well to consult the monumental work of A.E. Waite entitled *The Holy Kabbalah*. The eighth book of this valuable work is devoted to this mystery, and Mr. Waite's position is, in his own words, this: "The Secret Doctrine of the *Zohar* concerning the Holy Shekinah is the Mystery of Sex at its highest and she herself is the Mystery of the Oral Law. It is intimated that behind this Mystery there appears to be an authentic doctrine of Knowledge, based on experience."[3]

To confirm the conclusion that our Father, Brother C.R.C., is really the Gnostic "Jesus Christ," who is both the "Fish" and the "Son of the Fish," an erudite reader of the manifestoes would have noticed that the Founder of the Fraternity is said to have lived 106 years and that he was born in the year 1378. The first of these numbers is significant because 106 is the value of the letter name, NVN, nun, as ordinarily reckoned, with each N taken as 50. The second is significant for various reasons, but first of all because 1378 is 13 (the number of AChD, *Achad,* "unity," and of AHBH, *Ahebah,* "love,") multiplied by 106. Thus, it suggests the multiplication of that Divine Unity, which is God and which the apostle declares in so many words to be Love itself, by the power of generation corresponding to the sign Scorpio and the letter Nun. And here we may call to mind the injunction recorded in Genesis 1:28: "Be fruitful and multiply."

The number 1378 is also 26 (the number of IHVH, *Jehovah,* the Name of Names) multiplied by 53, the number of ABN, *Ehben* (Stone). Alchemists would have noticed this, because they thought of their Stone as something that had the power of multiplication. They were all agreed that their mysterious First Matter, from which the Stone is confected, is an absolute unity. That they thought of this First Matter as being a principle of love is shown by their often calling it their "Heavenly Venus." Thus, the Stone itself comes forth from the First Matter, but so does everything else. And since the Stone, once made, had the power of transmutation and multiplication, whatever its power was projected upon must necessarily have had its origin in that One Thing of which the *Emerald Tablet of Hermes* speaks when it says: "All things are from One." Thus, all things are forms of the One Thing; hence, it follows that whatever is transmuted or multiplied by the Stone is really an aspect of the One Thing, which One Thing is actually the supreme Reality denoted by the name of God, Jehovah.

Inspection of the number 1378 would have shown any erudite European that the first digit, 1, represents Unity, which Qabalists call "the Crown," or Primal Will. The second digit is that great mystery number, 3, full of meaning even for exoteric Christians and even more important in Qabalah and alchemy. The third digit, 7, Qabalists call "Victory," and it has so many occult meanings that one might write a large book on this one number. The last digit, 8, is called "Splendor" in the Qabalah and is a number associated with Hermes, the reputed founder of alchemy, as well as with Christ.

Furthermore, the first three digits are the number 137, and this is the value of QBLH, *Qabalah,* the arcane doctrine that the manifestoes

---

[3]Arthur Edward Waite, *The Holy Kabbalah* (Hyde Park, N.Y.: University Books, 1960), Introduction, p. xxi.

describe as being the philosophy of the Fraternity. Combined with the last digit, 8, associated with Hermes and Christ, the number 137 would inevitably suggest a combination of the Qabalah (137) with Christian Hermeticism—which is precisely what true Rosicrucianism is.

Again, the total resulting from the addition of the digits is 19, and the Founder is mentioned by his various initials exactly 19 times in the *Fama*. This number 19 is the number of the Hebrew proper name ChVH, *Chavvah* (Eve), meaning primarily "to manifest, to show forth." Furthermore, the digits of 19 add to 10, the number of the Qabalistic Sephiroth; and the digits of 10, in turn, add to 1. Thus, the birthdate of Brother C.R.C. indicates that he is the promised "seed of Eve" and intimates that he comes forth from that source of all power that is represented in Qabalism by the ten Sephiroth and that is held to be the Absolute Unity of which they are emanations.

In 1614, Freemasonry was not organized as it is today, but there is no doubt that many essential traditions of Freemasonry and rites exemplifying them were known then. Hence, it is interesting to note that MLK ShLMH, *Melek Shelomoh* (King Solomon), adds to 465; ChVRM MLK TzVR, *Khurum Melek Tsore* (Hiram King of Tyre), adds to 640; and the number of ChVRM ABIV, *Khurum Abiv* (Hiram Abiff), is 273. Thus, the names of the three original Master Masons have a numerical total that is the same as the birthdate of Brother C.R.C.: 1378.

Moreover, 1378 is the "theosophic extension" of 52, or sum of the numbers from 1 to 52 inclusive. Thus, it is the fifty-second in the series of numbers termed "triangular" by the Pythagoreans, because they may be represented by dots arranged to form an equilateral triangle. As the theosophic extension of 52, the number 1378 represents the full manifestation of the power of the name Jehovah, because that name spelled "in its plenitude"—that is, with the names of its four letters instead of single characters, IVD-HH-VV-HH, *Yod-Heh-Vav-Heh*—adds to 52. Thus, 1378 is a numeral symbol of the full power of God the Father.

As the extension of 52, C.R.C.'s birthdate is also the numeral symbol of the full power of the Qabalistic noun AIMA, *Aima* (Mother). This word is a name specially applied to the third Sephirah—Binah, or Understanding—and its value is also 52.

Fifty-two is also the value of BN, *Ben* (Son). This is the Qabalistic designation of *Tiphareth* (Beauty), the sixth Sephirah. Hence, 1,378 is a numeral symbol of the complete manifestation of the powers of the Son.

In other words, 1,378 represents numerally the full powers of the Qabalistic triad—Father, Mother, Son. The Qabalistic Father is Wisdom, and on the Tree of Life, this Sephirah is one of three Sephiroth composing the Pillar of Wisdom. The Qabalistic Mother is Understanding, but the Pillar on the Tree to which this Sephirah belongs is known as the Pillar of Severity or Strength. The Middle Pillar on the Tree is usually called "Mildness" by

Qabalists, but sometimes it is known as the Pillar of Beauty, from the Sephirah Tiphareth, which is its central point.

Our Masonic readers will know that Freemasonry associates King Solomon with a Pillar named Wisdom; Hiram, King of Tyre, is connected with a Pillar named Strength; and to Hiram Abiff, the Widow's Son, is attributed a Pillar named Beauty. These three pillars are said to be the supports of the Lodge, and leading Masonic authorities are agreed that the Masonic symbolism of the pillars is very old, preceding the Masonic revival of 1717. Mackey says, erroneously, that the Rosicrucians knew nothing of these pillars, and his statement is the more surprising because he was of the opinion that Masonry derived its conception of Beauty as one of the supports of the Lodge from the Qabalistic *Tiphareth*.[4]

But since the names of the three Ancient Grand Masters, as we have shown, add to 1378, and three pillars associated with the Grand Masters are directly connected with three Qabalistic names that correspond to the same three Pillars on the Tree of Life, we submit that when the Rosicrucians chose 1378 as the symbolic birthdate of the Son who was the Founder of the Order, they were intimating to the initiated that he was none other than that Son (BN, *Ben*) whose unity with his Father and Mother is indicated by the fact that the names of all three correspond to 52, the number that has 1378 for its theosophic extension.

A Widow's Son is the leading figure in the old Egyptian religion. He is Horus, son of Isis and Osiris. In the Egyptian language his name was Khoor, and it was spelled with two hieroglyphics that correspond exactly to Greek Chi and Rho and may also be represented, as to sound, by Hebrew Kaph and Resh, or German *C* and *R*. The Egyptian name of Horus, therefore, agrees exactly with the Chi and Rho of the monogram of Christ, already considered in this chapter.

Moreover, Plutarch informs us that the Egyptians attributed Khoor or Horus to the hypotenuse of the celebrated Pythagorean Triangle, which Masons revere as an invention of Pythagoras but in their monitors term the Forty-seventh Problem of Euclid. According to Plutarch, the vertical line of this triangle, three units long, represents Osiris, the Father; its base of four units corresponds to Isis, the Mother; and Horus, the Son, is the hypotenuse of five units. Observe that the parts of this triangle are assigned by the Egyptians to Father, Mother, and Son, just as the Pillars of the Qabalistic Tree of Life also are associated with a triad of Father, Mother, and Son. Note also that the Egyptian hero Horus, like the Masonic hero Hiram, is the son of a widow.

Figure 1 on page 48 is a diagram of the Pythagorean Triangle with the three Egyptian god names attributed to it, according to Plutarch's statement. Freemasonry preserves the tradition that when Pythagoras

---

[4]Albert G. Mackey, *An Encyclopaedia of Freemasonry* (Philadelphia: L.H. Everts & Co., 1886).

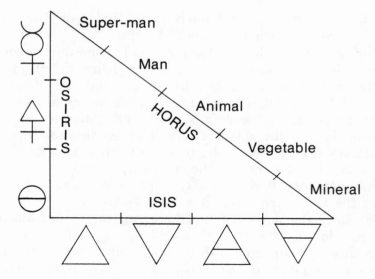

Figure 1. The Pythagorean Triangle

discovered the secret of this triangle he shouted, "Eureka!" This Greek word
is itself a formula for the triangle, since its number is 534, whose digits
express the unit value of the three sides of the triangle.

   To a Hermetic philosopher, this triangle is a summary of the Great
Work. Thus, Thomas Vaughan, in *Coelum Terrae*, says of the alchemical First
Matter: "Some few (but such as know her very well) have written that she
is not only one and three, but withal four and five, and this truth is
essential." The Pythagorean Triangle is the only symbol (with the exception
of one other, also Egyptian) that corresponds exactly to this description.
That other symbol is the Great Pyramid, a single solid, having triangular
faces (3), a square base (4), and five corners, including the apex (if the
uppermost part, now unfinished, is completed to make the perfect triangular form). The Pyramid also represents 5 by the number of its faces—
four triangles and one square.

   The Pythagorean Triangle is related to alchemy for other reasons.
Both Osiris the Father and Horus the Son were solar deities, and Isis the
Mother was a moon goddess. Thus, the triangle represents the Great Work,
declared to be an operation of the sun and moon.

   Again, the alchemists held that their work depended on three
principles, which they named Mercury, Sulphur, and Salt. Of these,
Mercury was the principle by whose aid the work of the Sun and Moon was
performed, and without Mercury nothing could be done. The alchemical
books also make it clear that Sulphur is the second principle, and that it
therefore occupies an intermediate place between Mercury and Salt. Salt is
also indicated as being the principle of fixation, just as Mercury is the
volatile state of the Matter. Hence, in our diagram (Figure 1) we assign

Mercury to the upper segment of the Osiris line, Sulphur to the middle segment, and Salt to the lower segment.

To the line corresponding to Isis, the mother, we have assigned the four elements—Fire, Water, Air, and Earth. These elements, need we say, are not the ordinary physical things that go by their names. This the alchemists make clear by taking care always to speak of "our" Fire, or "our" Earth, just as they always speak of "our" Sulphur, "our" Gold, or "our" Mercury, in order to indicate that what they are so naming is always to be understood as being other than the common substance.

Finally, to the hypotenuse of the triangle are attributed the ascending kingdoms of manifestation. Nearest the base and nearest to the element of "Earth" is the mineral kingdom. Above that is the vegetable kingdom, followed in order by the kingdoms of animal and human life. To the uppermost segment of the hypotenuse the fifth, or divine, kingdom is assigned. It is what Jesus called "the kingdom of God." Hence, the hypotenuse of the triangle represents the progressive upward movement of life, corresponding to the old Qabalistic aphorism: "First the stone, then the plant, then the animal, then the man, and after man—the god." Horus the Son is the cosmic Life Spirit, ascending this evolutionary ladder of form, one kingdom emerging from another.

This Pythagorean Triangle is remarkable, not only because of the properties of its three boundary lines, but also because of its interior angles. Of these, the first is the right angle of ninety degrees, formed by the junction of the descending line of Osiris to the horizontal base, or Isis. In Hebrew, 90 is the value of the word MIM, *Mem* (Water). Thus, the angle joining the lines of Osiris and Isis may be represented by the alchemical aphorism: "Our Sun and our Moon are conjoined in our Water." Paracelsus tells us: "The element of water is the mother, seed, and root of all minerals." In another place he writes: "The son of Hamuel says that the Stone of the philosophers is water coagulated, namely, in Sol and Luna. From this it is clearer than the sun that the matter of the Stone is nothing else but Sol and Luna."

Other Hermetic philosophers concur, but they are careful to assure us their "Water" must not be mistaken for the physical compound that goes by that name; rather is it that to which the apostle refers in his cryptic statement: "There are three that bear witness on earth, the spirit, the water, and the blood; and these three agree in one."

The spirit is the Life-breath, the descending power represented by the line of Osiris. The water is the generative potency representing the union of the Father and the Mother, male and female. (Here it may be well to remind you that Scorpio, the sign of generation and regeneration, is a *watery* sign.) The blood is the union of spirit and water, or rather, the consequence of their union. The blood is that which is manifest in the ascending scale of the evolution of forms. The life is *in* the blood, according to Moses, but even modern biology tells us that forms come from water.

The angle formed by the hypotenuse and the base, or by the conjunction of Isis with Horus, is one of 37 degrees. By the minute computations of modern mathematics, it is 36 degrees, 52 minutes, 11.54 seconds. The ancients, however, knew nothing of such computations. They knew of the division of the circle into 360 degrees. They had protractors. But higher mathematics are of comparatively recent invention. Thus, the fact that when this angle is measured with a protractor the naked eye cannot detect any variation from 37 degrees is the fact the old mathematicians reckoned with, and it is the basis of the whole symbolism.

This number 37 is of tremendous importance in Christian secret doctrine. Bond and Lea, in their *Apostolic Gnosis,* give a whole series of names and epithets of Jesus Christ, all multiples of 37, ranging from 37 itself up to 3996, or 37 × 108. They list more than five hundred different examples of Greek Gematria corresponding to the number 2368, or the number of "Jesus Christ" in Greek. In Chapter I of the first part of the work they say:

> It needs but a superficial acquaintance with the works of the medieval cabalists to convince the student that these men were engaged not merely in a pious exercise, but were consciously following a tradition preserved among the learned from times of great antiquity. The existence of such a tradition implies that the identity of number found to subsist between various words and phrases in the sacred writings was no mere accident, but expressed a real correspondence with the symbolic sense and doctrinal significance of the phrases thus found to tally. A similar association of meaning was traced in anagrammatic renderings of names and words. ...The doctrinal value of such countings was admitted equally by Jew and Christian, and had a singularly powerful influence on both sides.[5]

In Hebrew, 37 is the number of the proper name Abel (HBL), the second son of Adam, slain by his brother Cain. Even in exoteric Christian theology, Abel is understood to be the Old Testament prototype of Christ. As a common noun, his name means "transitoriness, impermanence, emptiness." The writer of Ecclesiastes uses it to express the changeful nature of manifested existence, and the noun is translated "vanity" in the English Bible. Thus, a literal rendering of Ecclesiastes 1:2 might be: "Abel of Abels, everything Abel."

When the Old Testament was translated into Greek, the word chosen to designate the arks of Noah and Moses was *he thibe,* and the Greek numeration is 37. Both arks, of course, are types of Christ as Savior, but they have profounder meanings than this superficial, though correct, symbolism. What is to our purpose here is that *he thibe* is merely a

---

[5]Frederick Bligh Bond and Thomas S. Lea, *The Apostolic Gnosis* (Oxford: B.H. Blackwell, 1919), 34.

transliteration of the Hebrew noun ThBH, *taybaw*, which itself belongs to the 37 series because its number is 407, or 37 × 11. But 407 is also the number of *he kleronomia* (The Inheritance) by Greek Gematria.

The ark of Moses was the means of saving his life, that is, of continuing the hereditary line represented by his existence. Similarly, the ark of Noah was the means of continuing the life of men and animals, male and female, during the flood. The two arks are symbols of the same thing, and they are directly connected with the idea of inheritance and salvation. Thus, we find the Dominical number, 8, which is also the Hermetic and Rosicrucian number, specifically connected with the ark of Noah, in which eight human beings were saved. In the Jewish dispensation, this number 8 was *the* number of the covenant, and that covenant was symbolized by circumcision, performed on the eighth day.

Dr. Bullinger, in *Number in Scripture*,[6] calls attention to many examples of the contrast between the number 8 and the number 13. His theological prepossessions kept him from discovering the deeper meanings, but he did uncover enough to make it clear to us that when the *thirteenth* Tarot Key was named Death and assigned to the *eighth* sign of the zodiac, there was a real reason for the choice. Dr. Bullinger correctly identifies 13 and its multiples, as applied to *unregenerate* humanity, as being used in Scripture to indicate apostasy, rebellion, disintegration, revolution, or some kindred idea. He shows also that the various people in the Old Testament who are represented as rebellious against God are all connected in one way or another with 13 and its multiples, whereas those who are on the Lord's side are similarly connected with 8 and its multiples. But Dr. Bullinger's adherence to traditional orthodoxy makes him miss the point that 13 is also a symbol of divinity, throughout the Old Testament. For most of the principal names of God in the Hebrew Scriptures are multiples of 13, and we have already shown that 13 is the number of two Hebrew words, one of which means "unity" and the other signifies "love." Thus, if these two words be added together, since each is a 13, their sum is 26, and this is the number of the Name of Names, Jehovah, Whom Moses revealed as One and Whom Jesus revealed as Love. And 26 is not only 13 doubled, but the digits of 26 add to 8.

Similarly, as our quotation from Thomas Vaughan shows, the alchemists who spoke of their First Matter as 1, which is *also* 3, 4, and 5 signified the number 13 by so declaring, since 13 is 1 + 3 + 4 + 5. So too our Pythagorean Triangle corresponds to 13, because it is 1 as a figure, and 3, 4, and 5 as to the number of units in its three lines.

Again, Moses was the Grand Hierophant or High Priest of Jehovah. As such, he was the light-bearer to the twelve tribes of Israel, who are identified with the twelve signs of the zodiac by all Qabalists and by all Gnostic Christians. When he died, the tribe of Levi became his representa-

---

[6]E.W. Bullinger, *Number in Scripture* (London: The Camp Press, 1952).

tive, but there were still twelve *other* tribes. And the very name Moses is MShH, or 345, according to Hebrew Gematria, so that our triangle also represents that leader of Israel, the digits of whose name add to 12; so that Moses as an individual or 1, plus the digits of his name also make 13. And of course the reader will by this time have anticipated that other 13, composed of Jesus, the light-bearer of the New Dispensation, and the Twelve whom He chose as spiritual representatives of the Tribes of Israel.

But to return to the angular relationship between the base and the hypotenuse of our Pythagorean Triangle, observe that this relationship is always expressed by the number 37. If we suppose the hypotenuse to be a line beginning at the end of the Isis line, and then ascending until it unites with the upper extremity of the Osiris line, we shall have a representation of the transitory evolution of form.

The segment of the hypotenuse nearest the base is a symbol of the mineral kingdom. An arc drawn downward from the upper end of this segment meets with the base at the end of the segment of the base marked *Earth*. Even so, the first stage of the development of the Life-force through form produces the seemingly dead things of the inorganic world, the kingdom of stone corresponding to the alchemical element earth. But recently science has made discoveries that demonstrate the truth of the old alchemical elementary notions and the truth of the idea that even metals have "seed." Life is rigidly restricted in the mineral kingdom, but all the potentialities of life are there. As Jesus said: "God of these very stones can raise up children unto Abraham."

The second segment of the hypotenuse is assigned to the vegetable kingdom. An arc drawn downward from the upper end of this segment encounters obstruction at the base line at the end of the segment marked *Air*. This serves to remind us of the fact that one main characteristic of the vegetable kingdom is that plants, though they are rooted in the earth as a rule, rise into the air and derive their sustenance from the atmosphere as well as from the soil. Plants, then, make use of two of the alchemical elements, and we all know that plants are alive.

The third stage on the ascent of the hypotenuse is that attributed to the animal kingdom. An arc drawn downward from this cuts the base at the end of the segment marked *Water*. Here again we are in accord with the facts of nature. The principal constituent of animal bodies is water. Blood has been described by more than one biologist as actually a modification of seawater. The same biologists tell us animal life had its beginnings in the sea, and they trace not a few of our physiological peculiarities to the marine existence of our evolutionary ancestors.

The fourth stage of the ascending hypotenuse corresponds to the genus *Homo sapiens*, or what St. Paul calls the "natural man." He is evolved from the kingdoms preceding his appearance, but his relation to Mother Nature is fundamentally the same. The angle of 37 degrees is here in this segment, just as in lower parts of the ascending line. But now an arc drawn down from the upper extremity of the fourth segment of the hypotenuse cuts the base line at the end of the segment marked *Fire*. More than this, the arc in question coincides at the base line with the point where the base and the perpendicular are joined. Again this agrees with fact, because man is the only creature on this planet who knows how to master fire. He is also the only creature possessed of sufficient intelligence to understand the secret of generation represented by the union of Osiris and Isis.

This is not to say that all men understand that secret. It says only that human intelligence at its highest, as represented by the *upper* end of the segment corresponding to man, has power to understand. They who penetrate into the heart of this mystery, which is the ultimate of the occult secret of Cosmic Fire, discover how to carry themselves beyond the limits of *Homo sapiens*, the natural man, into the fifth kingdom. Knowing the secret of generation (and that secret is summarized in what Jesus said about stones and the children of Abraham), they know also the secret of regeneration. Thus, they can use the law that has evolved man out of the lower kingdoms to take man farther, out of the limitations of his natural state. And the technique by which this is accomplished is the Great Art of the Rosicrucians, the Great Work of the Hermetic philosophers, the true *Disciplina Arcana* of the Gnostic Church.

Out of the raw material of the natural man, the divine man is unfolded. Out of the corruptible body of the natural man is made the truly incorruptible body of the spiritual man. This incorruptible body is sometimes called the solar body, and various other names have been given to it. What we wish to emphasize here is that it is an actual body and that it is made here on earth, not in a far-off heaven after death.

They who follow the Way of Liberation until they reach its term, in our triangle represented by the upper end of the Horus line, reach the point that is also the beginning of the Osiris line. The end, or goal, of the ascent of the Son is union with the Father. It is also release from the domination of the "elements." Thus, an arc drawn downward from the extreme end of the hypotenuse, like the other arcs we have noticed, encounters no obstacle, but continues its sweep around the center where the line of Isis joins the line of Horus, until it has formed the full circle shown in Figure 2 on page 54. That circle is a symbol of God. It is also a symbol of eternity, since it has neither beginning nor end.

Because it has a radius of 5, this circle has a diameter of 10, and thus its circumference is 31.42+. Taking this last as a symbolic number, we may understand it as 32, which it most nearly approximates. Thus, the diameter of the circle is the 10 that Qabalists associate with complete manifestation, because 10 is the number of the Sephiroth. The circumference of 32 also is associated with precisely the same idea because of the opening words of the *Book of Formation*: "In thirty-two mysterious paths of

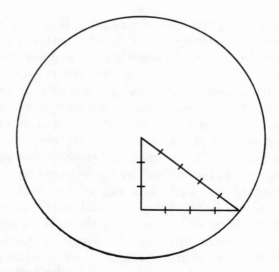

Figure 2. The Circle of God

wisdom did the Lord write....He created His Universe by the three forms of expression: Numbers, Letters and Words."[7]

In short, to arrive at the completion of the Great Work is to pass out of the limitations of Time into the Freedom of Eternity, where Past and Present and Future meet in a timeless *Now*, just as any point of the circumference of a circle is at once Beginning and End, Alpha and Omega, Aleph and Tav, *A* and *Z*. Thus, it is said that the true meaning of the word *Azoth*, used by alchemists, is to be discerned in the fact that its first letter may be taken either as Alpha, Aleph, or *A*, its second letter as the final letter of the Latin alphabet, its third letter as the last of the Greek alphabet, and the concluding *Th* as Tav, the last Hebrew letter.

Throughout the ascent, the relation between Horus and Isis, Son and Mother, developing Form and Nature, the womb of all forms, is expressed by the 37-degree angle. This relation does not change, even when the Great Work is completed, but something is added. The son, Horus, is conjoined with the uppermost point of Osiris, the father. That is to say, the Son becomes "One with the Father" at the Point whence the descent of the Osiris line begins. That Point is the beginning of the Osiris line. It is the "Small Point" that Qabalists also call *Kether* (the Crown). It is the point at which the boundless expanse of the Limitless Light condenses itself when a cycle of creation begins. It is the changeless *One*, which is the Center of Eternity.

The angle at this point is an angle of 53 degrees, the complement of the other angle of 37 degrees at the junction of the base line with the

---

[7]*Book of Formation*, translated by Stenring (Philadelphia: David McKay Co., 1923), 1:1. All subsequent quotations from the *Book of Formation* are taken from this translation.

hypotenuse. Here an interesting fact emerges. Even when the hypotenuse has progressed no higher than the first segment, the entire length of that segment is pointing directly at the Osiris line. It is aimed at that point though it has not yet reached it. Thus, the angle of 53 degrees is implied, though not expressed, at every point along the hypotenuse. Thus, along the line of the hypotenuse, the formation of the angle of 53 degrees is always the end aimed at, the objective, the goal.

This number 53 is the value of the Hebrew noun ABN, *Ehben* (Stone), and when the *Fama* was written, Qabalistic alchemists used this very word to designate the Philosophers' Stone. For example, it appears in an illustration in Khunrath's *Amphitheatrum,* where the letters of ABN are written in the interior angles of an equilateral triangle that surmounts the head of a winged dragon. The dragon sits on top of a mountain in the center of a seven-sided enclosure you will find described at greater length in Chapter VIII. We cite it here as one of many examples to be found in the occult literature of the period.

The word ABN, *Ehben*, has a peculiarity that recommended it to Qabalists. The first two letters, AB, spell *Ab* (Father), and the last two, BN, spell *Ben* (Son). As a Qabalistic alchemist might phrase it: "In the Stone (ABN) the powers of the Father (AB) and the Son (BN) are conjoined."

The power of the Qabalistic "Father" is the power of the second aspect of the Life Power, the Sephirah named *Chokmah* (Wisdom). *Chokmah* is named AB, *Ab*, by Qabalists, and the special power of *Chokmah*, the secret force of Wisdom, is named ChIH, *Chaiah*, the Life-Force. This is that same *Chaiah* that, when multiplied by *Ehben*, is 23 × 53, or 1219, which in Greek Gematria is *Ichthys* (the Fish)—NVN, Nun, the letter corresponding to Scorpio. Here we may note that Wisdom is clearly indicated as the one goal of the Rosicrucians, and as the one thing to which persons desirous of association with the Order should aspire, by these words of the *Confessio*: "To the false and to impostors, and to those who seek other things than wisdom, we witness...we cannot be betrayed by them to our hurt, nor known to them without the will of God."

The writers of these words announced themselves as Qabalists. We are not, therefore, reading into what we have just quoted anything whatever when we say it indicates definitely that the Qabalistic "Father," or AB, *Ab*, is there indicated as the one and only proper goal of the Rosicrucian quest. And since we know that Qabalists associate AB, *Ab*, with *Chaiah*, the Life-force, we are reminded that Gnostic Christianity is also a quest for life, and life more abundantly, as innumerable passages in the New Testament bear witness.

Again, the word BN, *Ben* (Son) is, as we have said, the sixth aspect of the Life Power, *Tiphareth* (Beauty). But Qabalists also assert that BN, *Ben*, is the special name of the "secret nature" of *Assiah*, the world of action, the physical plane. Here we find the Qabalah saying just what St. John says at the beginning of his Gospel when he writes: "That which hath been made was life in Him, and the life was the light of men." So Moulton translates the Greek in his *Modern Reader's Bible*.[8] Forget the Biblical and theological associations for the moment and consider the plain meaning of the words. Everything that exists is declared to be made by the Logos (that is, the Son). There is nothing not so made. And then it is declared that the "stuff" from which everything was made was the vital essence of the Creative Thought, which vital essence (that is, *Chaiah*) was (and is) the *light* of men. Get rid of the idea that these are mere figures of speech. They are as explicit a statement of actual fact as it is possible for human words to frame. The "stuff" of the physical plane is light, and the essence of light is vitality. Nothing is that does not live.

That fundamental life is what is meant by the Hebrew word RVCh, *Ruach*, which, like words of similar import in many other languages, signifies breath, vitality, and that in man which is sometimes called the rational soul, or animus. This last aspect of it is precisely what the Qabalah associates with *Tiphareth*, and *Tiphareth* is also *Ben*, the Son. So the union of powers of AB and BN in ABN, *Ehben* (the Stone), is the conjunction of the divine Life-force with the rational soul of man. Note also that since this conjunction is the combination of the Sephiroth numbered 2 and 6 (the digits of 26, or IHVH, *Jehovah*), it is symbolized by the number 8.

Similarly, the number of ABN, *Ehben*, being 53, the addition of its digits is also 8. Futhermore, if we read the digits from right to left, or from *units* to *tens*, as is customary in occult arithmetic, 53 expresses 3 working through 5. Thus, the two digits of this number are those that express the numeral proportion between 888, the name Jesus, and 1480, or Christ. For a properly instructed Qabalist, therefore, this word *Stone* would be in many respects an obvious symbol of Jesus Christ.

Now, in the Gospels of Matthew, Mark, and Luke, the words of Jesus Himself are reported as comparing Himself to the "Stone rejected by the builders," mentioned in the twenty-second verse of the 118th Psalm. In Acts 4:11, St. Peter tells the Jewish rulers that Christ is this Stone, and the same thought is repeated in the second chapter of St. Peter's first Epistle. All this was certainly known to the persons to whom the *Fama* was addressed. Henry Khunrath, for example, had said (in his *Amphitheatre of Eternal Wisdom*, published in 1609) that the Stone of the Philosophers is identical with *Ruach Elohim*, the Spirit that brooded over the deep at the beginning, and a central point of Christian doctrine is that this same Spirit is one with Christ. Also published in 1609 was *The Sophic Hydrolith*, an alchemical text that declares:

> This tried, blessed, and heavenly Stone Jesus Christ was
> longingly expected from the beginning of the world by

---

[8]Richard Green Moulton, ed., *Modern Reader's Bible* (New York: MacMillan, 1908).

the Fathers and Holy Patriarchs; God-enlightened men prayed that they might be accounted worthy to see the promised Christ in His bodily and visible form. And if they rightly knew Him by the Holy Spirit, they were comforted by His presence in their lives, and had an invisible Friend on whom they could stay themselves, as upon a spiritual fulcrum, in trouble and danger even unto the end of their life.

But although that heavenly Stone was bestowed by God as a free gift on the whole human race, the rich as well as the poor (Matth. 11, 6); yet to this very day comparatively few have been able to know and apprehend Him. To the majority of mankind He has always been a hidden secret, and a grievous stumbling block, as Isaiah foretold in his eighth chapter: "He shall be for a stone of stumbling and a rock of offence, a gin and a snare, so that many shall stumble and fall, and be broken, and be snared, and be taken." The same was revealed to the aged Simeon, when he spake thus to Mary, the Mother of the Corner Stone: "Behold, He shall be for a fall and rising again of many in Israel, and for a sign that shall be spoken against." To this St. Paul also bears witness (ad Rom. 9.): "They fell from the Stone of offence, and the rock of stumbling. He that believes in Him shall not be confounded." This Stone is precious to them that believe, but to the unbelieving "a stone of offence and stumbling, seeing that they are broken against the word, and believe not in Him on whom they are founded (Eccl. 43)." In all these respects the Precious, Blessed, and Heavenly Stone agrees most wonderfully with our earthly, corporal, and philosophical Stone; and it is, therefore, well worth our while to compare our Stone with its Heavenly prototype. We shall thus understand that the earthly philosophical Stone is the true image of the real, spiritual, and heavenly Stone, Jesus Christ.

Thus, the fact that the number of degrees in the angle uniting the line of Horus, the Son, to the line of Osiris, the Father, is the number 53 (the number of ABN) reminds us that Jesus Christ, the Stone, said: "I and the Father are one." Jesus is also called the Stone at the *head of the corner*, or the Stone at the *summit of the angle*. This is just what is suggested by the union of the hypotenuse of the Pythagorean Triangle with the upper extremity of its vertical side.

We have seen that this triangle is one of the symbols of Free-masonry and have seen also that the birthdate of Brother C.R.C. is 1378, the number resulting from the Masonic titles of the three ancient Grand Masters. One of those Masters who is the central figure of the Masonic legend is Hiram Abiff, whose name in Hebrew is ChVRM ABIV, *Khurum Abiv*. Some modern Hebraists are of the opinion that *Abiv*, or Abiff, is not part of Hiram's name; but many others, together with the Masonic Fraternity, agree with Luther that this master workman did have this precise cognomen. At any rate, when the Rosicrucian manifestoes were published, this was received opinion among alchemists, Freemasons, and Qabalists. And we have already spoken of the number of this name, 273, which is the total value of the phrase, ABN MASV HBVNIM, *Ehben masu ha-bonim* (the stone refused by the builders), as written in Hebrew in Psalm 118:22. It is also the number of the words AVR GNVZ, *aur ganuz* (Hidden Light), GOR, *gawar* (rebuked), and GRO, *gawrah* (took away, diminished).

According to the Masonic legend, Hiram the Builder was assailed by three villains, who demanded that he impart to them the Master Masons' word. He refused, on the ground that the time to do so had not yet come, since the Holy of Holies in the Temple was not yet completed. This is an important point, indicating the real reason certain "words" or "thoughts" cannot possibly be imparted to persons who are as yet in the unfinished state symbolized by the uncompleted Temple. When the Holy of Holies is completed and the ark has been set therein, the "word" can be and is given to the aspirant. These villians typified the importunity of the unworthy, clamoring to receive that for which they have not made themselves ready. So the Grand Master Hiram Abiff rebuked (GOR) those who assailed him. For doing this, he met his death and thus, as one slain (like Abel and Christ) by his own brethren, symbolizes the rejected Stone, which nevertheless is to become the summit of the corner.

Hiram's death caused the loss of the Master Masons' word, and that Lost Word is the Hidden Light. By his death Hiram took that light away with him. Thus, the Masonic legend corresponds accurately to *aur ganuz* and to *gawrah*, as well as to the Stone and to *gawar*, "rebuked."

Freemasonry also lays great stress on immortality, and this is done in connection with the legend of Hiram. Thus, it is not surprising to find that 273 is the value of the Greek word *athanasia*, which means "im-mortality." Nor will it escape the attention of the reader that the Stone of the alchemists is also the Universal Medicine, or Elixir of Life. In the *Confessio* it is asked: "Were it not an excellent thing to live so as if you had lived from the beginning of the world, and should still live to the end thereof?" Careful reading of the promises of Jesus makes it perfectly evident that he offered the gift of eternal life as a possession to be enjoyed here on earth, before the death of the physical body. For "eternal life" is precisely the state of conscious existence characterizing those who have passed out of the Fourth

Kingdom, the kingdom of the natural man, into the Fifth Kingdom, symbolized by the fifth segment of the line of Horus on the Pythagorean Triangle.

The number 273 is also the number of the Greek *he kleis* (the key). Specifically, this is the Key of the Gnosis, or Key of Knowledge, which Jesus accused the scribes of having taken away, in Luke 11:52. It is also the "Key of the House of David"—MPThCh BITh DVD, *maftayakh beth David*—mentioned in Isaiah 22:22 and also alluded to in Revelation 3:7. The Hebrew of this term adds to 954, which is 53 × 18. Since 18 is the number of Ch I, *chai* (life, health), and 53 is the number of *ABN, Ehben* (Stone), the multiplication of life by the Stone is indicated by this term, and there is no question that Qabalistic alchemists so understood it.

In Hebrew the noun MPThCh, *maftayakh* (key), is the number 528, and this is primarily important because it is the sum of the numbers from 1 to 32 inclusive, or the theosophic extension of 32. Thus, it is a numeral symbol of the full manifestation of the Thirty-two, which every Qabalist would understand as a reference to the full expression of the powers of the paths constituting the Tree of Life. Furthermore, this is the key of the House of David, and that house is the Temple not made with hands, eternal in the heavens. Thus, the Key is the secret that gives power to open the Temple and enter therein, even to the Holy of Holies. Here is a clue the reader will do well to follow in his meditations.

Returning now to Brother C. R. C., we note that these initials, as Hebrew letters, have a total value of 240. This is the number of the noun RM, *rawm* (high, lofty), which is applied to the spirit of Brother C. R. at the beginning of the story. The same word refers also to *Kether*, the uppermost Sephirah on the Tree of Life. It might also be applied to the upper end of the hypotenuse in the Pythagorean Triangle, which is the highest point on that symbol. Furthermore, the same word is a component part of the name ChVRM, *Khurum*, or Hiram, which combines or coalesces the two words KhVR, *Khoor* (white) (applied also to the Egyptian Khoor, Horus, as god of light) and RM, *rawm* (high). Thus, C. R. C. is that Height which is also termed the White Head by the Qabalists, or *Kether*, the Crown.

There is no Hebrew word spelled CRC (or Kaph Resh Kaph), but the same letters do spell KKR, *kikkawr*, and furthermore, Gesenius traces this word to a Syriac root meaning "to surround," which is actually spelled KRK. *Kikkawr* means primarily "a circle." Hence, it is closely related in meaning to *Kether* (the Crown) because, *Kether* is derived from a Hebrew root also meaning "to surround." A crown, in its simplest form, is a metal circlet, surrounding the head of a ruler. Thus, the primary meaning of *kikkawr* is actually related in Hebrew to the word chosen by Qabalists as a name for the first Sephirah. Later, we shall find that this Sephirah is regarded as the root or origin of the whole Tree of Life, that it is the universal I AM, or Cosmic Self, and that in the system of Rosicrucian Grades it is the highest of all. All this agrees with what the *Fama* has to tell us concerning our Father, Brother C.R.C.

When we come to the initials by which our Brother and Father is distinguished after he has completed his initiation by his two years at Fez, we do not have to make any transpositions of letters. For R.C. is RK, *roke*, a Hebrew noun meaning "tenderness, as of a green shoot" and also, as descriptive of character, "tender, compassionate."

Compassion is a distinquishing feature of the true adept. Thus, the agreement of the Brethren says that "R.C. was to be their seal, mark and character." That the Christ is compassionate is shown again and again by the Gospels, and we have heard much over the years of certain wise men of the East whose main title to human consideration is that they are Masters of Compassion.

The number of RK, *roke*, is 220, according to Hebrew Gematria. And since this is 22 × 10, it is the multiplication of the number of the Sephiroth (10) by the number of the letters of the Hebrew alphabet (22), so that 220 is a numeral symbol of complete manifestation of all the powers represented by the Tree of Life. Furthermore, the initials R.C. are introduced into the narrative at the time that the hero of the allegory is himself twenty-two years of age, for he was sixteen when he went to Damcar, where he spent three years. Thus, he was nineteen, or in his twentieth year, when he visited Egypt and during his journey from Egypt to Fez. At Fez he remained two years, so that he was in his twenty-second year when he left Fez. Twenty-two is the "magical age" of full initiation, because one who has completed his occult education has made the full round or circle of the secret sciences; and in ancient geometry the number 22 was taken as the special number of the circumference of a circle, because 22 is the nearest whole number expressing the circumference of a circle having a diameter of 7.

The number 220, the value of R. C. (and of C. R., which is the next set of initials used in the story), is the first of those numbers called "amicable" or "friendly" by the Pythagoreans. This would be known to the erudite of Europe who had studied such works as the writings of Nichomachus, Iamblichus, and Boetius.

Amicable numbers are those in which the aliquot parts or submultiples of the first add to a second number that, in turn, has aliquot parts or submultiples whose sum is the first number. The first pair of amicable numbers is 220 and 284. The aliquot parts of 220 are 1, 2, 4, 5, 10, 11, 20, 22, 44, 55, and 110. The sum of of these numbers is 284. The aliquot parts of 284 are 1, 2, 4, 71, and 142. The sum of these is 220.

Now in Greek Gematria, 284 is the number of *agathos* (good), *hagios* (sacred, holy), and *theos* (God). Really, the three words are simply different ways of saying the same thing. Thus, that to which 220 is amicable, or friendly, is God Himself. And since the parts of 284 add up to 220 and the parts of 220 add up to 284, we have here a numeral symbol of just what is implied in the union of the hypotenuse with the vertical line of the Pythagorean Triangle, and by the coalescence of the words *Father* and *Son* in the Hebrew for *Stone.*

Again, 220 is the number of the Hebrew word BChIR, *bawkheer,* meaning "chosen, elect," applied throughout the Old Testament to Israel and transferred by Gnostic Christianity to the Spiritual Israel, who receive the sacred inheritance not according to the flesh but according to something higher. The elect, throughout the New Testament, are the saints, the sacred ones, who are the few selected from the many who are called.

They are characterized by compassion, and they are pure, clean, honest, and free from all pollution. Thus, their natures are described by the Hebrew adjective THVR, *tahoor* (clean, pure, elegant), which is also specially attributed by Qabalists to the mode of Intelligence or the type of consciousness peculiar to the ninth Sephirah, *Yesod* (the Basis or Foundation). The nature of this purity, moreover, is clearly indicated by the fact that *Yesod* is the Sephirah said to represent the reproductive organs of Adam Kadmon, the archetypal man. And THVR is 220.

The number 220 is also associated with *Yesod* in another way. For in Isaiah 28:16, where the prophet, in the name of Jehovah, speaks of laying a *Stone* in Zion for a foundation, the Hebrew for "a sure foundation" is MVSD MVSD, *musawd musawd,* and these two words add to 220.

Tenderness, compassion, and purity are the marks of the elect. They are also the qualities that are truly "amicable" to goodness, holiness, and divinity. That which enters into compassion and purity is what makes divinity. If we attempt to define holiness and goodness, we find ourselves invariably speaking of sympathy, love, and purity. Thus, to find our Father and Brother designated by initials that give us a word and a number related to these very ideas is to find a clue to that same hero's true identity. He is and can be none other than the Christos whose throne is in the midst, the Anointed Ruler who governs the universe from its Center, that Center which, because it is everywhere, must be in man the innermost secret place of his own being.

This is confirmed for us by the other arrangement of the same initials, C. R., which spells the Hebrew noun, KR, *Kar,* meaning "lamb." As composed of the same letters, this word has all the Gematria that has been explained in connection with the word *roke,* and who does not know that the Lamb is one of the great Gnostic Christian symbols, as well as a favorite symbol of the exoteric Church? Who does not know that the Lamb is the Son who is one with the Father and therefore mentioned again and again in the manifestoes as "Our Father, Brother C. R."? Who in this day does not know that the distinguishing badge of the Masonic Fraternity, a symbol of innocence and goodness, is a white lambskin apron? And who does not know that the New Testament says definitely that the Lamb sits on the throne in the midst of the New Jerusalem, ruling all things from that central position and illuminating all from that same center? Read the twenty-first chapter of Revelation to refresh your memory, and do not fail to notice how the elect are described in the last verse of the chapter. Nothing could be more explicit.

What is probably not so well known is that in Rabbinic Hebrew the word VRDI, *varedi*, is an adjective meaning "of a rose," that is, none other than "rosy." This word also adds to 220 and is of particular importance to our present inquiries, for although, as we have shown, the hero of the Rosicrucian allegory is nowhere mentioned by name, and the supposition that he was "Christian Rosenkreutz" can be traced directly to an author who was, if anything, antagonistic to the whole Rosicrucian idea, there is no question that the Fraternity itself was known, from its first manifestoes, as the Fraternity of the Rosy Cross. Thus, our discovery that a Rabbinic Hebrew adjective having the value 220, which is the value of R. C. and C. R., actually means "rosy" does have a direct bearing on our research.

The fourth designation of the Founder, used only once in the *Fama*, is Brother C., that is, Brother Kaph. Here we may note that the letter Kaph is associated by Qabalists with the Intelligence of Desirous Quest, and certainly the allegory of the *Fama* is a narrative of just that. Furthermore, the number of Kaph is 20, and that is the number of the word AChVH, *akhavaw*, which means "brotherhood, fraternity." This too is borne out by the general meaning of both the *Fama* and the *Confessio*. And 20 is also the number of the verb ChZH, *khawzaw* (to gaze at, to penetrate, to pass through, to comprehend, to see prophetically, to prophesy). We believe the applicability of all these meanings to the text of the *Fama* and to the character of its hero needs no demonstration. As a noun the same letters, with different vowel points, are pronounced *khozeh*, which means (1) a prophet, a seer, an astrologer, and (2) an agreement, a compact. These meanings too are supported by the text of the allegory. And they all point to Brother C. as the Indwelling Christ.

Down through the ages, that Indwelling Ruler has been described just as He is described in the *Fama*. And always He has been represented by the names in which the letters *K* and *R*, or sounds corresponding to them, are prominent.

For the Hindus, he was Krishna, whose name begins with *K* and *R* and who says, in the *Bhagavad-Gita*: "I am the Self, dwelling inwardly in all beings; I am the beginning, I am the middle, and end also, of beings. Of the sons of the Mother, I am Vishnu, the Preserver; I am the word of those that speak. I am the father of this world, the mother, the guardian. I am the way, the supporter, the lord, the witness, the home, the refuge, the beloved." Krishna also declares himself to be the one teacher and, as author of the Vedas, the source of all knowledge, including knowledge of the healing art. In one of his incarnations he is especially associated with the symbol of the fish. The number 8 is connected with him, because he was said to be the eighth son of Vasudeva and Devaki. He is also related to the symbolism of the Ram or Lamb, because as the beginning of all he is associated with Agni, the god of fire, represented in Hindu religious symbolism as a lamb carrying a notched banner, exactly like the Agnus Dei shown on Roman Catholic medals, the only noticeable difference between the two symbols being that Agni's notched banner shows a swastika and the banner of Agnus Dei is blazoned with an equal-armed cross.

For the Egyptians, he is Horus, the avenger of His Father, yet as the Pythagorean Triangle and Egyptian religious hymns make clear, one with that same Father. Hence, since Osiris is judge of the dead, Horus, as one with Osiris, judges them also. So does Krishna, and so, in the Christian doctrine, does Jesus Christ.

Again, he is *Khurum Abiv*, in whose name we can hear the echo of the Egyptian Khoor. Hiram is the Stone rejected by the builders, yet he is raised after his body has reached an advanced stage of dissolution. This detail of the Masonic legend is particularly important to alchemists.

We do not mean by saying this to be understood as holding the belief that Krishna and Horus and Hiram Abiff were previous incarnations of Him who appeared in Palestine as Jesus Christ. There are some who hold this opinion, and they advance ingenious argument in support of their beliefs. To us it appears more probable that the Universal Mind made itself known in the historic character Whose life is detailed in the New Testament. We believe the Christos, the Christ, is universal, ageless, timeless. We believe the Logos or Word manifested itself again and again under various veils, down through the ages. But we believe, though we seek neither to persuade nor to force others to accept our belief, that in very truth the Logos was incarnate and given historic human embodiment through the life of Jesus Christ. This, moreover, is the belief most clearly expressed by the writers of the *Fama* and *Confessio*. It subtracts nothing from Jesus Christ to say that knowledge of the Indwelling Christ is veiled in the stories of Krishna, Horus, and Hiram Abiff. Rather it adds something when we realize that this Central Presence has never been without a witness. And thus we can understand why St. Augustine said the true religion has always existed, since the beginning, and only began to be called Christian after the time of Jesus.

Our Brother C. R., then, we regard as being none other than Christ. He is both Father and Brother. He is all-comprehending. He is the true founder of that fraternity of the Compassionate, whose only mission is to heal. He is the Friend of all. He is the Great Physician. He is the establisher of that perfect Order that leads all who enter it, step by step and grade by grade, to the comprehension of the highest knowledge attainable by mankind.

How his power and wisdom are manifested in the transformation of the natural man, a denizen of earth, into the spiritual man who is a citizen of heaven is the real theme of Gnostic Christianity and of the

Rosicrucian manifestoes. For in the temple of human society, there is a Holy of Holies, and that adytum of the Indwelling Divinity is a true House of the Holy Spirit.

It is a society within human society, which by superior wisdom and power actually rules the world and shares in the administration of the Kingdom of God on earth. Its members live in every part of the globe. Some are humble, and their attainments extend just a little beyond those of ordinary human beings. Some are great adepts, charged with powers and responsibilities beyond our ability to imagine. But all may be known by one certain mark and character. All are "Brothers of R. C." All are sympathetic, compassionate, tender. They rule, but the law whereby they rule is the perfect Law of Liberty, the Law of Love.

CHAPTER VI

THE JOURNEY, THE INITIATION, AND
THE FOUNDING OF THE ORDER

UR FATHER AND BROTHER C.R.C., we read, was a member of a German noble family. If we remember that the *Fama* and *Confessio* were written by wise men who knew the occult history of humanity, we shall understand this statement, for more recently other teachings of that same school have furnished us with a great deal of knowledge concerning the life waves of man. From this later instruction we can determine the true import of the designation "German." When the manifestoes were published, the Life Power had brought into manifestation, or evolved, five life waves of humanity, and the Indo-Germanic peoples were among the first to help root the new developments of this Fifth Lifewave into the consciousness of humanity as a whole. Thus, the story of the *Fama* is one addressed to members of this Fifth Lifewave and has to do with its problems and opportunities.

To emphasize this, the *Fama* goes on to say that in the *fifth* year of C.R.C.'s age he was placed in a cloister. The cloister, as the derivation of the noun from the Latin *claustrum* (bar, bolt, bonds) plainly indicates, is the state of relative bondage that precedes the work of liberation. To be placed in a cloister is to be shut away from the world, to be separated from the rest of mankind. Yet what is shut away is actually the essentially free Spirit. Free in itself, the Christos assumes the burdens of apparent limitation imposed by its incarnation in human personality. Hence, this passage of the *Fama* is of the same fundamental import as this declaration from St. John's Gospel: "The Logos became flesh, and tabernacled among us; and we beheld his radiance, a radiance as of a Son one-begotten from a father, full of grace and truth."

C.R.C is said to have been placed in the cloister in the fifth year of his age because it is a common device in occultism to represent by the term *age* a grade or experience. Thus, various ages are assigned to the degrees of

Freemasonry. In this instance, the fifth year is indicative of the Fifth Lifewave and of the five senses underlying the self-conscious awareness characteristic of that lifewave. This self-conscious awareness is also the cloister; that is to say, our sense of personal identity as apparently separate human beings is based on the five subtle principles of sensation. As the indwelling Self manifests through these, it seems to be divided into as many parts as there are human beings.

This appearance is an illusion, but so long as the *delusion* having its origin in the *illusion* persists, the person seems to himself to be separate from God, separate from his fellowmen, and separate from the various things constituting his environment, which things he calls Nature and conceives as an entity not himself, opposed to him. This state of delusion, and the five-sense, three-dimensional consciousness from which the delusion springs, are often referred to in occult books as *poverty*. Thus, we understand why the *Fama* says Brother C.R.C. was placed in a cloister "by reason of his poverty." It is this semblance of poverty, based on the limitations of the five-sense consciousness, that seems to shut away the essentially free God-Self in its tabernacle of flesh.

The members of the Inner School, however, because they have traced the history of human evolution, know this apparent separateness has its uses. Five-sense consciousness is not in itself an evil. What is evil is remaining in it too long. Among its uses are what the *Fama* hints when it says Brother C.R.C. learned in his cloister the Greek and Latin tongues. The archaic English of the text says he learned the two languages "indifferently," but we must not understand by this that he was but poorly grounded in them. The old meaning of the adjective *indifferent* is "without difference," and the *Fama* intends us to understand that in the five-sense consciousness one may learn the language of science (Latin) and the language of philosophy and religion (Greek) equally well. In the cloister of the sense life the Self gains the preliminary knowledge of the laws and meaning of what the senses report. Without this preliminary training it is impossible to go on and receive the higher instruction. This higher instruction, by which one becomes acquainted with the secrets of occult science and philosophy, is imparted in what the *Fama* calls "Arabic," meaning the language of initiation.

Would-be occultists all too often lose sight of what is intimated by this passage in the story of Brother C.R.C. The reader will do well to get Manly Hall's excellent *Essay on the Fundamental Principles of Operative Occultism*, in which it is laid down as a first principle that he who would become a practical occultist must realize the value of education.[1] Mr. Hall points out that Pythagoras demanded proficiency in music, mathematics, and astrono-

---

[1]Manly Hall, *Essay on the Fundamental Principles of Operative Occultism* (Los Angeles: The Philosophical Research Society, 1962). This work is available under its new title, *Spiritual Centers in Man.*

my from all who sought his instruction. The discipline of the mind is necessary as a first step. Occult training of the right sort is based on the foundation of ordinary science and philosophy.

This foundation laid, then comes the step indicated by the statement that Brother C.R.C., "(upon his own earnest desire and request), being yet in his growing years, was associated to a Brother, P.A.L., who was determined to go to the Holy Land." There are two meanings here, and both apply to the work of initiation.

According to the context, Brother C.R.C. was at this time about fifteen years old. This is the period of adolescence, the time when the subtle force symbolized as the serpent, the scorpion, and the eagle begins to bring about the physiological changes and mental transformations characteristic of puberty. It is the time when boys and girls begin to think "long thoughts," when they are stirred by a desire for new experiences, when their longing for wider horizons begins to manifest itself, when they seek adventure.

These inner stirrings are closely related to occult and mystical experience, as psychologists are beginning in these days to understand. Those among them, however, who try to make themselves and others believe that mysticism and occultism, the quest for reality beyond mere sensation, the search for truth transcending ordinary reasoning, are *nothing but* obscure activities of the sex life, fall into a serious error that has led many astray. The serpent power at work in the beginnings of initiation is truly the force termed *libido* by analytical psychology. Yet the impulses and emotions connected with the perpetuation of the race by reproduction constitute only a part of its potencies.

The deeper occult significance of the passage we are studying is revealed by the age of C.R.C. at this period. He was fifteen years old, and 15 is the "theosophic extension" of 5, or the sum of the numbers from 1 to 5. Thus, 15 represents the completion of the preparatory cycle of five-sense training. Furthermore, 15 is the number of the Hebrew noun ABIB, *Abib*, the name of the month of Exodus and Passover, which is appropriate at this point in our occult narrative, when C.R.C. is about to leave his cloister. Fifteen is also the number of the Hebrew divine name IH, *Jah*, which Qabalists attribute to that aspect of reality they name *Chokmah* (Wisdom), the second circle of the Tree of Life. This does not mean that C.R.C. had attained the Grade corresponding to the second circle. It does mean that the impulse that stirs us into activity when we begin to long for something higher than five-sense experience is one that originates in the Celestial Wisdom. This point on the Tree of Life is known also to Qabalists as "the Father," and it is the image of the Father in our minds that actually moves us, like the Prodigal Son, to leave the limitations of five-sense life and make a journey back home to the Holy Land.

At this stage of the unfoldment of the powers of the Christos comes what is indicated when the *Fama* speaks of Brother P.A.L. The name of this Brother is a simple Qabalistic puzzle. First of all, it is simply a rearrangement of the letters of the name of the first letter of the Hebrew alphabet, ALP, *Aleph*. This is the letter placed on the Tree of Life in the path connecting the first and second circles, Crown and Wisdom. The number next to the letter is zero, that of the Tarot Key named *The Fool*. This shows us what Brother P.A.L. really is, for the Tarot Fool is a symbol of the Life breath in man, working at superconscious levels. As Arthur Edward Waite rightly says, this Tarot Key represents the spirit in search of experience, and the Fool is "a prince of the other world on his travels through this one."[2]

Second, the letters of P.A.L. may be arranged so as to spell PLA, *pehleh*, a Hebrew adjective meaning "marvelous" or "miraculous," applied by Qabalists to the number 1, the Sephirah named Crown. This aspect of the Life Power is represented by the circle at the top of the Tree of Life, which corresponds to the highest Grade of the Invisible Order. Qabalistic psychology attributes to the Crown the highest principle of man, which it calls IChIDH, *Yekhidah*. This word means literally "the indivisible." The indivisible Unity is the Universal Self, the same as the Atman of Hindu philosophy. *Yekhidah* must be carefully distinguished (though *not* separated) from the Christos seated in the heart of human personality. On the Tree of Life, the particular place of the Christos is in *Tiphareth*, the Son, in the sixth circle. The Universal Self, *Yekhidah*, is what Jesus called "The Will of my Father."

When the cycle of five-sense life is fulfilled, as suggested by the number 15, the overshadowing presence of the Father stirs up our superconscious life and moves us to earnest desire and longing to go to the "Holy Land" of supersensuous experience. Thus, even in our cloister, we find ourselves associated with Brother P.A.L., who represents the power of the Crown of Primal Will, radiating from the indivisible I AM called "Father" by Jesus, through the path of the letter Aleph, to which the Qabalah attributes the essential Spirit, or Life-breath, veiled by the outer forms of human personality.

Do not be confused because PLA is connected with the first *circle* on the Tree of Life, whereas ALP is attributed to the *path* leading from the first circle to the second. The path is essentially identical with the circle from which it emanates, even as the rays of the sun are essentially identical with the sun itself. Hence the B.O.T.A. Tarot shows a white sun in the sky behind the Fool, as an intimation that this prince of the other world comes forth from the White Brilliance of *Kether*, the Crown. And Mr. Waite, who employs the same symbolism, says: "The sun, which shines behind him, knows whence he came, whither he is going, and how he will return by another path after many days,"[3] thus intimating that the sun is a center of consciousness because it *knows*.

[2]Arthur Edward Waite, *The Pictorial Key to the Tarot* (London: William Rider & Son, Ltd., 1911; York Beach, ME: Samuel Weiser, Inc., 1973) 152, 155.
[3]Waite, *The Pictorial Key to the Tarot*, 152, 155.

The main point to remember now is that this part of the allegory has to do with the first stirrings of a longing for higher things. The physiological aspect of those stirrings is related to the serpent power. The spiritual motivation comes from the awakening of our desire by an impulse originating in the universal and *indivisible* Self. Unless this eager longing is stirred, the indwelling Christos remains locked in the cloister of the five-sense life. Thus, all mystery rites agree with Freemasonry that the *first preparation* of a candidate for initiation must be in his heart.

At the beginning of the journey, the intended destination is Jerusalem. The name of this city means "Abode of Peace." The desire to visit Jerusalem typifies the longing for contentment, the hunger for rest from strife, the quest for peace. These usually are the dominant motives animating us when we seek entrance to the Way of Initiation.

Here, also, something is intimated that shows the real purpose of the manifestoes, despite their outward parade of sectarian Christianity. At the period when the allegory says Brother C.R.C. began his journey, the last crusade had been abandoned only a little more than a hundred years earlier, and Jerusalem was a place of pilgrimage to the Holy Sepulchre. Thus, a pilgrimage to Jerusalem was a type of that reverence for the dead forms of the past that, oddly enough, is often associated with the states of mind found in those who are just beginning their quest for truth.

Thus, occult students encounter all sorts of "Ancient Orders," making various claims to unbroken historical descent from India, Egypt, or even from Atlantis. Possibly the Uranian influence that astrologers associate with occult research may have something to do with this delight in whatever seems to be old, for astrologers hold that Uranus has great influence over antiquarian research.

Such research has its value, but it is easy to exaggerate the importance of antiquity. Truth never grows old, and reverence for the forms of the past often degenerates into superstition, which is fertile soil for the seeds of imposture. "Why seek ye the living among the dead?" is a question that might be asked of many persons who believe themselves to be specially favored because they have entered the ranks of some society claiming direct connection with seers and sages of other days.

The allegory goes on to say that Brother P.A.L. died at Cyprus. This is a subtle occult hint. P.A.L., remember, is the spiritual impulse, originating in the Will of the Father, and working at superconscious levels. To say P.A.L. dies, however, does not mean that this impulse is extinguished. In occult literature and especially in alchemical writings death means transmutation. What is meant here is that the superconscious impulse is transmuted into the special activity of a certain center, indicated by the name *Cyprus*.

Cyprus is the most easterly island of the Mediterranean Sea. Its name is the Greek root of our English noun *copper*, which was called the Cyprian metal because in that island were the copper mines that supplied the ancient world.

Copper is the metal the alchemists named Venus, and Cyprus, where this metal was mined, was the fabled birthplace of the goddess Aphrodite, a Syrian goddess, identified by mythologists with Astarte, or Ishtar, the Great Mother whose worship was introduced in Cyprus by the Phoenicians and whom the Romans later identified with Venus. The Hebrew name of this goddess is *Ashtoreth* (spelled, OShThRTh), the goddess of the Sidonians, whose name adds up to 1370, a number that is the sum of the values of the Hebrew words for Wisdom, Strength, and Beauty.

Cyprus was a great center of the cult of this goddess, and when the cult degenerated (as all cults tend to do), the adjective *Cyprian* came to be representative of all that is sensual and profligate. The original worship, however, was probably pure enough, though it had not a little in common with our more emotional forms of religion.

To a Qabalist this reference to Cyprus would have been suggestive, because the Qabalah associates both the planet Venus and the metal copper with a Hebrew letter to which the direction *east* is attributed also. Traditionally, the east, as the place of dawn, is the womb of light. Thus, this direction is associated with the beginnings of spiritual illumination. Hence, Freemasons say they travel east in search of light, and in the Masonic Lodges the chair of the Master and the pillar of Wisdom are in the east, just as the altar is placed in the eastern quarter of a Christian church. It is also true that the dawn of occult knowledge and mystical experience is represented by the literatures we call Oriental or eastern.

Moreover, since the *Fama* is intended to reveal to its readers certain secrets of the Microcosm, we may understand by the Mediterranean Sea that inner something alchemists call "our Sea," placed in the middle of the earthy vehicle of personality. That sea is the inner life, and the "islands" in it are certain interior centers. The Hindus called these centers *chakras*. The alchemists called them metals, which they named after the Sun, the Moon, and the five planets known to the ancients. In *The Apocalypse Unsealed*, James M. Pryse brings forward evidence which, if not altogether conclusive, seems to indicate that there may be some connection between these centers and the seven churches in Asia.[4] Yet other occult writers call these organs "interior stars," as does the school to which this book is largely indebted.

The Venus center, symbolized by Cyprus, is a nerve plexus in man's throat. It is the most *easterly* island because it is nearest to the original sources of power. It is the link between four lower centers in the body and two higher centers in the head. Through the Venus center, an alchemist would say, the sun rises to be joined to the moon, for the sun center is the cardiac plexus in the upper trunk, and through the sun center the physical organism receives what a yogi philosopher would call *undifferentiated Prana*. This is a form of radiant energy, in its physical aspect originating in the sun

---

[4]James M. Pryse, *The Apocalypse Unsealed*.

in the sky. The same force also has a metaphysical aspect, so that through the sun center in the trunk we make contact, at one and the same time, with the pure radiance of the physical sun and with its metaphysical counterpart.

This radiance, however, must not remain confined to the body. It must rise into the head, to be combined with the forces of the centers known as those of the Moon and Mercury. The solar energy rises through the Venus center in the throat. Hence, there can be no beginning of true occult development until Brother P.A.L., who represents the metaphysical power of the spiritual sun, "dies at Cyprus," which means that the superconscious impulse received through the sun center is changed into the awakened functioning of the Venus center.

Here we may note that the letter name ALP, aleph, means "Bull," so that it connects astrologically with the throat, inasmuch as astrologers say the region of the throat is governed by the sign Taurus, the Bull, which sign is ruled by the planet Venus.

Observe that the state of consciousness produced by the awakening of this center is predominantly emotional. The desire nature is stirred into intense activity. Little or no progress in practical occultism is made by persons having no stronger motive than intellectual curiosity. The feelings must participate. The inner door must open, so to speak, toward the heart rather than toward the head. This, however, is at the *beginning* of the work. Later the same door must swing the other way, to let the force from the heart center rise through the throat to enter and energize the brain. But at first there must be deep and genuine *emotion* if there is to be any effective action. This is the great practical lesson of this part of the *Fama*.

After Brother P.A.L. dies, Brother C.R.C. continues toward Jerusalem. The first impulse has been modified, but the desire for peace persists as the dominant motive. So the journey continues in its original direction until Damascus is reached. Here Brother C.R.C. is halted for a time "by reason of the feebleness of his body."

The place name *Damascus* means "work." Every beginner in occult practice finds that he has many purely physiological adjustments to make. "Sound mind in sound body" applies with special force to esoteric training. A practical occultist must have a strong and pure physical vehicle. To make a sound body takes work, and this work is indicated by the significance of "Damascus."

While this work goes on, Brother C.R.C. gains favor with the Turks "by reason of his skill in medicine." Taken literally, this is preposterous. At this time, according to the story, C.R.C. was only a little past fifteen years of age, and he was a Christian. Furthermore, he had not studied medicine, which he learned after he left Damascus. To fancy that a German lad, however precocious, could gain favorable notice from Mohammedans, who held all Christians in contempt, by practicing an art he had not yet begun to learn betokens a state of mind comparable to that of a person capable of sincerely believing the moon is made of green cheese.

What the *Fama* means is that as one result of the work of physical reconstruction, which takes time and effort, he who is preparing himself for initiation gains unusual skill in controlling the functions of his body. There are various systems of practice to this end. They include the establishment of correct habits of diet, the proper use of water, rhythmic breathing, and such control of the muscles as will enable the student to maintain a chosen bodily posture, without moving or suffering any discomfort, for at least an hour.

The occult school that published the *Fama* and the *Confessio* knew the laws governing the evolution of the human race. They knew that Turks are Mongolians, primary members of the Fourth Lifewave. What they said of the friendliness of the Turks to Brother C.R.C. is an allusion to the fact that the preliminary practices mentioned above do awaken physical and mental powers that were highly developed in the evolution of the Fourth Lifewave. During the evolution of the Fifth Lifewave, these powers have been submerged temporarily in subconsciousness. Let it be understood, however, that the purpose of the preliminary training represented by the sojourn of Brother C.R.C. in Damascus is by no means the awakening of these Fourth Lifewave powers. Such awakening does come as a byproduct of the work, but the real object of these practices is the cleansing of the physical vehicle, to the end that it may be prepared for initiation.

During this period of training, chastity in thought, word, and act is imperative. There are no exceptions whatever to this rule. They who neglect it may not only never get beyond Damascus but are in danger of worse things, for the practices that bring the body under control release potent physical and psychical forces. Unless they are controlled, they get out of hand, sometimes causing dreadful sexual perversions, insanity, or other manifestations of disease. Thus, the rule of continence of mind and body is absolute at this stage.

In consequence of this training comes the result described in the statement that Brother C.R.C. "became acquainted with the Wise Men of Damcar in Arabia, and beheld what great wonders they wrought, and how Nature was discovered unto them." This refers to the first awakening of interior hearing and interior sight. Interior hearing comes first, as a rule, and by means of it we "become acquainted with the Wise Men." The immediate cause of this interior hearing is the functioning of the body area under the governance of the zodiacal sign Taurus, which rules the ears and throat. As the body is purified and the Venus center in the throat begins to perform its subtler functions, which include the release of certain substances from the endocrine glands in the throat into the bloodstream, one begins actually to *hear* the Wise Men.

Students of Tarot will recognize the connection between this part of the Rosicrucian narrative and the practical meaning of Key 5, The Hierophant, which corresponds to Taurus. After the interior hearing is in some measure developed, it is followed by interior vision, which at this stage is purely mental and not to be confounded with what is ordinarily termed clairvoyance or with "astral vision." It is a heightened mental perception, whereby one *sees with the mind's eye* the nature of the powers of truly liberated humanity and sees also that full liberation reveals what is hidden by the veil of outward and illusory appearances.

Such inner hearing and vision constitute true intuition, or inner instruction, but this instruction is by no means the same as the actual initiation. It does, as the *Fama* says, "stir up the high and noble spirit of Brother C.R.C.," by giving the mind a realization of the tremendous possibilities, which may be developed into actual realizations as a result of further experimental work.

What follows is a fixed determination to prosecute that work to its completion. To accomplish this an even stricter continence of mind and body must now be established, which is indicated by the bargain our hero strikes with the Arabians. The "certain sum of money" mentioned in the text is a symbol, like the "coins" of which we hear from certain writers on alchemy. This "money" stands for one's personal energies, mental and physical, inasmuch as all money is really a symbol of one's powers and activities. Furthermore, since cattle were the universal medium of exchange in the ancient world, "money" really means just what is meant by Brother P.A.L. and by the letter Aleph, the Bull. It is the driving force of the student's whole organism. The vow of absolute chastity taken at this point is indicated by the place name *Arabia*, which signifies "sterility." It refers to more than formal physical continence, more than merely refraining from the exercise of the sex function, more than keeping the mind free from images relating to that function. To receive initiation demands utter *receptivity*, and that receptivity cannot be established or maintained unless, for this period, there is utter abstinence from any kind of creative activity, mental or physical.

Mind and body must lie fallow. Be sure you grasp this essential point. Even the tendency of subconsciousness to develop systems of imagery must be curbed. This is the object of the practices, beginning with concentration, that are explained in detail in such works as the *Raja Yoga Sutras* of Patanjali. Body and mind must be still. "Be still and know that I am God" relates to this stage of the work. In the books of the alchemists it is sometimes called the black stage of the Great Work. For it must be remembered that the Rosicrucian philosophy has been identified as the Qabalah, and since *Qabalah* means "the Reception," we must realize that before we can become partakers in this Wisdom we must prepare ourselves by becoming adequately receptive.

Thus, the temple of initiation is also in Arabia, and it is there Brother C.R.C. meets the Wise Men. Yet the bargain with the Arabians is for a "certain sum of money." Furthermore, Brother C.R.C.'s sojourn at the temple is for a definitely limited time. The utter sterility that is necessary in order that one may pass safely through the trials of initiation is by no means imposed for life. It is an indispensable *preliminary* training in self-control, and this training is what Jesus meant by His cryptic statement that some persons make themselves eunuchs "for the kingdom of heaven's sake." More than one Christian has taken this statement literally, among them Origen, who, of all persons, might be supposed to know that Jesus spoke in metaphorical terms.

This temporary sterility establishes in the body a tremendous physical reserve of life force, and in the mind a like reserve of the subtler manifestation of the same force. After initiation, however, one leaves Arabia; that is to say, one returns to a more normal course of life. Not even celibacy is required once the trials of initiation have been passed. Hence the *Confessio* says explicitly that some of the Fraternity have children. Similarly, the name of the patriarch who walked with God, Enoch, signifies "initiate," yet the Bible records an imposing list of his posterity.

The location of the temple of the Wise Men is given as Damcar in Arabia. Not long after the manifestoes appeared, hostile critics pointed out that no such place was shown on any map and that no tradition of such a city or temple was to be found outside the *Fama* and the *Confessio*. They were right as to their facts but wrong as to their conclusion that the story was a hoax. Damcar has no geographical location. Mr. Waite says the name seems later to have been regarded as a misprint for Damas, meaning Damascus.[5] This was the opinion of a more ingenious than critical American writer, who suggested that Damcar means Damascus-Cairo. The objection to this is that Damascus is in Syria and Cairo in Egypt, to which country, the story says, Brother C.R.C. went after he had left Damcar.

The key to the puzzle is in the name Damcar itself and would have been plain to any competent Qabalist in 1614. This place name is a made up combination of two Hebrew words. The first is DM, *dam*, meaning "blood." The second is KR (that is C.R.), *car*, meaning "lamb." Thus, the name is Hebrew for "Blood of the Lamb," a phrase familiar to all Christians.

In the work just referred to, Mr. Waite says: "A Rosicrucian secret Ritual of the nineteenth century affirms that Damcar is a Hebrew word, signifying Blood of the Lamb—i.e. DM is Blood and KR is Lamb. In Talmudic Hebrew KAR denotes an ass and therefore the alleged signification might be as reasonably Blood of the Ass."[6]

This is Mr. Waite at his worst. It deserves the sharper condemnation because it appears in a book whose general excellence demonstrates that Mr. Waite knew better. He need only have consulted a Hebrew dictionary to find KR, *car*, is good Scriptural Hebrew for "lamb," used in Deuteronomy 32:14 and in many other places. It happens that Mr. Waite had a special dislike for the Rosicrucian society whose ritual he ridiculed. He

[5]Waite, *The Brotherhood of the Rosy Cross* (London: William Rider & Son, Ltd., 1924), 127n.
[6]Waite, *The Brotherhood of the Rosy Cross,* 127n.

had good grounds for his dislike, but he went too far with his prejudice, for he knew perfectly well that along with much that is bad these rituals contain a great deal that is good. Furthermore, the criticism is not only prejudiced but definitely disingenuous, so that an instructed reader might be tempted to apply the Talmudic word KAR to Mr. Waite himself, rather than to the writers of the ritual he criticized.

Spelled in Hebrew, Damcar is DMKR, and its number, 264, is that of the name of the River Jordan, IRDN, which river is associated by Qabalistic alchemists with the "Water of Minerals." More than one esoteric interpretation of the Scriptures associates Jordan with the bloodstream of man.

The Lamb, as we have already seen, is a symbol for the Christos, common to Hindu and Christian typology. Initiation begins a process by which the powers of the Christos are liberated and brought into expression. This process results in the perfection of a personal vehicle adequate for the transmission of these powers outward from the causal plane into manifestation in the physical world.

The practices of initiation modify the chemistry of the initiate's own blood. The abode of the Wise Men in Damcar is the initiate's own body. Thus, it is like Solomon's temple in Freemasonry. Many have said that the Biblical account of Solomon's temple is allegory, inasmuch as a building erected without sound of hammer is more likely a spiritual than a material edifice. It is, as Freemasonry says, "a temple not made with hands, eternal in the heavens." Here be on your guard. The temple is not a metaphysical structure but a physical one. Truly it is not made with hands, for its builders have no hands. Truly, also, is it in the heavens, but this is because it is the vehicle of a consciousness that knows itself to be what Rosicrucians call "a citizen of heaven."

We read that Brother C.R. learned his medicine and mathematics at Damcar, because the physical work of initiation is based on occult mathematics; that is, on the actual geometrical proportions governing the manifestation of all forms in nature. The initiatory work is also a work of occult medicine, because it has to do with control of forces whose first awakening is represented by the passage in the *Fama* that tells us of the friendliness of the Turks at Damascus. The activities of these forces determine the state of the body chemistry, and they also build cells into bones and tissues. The practical work of initiation, in short, is the perfection of a physical body by means of the mental direction of spiritual forces. When the bodily vehicle is perfected, the spiritual powers find free and harmonious expression on the physical plane. This is one reason there are not many Masters. Most persons are too lazy to do the work and waste their lives trying to find some "easy way."

Brother C.R.C. came to Damcar at the age of sixteen. At this age the physical transformations of puberty are completed, so that it is safe to begin the undertaking that prepares the body for occult initiation.

The number 16 has yet another meaning, illustrated by the 16th Key of Tarot, entitled The Tower. This Key depicts the overthrow of a tower, which is destroyed by a lightning flash. It may be interpreted briefly as representing the overthrow of the structure of false knowledge reared on the foundation of delusion that supposes each human personality to be a separate entity. The lightning flash knocks a crown from the tower, to represent the destruction of the false notion of independent personal volition, since in symbolism a crown always stands for *will*. When we have arrived at the occult age of sixteen, we have awakened to the fundamental truth that there can be no such thing as personal independence, no such thing as personal autonomy, no such thing as personal separateness.

Furthermore, the number 16 is the square of 4, or the multiplication of 4 by itself. Geometrically, this is represented by a square having sides of 4 units, and such a square has the peculiarity that the number representing its area is also the number of units in its boundary. On this account the number 16 was anciently esteemed as a numeral symbol of the heavenly order, and was particularly associated with Jupiter, the wielder of the thunderbolt. It is this weapon of Jove that destroys the tower of Tarot Key 16. What is meant is that the overthrow of false knowledge is brought about by an influx of light from above, by a sudden perception of the true nature of things. And so Brother C.R.C. is said to have been sixteen years old, to intimate that one must have reached the point where the unfoldment of higher consciousness from the Christos within manifests itself as the destruction of the error of separateness, before one may progress to the higher Grades of initiation. He who is deluded by the false notion of personal separateness, he who still believes in personal autonomy and personal free will, is not yet of the "age of sixteen" and cannot receive the higher instruction, because he cannot possibly be receptive to it.

After mentioning C.R.C.'s age and his "strong Dutch constitution," the *Fama* continues: "There the Wise Men received him not as a stranger, but as one whom they had long expected; they called him by his name, and showed him other secrets out of his cloister, whereat he could not but mightily wonder." As soon as the work of initiation really begins, one discovers that he is by no means alone in his quest for truth. A more vivid and direct contact is established with the Masters of the Inner School, but it must be remembered that this contact is made in Damcar. What is represented here is not an astral journey, not a departure from whatever place one's physical body happens to occupy at the time of the experience.

What really occurs is that one's interior mechanism of reception becomes so finely attuned that the entire interior sensorium awakens. To all intents and purposes one not only sees and hears the Masters as if from a distance but has also an experience of their actual presence. This experience is so difficult to distinguish from objective sensation that St. Paul wrote of it: "I knew a man in Christ above fourteen years ago, (whether in the body I cannot tell; or whether out of the body, I cannot tell: God knoweth;) such an one caught up to the third heaven." [2 Corinthians 12:2]

During such experience the initiate is made to understand that his occult progress has been under observation for years, even before he was consciously aware of an urge to follow the path. The deeper significance of his five-sense consciousness and its experiences is made clear to him. A host of impressions that have been stored in subconsciousness are brought to the surface, and he sees the meaning of many events in his life. Misunderstandings are cleared up. Things that might have seemed to have light importance when they occurred are more correctly evaluated. This course of occult retrospection, under the guidance of Masters of the Inner School, provides one with some of the most valuable lessons in the whole period of training. Sometimes it includes recollection of events in previous incarnations but not always. The purpose of the work is not to satisfy curiosity but rather to illustrate principles by reference to the initiate's own personal history.

Remember, the Wise Men are actual human beings. They constitute the Third Order of the Invisible Rosicrucian Fraternity. They are designated as Masters because they actually do exercise mastery over all things and creatures that are natually subordinate to man. Yet in speaking to them one does not call any of them by the name "Master." One obeys the New Testament command: "Neither be ye called masters, for one is your Master, even Christ." We address them as either "Brother" or "Sister," for among those who have attained this stage of spiritual unfoldment are women as well as men.

The Masters of the Third Order become visible to human eyes when those eyes, as the *Confessio* puts it, "have received strength borrowed from the eagle." The *eagle* is the nerve force that finds outlet ordinarily in the reproductive functions governed by the sign Scorpio. This force must be sublimated before it may be expressed through the bodily centers that are the organs of initiatory experience. Attempts to bring about this sublimation before body and mind have been purified by preliminary practice are fraught with danger. The body must be cleansed. The mind must be controlled. The bloodstream must be charged with subtle substances from glandular secretions controlled by the subconscious powers called "Turks" in the *Fama*. All this must be done in Damascus, before one goes to Damcar. The work in Damascus changes the blood chemistry and modifies the structure of certain areas in the brain.

In our times, a greater number of persons may be expected to have this experience than at any other recorded period in history. The present state of the human consciousness, together with certain cosmic conditions that have not obtained on earth since a time long prior to any external record of human experience, are especially favorable to real initiation. Beyond a certain point, the details of practical methods may not be explained publicly, yet every reader of these pages may undertake the preliminary work of purifying mind and body. When such a person is ready, when he gives the right knock, when he asks at the right door, when he meets the tests that show him to be duly and truly prepared, he will get in touch with those who can give him instruction, which it is inadvisable to publish at present. The tests are strict. They are also subtle, so that many are tried and fail, without knowing what has occurred. Also, many pass their tests triumphantly without realizing at the time the true nature of their experience; but when they "come to Damcar" they learn things "out of their cloister," and like the hero of this allegory, "they cannot but mightily wonder."

Brother C.R.C. begins his work at Damcar by perfecting himself in the "Arabian tongue." This refers to the initiate's instruction in what is actually a kind of occult language, which combines sound and meaning in ways different from the speech that expresses five-sense consciousness. This "Arabian tongue" is by no means any variant of ordinary Arabic. It is a mode of expression that becomes possible in no other manner than through the exercise of the subtler senses, which become active during the period of temporary celibacy. At this time one has unusual insight into the secrets of nature, and putting this experience (or as much of it as can be recorded in words) into an orderly, scientific, well-organized form of statement is what is meant by the translation of Book M (*Liber Mundi* or *Book of the World*) into good Latin. This translation Brother C.R.C. is said to have brought with him, because even after the initiatory experiences are over, the knowledge gained thereby is never lost. This knowledge included grasp of the principles of occult healing and occult mathematics.

The *Fama* says all this took three years. It does require just about that time, provided one has sufficient leisure to undertake the work. For those who are, or who seem to themselves to be, too much involved in duties and other outer concerns of life to devote the greater part of their waking hours to occult practice, the period of the sojourn at Damcar is somewhat lengthened.

Here let us anticipate an objection to what has been said about the meaning of "Arabia." Some readers may hastily conclude that such strict continence is beyond human possibility. Actually it is not, even in the most literal sense, when one desires initiation sincerely enough. Even persons in the midst of a busy external life can, if they understand the principle, maintain the physical conditions required, without any clamping down of a lid of repression on the desires of the flesh. What may seem more difficult is the curbing of mental imagery and the abstention from developing systems of creative expression.

With respect to this, we find that what seemed to be a perfectly lucid explanation is influenced by our long familiarity with the cryptic writing of the adepts. So we add that the real object of this practice is attained when one stops identifying his personality as the source of any activity whatever. To realize at all times the truth of the words "I do nothing whatever of my personal self" is to become a true "Arabian." If you grasp the full meaning of this explanation, you will see that no matter what the requirements of your outer life may be, you can make ready for Damcar and go there, and this is true of every person in the world. This work is for all. Whosoever will may partake of the water of life freely. Yet it is also true that though many are called, few are chosen, for though the *Fama*, like every work of true occultism, says: "We offer our treasures freely," it also makes perfectly clear the truth that none but the worthy may receive the gift.

It will be seen that these initiatory practices at Damcar have to do with the perfection of what amounts to a new vehicle for the God-Self or Christos, our Brother C.R.C. Hence, the three years bring the hero of the story to the magical age of nineteen.

This age is symbolized by the 19th Key of Tarot, which shows a little boy and a little girl dancing hand in hand in a fairy ring, with their backs to a wall built of five courses of stone. Over them shines a sun with a human face. The children typify the regenerated human personality, which turns its back on the wall of the limitations of the five-sense consciousness, and begins to learn the first steps of the dance of life—in the fairy ring or circle of true Christ-consciousness.

The number 19, furthermore, is the number of the Hebrew proper name ChVH, *Chavah*, translated "Eve" in English Bibles. Mother Eve personifies what Hindu philosophy calls Prakriti and what the Egyptians worshipped as Mother Isis. She is Nature, the alchemical Woman, and the alchemical Moon, or Silver. In the Tarot Key just described she is pictured as a little girl, and the little boy is a symbol of the regenerated self-consciousness. The two are shown hand in hand, because at this stage of development the manifesting power (Eve, Isis, Prakriti) is transformed from the dark, terrible Mother into what is hinted at in Proverbs 7:4, which reads: "Say unto wisdom, Thou art my sister; and call understanding thy kinswoman." A Qabalistic book, *The Lesser Holy Assembly*, comments on this passage as follows:

> It is written, Prov. 7:4: "Say unto Chokmah, thou art my sister." For there is given one Chokmah (*male*), and there is also given another Chokmah (Female). And this Woman is called the Lesser Chokmah in respect of the other. And therefore is it written, Song of Solomon 8:8: "We have a little sister and she hath no breasts." For in this exile She appeareth unto us to be our "little sister." At first, indeed, she is small, but she becometh great and greater, until she becometh the Spouse whom the King taketh unto Himself.[7]

---

[7] *The Lesser Holy Assembly*, Chapter 21, verses 728-731, from the *Zohar*, translated by S.L. MacGregor Mathers in *The Kabbalah Unveiled* (London: Kegan, Paul, Trench, Trubner & Co., 1926; York Beach, ME: Samuel Weiser, Inc., 1968), 335-336.

Nature is terrible to those who do not understand her. To the initiated, regenerated personality she is a joyous companion in the dance of life. Qabalists identify her with Wisdom, the second circle on the Tree of Life. Ordinarily, Wisdom is called "Father" and is thought of as male; but as the recipient of the influx from the Primal Will or Crown, *Chokmah* is the "little sister" who grows until she becomes the Spouse, or Bride. To Wisdom, or *Chokmah*, Qabalists assign "the highway of the stars," or the vast order of the heavenly spaces, which flows into our human life through the tides and currents of what is commonly denominated "astrological influence." To the greater number of human beings, this heavenly order seems to be a fatal bond, restricting their freedom. Thus, many lovers of liberty, mistaking both the true nature of what they love and the true meaning of astrological influence, repudiate the ancient wisdom concerning man's relationship to the stellar order. The ignorant, destructive notion of astrology held by many astrologers is largely responsible for this repudiation.

When one becomes a true initiate, the heavenly order is called "little sister," for it is perceived as being the macrocosmic manifestation of the perfect law of liberty proceeding from the God-Self dwelling within, at the center. Our dance of life then accommodates its measures of personal activity to the music of the spheres. The mask of terror worn by the "mysterious power," Prakriti, is torn off. We see her as the kinswoman who is also the beloved, our partner in the dance.

Brother C.R.C.'s twentieth year is described as having been occupied with a journey from Damcar to Egypt, a short stay in that country, and another journey to the place where he completed his work. Of the journey to Egypt we learn that it was across *Sinus Arabicus*, the Arabian Gulf. Here is an intimation that the period of celibacy represented by Arabia has come to its end.

Egypt, land of darkness and captivity, is the automatic region of subconsciousness. C.R.C. goes there, as did Joseph, Pythagoras, Jesus, and many another. His work in Egypt represents the initiate's investigation of the modes of power developed in man during the course of his evolution through the vegetable and animal kingdoms. An initiate is able to receive conscious awareness of this experience. Such revival is one of the meanings of Tarot Key 20, which corresponds to the magical age of C.R.C. while he was in Egypt. This Tarot Key shows three figures, representing the Egyptian triad—Osiris, Isis, and Horus—rising from their coffins. Thus, it is a picture of a revival of the god-powers of "Egypt," or the subconscious forces of human personality.

Patanjali, the great Hindu teacher of mind control, speaks of this revival of subconscious knowledge when he says one may so meditate as to gain understanding of the properties of all plants and knowledge of the meaning of all animal sounds. Observe, however, that such exploration of the automatic consciousness is dangerous if undertaken before one has gone through the training represented by Brother C.R.C.'s three years at Damcar. Hence, the *Chaldean Oracles* give to those who are tempted to premature investigation of the "mysteries of Egypt" this solemn warning:

> Stoop not down into the Darkly Splendid World; where-
> in continually lieth a faithless depth, and Hades wrapped
> in clouds, delighting in unintelligible images, precipitous,
> winding, a black, ever-rolling Abyss; ever espousing a
> body unluminous, formless and void.
>   Stoop not down, for a precipice lieth beneath the
> earth, reached by a descending ladder which hath seven
> steps, and therein is established an evil and fatal force.[8]

The psychic powers of "Egypt," the region under the surface of the earth, or beneath the plane of ordinary sensation, are powers unquestionably marvelous. They need investigation, but that investigation should not be unduly prolonged. Hence, Patanjali tells us that the *Siddhis*, as the Hindus call these powers, are actually an obstacle to real advance along the Path of Liberation. So the *Fama* says C.R.C. spent no long time in Egypt.

Truly are the powers of this region described as "darkly splendid." Note that they are associated with Hades, the Greek name for the abode of the spirits of the departed. Thus, "Egypt" is to be understood as that region of activity that is commonly the field of investigation in psychic research. It is also the region whence come the powers of mediumship exploited by Spiritualism. There is a tremendous attraction in these powers, and their dark splendor has lured many a seeker away from the true path.

The *Oracle* says truly that this region is the abode of an evil and fatal force. For the powers of subconsciousness, developed during stages of evolution below that of humanity, are evil in the sense that it is always evil to go back to a lower level of development. They are powers, moreover, that work according to a Law of Averages from which man escapes by exercising his power of conscious self-direction. They are powers belonging to what Jacob Boehme calls "the astral sphere," from which the higher wisdom releases us.

The ladder of seven steps leading down into this region is the same ladder up which these powers, in a right system of occult training, are made to ascend. The warning is that *we* should not descend the ladder, that *we* should not stoop down. The rungs of the ladder are the interior centers otherwise represented as the churches in Asia, as the interior stars, or as the *chakras*. The purpose of the warning is that the ladder should be ever one of ascent, permitting the rising or sublimation of the "Egyptian" powers.

---

[8]*Chaldean Oracles of Zoroaster*, edited and revised by Sapere Aude (W. Wynn Westcott). Reprinted by Occult Research Press, New York. page 46.

The greater number of "occult failures," as they are called, are persons who have gone down into "Egypt" and have been fascinated by the lure of its shadowy glamour. In the Bible they are personified by the Israelites whose prolonged sojourn in Egypt led to their being subjected to intolerable slavery. Occult failures are often persons who attract attention by exercising psychic powers that really belong to lower than human levels of evolution.

Psychism of this kind is so great an obstacle to liberation that Buddha not only agreed with Patanjali as to its dangers but actually made the exercise of such powers in any form of miracle working cause for expulsion from the Buddhist brotherhood. Yet C.R.C. goes to Egypt for a short time. Psychic powers must be investigated, and the laws of the subhuman forces that are part of our makeup must be understood. There is a danger here, but it must be met, not avoided.

Cowardly refusal to make oneself acquainted with subhuman powers is not the way to mastery. We must know them in order to control them. The business of the occult teacher is to warn his pupils against the dangers of "Egypt," and even Buddha's strict rule is only against the public performance of marvels of thaumaturgy and against public claims to the possession of the *Siddhis*. But that teacher is remiss in his duty who utters words of discouragement. It is both false and cowardly to make people *afraid* of the "powers of Egypt." It is even worse to malign those powers as being in themselves evil. We repeat, the evil is in returning to the level represented by those powers, not in the powers themselves. What is a positive good for a tiger or an elephant becomes an evil for man, if the exercise of that power lowers the man's consciousness to the elephant or tiger level. Readers with some degree of discrimination soon learn to detect the difference between honest warnings against the dangerous glamour of "Egypt" and the sort of thing so often said by persons whose principal stock-in-trade is a false pretense to the possession of some measure of psychic power, which pretense they protect from exposure by the transparent device of telling their dupes that only after incarnations of preparation may such powers be safely exercised. In effect they say: "We have these powers, of course, but you must not expect to develop them. No, just you rely on our revelations. We'll tell you all about the Masters. We'll let you into the secrets of the invisible. We'll let you buy our books and fill your minds with fancy pictures of angels and elementals and mysterious 'initiations.' But whatever you do, don't think of looking for yourself! You're not ready!"

Even when this sort of thing is not merely a device to prevent the exposure of pretenders and is uttered by persons who sincerely believe in their own psychic powers, it is pernicious. For it has a tendency to encourage reliance on the authority of others in those who pay attention to it, and it undermines the student's self-reliance. If to such warnings there is added, as often happens, outright condemnation of psychic forces as intrinsically evil, even more harm is done.

His studies in Egypt completed, Brother C.R.C. sailed over the entire Mediterranean Sea to Fez. This city is at the western end of the sea. It is therefore in contrast to Cyprus, where the first work of transmutation occurred. Fez is also at the other end of the sea from Egypt, and if we remember that this sea is in the microcosm, we shall understand the allegory.

In the fourteenth century, Fez was the intellectual center of the world. A great university was there, with a fine library, to which men of learning repaired from every land. In this allegory, therefore, Fez corresponds to the intellectual powers associated in occultism with Mercury or Hermes. These are the powers expressed through organs in the head of man, and when the *Fama* was written, the whole world knew that the characteristic Turkish headdress, the fez, was named after the city. Thus, the hint is plain enough.

The *Fama* says those at Fez excelled in mathematics, medicine, and magic—and all of these are departments of Hermetic Science. It also says that in Fez Brother C.R.C. "did get acquaintance with those who are commonly called the Elementary Inhabitants, who revealed unto him many of their secrets." These are the conscious entities of the *nonhuman* manifestations of the Life Power, sometimes denominated the *Deva Evolution*. Among them are entities at work in the phenomena of inorganic chemistry, as well as entities working through plants and animals. To occultists of the seventeenth century Paracelsus made these known by the following names: salamanders, inhabitants of fire; undines, inhabitants of water; sylphs, inhabitants of air; gnomes, inhabitants of earth. Much information concerning them, veiled in language full of absurdities if taken literally, may be found in the *Comte de Gabalis*, first published in Paris in 1670.

What needs to be said at this point is that numerous amusing misconceptions concerning these "Elementary Inhabitants" are current among readers and writers of occult books. The *Fama* gives us a strong and pertinent hint when it says that Brother C.R.C. made the acquaintance with those who are "commonly called the Elementary Inhabitants," as if the common designation might be a veil for a more accurate description known to the authors of the manifestoes. Furthermore, since this "acquaintance" was made at Fez, we may pause here to ask ourselves if this be not a hint that the acquaintance itself was an intellectual conception, rather than any form of psychic perception.

Benvenuto Cellini says in his autobiography that his grandfather once saw a salamander. But the good goldsmith stretched a stout longbow on occasion, and since his grandfather must have lived before the days of Paracelsus, who seems to have invented the name *salamander* as a designation for the inhabitants of fire, one cannot but wonder as to the accuracy of the tale. In our own times, we hear of the head of an occult order who had a "tame salamander" in her home for a period of some months; but one knows this person to be a subtle Qabalist, and it is probable that there is more to her story than appears on the surface. We may well remember that long ago Madame Blavatsky wrote in *Isis Unveiled* that for the production of physical phenomena an adept "summons the nature-spirits as obedient *powers*, not as intelligences."[9]

At this point in the Rosicrucian allegory there is a plain intimation that the errors of what passes for science in our times are chiefly attributable to the fact that true observation and correct inference require something more than laboratory apparatus. The physical and psychical constitution of the observer must be taken into account. It *is* taken into account by all trained researchers, who always allow for what is termed "the personal equation." Yet this allowance is often insufficient. Until one has passed through the stages of physical and mental development represented by the earlier work of Brother C.R.C., the study of the phenomena of the inorganic phases of life expression leads more often to gross error than to truth. The materialism of our times is evidence of this.

Human knowledge of physics, chemistry, astronomy, biology, and like sciences is extraordinary in its accumulation of facts and has led to marvelous results. Knowledge of facts, however, is not wisdom, and in our day grasp of the meaning of many facts is sadly wanting. The whole world is sick with the errors of misinterpretation. The popular notion is that science is exact, but some of the leading scientists confess that in large measure they are groping in the dark.

Thus, the *Fama* says: "Of those at Fez he often did confess that their Magia was not altogether pure, and also that their Cabala was defiled with their Religion." Even so, among scientists today the "religion" of materialism, not less dogmatic and authoritarian than any other form of religion, interferes with proper reception of truth. Hypothesis follows hypothesis, book follows book. A "truth" accepted today, and taught everywhere in schools and universities, is tomorrow an exploded fallacy that is abandoned for a more fashionable doctrine.

As for the magic, or applied science, of our day, what shall we say of the use of electricity and poison gas to kill men whose evil deeds are direct consequences of the materialism taught in our schools, or of the worse type of materialism that is taught by example in those unofficial but terribly efficient schools, the slums of our great cities? What shall we think of chemical warfare and of the destruction of helpless civilians by bombs dropped from airplanes? What of food adulteration, of the production of tons and tons of worthless goods, of the slavery that misuse of machinery imposes on thousands of men, women, and even little children? All in the name of science and progress! Not to speak of the black magic of lying advertising and propaganda sent everywhere by a cynical press, which publishes Bible texts on its editorial pages and the lures of swindlers in its

---

[9]H.P. Blavatsky, *Isis Unveiled* (London: Theosophical Publishing House, 1923), 1:457.

advertising columns. And now that radio and television, even more irresponsible than the press, have invaded our homes with all the evil arts of suggestion turned to the basest uses, we are reaping the fruits of mere knowledge when that knowledge is used by persons devoid of spiritual understanding.

True occult science avoids these errors and their consequences. It trains the observer so that he can read the Book of Nature and make adequate translations from it. Thus, it prepares its initiates for the most difficult of all investigations—the exploration of the mysteries of the inorganic modes of existence. Rightly prepared by the study of kingdoms of nature more like himself, in which the spark of consciousness is not so heavily veiled by the limitations of physical form, an initiate of occult science approaches the investigation of the inorganic plane prepared to detect even here the same fundamental laws of consciousness he has discovered in operation elsewhere.

Furthermore, though he may discover errors and contaminations in the works of uninitiated scientists, he is able to make good use of their labors. A true occultist is no enemy of the Darwins, the Huxleys, the Steinmetzes, or the Millikans. He gladly uses the results of their investigations, because he has a touchstone that enables him to separate the gold of truth from the dross of error. He rejoices in every new discovery of the physicists, the chemists, the biologists, and all the others who study man and his environment according to accepted scientific procedures, because therein he finds, to employ the quaint phrase of the *Fama*, "still more better grounds for his faith."

At the end of two years Brother R.C. departed the city Fez. At this paragraph in the story occurs the first use of the initials R.C., instead of C.R.C., as if to direct the attention of those who had the Qabalistic keys to the *Fama's* puzzles to the truth that the completion of occult training develops in man the character of compassion or tenderness (RC, *roke*). The age of our Brother at this time is twenty-two years. This number is appropriate, because in occult mathematics 22 represents the circumference of a circle, and the completion of a cycle of manifestation is therefore numerically symbolized by 22. Furthermore, as we have seen that the circle symbol is also connected with the initials C.R.C., what is intimated here is that the full powers of the God-Self are now ready to manifest through their regenerated and perfected personal vehicle, the distinguishing mark of which is tenderness and sympathy.

Qabalists are familiar with the twenty-two Hebrew letters, the twenty-two phases of consciousness, and the twenty-two expressions of *Mezla*, the influence flowing down the paths of the Tree of Life from *Kether*, the Crown. The twenty-two connecting paths of the Tree are represented also by twenty-two Keys of Tarot. At the magical age of twenty-two, one has become a Master of these paths, and is, so to speak, a living embodiment of all that is represented by the diagram shown in our frontispiece.

What follows in the story is always true. When one's occult training is finished, the first effect of the sympathy and compassion it engenders is a desire to share one's knowledge with others. Yet as the story shows, one must be careful in selecting those to whom the higher wisdom is to be imparted. Therefore, secrecy has ever veiled the dazzling light of arcane teaching. The proper way to communicate wisdom of the subtler sort is not by indiscriminate open teaching. This invariably has no other result than to excite ridicule, provoke bitter antagonism, and invite persecution.

Spain was chosen by the authors of the *Fama* as being typical of religious and scientific traditionalism. All the world knows how that proud country, once mistress of a great empire, has fallen on evil days because of its unreasoning obedience to tradition. For centuries creative art and thought have been stifled by the weight of spiritual and mental tyranny over the minds of the natives of the land that gave us Velázquez and Cervantes. The spirit of reliance on the dead past has throttled Spain, and it is the perfect type of the causes of antagonism to occult science found elsewhere.

The causes of that antagonism are the same today as when the *Fama* was written. It matters not how willing a practical occultist may be to show "new growths, new fruits, and beasts." Such things, being outside the range of ordinary experience, are a laughing matter to minds accustomed to the narrow limits of traditional orthodoxy, whether in religion or in science. On this account even so extraordinary a person as H.P. Blavatsky found, to her sorrow, that phenomena, however wonderful, never convince anyone who is determined not to change accustomed opinions and prejudices. Only an exceptional person is willing to acknowledge an error to which he has grown accustomed, especially if it has been the means of bringing him fame and money.

At this point in the story a detail is introduced that has a bearing on the general thesis developed in the *Fama* and the *Confessio*. It is said the new growths, new fruits, and beasts "did concord with old philosophy"— that is, they were new demonstrations of ancient principles. So it was also with the phenomena of Madame Blavatsky, which were produced to arouse interest in her presentation of a most ancient secret doctrine. The central thesis of the Rosicrucian manifestoes is that they propose a reformation of the arts and sciences in order to correct faults that have crept in with the passage of time. The amendment of philosophy they present for our consideration is not an innovation. It is a return to something that has been forgotten by the greater part of mankind, although it has been kept alive, generation after generation, by the Inner School.

The external evidences of the validity of this ageless doctrine do change from age to age. Thus, Brother R.C. had new things to show, but they agreed with the old philosophy. Nevertheless, the wise men of Spain and of other nations would have none of his teaching. Here is a lesson for all persons imbued with the missionary spirit. Mere willingness to impart truth is not enough. Those who are to receive it must have adequate capacity. In the Orient this is well understood, and many tests of a would-be pupil's competence are made before he is given any of the deeper instruction. What the *Fama* calls "the true and infallible Axiomata" sound like nonsense to a person incapable of grasping what they mean. As a matter of fact, many of these axioms of Rosicrucian doctrine are indeed *non-sense*, in that they run counter to the testimony of superficial sense experience. Thus, the Tarot, which presents many of the Rosicrucian Axiomata in pictorial form, begins with a Key named The Fool, to intimate that the instruction developed in subsequent pages of that picture book of Ageless Wisdom is a doctrine regarded by the worldly wise as being utterly foolish.

The Rosicrucian Axiomata, moreover, are said to direct us to "the only middle point and center." Occult wisdom leads always away from the "many-ness" of the outer world to the unity at the heart of being. This, incidentally, is the inner significance of the American motto, *E pluribus unum*, which appears on the Great Seal of the United States. The same American national coat-of-arms exhibits other indications that it was composed under the influence of Rosicrucian doctrines transmitted through Freemasonry. The direction of occult wisdom toward an inner center furnishes another reason for the difficulty that an average exoteric scientist experiences when he tries to understand esoteric teaching. All of his training has led him away from the inner center toward the many divisions of the surrounding field of environment. Not many scientists realize that no matter what the field of research, the real object of study is the inner life of man.

According to the *Fama*, the knowledge Brother R.C. was ready to impart gives accurate indication of the trend of future events, and this in considerable detail. It shows how the present and the future may be brought into harmony with the past. It is the cure for the faults of the Church and for the errors of moral philosophy. More than this, the possessors of this knowledge may be described as a society having vast material resources also, namely, "gold, silver, and precious stones, sufficient for to bestow them on kings for their necessary uses and lawful purposes."

These words must have aroused the interest of a great many readers when the *Fama* first made its appearance. Among them must have been a considerable number who had no other purpose than the acquisition of material wealth. The same motive animates hordes of seekers today. Yet both *Fama* and *Confessio* warn us that none who entertain such unworthy motives will be able to make contact with the Order.

Then why mention the matter at all? First, as a test. Sometimes the existence of base motives is unrecognized by persons who are sub-consciously influenced by them. To such readers the mere mention of great wealth would be sufficient to set up subconsious responses that would inevitably betray themselves in the letters that seekers were invited to address to the Fraternity. Second, because unusual control of the means for material supply is actually one of the results of occult wisdom, and those who do make contact with the True and Invisible Order do share in the benefits of such control, even though they are not primarily interested in such benefits. Third, because these gifts are for "kings," but by this term is not meant the occupants of earthly thrones. The kings here indicated are those persons who have come to know the true royalty signified by the word *man*. For all such the fundamental laws of life offer material riches beyond the dreams of avarice. Besides this, what is said at this place in the *Fama* refers also to the occult or alchemical gold, silver, and precious stones. The latter are the transformed and perfected interior centers mentioned heretofore. Yet we trust we have made it perfectly clear that the words of the *Fama* are to be taken literally as well as figuratively when it speaks of the unlimited riches at the Order's disposal, riches that, as we read in another paragraph, can never fail or be wasted.

The *Fama* goes on to render due credit to the wise men of other ages. It shows that the world's need ripens human beings equipped to deal with problems as they arise. "The world in those days was already big with those great commotions, laboring to be delivered of them, and did bring forth painful [painstaking], worthy men, who brake with all force through darkness and barbarism, and left us who succeeded to follow them." The *world* brings forth such men; that is, the activities of human beings are not mere functions of personality. They are manifestations of a cosmic process, at work through human thoughts, words, and deeds.

The Triangle of Fire mentioned in this connection is a very old occult symbol. It links up with the lamb symbolism, which is related to the Hindu god, Agni, the personification of the powers of fire. This *Trigono igneo* also is connected with the symbolism of the Great Pyramid, which the ancient Egyptians called "The Light" and which is a stone emblem of the Eternal Flame. That the same symbol appears twice on the reverse of the Seal of the United States (as an unfinished pyramid and as a radiant triangle enclosing an eye) is another evidence that the structure of government intended by the founders of the American republic presented itself to their minds as a piece of *Egyptian Masonry*. In this connection we should remember that the Rosicrucians are often termed Fire Philosophers.

Note also and ponder well the saying that the worthies mentioned "brake through with all force." In various parts of the manifestoes are similar unobtrusive but unmistakable hints that their authors recognized the truth that there is sometimes necessity for forcible overthrow of darkness and barbarism. They were, in short, of like minds with Washington, Franklin, and the writers of the Declaration of Independence, and of like mind with Abraham Lincoln, who proclaimed it as the right of any free people to overthrow its form of government by peaceable means, if possible, and if not, by force. We shall touch on this point again, as we progress with this interpretation.

In view of assertions often made that the Rosicrucian philosophy is merely a reflection of the theories of Paracelsus, the next paragraph of the *Fama* requires careful consideration. Paracelsus is there acknowledged as one who had a natural vocation in the right direction. His diligent reading of Book M, or *Liber Mundi*, the Book of Nature, is conceded, and acknowledgment is paid to his genius. Yet nothing could be more explicit than the statement that he "was none of our Fraternity" not the declaration that he lost his time with a free and careless life. And here the context shows that "free" has the old sense of "irregular," almost approaching the meaning of "libertine."

This judgment of Paracelsus is borne out by the history of that genius and is even more clearly established by his books. The defect in Paracelsus that spoiled him was his overbearing egotism, exhibited in arrogant impatience with colleagues and as a fixed idea that he, and only he, could amend the errors of philosophy. Besides, Paracelsus was lacking in self-control and drank altogether too much. Thus, he lacked two essential characteristics of a true Rosicrucian, being both uncompassionate and intemperate.

To return, with the *Fama*, to Brother C.R., we read that he refrained from further attempts to call attention to his unusual knowledge. In this connection occurs the phrase previously cited, wherein men are called "citizens of Heaven." Today this may seem commonplace enough, after years of widely circulated occult instruction have made the thought familiar. In 1614, when the general opinion was that man was a mere worm of the dust, it must have brought forth a quick response from many a reader's heart. Even now, when materialism would have us believe the whole human race to be merely a negligible incident in a series of cosmic accidents, this Rosicrucian estimate of man's true nobleness and worth is cheering. For those whose minds are yet darkened by the old, gloomy, traditional theological doctrine that man is a vile creature, tainted with original sin, here is light. In fact, we may all do well to think of ourselves as having a rightful share in the universal government, as having our abode in heaven, rather than as being merely denizens of earth and slaves to its changing circumstances.

The *Fama* goes on to say that our Father and Brother built a fitting and neat habitation, thus bringing him into the circle of Master Builders with Hiram and with Jesus the Carpenter. The habitation is the perfected body of the adept, which he is able to build because he has gained the necessary knowledge and power. The very adjectives employed in describing this habitation have the flavor of precision, order, and purity. In this house Brother C.R. "ruminated his voyage and philosophy, and reduced them together in a true memorial." It takes time to digest the initiatory experience and training and to develop its consequences. One has to chew the cud of reflection to get the full value.

The *Fama* says he spent much of his time in mathematics, because from occult arithmetic and geometry one gains the basic knowledge that makes possible what is described as the making of "many fine instruments." These instruments are made in the "house." They are the instruments of the alchemist's true laboratory, sometimes called the "secret vessels" of the art of transmutation. They are, in fact, the same as what in other connections are described as the metals, or as the interior stars.

So at first with a vain missionary enterprise and then in more intelligent pursuits just described, our Brother C.R. is said to have passed five years, which brings his magical age to twenty-seven. The number 27 is important in occultism as the *second* cube, or 3 × 3 × 3. Qabalists would have recognized it as the number of the Hebrew adjective ZK, *zak*, meaning "clean" or "pure." This is appropriate at this point in the narrative and agrees with the adjectives used to describe Brother C.R.'s house. Furthermore, though it is designated by another adjective, the idea of purity is associated with the aspect of the Life Power that Qabalists call *Yesod*, meaning "Basis" or "Foundation." *Yesod* is the ninth Sephirah, corresponding to the ninth circle on the Tree of Life. Note that 9 is the sum of the three 3s, which, multiplied together, produce 27, and that the digits of 27 also add to 9.

Thus, the number 27 is appropriate to designate the magical age at which Brother C.R. becomes the Foundation or Basis of the Fraternity and at which his idea of the reformation of the arts and science took clear form in his mind, together with a definite theory on which to proceed in carrying out the work. This last is in relation to the fact that the name of the Rosicrucian Grade corresponding to *Yesod* is Theoricus (or Theoreticus) and that in this Grade the fundamental theory of the Great Work is explained.

Furthermore, 27 is the third cubical number, 1 being the first and 8 the second. And we shall see later that the constitution of the original Fraternity was such that it may be represented by the symbolism of the cube, as were the Holy of Holies in the Jewish tabernacle and temple and as is the heavenly city, described in the twenty-first chapter of Revelation.

The number 27 is also that of the noun ChIDH, *kheedaw*, meaning "intricate speech, a riddle, an enigma." This is the best possible description of the magical language and writing with which the Brethren began at once to busy themselves. Again, 27 is the number of the verb BKH, *bawkah*, whose original meaning was "to drop, to distil, to flow in drops." This describes the Hermetic work and suggests also the measured outpouring of energy involved in such an undertaking as the text describes. Furthermore, BKH also means "to weep" and hints at what is the real motive of the Masters of the Inner School, a motive that distinguishes them sharply from men like Paracelsus, however brilliant such men may be. The Masters are moved by compassion for the errors of the unenlightened and by sympathy for sufferers from the consequences of those errors. Because these men are like God, they love the world. Therefore, they work without ceasing for the purification and regeneration of the human race.

The three cofounders of the Order are said to have been called by Brother C.R. out of his first cloister. Here is another example of sheer nonsense, if one takes the story literally. For if these were men bound by monastic vows, Brother C.R. would have had no authority over them, nor could they have responded to his call. If we understand them to be types of powers that are present even in uninitiated humanity, powers belonging to ordinary self-conscious awareness, we can understand what is meant. Observe that Brother C.R. is said to have borne them great affection. The higher order of knowing does not demand of us that we abandon or belittle the powers of ordinary self-consciousness. Quite the reverse. The higher order of knowing enables us to be rid of the limitations of the lower consciousness and helps us to cleanse our personal mind of the errors and delusions engendered by those limitations. But within their limits, these lower activities can be called on to do good work when the God-Self within has unfolded its higher potencies.

This meaning is further elucidated by the Qabalistic significance of the initials of the cofounders, which are as follows:

G.V., Hebrew GV, *gav*, meaning "middle," or "center."

I.A., a transposition of Hebrew AI, *ahyee*, meaning "where? how?" I.A. is also the Notariqon or Qabalistic abbreviation for the phrase IHI AVR, *yehi aur*, meaning "Let there be light."

I.O., adding to 80, the number of the letter Peh (the mouth), and the number of *Yesod* (Foundation or Basis), the name of the ninth Sephirah.

Brother G.V., then, stands for concentration, which leads to the establishment of equilibrium, because by concentration one establishes the true *center* or *middle* in personal consciousness. From that center a definite radiation is projected, and to do this effectively one must ask both *where?* and *how?*, which is what the transposition of the initials of I.A. suggests. The same initials, in their original order, are the first letters of the two Hebrew words meaning "Let there be light," and the establishment of light presupposes choice of a field of operation, involving a definite *where*, and a choice of some method of work, involving an equally definite *how*. Finally, any specific work has for its foundation or basis some particular form of self-expression, as suggested by the numeral values of the words corresponding to 80, or I.O.—concentration, self-interrogation followed by decision as to ways and means, and then definite expression. These are the three Brethren, and they are all "out of the cloister," for they are, all of them, personifications of powers of the human mind, working at the level of self-conscious awareness.

The values of these various initials total 100, which is the number of: KLIM, *kaleem*, meaning "vases"; MDVN, *madown*, signifying "effort" or "extension;" KP, *Kaph*, "a grasping hand," the name of the letter assigned to

Key 10 in Tarot, which Key is a symbolic representation of the actual constitution of the Invisible Order; and finally, the single Hebrew letter Q, or *Qoph*, which represents the Corporeal Intelligence, symbolized by the eighteenth Key of Tarot.

Moreover, 100 is a square number, and thus corresponds to the figure suggested by the fact that the three Brethren, with Brother C.R., were the beginning of the Fraternity, so that *four* persons were engaged in laying the foundation. As the square of 10, moreover, 100 would have indicated to any Qabalist who read the *Fama* that the basis of the Fraternity is to be sought in the powers of the ten Sephiroth.

Into concentration, decision, and expression (the three Brethren) the God-Self (Brother C.R.) pours its power and wisdom, as water is poured into vases (KLIM). Through their activity and effort, the light of instruction is extended or radiated (MDVN). They established the constitution of the Order in accordance with the comprehension (*Kaph*) of the principle of *concentric circles*, illustrated in Tarot by the threefold subdivision of the Wheel of Fortune on Key 10. The field of their operation is the Corporeal Intelligence, or body-consciousness (Q), of humanity. In confirmation of this, we find the *Fama* saying that the only profession of the Brethren was to heal the sick. That healing is accomplished by spiritual means, through the establishment in human consciousness of the perfect pattern of the Heavenly Man, which pattern is presented as a diagram by the Qabalistic Tree of Life.

If we take the initials of the Founder as being C.R. (or R.C.), their value is 220. This, added to 100, the number representing the combined initials of the three cofounders, makes 320. This is the number of the Hebrew noun ROIM, *rayim*, meaning "friends, associates," which is certainly appropriate to this part of the allegory.

If the Founder's initials are taken as C.R.C., they add to 240, and this, combined with the number of the cofounders' initials, makes 340, the value of ShM, *Shem*, meaning "name" and used by Qabalists to designate the Great Name, IHVH, *Jehovah*, which is the last word of the *Fama*. The number 340 is also the value of SPR, *sepher*, meaning "book." Any association of four persons would have suggested to a Qabalist the four letters of IHVH, or the Name of Names. The *Fama* tells us also that the first work of these Brethren was the making of the magical language and writing, with a large dictionary. They also began the Book M. Thus, their combined labors, which were dependent on the wisdom they received from Brother C.R.C., are well represented by SPR, *sepher*, or "book."

At the same time they were occupied with healing, for it is said their work on Book M was hindered by the unspeakable concourse of the sick. This last means also that at the beginning of any occult work the progress of the undertaking through its early stages is always hampered by the "sickness" of the very persons it is designed to help. Read *The Mahatma Letters to A.P. Sinnett*, and you will see how a spiritual movement goes through these labor pains. Even better is a careful study of the beginnings of Christianity, as outlined in the New Testament.

During this period, says the *Fama*, Brother C.R.C.'s new building, The House of the Holy Spirit, was finished. This indicates the real nature of the undertaking announced by the manifestoes. The *Domus Sancti Spiritus* is not the same as the "neat and fitting habitation" Brother C.R. made for himself. It is another building, described later as the meeting place of the Order. In the last paragraph of the *Fama* it is mentioned again, where we read: "Also our building, although one hundred thousand people had very near seen and beheld the same, shall for ever remain untouched, undestroyed, and hidden to the wicked world.

Yet there have been critics who say the manifestoes must be a hoax, because nobody ever saw The House of the Holy Spirit! In truth, it is probable that considerably more than a hundred thousand persons have seen it by this time. Thousands of others, though some nearly see it, do not, after all, behold that glorious structure. Let it be ours to affirm that it is a real building, though unseen, more marvelous than any of this world's other wonders. Let it be ours to declare that the way to it stands open today, as in the past, and that none shall fail to find it who seek diligently *in the right direction*. And the path that leads to it is the path pictured in the eighteenth Tarot Key.

Four more Brethren were now drawn into the work. These four represent the elements required, in addition to those already mentioned, in order to complete the establishment of any organized effort to communicate occult instruction.

The first is designated by the same initials as those of the Founder, R.C., which stand for the word *roke*, or compassion. Tenderness must come first and foremost in work of this kind. Sympathy with human suffering, understanding of human problems through ability to put oneself in another's shoes, unselfish desire to lift the heavy burden of ignorance from the minds of the unenlightened—these are primary requirements.

It is not simply the wish to give a treasure, not simply the desire to be bountiful, that must animate a work such as this. Utmost patience with human shortcomings is needful, for that patience will be sorely tried, again and again and again. The stupidity of the crowd is almost beyond belief, yet the stupid ones must never be blamed. Hate and antagonism will be encountered, coming from those most in need of help and guidance, yet these must be forgiven, because they are the natural fruit of ignorance. Fickleness and desertion in the face of seeming dangers are to be expected from those who are not yet well grounded in the work. Hardest of all for some to bear is a spectacle all too common in these days, the spectacle of seekers for light running madly after charlatans and impostors who are but purveyors of lies and traffickers in deception. Yet even the charlatans must be forgiven and understood, even though one is in duty bound to expose their tricks and condemn their charlatanry.

The next Brother is B. This initial corresponds to the Hebrew letter Beth. As you will see from the diagram of the Tree of Life, this letter is assigned to the path connecting circle 1, the Crown, with circle 3, Understanding. In Tarot, Beth is represented by Key 1, The Magician, a symbol synthesizing all of the powers of human self-consciousness. This letter and Key also are related to Mercury or Hermes, and thus, to alchemists, the letter *B* stands for the active agent in the Great Work, for alchemical books say the Great Work is a work of the Sun and Moon, performed by the aid of Mercury.

Brother B. is described as being a skillful painter. In the list of the Brethren following the *Elogium* he is designated as *Fra.* F.B.M.P.A., *Pictor et Architectus*, and the value of this extended designation is 129, for the *F* in German corresponds to Hebrew Vav. Thus, the extended meaning of his initials corresponds to the Hebrew phrase IHVH HVA ALHIM, *Jehovah Hu Elohim* (Jehovah He is God), for upon conscious recognition of what this phrase implies all adequate planning for such building as is indicated by the allegory of the *Fama* must be based. Brother B. is also the one who works with colors, which further identifies him with the Mercury of the alchemists, which they call their tingeing, or coloring, agent.

To a Qabalist, moreover, the letter *B* would suggest the power of initiative, inasmuch as *B* is the first letter of the first Hebrew word in Genesis. To communicate occult instruction, one must have at his command the quality of strong initiative, combined with ability to make definite, specific plans, and the ability to set forth the subject in its proper colors. Dull, abstract statement of bare principles will not suffice.

Consider in this connection the method of Jesus. No man ever spoke as he did, and he held vast audiences enthralled as he illustrated his doctrine by vivid human-interest stories. Cold, academic precision always fails to arouse the enthusiasm necessary to heal the fatal sickness of human ignorance. To hear some professed occultists talk, one might suppose they had kept their minds and hearts in cold storage for years on end. It takes a *skillful painter* to limn the picture of reality so that the dull, half-blind eyes of sense-bound humanity can make it out.

Third in order of these second four Brethren is Brother G.G. His initials spell the Hebrew noun GG, *gawg*, meaning "roof," so suggesting both shelter and secrecy. Thus, the doorkeeper of a Masonic lodge bears the significant name of "tiler," and to "tile" the lodge is to make sure that none are admitted save those having the right to enter. Hence, Brother G.G. represents the human virtue of prudence. He also represents the principle of secrecy, as necessary today as ever before, if genuine occultism is to be propagated successfully.

The modern intellectual mind chafes against secrecy. "Why not tell all?" is a question often asked. Those who ask it forget that the essence of anything truly occult is that it is *hidden*—hidden not only by the ignorance that keeps men from seeing but hidden also by those who are custodians of certain kinds of knowledge. It is hidden primarily out of compassion for those persons whose minds are unprepared to grasp the real meaning of occult doctrines. These are doctrines that are susceptible to misconstruction if their true import is not fully apprehended. To give them to the unprepared is to violate the old alchemical maxim that before one uses the Philosophers' Stone to transmute metals, the metals must first be purified. He who rashly communicates to another what that other is almost certain to misunderstand, and consequently misapply, is responsible for the consequences. Eagerness to learn is by no means adequate assurance of *readiness to understand.* Thus, the *Fama* says Brother C.R. bound the Brethren to be not only faithful and diligent but *secret* also, and it speaks of the Brethren taking their knowledge into the world in order that it might be examined *in secret* by the learned. Similarly, in the ministry of Jesus, "Brother G.G." appears side by side with "Brother B." For although Jesus held the multitudes spellbound with His verbal moving pictures, He withheld from all but a tested few the subtler meanings of his brilliant, colorful discourses.

The last of the four new Brethren is P.D. These initials do not spell a Hebrew word, but they correspond to the letters Peh, attributed to Mars, and Daleth, attributed to Venus. Thus, they suggest action (which is expression, since Peh means "mouth") and imagination (which is the door, or Daleth, leading out of any given situation into another). The values of these letters add to 84. This is the number of ChNVK, *Enoch,* the patriarch whose name means "initiate," and of DMM, *damam* (to be silent), reminding us of the last and therefore most emphatic of the four ancient occult admonitions: Know, Will, Dare, Be Silent.

Action that expresses vivid imagination is indispensable, yet the most effective action is free from noise. Silent action speaks louder than any words. The *Fama* says, moreover, that Brother P.D. was their secretary, and his initials (*P*, the "Mouth," and *D*, the "Door") are certainly appropriate in this connection, for a secretary receives letters and applications, and communicates the responses of the Fraternity. It is he who keeps the records of the work and all the archives. He must be gifted in expression, because he is the mouthpiece of all. He must be possessed of imagination, because he has to understand the problems of others. He must be a true initiate, walking with God, like Enoch. He must be silent in the face of criticism, silent before enemies of the work, silent in the presence of the unprepared, and, hardest of all, silent when the silly ignorance of others tempts him to speech where speech would do no good.

The numbers of the initials of these four additional Brethren add to 312, which is 12 × 26. To a Qabalist this would suggest the complete expression (12) of the powers of the One Reality, designated by the Ineffable Name, IHVH, or 26. Again, 312 is the number of the verb ChDSh, *khodesh,* meaning "to renew" or "to rebuild," and this describes the work undertaken by the Fraternity.

The total number of the original members is 8. We have seen that this is the number of Krishna, of Hermes, and of Christ. As the number of points bounding a cube, 8 reminds us of the cubical Holy of Holies and the cubical New Jerusalem. Qabalists would be familiar with these words, all adding to the number 8: AGD, *aged* (to bind, to combine), DBB, *dabab* (to move slowly, to cause to speak, to quote from departed authors), and BAH, *beah* (the entrance, the threshold). Is it not evident that these all have to do with the beginning of an enterprise such as that described in the *Fama?*

If the Founder's initials are taken as C.R.C., then the total value of the initials of the eight original Brethren is 652, which is significant to a Christian Qabalist because it is twice 326, and 326 is the value of the Christian Qabalistic spelling of Yeheshua, or Jesus: IHShVH. This is a spelling found in innumerable Qabalistic writings contemporary with the *Fama* or published within the next fifty years. It has, of course, a direct bearing on the Rosicrucian motto: *Jesus mihi omnia,* to be explained hereafter. Also, 652 is the value of the Hebrew phrase: KTzL IMINV OL-HARTz, "He hath made the earth by his power" (I Chron. 29:15), which is appropriate enough if we consider that the Order, as raised to a cube by the second four Brethren from the square suggested by the first four, is a symbol that from the days of Pythagoras has been associated with the earth.

If the initials of our Father and Brother are taken as C.R. (or R.C.), the total value of the initials of the eight founders is 632, which is the value of BLTShATzR, Belteshazzar, the Babylonian name of the prophet Daniel; and Qabalists would recognize the close connection between the Rosicrucian ideas and those that are expressed in Daniel's prophecy.

Finally, if our Brother and Father is indicated simply by the initial C., the total value of the initials of the eight founders is 432, and this is the value of the noun ThBL, *taybale,* which would be recognized by Qabalists as the special name of the "earth of Yesod." It has connection also in Greek Gematria with *onoma kainon,* "a new name," used in Revelation 2:17.

Thus, no matter what combination we use, the initials of the four original founders, combined with those who were later drawn into the work, give numbers that are applicable to the very thing that is described in the *Fama* as being the beginning of the Order.

When the preparatory work is finished, the Brethren fare forth into the world. This shows, first of all, that practical occultism not only does not demand of those proficient in it that they should permanently seclude themselves but actually requires that they should mingle with their fellowmen. Only by actual contact with the affairs of daily life may occult knowledge be tested. Again, there is more than a hint here that the tendency to organize little, exclusive cliques and circles of the supposedly "elect" is contrary to the fundamental principles of Ageless Wisdom. By contact with humanity we are more likely to find those who are ready for occult instruction. Even the friction developed by encountering persons who have decided views other than our own is good for us. It keeps our knowledge bright. Nothing is more stultifying to real intelligence than to become one of a little group of serious thinkers that is really nothing more than a mutual admiration society.

The activity of the light-giving Spirit of Truth does not end with the personal liberation of the initiate. He becomes a center of illumination for all who come within his sphere of influence. The only restriction put on him is that his light can be received by none but those who are ready to receive it and who put themselves in a position to do so.

CHAPTER VII

THE ROSICRUCIAN AGREEMENT

THE SIX POINTS OF THE Rosicrucian agreement are clearly stated in the *Fama*, yet we should remember that this is evidently a Hermetic book, written by persons accustomed to the cryptic method of expression used by alchemists. In reading it, therefore, we must bear in mind Jean d'Espagnet's warning "Let a Lover of Truth make use of few authors, but of the best note an experienced truth; let him suspect things that are quickly understood, especially in Mystic Names and Secret Operations; for truth lies hid in obscurity; for Philosophers never write more deceitfully than when plainly, nor ever more truly than when obscurely."

The first point of the Rosicrucian agreement was "That none of them should profess any other thing than to cure the sick, and that gratis." This point has to do with the attitude a Rosicrucian takes before the world. He makes open avowal, or profession, of but one thing. He makes no open claim to the possession of secrets, no public announcement that he is an initiate, no pretensions whatever to occult authority. He comes before the world in just one role, that of healer.

His healing art has to do with the cure of souls as well as bodies. The physical work, however, is emphasized. The healing activities of those who are in touch with the Invisible Order begin with the physical body. The perfection and renewal of the powers of the human body are of primary importance, as we have seen before, in considering C.R.'s sojourn in Damascus.

The healing of mind and soul are equally important. The Inner School possesses a vast fund of practical knowledge bearing on this work. Hermetic and Qabalistic psychology is before all else practical. What our academic psychiatrists and analytical psychologists are doing today is clumsy fumbling when compared to the technique developed by the Masters of the Invisible Order after thousands of years of research and experiment.

There is also a social aspect to healing. The ills of the body politic and the diseases of the race mind fall within the province of this first Rosicrucian point. Yet the Rosicrucian remedies for these ills are to be applied, first of all, to the individual members of the human race. No true Rosicrucian would ever try to cure a social disorder by the favorite modern device of passing a law—and then forgetting to execute it. Thus, the *Fama* says "our philosophy" has in it but little of Jurisprudence.

Finally, a true Rosicrucian gives his healing service free. He has no fees for it. He does not try to gain a livelihood by it. He will not take a salary for his work in the cure of bodies and souls. Lest this be mistaken for a criticism of our physicians, on the one hand, and of our ministers, on the other, let it be understood that no criticism of these *persons* is intended. There are more self-sacrificing physicians and ministers than there are self-seeking ones. The system is wrong, not the men. Fortunately, the time seems to be rapidly approaching when the system will be changed. Then it will be possible for those who are truly called to heal souls and bodies to do so freely, and the whole world will be the better for the change.

The second point was "None of the posterity should be constrained to wear one certain kind of habit, but therein to follow the custom of the country." This disposes at once of the pretensions of self-styled Rosicrucians who appear in public in outlandish costumes or circulate photographs of themselves in which they are shown wearing mystic "jewels" bearing witness to their grades of Rosicrucian attainment. True Rosicrucians do sometimes wear symbolic garments, because they are appropriate and even necessary in certain types of ceremonial working, but such work is done in private convocations, never in public.

A true Rosicrucian does not seek to seem different from his neighbors in matters of outward form. The difference is in his inner life. Eccentricity of dress or conduct is evidence that a person given to it is probably not a true Rosicrucian.

This second point refers also to Rosicrucian methods of procedure. The customs of a country are also the customs of a period. As times change, methods naturally alter. Here is another way to distinguish real Rosicrucians from the self-deluded and from outright pretenders. Counterfeit Rosicrucianism is quite likely to betray itself by its appeal to precedent. "Look at our ancient warrants! See, we have charters from this one, or from that one! Ours must be the only genuine, for we adhere without deviation to the procedures, to the terminology, even to the spelling, of the past."

We do not mean to say that genuine Rosicrucian practice does not include many procedures that were customary long ago. These are adhered to, however, not because they are old but because they work. Furthermore, no Rosicrucian is *constrained* to adopt a particular method. He may make as many experiments as he likes. He may attempt new forms of presentation. He may devise new symbols and ceremonials. The dead hand of the past is never laid on him. His one duty is to adapt the changeless principles of the

Great Art to the ever-changing conditions of the period in which he lives. No form is ever sacrosanct in the eyes of a true Rosicrucian, for he is trained to look behind forms to their essence. He is conservative as to principles, because true principles, being eternal, are ageless. He is progressive as to forms but is not a rash innovator, proposing outer changes to which most of his contemporaries would find it difficult to adjust themselves.

The third point was "That every year, upon the day C., they should meet together at the house *Sancti Spiritus,* or write the cause of absence." According to a tradition preserved in some societies working according to the fundamental Rosicrucian pattern, the "day C." is a festival of the Roman Church, the day of Corpus Christi, or day of the Body of Christ. If we remember that this is distinctly a Roman Catholic festival, we may entertain some doubts of the tradition, since the anti-Roman tone of both the *Fama* and the *Confessio* is so obvious that it seems unlikely the authors of these books would have meant by "day C." a festival of the branch of the Christian Church which was antagonistic to Rosicrucianism in the seventeenth century and is not less antagonistic today.

Other societies, also working according to the basic Rosicrucian Philosophy, interpret "day C." as being the hundredth day of the astrological year, counting the time from the day the sun first enters Aries, at the vernal equinox. On years when the sun enters Aries on March, 21, "day C." by this calculation falls on June 28. As the calendar date of the sun's entry into Aries varies, the calendar date of day C. also will vary but will be always the day when the sun is passing from the sixth to the seventh degree of the sign Cancer.

There are good astrological and other occult reasons in favor of this interpretation of the third point. Most of them, however, are so technical that they seem likely to be of little interest to the average reader of these pages. Nevertheless, one sheds some light on another detail of this third point. In Qabalah the sign Cancer is attributed to the letter Cheth, which letter represents also "The Intelligence of the House of Influence." This is exactly what is meant by the House of the Holy Spirit.

Here we should remember d'Espagnet's counsel. The notion that the House of the Holy Spirit is open on but one day of the year would be far from true. Those who know the way to it may visit it as easily in January as in June. Yet it may not be saying too much to declare that the hundredth day of the astrological year is actually a date of special importance, on which Rosicrucians from all over the world do "meet" in the House of the Holy Spirit. This they can do, even though their physical bodies may be separated by thousands of miles. On this special date, however, it sometimes happens that the duties of one of the Brethren prevent his attendance at the Great Convocation. In such case he communicates the reason for his absence to the other members of the Order, and this is what is meant by "writing the cause of his absence."

The fourth point was "That every Brother should look about for a worthy person who, after his decease, might succeed him." This does not mean that a Rosicrucian is limited to the selection of a single pupil. There are today members of the Invisible Order whose powers of organization make them heads of groups numbering hundreds or even thousands of aspirants. On the other hand, to find a person able to take up one's special part of the work and carry it on with full knowledge of all that is required and full power to meet these requirements may well take a lifetime of patient search.

The fifth point was "That the word R.C. should be their seal, mark, and character." Note that the text says "the *word* R.C.," though it separates the initials by periods. We have seen that the word is *roke,* meaning "tenderness" or "compassion." Sympathy and forbearance are the seal and character of every true Rosicrucian. Harshness in speech or action is incompatible with the work of the Invisible Order. True Rosicrucians understand the human heart, because they know how great are their own struggles to maintain balance in the midst of the swirling conflicts of the world's emotional life. They are tender without being weak, compassionate without unduly identifying themselves with the woes of others, and, firm to correct error without feeling any condemnation for those who err.

The sixth point was "The Fraternity should remain secret one hundred years." This has reference to a matter that does not seem to us to be suitable for public exposition. We are permitted to offer one clue to it. The number 100 is that of the Hebrew letter Qoph, which has to do with the Corporeal Intelligence. As that intelligence is manifested through the average human being, in the Piscean Age (which is also represented by Qoph, because that letter corresponds to the zodiacal sign Pisces) it is what hides the Invisible Order from human sight.

The Piscean dispensation draws rapidly to its close. As it does so, there are evidences that a remarkable transformation is due to take place in the constitution of the physical bodies of many persons now living. During the Aquarian dispensation, now relatively close at hand, this physiological change will be even more general than it is at present. Then it will be possible to speak more openly, because a greater number of persons will be able to understand, since they will have a wider range of perception than is common at present.

A little farther along in the *Fama* we read of "dark and hidden words and speeches of the hundred years." This refers to the same esoteric doctrine touched on in the sixth point of the Rosicrucian agreement. Even in what may be called the outer circle, comprising the lower Grades of the Invisible Order, this doctrine is stated in cryptic language, though there are intimations that it is more explicitly explained to members of the higher and inner circles.

The essence of the doctrine, however, is not secret. It is the simple truth that to exercise any power of human consciousness we must be provided with suitable organs. The Rosicrucian Order is invisible because most persons have not reinforced their vision with strength borrowed from the eagle. The Fraternity remains secret for one hundred years because "one hundred years" is a symbolic number relating to the structure, chemistry, and functions of the human organism, which has undergone a gradual change during the entire Piscean dispensation. As the Aquarian dispensation draws nearer and nearer, this change is completed for an increasing number of persons, who, with different bodies, are enabled to make conscious contact with the Invisible Order.

Such is a brief explanation of the six points of the agreement. It does not pretend to be exhaustive or final. Its purpose is to put the reader on the track of the method of interpretation, to turn his face in the right direction. According to his gifts and his desire for more light, he will find other intimations of deeper meanings, if he will meditate on these six articles.

CHAPTER VIII

THE VAULT OF BROTHER C.R.C.

HE STORY OF THE DISCOVERY of the vault of Brother C.R.C., the description of its proportions, and the various details as to its construction now claim our attention. A book intended for general circulation cannot explain all this vault symbolizes. Certain points must be reserved for the instruction of selected aspirants to initiation. Yet within the limits imposed by certain obligations, we shall endeavor to expound the inner meaning of this part of the Rosicrucian allegory.

The Brother who discovered the vault is designated by the initials N.N. That is, he represents a "double Nun," or the double function of the occult force associated in Qabalah with the Hebrew letter Nun, or *N*. This force is governed by the zodiacal sign Scorpio. Thus, Brother N.N. is a type of the awakened consciousness resulting from the sublimation of this occult force and from its expression through the higher brain centers whose activity makes illumination possible.

Taken as Hebrew letters, the two initials add to 100. Thus, they have the same Qabalistic meaning as the combined initials of Brothers G.V., I.A., and I.O., explained in Chapter VI. The number 100 also refers to the mystery of the sixth point of the Rosicrucian compact, as explained in Chapter VII, because the double operation of the force corresponding to the letter Nun and to the sign Scorpio is actually the basis of the practical work of organic transformation.

Brother N.N. is said to have been the successor to Brother A., after A. had died in *Gallia Narbonensi*. Note here that Brother N.N. comes into office as a result of the death of Brother A. The letter is really Brother *Aleph*, or Brother A.L.P., to use initials corresponding to the full spelling of the name of the first Hebrew letter. Here we see that Brother A. is simply another variation of Brother P.A.L. We notice, too, that after the death of Brother A., his successor made the discovery of the vault, where all the wisdom of the Order is summarized, while he was in the course of altering his building in order to make it more fit. This is an echo of what has been said concerning Brother C.R.'s sojourn in Damascus, by reason of the feebleness of his body. Just as C.R. hears of the Wise Men and goes to them after he has worked in Damascus, so Brother N.N. finds the vault, which conceals the wisdom of those same sages, after Brother A. has died and after Brother N.N. has begun to alter his house.

Brother P.A.L. died at Cyprus, but Brother A. died in that part of France including the provinces of Languedoc and Provence. Here is an allusion to the Gnostic Christian secret societies that under the name of Albigenses were so bitterly persecuted by Rome. The Roman Church practically exterminated the Albigenses, yet their secret doctrine was by no means destroyed. There are traces of it in Dante's *Divina Commedia*, in Jean de Meung's *Roman de la Rose*, and in Boccacio's *Filocopo*.

The *Roman de la Rose* contains much alchemical wisdom, and its author wrote an important alchemical treatise entitled *A Demonstration of Nature*. In the *Roman de la Rose* is a description of a castle surrounded by a sevenfold wall covered with symbolic figures. He who was desirous of admission to the castle had to be able to explain the meaning of these figures. The hero of the romance is named Amant (that is, "Lover"), and in the *Fama* Brother C.R.C. is called "our loving Father." Amant comes to a beautiful garden, and at the center of the garden he finds a rose. This rose is transformed into a maiden:

> Through the magic power
> Of Venus, in that selfsame hour
> A wondrous miracle befell.
> The Rose became a damozel
> Of form and beauty past compare,
> Clothed in her own rich golden hair.

The Gnostic Christians of Languedoc and Provence knew the Great Secret and hid one of its important keys in the symbolism of the rose. Thus, among books written by Albigensian authors, we find one entitled *The Root of the Fragrant Rose* and another named *The Leaves of the Rose*.

The rose is the flower of Venus, and we have just seen that in the *Roman de la Rose* the magic power of Venus effects the transformation. As we progress with our study of the Rosicrucian allegory, we shall see that this magic power of Venus is hinted at in more than one place. We have indeed already noticed this in connection with the death of P.A.L. at Cyprus, and the occult meaning of that death has been explained. Thus, when we read of Brother A., or Brother Aleph (ALP), dying in the part of France where Gnostic Christianity hid its wisdom "under the rose," we shall not be slow to take a hint that must have been plain enough to many of the erudite of Europe.

Since Brother N.N. becomes head of the Fraternity after A.'s death, by this succession he takes the place of the original C.R.C. That is to say, at this point in the allegory, Brother N.N. symbolizes the operation of the God-Self, just as did C.R.C. in that part of the narrative that has to do with the journey and initiation.

Thus, we read that after certain preliminary work had been done, it was in N.N.'s mind to travel, but before he went on his journey he thought best to make some repairs in his building. All this, as we have said, is a variation of the first part of the allegory.

While N.N. was making these repairs, he came upon the Memorial Table, which was cast of brass. Attached to this table was a nail, which, when it was pulled out, took with it a stone, leaving an opening that exposed the hidden door.

The *Fama* uses the noun *brass* as does the English translation of the Old Testament, to indicate not the mixture of copper and zinc nor any other alloy but, as the original Hebrew shows, the metal copper, which the alchemists call Venus. The Hebrew noun is NChShTh, *nekosheth,* and its number, 758, deserves special attention, as we shall see presently. We may compare this Memorial Table to the Emerald Table of Hermes, for as brass or copper is the metal of Venus, so is the emerald the precious stone of the same planet.

The nail refers to the Hebrew letter Vav, for the meaning of the letter name *Vav* is "nail" or "hook." This letter Vav, moreover, is the Hebrew letter corresponding to the zodiacal sign Taurus, ruled by Venus. In Taurus, according to astrologers, the Moon is exalted. Now, in occult psychology the Moon is a symbol for memory, and Venus has to do with imagination. Hence, in Tarot, the letter Vav and the sign Taurus are represented by the fifth Key, named The Hierophant; and the basic meaning of this Key is the revelation of truth through intuition. Intuition is personal recollection of some aspect of truth that the Universal Mind has never forgotten. This recollection is presented to consciousness in some sort of mental imagery. Thus, intuition is what links personal consciousness to the Universal Mind and results in the discovery of some aspect of hidden wisdom. Even so, in our allegory, the Vav, or nail, brings with it the Stone, which reveals the hidden door to the Rosicrucian "compendium of the whole universe."

The nail, moreover, as the letter Vav, is a symbol for all the intricate Qabalistic doctrine associated with this letter. Vav is the third letter of the divine Name of Names, IHVH, Jehovah. Qabalists connect it with the Microprosopus, or Lesser Countenance, the soul of the lesser world, also identified with the First-formed Adam. Microprosopus, on the Tree of Life, corresponds to the six Sephiroth from *Chesed* to *Yesod* inclusive but is particularly centered in the sixth Sephirah, *Tiphareth* (Beauty), attributed to the *central* or *middle* point on the Tree of Life. Thus, this letter Vav indicates the *centrum* mentioned in the *Fama* as the only point and center to which we are directed by true philosophy.

This middle point, *Tiphareth,* is named Adam, or Man; *Melek,* or King; and is known also as *Ben,* the Son. To reveal its secret is announced as the underlying purpose of the *Fama*, when it says the object of the manifesto is to reveal man's nobleness and worth and why he is called Microcosmus. For Microcosmus (or Microcosmos) is simply the Paracelsian adaptation of the Qabalistic Microprosopus, or Lesser Countenance.

The *Zohar* says that all is contained in the mystery of Vav, and thereby all is revealed. The same Qabalistic authority connects Vav with the Son of David, and this was interpreted by erudite Europe in the seventeenth century, as a reference to the Christos.

Attached to the nail was a stone. This is the same stone we have mentioned before. It is the Stone rejected by the builders. It is the Stone of the Philosophers. It is ABN, *Ehben*, signifying the union of the Son with the Father.

We have already said that Henry Khunrath published in 1609 a book called *Amphitheatrum Chemicum*, in which appears an illustration showing the word ABN, *Ehben*, enclosed in a triangle. This radiant triangle, with the letters ABN at its corners, is borne by a dragon, and the dragon is on top of a mountain. The mountain is in the middle or center of an enclosure, surrounded by a wall having seven sides, whose corners bear the words, reading from left to right or clockwise around the wall: Dissolution, Purification, Azoth Pondus, Solution, Multiplication, Fermentation, Projection. Thus, the inner wall summarizes the alchemical operations. Its gate has the motto *Non omnibus*, meaning "Not for all," as if to intimate that entrance into the central mystery is not for everyone.

Surrounding this inner wall is another in the form of a seven-pointed star, composed of fourteen equal lines. The gate to this outer wall is flanked by two triangular pyramids, or obelisks. Over one is the sun, and this obelisk is named Faith. Over the other is the moon, and this pillar is named Taciturnity, or Silence. Between the pillars, in the gate, is a figure bearing the caduceus of Hermes or Mercury, standing behind a table on which is written "Good Works." Below is the motto: "The ignorant deride what the wise extol and admire."

Thus, in Khunrath's diagram we have the same association between a seven-sided figure and a stone that occurs in the *Fama*. The mystic mountain, with the dragon at its summit, is also a Rosicrucian symbol, as one may see in Thomas Vaughan's *Lumen de Lumine*, where Section 2 is entitled "A Letter from the Brothers of R.C., Concerning the Invisible, Magical Mountain and the Treasure therein Contained." Incidentally, the title of this section is a clear enough intimation that Thomas Vaughan was in communication with the Invisible Order, although he says in one of his books that he has "no acquaintance with this Fraternity as to their persons." Vaughan further says, concerning the Rosicrucians:

> Every sophister condemns them, because they appear not
> to the world, and concludes there is no such society,
> because he is not a member of it. There is scarce a reader
> so just as to consider upon what grounds they conceal

themselves and come not to the stage when every fool cries: Enter. No man looks after them but for worldly ends, and truly if the art itself did not promise gold I am confident it would find but few followers. How many are there in the world that study Nature to know God? Certainly they study a receipt for their purses, not for their souls, nor in any good sense for their bodies. It is fit then they should be left to their ignorance as to their cure. It may be the nullity of their expectations will reform them; but as long as they continue in this humour, neither God nor good men will assist them.[1]

The stone is fastened to the nail, and the nail is fastened to the Memorial Table. Thus, the stone is removed because it sticks to the nail. This means that intuition follows right *recollection*, as the reader acquainted with Patanjali's *Yoga Sutras* or with books of instruction in mystical practice will understand. Right recollection enables us to discover the truth about ourselves, which truth is the Stone, ABN, *Ehben*, the rejected building stone: "Son and Father are one." This being brought forth as a consequence of intuition (cf. the words of Jesus to Peter, "Flesh and blood hath not revealed it unto thee," which are a direct clue to the meaning of Key 5, The Hierophant, called "The Pope" in old Tarot packs), the hidden door is revealed.

This door continues the Venusian symbolism. For "door" is the meaning of the Hebrew letter name Daleth, and Daleth is the letter of the planet (and metal) Venus. To Daleth is assigned the fourteenth of the thirty-two paths of Wisdom, called the Luminous Intelligence. This path is said to be "the institutor of arcana"—that is, the establisher of things shut up—because Daleth represents not the doorway but the *valve* of the door, the bar to entrance. The fourteenth path of Daleth is termed also the "foundation of holiness," or, more accurately, the "holy foundations." The word translated *foundations* is ISVDVTh, *Yesodoth,* the plural being in the feminine form. Here is a very plain intimation that by Venus and copper, alchemy refers to that feminine basis of manifestation that is recognized throughout the various versions of the Ageless Wisdom. It is described here in the plural, because in what is so designated is the root of the bewildering multiplicity of forms that does indeed act as a barrier to the aspirant's entrance into the secret place where the Great Treasure is hidden at the center. It is the same as what Krishna, in the *Bhagavad-Gita,* calls "My mysterious power, difficult to cross over." To pass this barrier, to open the door, is to clear the way to what the *Chaldean Oracles* call "the adytum of god-nourished silence."

---

[1] Thomas Vaughan, *Lumen de Lumine,* from *The Works of Thomas Vaughan: Eugenius Philalethes,* edited by A.E. Waite (London: Theosophical Publishing House, 1919), 29.

The meaning of this part of the allegory should now be clear. The combined powers of memory and intuition, the table and the nail, bring with them the stone of conscious union with the Higher Self, and thus the door of liberation is revealed. This is the door that leads to understanding of the mathematical and psychological principles at work in the construction of the universe. Thus, the *Fama* says that through this door the Brethren gained access to such a treasure of knowledge as would serve for the complete restoration of all arts and sciences.

Written on the door in large letters was the Latin sentence: *Post CXX Annos Patebo*, "After 120 years I will open." The number of years mentioned refers primarily to the perfected consciousness of the illuminated man. One hundred twenty years is the "magical age" of full insight into the mysteries. None but those who have reached this magical age may open the Vault of the Adepts. This is the full age of man, for the Bible says of man, "His days shall be a hundred and twenty years." It also gives 120 years as the age of Moses when he died.

This number is contrasted in Scripture with the seventy years of the ordinary span of human life, mentioned by the Psalmist. The difference between 120 and 70 is 50, so that we may say the magical age of 120 years is attained by adding 50 to the 70 years of ordinary human experience. The number 50 and 70 are, of course, symbolic. Fifty is the number of the letter Nun, symbol of the occult power that, when sublimated, leads to illumination. Seventy is the number of the letter Ayin, whose name means (1) "the human eye, as the organ of vision"; and (2) "outward appearances," or the superficial aspect of things.

In Tarot, the letter Ayin is represented by Key 15, named The Devil. Thus, this Key is a symbol of that Enemy of mankind that is mentioned in the manifestoes as the cause of all degeneration in the arts and sciences. Those who agree with Mr. Waite that the authors of the manifestoes were not adepts but merely some Lutheran Germans of the period, casting a net to see what fish they might catch for a projected secret society, will agree with him also that the Devil of the *Fama* is the orthodox Chief Stoker, horns, hoofs, and all. But we remember that the opponents of the Albigenses alleged that these Gnostic Christians said the Devil was Lucifer, a rebellious Son of God, who in his exile had created this world with its inhabitants. We remember also that according to the ideas of the old magicians, Lucifer presides over the East, which is also the direction attributed by Qabalists to the letter Daleth and so to Venus. And we have found so much already behind the literal veil of the *Fama* that possibly we shall be prepared to understand that this "Devil" of exoteric dogmatism is the Enemy in one sense only, which is that he personifies what appears to be antagonistic to our search for truth. He is what produces the appearance. He is the Dweller on the Threshold, barring the way that leads to the inner center. Thus, he is, we discover, the same in function as Daleth, the door that must be opened and passed before we can enter the Palace of the King.

Key 15 in Tarot, then, symbolizes the false appearances that delude mankind. Of persons who take at face value the appearances of the phenomenal world, the Psalmist says: "The days of our years are three-score years and ten." But when the process of initiation has added the borrowed strength of the secret force of the eagle (Scorpio or *Nun*), 50 is added to 70, and the magical age of the perfected man is then reckoned as 120 years. Thus, we read: "And Moses was a hundred and twenty years old when he died: his eye was not dim, nor his natural force abated." Notice here that the eye, corresponding to Ayin and the number 70, is given special emphasis, together with the natural force (in Hebrew, LCh, *layakh*, from a root signifying "moist") corresponding to Nun and 50.

Now 120 is the theosophic extension, or secret number, of 15—the sum of the numbers from 1 to 15 inclusive. In relation to the fifteenth Tarot Key, therefore, it represents the full expression or complete manifestation of the power represented by The Devil. So long as we are outsiders, what stands in our way looks like the Devil. But when we overcome our terrors and find out all there is within this forbidding figure, then we reach the magical age of 120 years. Key 15 represents the Great Magic Agent, the Astral Light, truly called Lucifer, the Son of the Morning. This is our Adversary, because it is the immediate cause of the manifold appearances that delude the ignorant. But when we strengthen our vision with force borrowed from the eagle, we are able to *see through* those very same illusions, and then we are no longer deluded by them.

Hence, 120 is also the number of the letter name *Samekh*, and the letter Samekh is illustrated by the fourteenth Tarot Key, called Temperance, which shows what some have called "The Holy Guardian Angel." This angel of the fourteenth Key is also the Son of the Morning and is so identified by a solar disc on his forehead. The letter to which this Key is attributed means "a prop, a support." When we pass the Dweller on the Threshold, when we strengthen our eyes, when we arrive at the magical age of 120, what frightened us before turns out to be our protector, our helper, our support through every difficulty.

In other words, the number on the door of the vault intimates that access to the Hidden Treasure is a consequence of the ripening of the full powers of human consciousness, under the guidance of the Holy Guardian Angel.

After the door was fully exposed, but before it was opened, the Brethren rested and consulted their *Rota*. The *Rota*, or Wheel, is actually the Tarot, which members of the Invisible Order had invented some four centuries prior to the publication of the Rosicrucian manifestoes. It is a curious coincidence that what is perhaps the most celebrated pack of Tarot Keys was painted by Jacques Gringonneur for Charles VI of France in 1393, the year Brother C.R. began his journey. Thus, the Tarot was already in circulation in Europe, and was being used for games and fortune-telling when the *Fama* and the *Confessio* were published. That there should not have been some among the erudite of Europe who would have known enough concerning its symbolism to identify it with the Rosicrucian *Rota* is difficult for us to believe, though we concede to incredulous readers of these pages that possibly we are urged to this conclusion by our knowledge of an occult tradition that the manifestoes emanated from the same Inner School that gave us these wonderful Keys.

The place of their invention, according to this tradition, was that same city, Fez, where Brother C.R. is said to have completed his initiation. And just as we write this we come upon this passage in Isaac Myer's *Qabbalah:* "It is stated in the beginning of the Tiqqooneh ha-Zohar that the book Zohar has existed from immemorial time at Fez in Africa."[2] This would indicate that Fez was regarded by Qabalists themselves as a center of their philosophy.

The *Fama* says this *Rota Mundi* ("Wheel of the World," an apt title for the Tarot) was held by the Brethren to be that one of the Rosicrucian books displaying the greatest degree of artifice. It is truly one of the most wonderful productions of human ingenuity and deserves the praise bestowed on it by Eliphas Levi:

> The Tarot is a veritable oracle, and answers all possible questions with clearness and accuracy; so that a prisoner devoid of books, had he only a Tarot of which he knew how to make use, could, in a few years, acquire a universal science, and converse with unequalled doctrine and inexhaustible eloquence. This wheel, in fact, is the key of the oratorical art, and of the great Art of Raymond Lully; it is the true secret of the transmutation of darkness into light; it is the first and most important of all the arcana of the *magnum opus.* By means of this universal key of symbolism all the allegories of India, Egypt, and Judaea are made intelligible; the Apocalypse of St. John is a Kabbalistic book, the sense of which is exactly indicated by the figures and numbers of the Urim, Thummim, Teraphim and Ephod, all summarized and completed by the Tarot; the sanctuaries of eld are no longer full of mysteries, and the signification of the objects of the Hebrew cultus may for the first time be understood.[3]

The Tarot has many uses. It is a symbolic alphabet. It is also a symbolic book. It may be used as an oracle, and this use is evidently what is suggested by the *Fama.* This oracular use of Tarot must not be confounded

---

[2]Isaac Myer, *Qabbalah* (York Beach, ME: Samuel Weiser, Inc., 1970), 48.
[3]Eliphas Levi, *The Mysteries of Magic* (London: Kegan, Paul, Trench, Trubner & Co., 1897), 285.

with vulgar fortune-telling. Those whom the *Fama* represents as consulting their *Rota* are also represented as being highly trained occultists. They could truly *divine* with Tarot, because they had learned its meaning as an alphabet, had studied it as a book, and had employed it also for its most important purpose, the development of higher powers of human consciousness.

The *Fama*, of course, is allegory, but it is also more than allegory. This does not mean that the story of the finding of the vault is to be taken as a description of an actual event. No such building existed as a physical structure, although there have been and are a considerable number of symbolic buildings, used in occult ceremonials, built in accordance with the *Fama's* specifications. Yet there is an actual Rosicrucian Order, invisible though it be, and all its members "find" the vault through the aid of Brother N.N. The Tarot is an actual thing, and so are the *Axiomata* and the *Protheus*, for these volumes of the Rosicrucian library are still to be consulted, if one knows where to find them.

We come now to the symbolism of the vault, described as being of seven sides and seven corners, every side five feet broad and eight feet high. In other words, the ground plan of the vault was a heptagon. Here is another piece of Venusian symbolism, for to the occultists of that period, the number 7 was particularly associated with Venus and with copper. The *Aesch Metzareph*, in the *Zohar*, had made this correspondence familiar to Qabalists and alchemists and had referred the magic square of 7 × 7 to Venus, as well as attributing Venus to *Netzach*, the seventh circle on the Tree of Life. When the *Fama* was published, all this was known to the erudite of Europe, for it had been included in the medley of things occult gathered together by Henry Cornelius Agrippa in his three books entitled *De occulta philosophia*, published in 1531.

The Hebrew name for Venus is NVGH, *Nogah*. Its value is 64, which is also the value of the Greek *aletheia* (truth) and the Hebrew DIN, *deen* (justice). Sixty-four is also the sum of ADM, *Adam* (45) and ChVH, *Eve* (19), so that it is a number representing the total of humanity. Any well-taught Qabalist would know these correspondences, and thus the heptagonal ground plan of the vault would have given such a reader of the *Fama* to understand that it was a symbol of the *heavenly* Venus, representing truth, justice, and the perfect balance of those powers of man that are represented by the mystical names Adam and Eve.

Such a reader would have known also that besides the heptagon two other symbols were used by Qabalists to represent Venus. These were two heptagrams, or seven-pointed stars. One of these stars has broad points, the other has sharp points. Thus, the *Fama's* description of the vault would have suggested the diagram shown in Figure 3 on page 114.

Before we begin to analyze this diagram, remember that the *Fama* says the vault had seven sides, and that the measures of each side were five feet and eight feet. It mentions the numbers in just this order: 7, 5, 8. Now recall that the Hebrew noun for copper, or brass, is *nekosheth* (NChShTh),

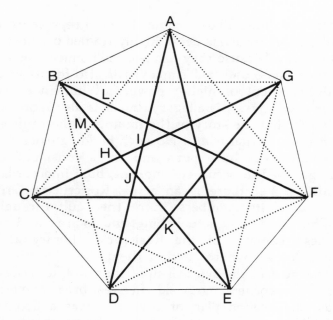

Figure 3. Seven-Pointed Star Forming Hexagon

and that it adds to 758. That is, the word is a formula for the vault, just as the exclamation "Eureka!"—said to have been uttered by Pythagoras when he discovered the properties of the right-angled triangle—is itself a formula for the construction of such a triangle, because the Greek spelling of *Eureka* adds up to 534, a number whose digits give the values of the hypotenuse (5), the shorter side (3), and the longer side (4).

Let it be remembered that the *Fama* itself describes the vault as a symbolic building. Then as we study the ground plan, we shall recognize all the numbers connected with it as being symbolic numbers; that is, they are always whole numbers, and thus they are necessarily approximate numbers. I mention this at the outset, because none of the numbers represented by this diagram, except 5 and 7, are exact in the modern mathematical sense.

If a heptagon containing two large heptagrams be constructed, as in our diagram, then there will be within it at the center a small heptagram enclosing a small heptagon. The points of this interior heptagram are the small triangles identical with the triangle IHJ, having sides of equal length, *HI* and *HJ*.

Taking one of these sides as our unit of measurement, we find it dividing all the lines equal to *AB* (one side of the ground plan of the vault) into five parts, and all lines equal to *AC* (which form the larger of the two great heptagrams) into nine parts. We find also that the distance *HI* is equal to the distance *LM* so that lines equal to *AC* are not only divided into nine parts but so divided that four of the nine parts fill the distance from *A* to *L*, one of them the distance from *L* to *M*, and the other four the distance from

M to *C*. Thus, the digital arrangement 414 is suggested, and this is found in the number 414.

The number 414 is the number of AIN SVP AVR, *En Soph Aur* (The Limitless Light), representing the great ocean of potential energy that is concentrated, according to Qabalists, into the whirling motion that begins a cycle of manifestation with *Kether*, the Crown. Thus, every line of the great star composed of lines AC, BD, CE, DF, EG, and FA, would suggest this Limitless Light.

Again, 414 is the number of the words ANI IHVH ALHI ABRHM ABIK, translated in English Bibles thus: "I am Jehovah, the God of Abraham thy father" (Gen. 28:13). This declaration occurs in the story of Jacob's dream of the ladder, and the ladder is understood by Qabalists to represent the Tree of Life or scheme of the ten Sephiroth.

Since the lines equal to *AB* constitute the boundary of the outer heptagon, and they are divided into five parts each by the unit of measurement we are now considering, their combined length will be 7 × 5, or 35. This number is that of the noun *gawbal* (GBL) meaning "boundary line," which is particularly appropriate here. Thirty-five is also the number of the magical word *Agla* (AGLA), found on many magical talismans and seals. It is not really a word, but its number must have been familiar to every seventeenth-century occultist, for one encounters it again and again in occult books and manuscripts of that period, and Knorr von Rosenroth includes it in his great Qabalistic dictionary. This made-up word is composed of the initials of the sentence AThH GBVR LOVLM ADNI, *Atah gebur le-olahm Adonai*, meaning "Thine is the power throughout endless ages, O Lord."

Furthermore, each of the lines in the diagram equal to *AB*, as representing the number 5, stands for the Hebrew letter Heh, the second letter of the divine name, IHVH, Jehovah. According to Qabalists, this particular letter Heh, the second in the divine name, is associated with Understanding (the third circle on the Tree of Life) and is called "the Mother." With this letter, they hold, creation took place, and their doctrine in this respect has many points of resemblance to the Hindu doctrine concerning *Maya-shakti*. So considered, the letter Heh stands for substance in contradistinction to essence, and it also represents the universal principle of production.

Our first unit of measurement, however, will not divide the lines corresponding to *AD* into seven approximately equal parts. But if we take the distance *IJ* (one side of the small interior heptagon) as our unit of measurement, then we find that this unit does divide the lines equal to *AD* into nine units; and that just as our first unit cut the lines equal to *AC* into parts suggesting the number 414, so does our present unit of measurement do the same thing to the lines equal to *AD*. Hence, not only the larger heptagram, with relatively broad points, but the smaller one (composed of lines *AD*, *BE*, *CF*, *DG*, *EA*, *FB*, and *GC*) would suggest the Limitless Light and Jehovah's declaration to Jacob.

With this second unit of measurement, moreover, we find that lines equal to *AB* are divided into exactly four parts instead of five. Thus, each would become the representative of the letter Daleth, which is 4 in the Hebrew alphabet. This would make each line a symbol of Venus again. So measured, furthermore, the boundary of the ground plan of the vault would be 7 × 4, or 28. This is likewise a Venusian number, because 28 is the sum of the numbers from 0 to 7, or the "theosophic extension" of 7.

Since by this unit of measurement, lines AD and AE are equal to 9, and line *DE* is equal to 4, the triangle *DAE* will have a perimeter of twenty-two units. This would have been most significant to Qabalists in the seventeenth (or any other) century, for 22 is not only the number representing the circumference of any circle, by an ancient *pi* proportion, but it is also the number of letters in the Hebrew alphabet, and all Qabalists know the doctrine of the *Book of Formation:* "Twenty-two basal letters: He designed them, He formed them, He purified them, He weighed them, and He exchanged them, each one with all; He formed by means of them the whole creation and everything that should be created [subsequently]."

By the first unit of measurement (*HI*), the line *DE* is equal to five units, and the distance *DK* is equal to four units. Thus, the triangle *DKE* would have a base of 5 and two equal sides of 4. The angles of this triangle are the same as the angles of the little triangle, *IJH*, forming one of the points of the small interior heptagram. They are also the same as the angles of the seven triangles forming the points of the large heptagram. Again, the same angles are to be found in all triangles identical with *CAF*, of which there are seven in the diagram. Since the *angles* of all these triangles are equal, no matter what their size, it follows that their other proportions are equal, and that in all of them the sides are to the bases as 4 is to 5. Thus, we discover that all lines equal to *AC* are to all lines equal to *AD* as 4 is to 5.

Therefore, all lines equal to *AB* are to all lines equal to *AC* as 5 is to 9; all lines equal to *AB* are to all lines equal to *AD* as 4 is to 9; and all lines equal to *AC* are to all lines equal to *AD* as 4 is to 5. In terms of the Hebrew alphabet this would mean that all lines equal to *AB* are to all lines equal to *AC* as Heh is to Teth; that all lines equal to *AB* are to all lines equal to *AD* as Daleth is to Teth; and that all lines equal to *AC* are to all lines equal to *AD* as Daleth is to Heh. Or in terms of the Ten Sephiroth, the formula would be: All lines equal to *AB* are to all lines equal to *AC* as Severity is to Foundation; all lines equal to *AB* are to all lines equal to *AD* as Mercy is to Foundation; and all lines equal to *AC* are to all lines equal to *AD* as Mercy is to Severity.

The properly instructed Qabalist should be able to take these two formulas and, especially if he knows the Tarot, work them out to their practical conclusions. They are rigorously exact in their application to the Great Work, but I do not feel myself at liberty to explain them. It is perhaps almost too much to have given them out, although in saying this I am expressing only my personal opinion and hasten to add that these formulas are now published because I have been specifically directed to make them known.

But we are not through with our similar triangles. Since they all have two equal sides of 4 and a base of 5, they represent the number 13 by the distance around their perimeters. Furthermore, the base is 5, and the sum of the two sides is 8, so that each of these triangles is a reminder of the exact proportions so insisted on by the *Fama* itself.

The number 13 is one of the most important in the Qabalah. It is the number of the two great key words AChD, *achad* (unity), and AHBH, *ahebah* (love). It is a prime factor in the numbers of the most important Hebrew divine names. It is the number of conformations in the beard of Microprosopus, described in the *Greater Holy Assembly*, chapters 11 to 23. Philo Judaeus says that 13 is important because it is composed of the first two square numbers, one odd, one even; that is, the square of 2 and the square of 3, or 4 and 9. Note that these numbers are emphasized in this vault geometry. Thirteen is also the diagonal of a rectangle of 5 × 12, or the hypotenuse of a right-angled triangle having a shorter side of 5 and a longer side of 12. Thus, the many repetitions of this number in the vault diagram would be of intense significance to any Qabalist and would sum up many secrets of his esoteric philosophy.

Furthermore, a triangle that has sides of 4 and base of 5 is a very close approximation to a cross section of the Great Pyramid. Thus, it would remind all rightly prepared occultists of that great symbolic building, which, like Noah's ark and Moses' tabernacle and Solomon's Temple, reveals fundamental *measures* of the universe.

Again, such a triangle's altitude is to its base almost exactly as 7 is to 11, so that it presents the same proportion that is shown in the Great Pyramid. This is such that if the height of the Pyramid be taken as 7, and each of its four base lines as 11, then the height is the radius of a circle whose circumference is 44, or the sum of the base lines. Yet another close approximation is that which makes the altitude of such a triangle to its base as 5 is to 8, and these two numbers are the ones emphasized in the description of the vault. The proportion of 5 to 8, moreover, is the nearest arithmetical expression of the Pythagorean Golden Section, or Extreme and Mean Ratio, which is defined as that division of a quantity that will make its lesser part to its greater part as the greater part is to the whole.

By the first unit of measurement, *HI*, all lines equal to *AC* are divided into nine parts, all lines equal to *AB* are divided into five parts. Thus, the outline of the "keystone," *BDEG*, would be 3 × 9 plus 5, or 32. Speaking figuratively, the Tree of Life, with its thirty-two paths, is certainly the keystone of Qabalism. Nor is this all. The number 32 is that of the Hebrew noun LB, *laib*, which means "heart" in all senses, including *life, the feelings and affections, understanding*, and the like. The same word also represents that which is within or at the midst.

Thus, the number 32 represents something familiar to occultists of many schools. To Freemasons, whose rituals preserve many vestiges of the Qabalah, the heart is the point of initial preparation for admission to the fraternity. That modern Masonry has well-nigh forgotten the deeper significance of this point must be admitted, but the truth remains that in the heart every man is first prepared to become a true Builder. And the essence of that preparation is inner harmony with what the Qabalists represent by the thirty-two paths. Or it might be even more accurate to say that not until the heavenly wisdom begins to stir in a man's heart is that man ready to seek initiation.

A great deal more might be developed in the way of mathematical analysis of this diagram, but I wish to touch on just one other point. The average reader of these pages will think I have said too much. Occultists who are duly and truly prepared will not require anything more than what has been given in order to work out further details for themselves. But the one more point leads to something we shall deal with at greater length in the next chapter, and it is this:

Our first unit of measurement, the distance *HI*, is one side of one of the points of the interior heptagram. According to the *Fama*, the length of this unit is one foot. Since there are fourteen such units in the outline of the interior heptagram, their combined length will be equal to the perimeter of a cross of six squares, in which each square has sides measuring one foot long. This cross, the basis of the only correct Rosicrucian cross, is also the pattern for a cube, and that cube would be a cube measuring one foot in all three directions. This establishes a direct correspondence between the proportions of the vault of Brother C.R.C. and the mystical cube that is described in the Apocalypse as the form of the New Jerusalem. For one foot is twelve inches, and the New Jerusalem is described as being twelve thousand furlongs in all three directions. In other words, the pattern cube for the construction of the vault of C.R.C. is one measuring twelve inches each way, so that each inch represents one thousand furlongs of the measurement of the New Jerusalem.

This cube symbol, as we shall see in the next chapter, is of utmost importance in the Qabalah and in Gnostic Christianity. Thus, it is not surprising to find it related to Brother C.R.C.'s symbolic building.

The sides of this vault are described as being rectangles measuring five feet by eight feet. Thus, the four lines bounding each side would have a total length of 26, and 26 is the number of the divine name IHVH, Jehovah. Hence, these proportions tell us that as one stands inside the vault, he is faced on every side by the Lord. This reminds us of Swedenborg's saying that one faces God always in the celestial world, no matter which way one turns.

The area of the seven sides of the vault is 7 × 40, or 280. This is also a Venusian number, since it is ten times the perfect number 28, or ten times the theosophic extension of the Venusian number 7.

The area of a heptagon with sides of five feet is almost exactly 91 square feet. This number 91 is that of the great divine name *AMN*, *Amen*, signifying faithfulness and fidelity. This word was also used by Qabalists as a divine name, which is attributed to *Kether*, the Crown, or first aspect of Reality. They also understood it to represent the combination of the divine names IHVH, *Jehovah* (26) and ADNI, *Adonai* (65). It is, of course, obvious that 91 is 7 × 13, so that it is the sum of the last two digits in 758, multiplied by the first digit, and we have seen that the whole symbolism of the vault is intimated in the Hebrew noun NChShTh, *nekosheth*, which means "copper," and adds to 758.

Since the top and bottom of the vault are equal heptagons, the area of the floor is like that of the ceiling, or *Amen* above and *Amen* below. That is to say, faithfulness above and faithfulness below. This would have been familiar indeed to students of alchemy, who had by heart the dictum of Hermes, "That which is above is as that which is below, and that which is below is as that which is above."

Every side of the vault has an area of forty square feet, so that the total area of the sides is 280 square feet. Add this to 182, the sum of the areas of the ceiling and floor, and the result is 462. This is the number MTzVTh IHVH, *Mitzvath Jehovah*, "the commandments of Jehovah" (Ps. 19:8). Observe that the Psalmist says the commandments enlighten the eyes, as if they were addressed to the visual sense. The number 462 is also the number of the place name BAR LChI RAI, *Beer-lahai-roi*, mentioned in Genesis 16:14, meaning "well of the living and seeing one." The *Zohar* says: "The 'well' is none other but the Shekinah; 'the living one' is an allusion to the Righteous One who lives in the two worlds, that is, who lives above, in the higher world, and who also lives in the lower world, which exists and is illumined through him, just as the moon is only illumined when she looks at the sun. Thus the well of existence literally emanates from the 'living one' whom 'it sees', and when it looks at him it is filled with living waters."[4]

The identity of numeration between this "well," which the *Zohar* explains as representing the sum-total of existence, emanating from the Righteous One, or the Supreme Unity, and "the commandments of Jehovah" points to an underlying identity of meaning. This is fairly obvious, for it is one of the fundamentals of the Qabalah that the universe is commanded into manifestation through the Word of God. Thus it follows that whatever is manifested is the visible presentation of the Divine Intention. Observe that the well of existence is also a well of vision, and that the Psalmist asserts that the commandments of Jehovah enlighten the eyes. So, too, the *Fama* veils its central mystery in the symbolism of this vault, a symbolism addressed to the eyes. And elsewhere, defining the qualifications of a true Rosicrucian, the *Confessio* declares: "Truly, to whom it is permitted to behold, read, and thenceforward teach himself those great

---

[4]*Zohar*, translated by Sperling and Simon, 2:38-39.

characters which the Lord God hath inscribed upon the world's mechanism, and which He repeats through the mutations of Empires, such an one is already ours, though as yet unknown to himself." Remember, too, that this number 462 is that which represents the total area of the vault, which the *Fama* describes as a compendium of the universe.

Fourteen of the boundary lines of the vault, considered as a solid, are five feet long. Seven of the boundary lines are eight feet long. Thus, there are twenty-one boundary lines in all, and their total length is 126 feet. This number 126 is a peculiarly magical number, for it is the sum of the values of three great mystery words, used over and over again in magical manuscripts known to the erudite of Europe. These words are: IHVH (26), *Jehovah;* ADNI (65), *Adonai;* and AGLA (35), *Agla.* Observe that their numbers are hinted at by the heptagon defined in the *Fama,* because the boundary of that heptagon is thirty-five feet, and its area is ninety-one square feet, so that the boundary represents *Agla* and the area represents Jehovah Adonai. And now we have the same names suggested by the total length of all twenty-one boundaries of the vault, considered as a solid.

The *Fama* goes on to tell us that although the sun never shone in this vault, it was enlightened with another sun, which had "learned this from the sun." The reference is, of course, to the microcosm—man. The Internal sun located in the ceiling (that is, in the upper part, or the head) does truly learn how to shine from the external sun. For our inner enlightenment is the conversion of energy drawn directly from the actual day star that is the physical center of our solar system. Illumination is not purely a spiritual or a mental process, if by spiritual or mental one means something nonphysical. The enlightenment is a physiological process. Something happens in the blood. Something goes on in the brain. Something alters cell function and cell structure, and the "something" that does all this is *light,* radiant energy sent to this planet from the actual physical sun in the sky.

Need I say that no true Rosicrucian believes illumination to be a *purely* physical process? Need I declare my firm conviction that illumination is a spiritual experience, and that (when one understands them) those mystics are perfectly correct who tell us that enlightenment is nothing less than a work of Divine Grace? Yet Grace has its physical as well as its metaphysical aspects, and the metaphysical manifestations do by no means exclude the physical. True Rosicrucianism does not fall into the ancient error of setting the spiritual against the "material." It does not seek escape from the material into the spiritual. Rather it seeks to expose the lie that there is any "material" whatever apart from the substance of pure Spirit. At the same time, though it denies there is a reality (matter) opposed to another reality (spirit), Ageless Wisdom finds useful and accurate the distinction between the terms *physical* and *metaphysical.* The "physical" is that range of spiritual activity that man perceives through his ordinary senses. The "metaphysical" is that range of spiritual activity that lies beyond ordinary sensation. Moreover, "beyond" may mean either above or below, so there may be whole fields of metaphysical reality that are relatively *interior* to those we know by means of our senses.

After its reference to the true source of the Inner Light, the *Fama* tells us of a round altar covered with a plate of brass (copper), on which was engraved *Hoc universi compendium unius mihi sepulchrum feci,* which may be translated "I have made this sepulchre as a single compendium of the universe." Here is a direct statement that the symbolism of the vault is cosmic—both macrocosmic and microcosmic. It links the vault with that other great sepulchre, the Pyramid, which is also a single compendium of the universe, and with Solomon's Temple and Noah's Ark.

The inscription is on a circular altar, for the circle is the fundamental symbol of cosmic perfection. To it is added the other inscription, *Jesus mihi omnia,* meaning literally "Jesus is all things to me." This inscription has a more profound content than a casual reader might suspect. The name Jesus signifies "Self-existence liberates." Thus, the *Fama*, by connecting this word of freedom with the word *omnia*, signifying "everything," intimates the characteristic Rosicrucian point of view, which is that everything contributes to liberation. The nature of things is to set free rather than to bind. Thus, the motto is the affirmation of the inherent tendency to liberty, as the very heart of the cosmic order.

Incidentally, it was because of this, we may believe, that Jesus promised so much to those who would pray "in his name," for whoever truly prays *in* that name prays in the recognition of the idea the name represents, and he prays effectively who is thoroughly imbued with the thought that the nature of things is liberative rather than restrictive.

In Qabalistic books published about the time the *Fama* made its appearance (for example, in the writings of Jacob Boehme and Henry Khunrath), the name Jesus is spelled IHShVH. This occult spelling puts the "holy letter," Shin, between the first and last two letters of IHVH, *Jehovah*. This makes the number of the word 326. The first two digits add to 5, and the last two to 8. Taken together, the first two make 32, the number of paths on the Tree of Life, and the length of the perimeter of one of the "keystones" in our diagram of the heptagons and heptagrams. The last two digits of 326 make 26, IHVH, *Jehovah*, which is also a Qabalistic summary of the Tree of Life.

The name Jesus Christ, in the Greek language, is spelled with letters that give a total numeral value of 2368. The word *Christ* is spelled in Greek with letters that add up to 1480. Now, the ratio of 1480 to 2368 is *exactly* the ratio of 5 to 8, for 5×2368 is 11,840 and 8×1480 is also 11,840.

Furthermore, 1480 is the value of the Greek words *Mathesis sphairas* (Doctrine of the Sphere), *Kaine philosophia* (The New Philosophy), *He aneogmene thura* (The Open Door), and *Lithos trisepapeiros* (Stone of the Three Boundless Dimensions). That these are all appropriate descriptions of the mystical Christos is evident. But they are also mentioned directly in the *Fama*, which

Table 2. Names and Epithets of Jesus Christ

Greek	English
Ho kubikos petros: Ho alethinos logos	The Cubic Stone: The True Logos
Ho kubidos petros Kuriakos	The Cubic Stone of the Lord
Teleios logos: teleios petros	Perfect Word: Perfect Stone
Teleios lithos: ho oikos epi ten petran	Perfect Stone: The House upon the Rock
Ourania basileia: Kubikos petros	Heavenly Kingdom: Cubic Stone
Hals kubos teleios: ho petros	Perfect Salt-cube: The Stone
Aletheia: Ho Nomos tes symmetrias	Truth: The Law of Symmetry
He petra he kubike: he zosa polis	The Cubic Stone: The Living City
Sion oros: domos Theou	Mount Sion: Abode of God
He oikodomia en Christo	The Building in Christ
Ho lithos akrogoniaios: Emmanouel	The Corner-Stone: Emmanuel
He polis chrusous	The Golden City

proclaims a *new philosophy*, which it compares to a globe or circle ("the Axiomata, which he knew would direct them, like a globe or circle"), so that it is truly a *doctrine of the sphere*. This doctrine is hidden in a vault, and the *open door* of that vault is compared to a door that will be opened in Europe. And the whole secret doctrine is summed up in the occult meaning of the cube, or *stone of three boundless dimensions.*

Again, 2368 is the value of 500 names and epithets of Jesus Christ, given by Frederick Bligh Bond and Thomas S. Lea in their book, *The Apostolic Gnosis*.[5] Some are listed in Table 2. Since 2368 is to 1480 as 8 is to 5, all the phrases that are represented by the number 1480 may be said to be symbolized by the shorter boundaries of each of the walls of the vault, and all the phrases that correspond to 2368 may be said to be symbolized by the longer boundaries. Note that the relation is between Christos (1480), the

---

[5]Frederick Bligh Bond and Thomas S. Lea, *The Apostolic Gnosis* (Oxford: B.H. Blackwell, 1919). I am indebted to this work for many of the examples of Greek Gematria cited in this book.

universal Christ-principle, and Jesus Christos (2368), the manifestation of that universal principle through an incarnate human being. Truly then does the *Fama* declare: "We confess to have the *knowledge* of Jesus Christ."

It is quite true that Bond and Lea make no direct mention of Rosicrucianism in their works on the Apostolic Gnosis. Yet it is also true that Frederick Bligh Bond, who was director of excavations at Glastonbury Abbey, holds this opinion: "The embodied consciousness of every individual is but a part, and a fragmentary part, of a transcendent whole, and ...within the mind of each there is a door through which Reality may enter as Idea—Idea presupposing a greater, even a cosmic Memory, conscious or unconscious, active or latent, and embracing not only all individual experience and revivifying forgotten pages of life, but also Idea involving yet wider fields, transcending the ordinary limits of time, space, and personality."[6] Furthermore, Mr. Bond put his theory to the test of practice, and through the joint labors of himself and a friend who has the gift of automatic writing, he discovered a hidden chapel at Glastonbury.

Thus, I submit that whatever may have started Bond and Lea to investigating the Apostolic Gnosis, Mr. Bond was certainly prepared to open what he calls a "door" through which he could recover precisely the knowledge that sheds so much light on Rosicrucianism and alchemy. My own work in this field has been of a similar sort, and I have, besides, enjoyed unusual opportunities for direct, objective instruction from a person who has demonstrated to me his possession of the practical and theoretical keys to the Rosicrucian mystery. Thus, what I am offering in this explanation of the Rosicrucian allegories is by no means the result of my own personal interpretations only. It is largely a development of instruction received from one who merits, if ever man did, the august title "Rosicrucian." The identity of this man is beside the point. To divulge it might add, for some readers, too great a weight of supposed occult authority to the contents of these pages.

Hence, this interpretation of the *Fama* and the *Confessio* is submitted entirely on its inherent merits. I am simply confessing my personal inadequacy to the unguided production of such an interpretation and humbly acknowledging my everlasting indebtedness to the source of my enlightenment. From that same source I have received assurance that we are now in a period of human history when much that hitherto has been forgotten by the world shall once more be brought to light. Wherever men and women address themselves earnestly and sincerely to the solution of life's great problems, Those Who Know are ready to give the answers. Thus, there is now available a great treasure of wisdom concerning the Bible, the Qabalah, the significance of the Great Pyramid, Tarot, and related matters, and through the work of the True and Invisible Rosicrucian Order, influencing the minds of honest and earnest researchers everywhere, that treasure is being given to the world.

---

[6]Frederick Bligh Bond, *The Gate of Remembrance* (Oxford: B.H. Blackwell, 1918), 19-20.

Some who are the agents of its distribution have conscious knowledge of the secret sources of their enlightenment. Many more believe themselves to be original discoverers in various fields of research. Among the latter are many of our men of science, many of our inventors, many of those who are devising better forms for our social and economic structures. But whether those who bring it before the world are *conscious* instruments or not, the treasure is available, and whoever will may enjoy it.

But to return to the *Fama*. It goes on to tell us that in the middle of the brass plate that covered the altar were four figures. What these figures were is not disclosed in the text, but an ancient Rosicrucian tradition says they were the four mystical creatures mentioned in Ezekiel and the Apocalypse. The passage in Ezekiel reads: "They four had the face of a man, and the face of a lion, on the right side: and they four had the face of an ox on the left side: they four also had the face of an eagle." [Ezekiel 1:10] The description in the Apocalypse is as follows: "And in the midst of the throne, and round about the throne, were four beasts full of eyes before and behind. And the first beast was like a lion, and the second beast like a calf; and the third beast had a face as a man, and the fourth beast was like a flying eagle." [Apocalypse 4:6,7] These are the "living creatures" depicted in the four quarters of the arms of the Masonic Fraternity. They are represented in the zodiac by Leo the lion, Taurus the bull, Aquarius the man, and Scorpio the eagle. These are the fifth, second, eleventh, and eighth signs of the zodiac, and the numbers designating their positions in the zodiacal order add to 26, the number of the name IHVH, *Jehovah*.

The first motto on the altar was written, according to the tradition previously mentioned, around a small circle containing the figure of a lion, corresponding, through the sign Leo, to the element of fire. This motto was *Nequaquam Vacuum*, meaning "Nowhere, not at all, a void." This is the negative declaration of the absolute fullness of space, a denial of apparent emptiness, wherever that emptiness may seem to be encountered. Its positive expression is the statement that all space is filled with the Divine Presence. Since the Bible says, "The Lord our God is a consuming fire," the Divine Presence is properly represented by the Lion and Fire. Furthermore, in the Qabalah, the element of fire is attributed to the Holy Letter, Shin, because the numeral value of that letter is 300, and 300 is the value of RVCh ALHIM, *Ruach Elohim*—literally, "The Breath of the Creative Powers," or as the English Bible puts it, The Spirit of God. In other words, the first motto indicates the fullness or *Pleroma* of the Divine Spirit, that all-pervading fire of life that the Orientals call *Prana*, as being the truth that necessitates the conclusion that nowhere is there any emptiness whatever.

The second motto, *Legis Jugum*, was written around a circle enclosing the figure of an ox. Exoterically, this means "The yoke of the Law" and refers to the Law of Moses, expounded in the Old Testament. But note that it is connected with the sign Taurus, and that a yoke is placed on the neck, ruled by that sign. We know today that the Sanskrit noun *yoga* and the Latin *jugum* are from the same ancient root. The esoteric meaning of this motto has to do with the Law of Yoga and particularly with the functions of a center located in the neck or throat, suggested in this Rosicrucian allegory by Cyprus in the story of C.R.C.'s journey and by *Gallia Narbonensi* in another place. In one sense, this motto is a reference to Jesus' declaration that not one jot or tittle of the law shall pass away until all be fulfilled. In a deeper sense it is an intimation that the Mosaic Law, which was a law of *sacrifice*, is itself a symbol of those preparatory processes of yoga, in which the seeker for enlightenment loosens the bonds of material form and appearance, represented by Taurus, the earthy fixed sign symbolized by the figure of the ox. There is no actual sacrifice, for what is given up is a delusion. Yet there is the semblance of death, as we learn from the *Fama*, for Brother P.A.L. dies at Cyprus, and Brother A. dies at *Gallia Narbonensi*. Yoga effects a transmutation (death) of the life force (P.A.L or A.) in the throat center, and the processes by which this is accomplished are the preliminary stages of yoga and of the alchemical Great Work. They are processes that kill the sense of separateness and thus awaken the realization of union (*jugum*).

The third motto, *Libertas Evangelii*, was written in the circle containing the figure of an eagle. Its exoteric meaning is "The liberty of the Gospels," and it refers to the "good news of freedom" that is the burden of the New Testament. That good news has for its essential principle the idea represented by the name Jesus, which means "the nature of reality is to set free." Jesus and Joshua are two forms of the same name, and the Old Testament tells us that Joshua, who succeeded Moses as leader of the Children of Israel, was the son of Nun; that is, his father's name was the same as the name of the letter connected by Qabalists with the sign Scorpio. Just as the leadership of Joshua follows that of Moses, so does the fulfillment of the ancient law by Jesus succeed its earlier manifestations of sacrifice. Similarly, after preliminary purifications of yoga and alchemy (The yoke of the Law) comes the liberation of the good news, which is heard by the initiate through the transmutation of the Scorpio energies. Thus, the Rosicrucian allegory tells us that when Brother C.R.C. had overcome the feebleness of his body during his stay at Damascus, he heard of the Wise Men at Damcar, went to their temple, and received from them good news, not only as to the significance of events that had happened while he was yet in the cloister of the sense life but also concerning the true meaning of the world of nature. This good news is associated with the eagle, as a symbol of the regenerated activities of the Scorpio force, connected with the element of water, always a symbol of purification. Hence, we find the alchemists directing their pupils to wash the matter many times, and then, they say, the Great Wonder will appear to you. Similarly, when this purification is accomplished, we have borrowed strength from the eagle and have eyes with which to see and recognize the great truth that everything in our environment works for liberty and not for human bondage.

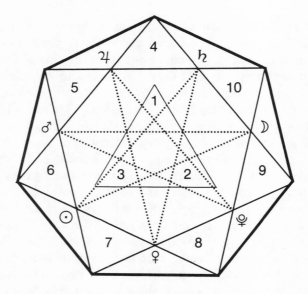

Figure 4. Diagram of the Ceiling of the Vault

The fourth motto, *Dei Gloria Intacta*, was written around the circle containing the figure of a man. It signifies "The Undefiled Glory of God." It refers to the occult conception that the real Inner Man is identical with and inseparable from the pure essence of the Life Power. That essence is correctly associated with the element of air, to which the sign Aquarius (the Man) is referred, because Spirit and Breath are correlated in all ancient philosophies. Furthermore, the adjective *intacta*, which I have translated "undefiled," means even more than this. The Inner Glory that is the essence of the real Man is not only untouched by the action of its outer vehicle of personality. It is truly *untouchable*. It can never be defiled. Here is a conception of man's spiritual nature far beyond that held by the exoteric churches, even today. Priestcraft flourishes by emphasizing the human sense of unworthiness. Esoteric Christianity has ever held to the idea hinted at when the *Fama* speaks, in its first paragraph, about bringing man to understand his own nobleness and worth.

This is the focus of the conflict between the Secret Church and the representatives of exoteric religion. That the conflict is less harsh and bloody in these times than in former centuries is due in no small measure to the unremitting efforts of the Invisible Order. It is not because the representatives of the older exoteric churches are any less bitter against what they are pleased to call heresy. It is rather that the cause of human liberty has robbed the representatives of exoteric religion of their former power. More about this in a subsequent chapter.

According to the rather obscure text of the *Fama*, the ceiling of the vault was "divided according to the seven sides in the triangle which was in the bright center." Some students of the Latin text think this should read:

"Divided according to the seven sides into triangles, with a triangle in the bright center." This reading seems to be borne out by a traditional diagram of the ceiling of the vault, used in some of the Rosicrucian ceremonial societies. This is shown in Figure 4.

In this Figure the planets are indicated by symbols placed in the small triangles adjacent to the sides of the vault.[7] Thus, the symbol of Venus is at the bottom of the diagram, next to that side of the heptagon corresponding to the door of the vault. The planetary symbols are arranged around the heptagon in their usual astrological order, so that if one begins with the symbol for Saturn, and reads around the heptagon to the left, the order is Saturn, Jupiter, Mars, Sun, Venus, Mercury, Moon.

In the points of the large heptagram are the numbers from 4 to 10. The number in each point immediately to the right of any particular planetary symbol (with the exception of Saturn) is the number of the circle on the Tree of Life said to be the sphere of that planet's action. Thus, 4 is to the right of Jupiter, 5 to the right of Mars, 6 to the right of the Sun, 7 to the right of Venus, 8 to the right of Mercury, and 9 to the right of the Moon. In every instance, the position of the observer is understood to be at the center of the diagram, facing the side corresponding to the planet mentioned. The one apparent exception is that the point of the heptagram containing the number 10 is at the right of the triangle containing the symbol of Saturn. But even this is only a superficial discrepancy, for Malkuth (10) the sphere of the elements is, according to the Qabalah, the seat also of a predominantly Saturnine influence.

If we begin with the symbol for Mars and take the planetary symbols as representing the metals of the alchemists, then by counting counterclockwise around the heptagon and skipping one symbol each time, we shall have the correct sequence of the atomic weights of the metals, thus: Mars, *iron*, 55.85; Venus, *copper*, 63.57; Moon, *silver*, 107.88; Jupiter, *tin*, 118.7; Sun, *gold*, 197.2; Mercury, *quicksilver*, 200.61; Saturn, *lead*, 207.22.

Again, if we begin with the Sun and trace the lines of the smaller, sharp-pointed heptagram in order, we shall find that the planets are placed at the points of this heptagram in the order of their days in the week: Sun, Sunday; Moon, Monday; Mars, Tuesday; Mercury, Wednesday; Jupiter, Thursday; Venus, Friday; Saturn, Saturday; and the last line takes us from Saturn back to the Sun.

The interior triangle bears the numbers of the first three aspects of reality, or Sephiroth: 1, *Kether*, the Crown; 2, *Chokmah*, Wisdom; and 3, *Binah*, Understanding. The top of this triangle is supposed to face East. Thus, the door of the vault is in the west.

---

[7]Because of an oversight, in earlier editions of this book the planetary symbols were incorrectly placed. This detail would be of little moment to the average reader, but it has important practical consequences, and it is deeply regretted that a careless reading of the proofs permitted the error to be so many times repeated.

Table 3. Correspondences of the Seven Spirits

Planet	Angel	Metal	Chakra
Venus	Anael	Copper	Throat center
Mercury	Raphael	Quicksilver	Cerebrum and pineal body
Moon	Gabriel	Silver	Pituitary gland
Saturn	Tsaphkiel	Lead	Center at base of spine
Jupiter	Tzadkiel	Tin	Solar plexus
Mars	Kamael	Iron	Center below navel
Sun	Michael	Gold	Heart center

The planetary angels corresponding to the seven sides of the vault, beginning with the door, and going around the heptagon counterclockwise, are HANIAL, *Anael* (Grace of God); RPAL, *Raphael* (God the Healer); GBRIAL, *Gabriel* (Man of God); TzPQIAL, *Tsaphkiel* (Contemplation of God); TzDQIAL, *Tzadkiel* (Righteousness of God); KMAL, *Kamael*, (Severity of God); and MIKAL, (Like unto God). These angels are personifications of the seven powers that are basic in manifestation. They are the Seven Spirits, whose power extends throughout the cosmos, influencing all things. In the human body they correspond to seven centers that are the *chakras* of the yogis and the metals of the alchemists. These correspondences are shown in Table 3.

The floor of the vault is similarly divided into triangles, but the triangle in the center points west instead of east and is black instead of white. The "Inferior Governors" mentioned in the *Fama* are the destructive forces that Qabalists call *Qlippoth*, or "Shells." The same considerations that lead the authors of the *Fama* to withhold the explanation of this part of the vault seem to me to be still valid, even though more than three hundred years have passed since the Rosicrucian manifestoes were published. Hence, to use their words, I "leave to manifest the same, for fear of the abuse of the evil and ungodly world."

The *Fama* says every wall of the vault was parted into ten squares. This is an obsolete use of the noun *square* meaning any rectangle, as when Freemasons declare that the form of their lodge is an "oblong square." The ten rectangles are formed by dividing each wall by a vertical line through the center and crossing this with four equidistant horizontal lines. Then each of the ten rectangles, according to the dimensions given in the *Fama*, will have two sides of 1.6 feet, and two sides of 2.5 feet. The proportion would interest any Qabalist, for 1.6 is to 2.5 as 32 is to 50. Thus, each rectangle suggests the 32 Paths of Wisdom and the 50 Gates of Understanding.

The "several figures and sentences" in these squares are the names of various Qabalistic attributions of the ten Sephiroth, represented by the ten circles on the Tree of Life. Each wall has a different arrangement, determined by the planetary nature to which that wall corresponds. Thus, the wall corresponding to Venus, which is also the door of the vault, contains in its rectangles all the correspondences relating to the various Venusian aspects of the ten Sephiroth. It would serve no useful purpose to give all these details here. Note that the *Fama* says they "are set forth *concentratum* here in our book"—that is, the essential principles of the Qabalistic philosophy elaborated in this diagrammatic scheme of the vault are set forth so clearly in the *Fama* that none of the erudite could fail to recognize them.

The text goes on to say that every wall had a door for a chest, in which the Brethren found various things. The English version is somewhat ambiguous, but careful reading shows the true meaning. It says: "especially all our books, which otherwise we had, besides the *Vocabulario* of Theophrastus Paracelsus of Hohenheim, and these which daily unfalsifieth we do participate. Herein also we found his *Itinerarium* and *Vita*, whence this relation for the most part is taken."

Arthur Edward Waite poked fun at this passage, asserting it to be an anachronism, because it mentions the vocabulary of Paracelsus, and the latter's *Itinerarium* and *Vita*.[8] But the text specifically says of the books found in the vault "which otherwise we had, together with the *Vocabulario* of Paracelsus," and I understand this to mean that although the vault contained the specifically Rosicrucian texts (and all this, remember, is allegory), the Brethren also had other copies of the same texts, which they used in conjuction with the vocabulary of Paracelsus. The authors of the *Fama* are here hinting, as they did before, that the work and discoveries of Paracelsus were useful to Qabalists. Even though he was "none of our Fraternity" and his writings, like the Magic and Qabalah of "those at Fez," were vitiated by some errors, he had diligently studied the Book M; and thus the Brethren of the Invisible Order found much that was valuable in his "vocabulary," that is, in his modes of expressing truth as he saw it.

The "looking glasses of divers virtues" refer to the power of self-reflection that is developed by practical work in occultism. In this work one comes to see himself from various points of view, and there is varying merit in each experience of this kind. The little bells refer to an experience that is repeated again and again in occult practice, hearing interior sounds that actually resemble the sound of small bells. Sometimes these interior sounds are so definite they seem to be the ringing of bells in external space, and there are some indications in occult literature that in the presence of an adept, the interior hearing of even an uninitiated person may be temporarily

---

[8]Arthur Edward Waite, *The Real History of the Rosicrucians*. This work was first published in 1887. By the time Mr. Waite came to write his *Brotherhood of the Rosy Cross*, he appears to have realized his blunder, for he does not repeat it in that book.

awakened, so that he hears what have been described as "astral bells." Similarly, the burning lamps are actually seen during the process of the awakening of the interior sensorium, for as one gains certain powers, which are described minutely in some of the books on yoga, there is direct perception of the *chakras,*, or interior stars, and this perception takes form as a vision of lights. Mr. Waite derides Wynn Westcott's suggestion that the artificial songs were mantras, but Dr. Westcott was close to the truth.[9] Incidentally, the German word translated "artificial" is *ettlich*, which really means "genuine." These songs are tonal sequences, heard within the "vault," or within the initiate's own inner house of life, and they are closely related to the "words of power" mentioned in various occult writings.

Underneath another strong plate of brass was hidden the body of "our careful and wise Father," described as "a fair and worthy body, whole and unconsumed." This "dead body" of C.R.C. is the same as the "dead Osiris" of the Egyptian Ritual. One does truly come upon it in the course of discovering the mysteries of the secret vault. What the *Fama* does not tell us is that this dead body is brought to life, yet personal experience of what is shadowed forth in this allegory of the opening of the vault culminates in that glorious resurrection.

The Book T, which was found in Brother C.R.C.'s hand, has been identified by some writers with the *Torah*, or Hebrew book of the law of Moses—that is, the Pentateuch. This, however, is expressly contradicted by the context, which describes Book T as the greatest treasure "next unto the Bible." Others have identified Book T as the Tarot, but we have already seen that the Tarot is the Rosicrucian *Rota*. Furthermore, Book T is described as a parchment, at the end of which is written the long Latin *Elogium*, signed by some of the Brethren. Such a parchment scroll would be a poor description of the Tarot, which consists of 78 detached leaves.

First of all, then, note that it is a parchment, that is, the skin of a sheep, dressed for writing purposes. A lambskin, in other words, and this is a plain hint that Book T is no actual volume but rather a symbol, connected with the symbols C.R. (The Lamb) and Damcar (Blood of the Lamb). If the title *Book T* be written in Hebrew, it becomes SPR Th, *Sepher Tav*. The number of this is 740, equivalent to HSPR HSPRIM, *Ha-Sepher Ha-Sepherim* (The Book of Books). What is this Book of Books written on lambskin? What else but the same book described in Revelation as being sealed with seven seals? James M. Pryse says of this book, described in the Greek of the Apocalypse as a scroll: "The scroll is a mysterious document which it has taken the God aeons to write, a Bible which, when rightly read, discloses cosmic and divine mysteries. It is simply the human body, and its seals are

---

[9]W. Wynn Westcott was former Supreme Magus of the Societas Rosicruciana in Anglia, a high degree Masonic organization, and one of the founders of the Hermetic Order of the Golden Dawn in London around 1888. From A.E. Waite, *The Brotherhood of the Rosy Cross*, 133n2.

the force-centres wherein radiates the formative force of the Logos. These seals are the same as the seven Societies and the seven lamp-stands. The expression 'written inside and on the back' refers to the cerbro-spinal axis and the great sympathetic system."[10]

In translating this passage from the Apocalypse, Mr. Pryse renders part of it thus: "And I saw a strong Divinity proclaiming with a great voice: 'Who is worthy to open the scroll and force open its seals.'" Then he goes on to say that the "strong Divinity," as shown by the adjective, is Kronos, the God of Time.[11] Thus, this strong Divinity is none other than Saturn, and in the Qabalah the planet Saturn is attributed to the letter Tav, or T. Thus, we may understand Book T to be the record of all time, written on the flesh of the human body, within and without. Rightly does the *Fama* warn us that this great treasure ought not to be delivered to the censure of the world.

The Latin *Elogium* is introduced by a short sentence, *Granum pectori Jesu insitum*, which may be translated "A seed planted in the breast of Jesus." This is followed by a long sentence, constituting the entire paragraph given in the *Fama*. Arthur Edward Waite summarizes the main points of this sentence as follows:

> (1) That C.R.C. came from a noble and illustrious family of Germany bearing that name; (2) that on account of his subtle conceptions and untiring labours he became acquainted with Divine and human mysteries by way of revelation; (3) that he collected a royal and imperial treasure in his journeys to Arabia and Africa; (4) that the same was serviceable not only to his age but to posterity; (5) that he desired to have heirs of the name, faithful and closely joined; (6) that he fabricated a little world corresponding to the great one in its movements; (7) that it was a compendium of things past, present and to come; (8) that after living for more than a century he passed away at the call of the Holy Spirit and not by reason of disease, yielding his illuminated soul to its faithful Creator; (9) that he was a beloved Father, a most kind Brother, a faithful Preceptor and an upright Friend; and (10) that he is hidden here from his own for one hundred and twenty years.[12]

At the end of the *Elogium*, after the names of eight of the Brethren, was written the sentence: "*Ex Deo nascimur, in Jesu morimur, per Spiritum Sanctum*

---

[10]James M. Pryse, *The Restored New Testament* (London: John K. Watkins, 1914), 319.
[11]Pryse, *The Restored New Testament*, 318.
[12]Arthur Edward Waite, *The Brotherhood of the Rosy Cross* (London: William Rider & Son, 1924).

reviviscimus, meaning "From God we are born, in Jesus we die, through the Holy Spirit we become alive again."

The *Minutum Mundum* is one of the inner secrets of the Invisible Order. All I may say of it is that it is quite rightly declared to be fabricated. It is a work of art and not a product of nature. The vault itself is in some sense its symbol, and it is, of course, none other than the microcosm, or regenerated and reintegrated personality of the initiate.

Summing up this chapter, then, we have found that analysis of the proportions of the vault shows it to be a summary of the principal points of the Qabalah. Like Solomon's Temple and the Great Pyramid, it is a symbol of the whole universe, and of the indissoluble *unity* of all things. The vault is the microcosm and the macrocosm. It is man's inner life and his cosmic environment too. But the story of the *Fama* clearly indicates that it is by entering the vault that its mysteries are to be discovered. The Path of Initiation leads within, toward the center, not toward the circumference.

CHAPTER IX

SYMBOLISM OF THE ROSE-CROSS

HE SYMBOL OF THE TRUE AND Invisible Rosicrucian Order is a cross of six squares, with a five-petaled rose at its center. This fundamental form may be varied by additional symbolic details, but the cross is always one of six squares, and the rose is always red, with five petals. To readers inclined to challenge this statement I can only say that whoever follows the procedure described in the *Fama* and the *Confessio* will sooner or later make direct contact with the Invisible Order. Such a person will then be in a position to verify this detail, together with many other points brought up in this book.

The cross of six squares is derived from the cube. It is the pattern for that regular solid. The cube itself is a symbol of truth, but truth expressed on the physical plane. Among the five regular solids, therefore, the cube is said to represent the element of earth. In the preceding chapter we have seen that the cross of six squares and the cube from which it is derived are related to the vault of Brother C.R.C. and that the cube symbol is of utmost importance in the Qabalah and in Gnostic Christianity.

In the Bible, the cube is directly connected with the *sanctum sanctorum* or Holy of Holies. This room contained the Ark of the Covenant on which rested the Shekinah or Divine Presence. In the Tabernacle, the Holy of Holies measured ten cubits in length, breadth, and height. In Solomon's Temple it measured twenty cubits in each dimension.

Within this *sanctum sanctorum* in Solomon's Temple was deposited the Ark of the Covenant, and between the cherubim of the Ark was the resting place of the Shekinah. In the second Temple, according to Josephus and the traditions of the Hebrew Rabbis, the Holy of Holies was either empty or it contained only the Stone of Foundation, standing in the place the Ark should have occupied.

Rabbinical and Masonic traditions agree that this Stone of Foundation was itself a cube. A clue to its real significance is to be found in the

Zohar, which says the Stone of Foundation is the central point of the universe, the nucleus of the world, the point out of which the world started. This involves a subtle piece of esoteric doctrine that has been grossly misunderstood by many.

If we ask, "Where is the center of the universe, at which is located the nucleus of the world?" the only logical answer is, "Everywhere." Thus, more than one philosopher has described God as a circle whose center is everywhere and whose circumference is nowhere. What the Qabalists call the "Small Point," or initial nucleus of creation, can be nothing other than the focus of the Originating Spirit at some point within its own Boundless Being. For Qabalistic psychologists, this Small Point is identical with *Yekhidah*, the Indivisible, or the One Self.

Hence, this point is symbolized as the Stone of Foundation within the Holy of Holies, but the Temple in which this stone is to be found is one not made with hands. We have already seen that the Hebrew word for Stone is one that combines the words for Father and Son. It is the verbal symbol for the essential identity of God and Man. They who, like Jesus, become *aware* of this identity, receive the Stone of Foundation. By means of it they come into the Divine Presence. Hence, the *Zohar* says: "King David felt great affection and attachment for this stone: it was of it that he said, 'The stone which the builders rejected is become the corner stone.' And whenever he desired to gaze at the reflection of the glory of his Master, he first took that stone in his hand and then he entered, as whoever wishes to appear before his Master can only do through that stone."[1]

What is meant here is that when one actually has the consciousness of union with the Indivisible, so that it can be put into practical application— "taken in hand"—then one comes into the presence of the Master Principle of the universe. That Master Principle is eternally the Originating Principle, as Judge Troward has so well shown in his books on Mental Science.[2]

Why should this Stone be described as a cube? This brings us to the Qabalistic and Gnostic doctrines of which I have spoken. If we begin with the knowledge that awareness of unity with the Originating Principle, of the identity of the Son with the Father, is a real experience of human beings involving the activity of an actual point within the human brain (the point that is meant by the *sanctum sanctorum*), we shall see that this point is at once a center within the brain of the man having the experience and at the same time a point in space, from which lines may be conceived as radiating in every direction.

In the *Book of Formation* we read: "He sealed the height, and turned toward above, and sealed it with IHV. He sealed the depth, and turned toward below, and sealed it with VHI. He sealed the east, and turned

---

[1]*Zohar*, translated by Sperling and Simon (London: The Soncino Press, 1931), I:244.
[2]For additional reading on the subject, see also other works by Thomas Troward: *The Creative Process in the Individual; The Law and the Word; Bible Mystery and Bible Meaning; The Hidden Power; The Dore Lectures;* and *The Edinburgh Lectures on Mental Science.*

forward, and sealed it with HIV. He sealed the west, and turned backward, and sealed it with VIH. He sealed the north, and turned to the left, and sealed it with HVI. He sealed the south, and turned to the right and sealed it with IVH."[3]

Here the Heavenly Architect is pictured as facing east. The first movement is from the center upward to the height, followed by a second movement downward to the depth. Then comes a forward movement to the east, followed by a backward movement toward the west. Then there is movement from the center toward the north, followed by movement from the same center toward the south. Each movement is accompanied by a manifestation of the three essential letters of the Divine Name, IHVH. Height is established by the Divine Name *Yaho*, IHV, equivalent in number (21) to AHIH, *Eheyeh* (Existence), the particular Divine Name associated with the number 1, and with the Small Point of Origination, which is eternally the *Center* of the universe. East is established by a gesture symbolizing movement of the Originating Spirit toward the past, which we associate with beginnings. The gesture associated with west is a movement into the future. Movements toward north and toward south complete the establishment of the six cardinal directions. As each is represented by one of the permutations of the same three letters, IHV, each has the numeral value 21. The Small Point is, therefore, in the very midst of Existence, the Center of the universe.

The sequential order of these six movements is to be understood as representing only the *logical* order. Actually, all of this must be conceived as simultaneous motion from the center, in all six directions at once. What is thus established by these six radiating lines is nothing other than the combination of three lines representing the coordinates of a cube; for if we speak of boundless height and depth, boundless east and west, and boundless north and south, as does the *Book of Formation*, the only image our minds can form is that of a perfect cube.

There is also a link of connection between this Qabalistic passage and the description of the vault in the *Fama*. It consists in the sixfold repetition of a group of letters whose value is 21, so that the six combinations of three letters are equivalent to 6 × 21, or 126. This is the number of feet in the boundary lines of the vault, which has seven lines of eight feet each, and fourteen lines of five feet each.

The same image of the cube was known to the early Christians, as we may see from a passage in the *Clementine Homilies*. This is supposed to be a report of St. Peter's words in his refutation of the false Gnosticism of Simon Magus. St. Peter says:

> The Place of God is "That-which-is-not," but God is
> That-which-is. The very subsisting God is therefore
> One, Who enthroned in more excellent form, is the heart

---

[3]These attributions are from the Kalisch *Sepher Yetzirah*, pages 16 and 17.

dually controlling both that which is above and that which is below, sending forth from Himself as from a centre the life-giving and bodiless power, all things with the stars of Heaven, air, water, earth, fire, and whatever there be aught else, boundless in height, unlimited in depth, immeasured in breadth, thrice to the boundless stretching forth His life-giving and provident nature. This, therefore, that, starting from God, is boundless in every direction, must needs be the heart holding Him Who is verily above all things in fashion, Who, where-soever He be, is as it were in the middle of a boundless space being the terminal of the All. Taking their origin therefore from Him, the six extensions have the nature of unlimited things. Of which the one taking its begin-ning from God is displayed upwards towards the height, another downwards towards the depth, another to the right, another to the left, another in front, another behind. And looking forth on these as on a number equal in every direction, God completes the world in six equal divisions of time, He himself being the Repose, and having as a likeness the boundless Aeon that is to be, God being the Beginning and the End. For at Him the six boundless lines do terminate and from Him they take their boundless extension.[4]

This Christian doctrine is precisely that of the Hebrew *Book of Formation*. It is, moreover, introduced by two paragraphs in which St. Peter declares that Jesus taught crucial things concisely, without much elaboration of detail, because he had selected a group of disciples to whom many of his doctrines were already familiar. The Rabbinic symbol of the Stone of Foundation was familiar to Jesus and his contemporaries, and Jesus himself made an allusion to the stone refused by the builders, as directly applying to his own mission.

The parallel between the *Homilies* and the *Book of Formation* may also be carried further. The *Homilies* speak of the Place of God as being at the center, and they compare it to the heart. The *Book of Formation* assigns the six directions to the first six of the double letters of the Hebrew alphabet, but to the seventh letter, Tav, it attributes "The Palace of Holiness which is in the midst." To this letter Tav, moreover, the planet Saturn is attributed, and as this planet rules the seventh day of the week, or Hebrew Sabbath, we find here a correspondence to the teaching of the *Homilies* that the center is the place of the Divine Repose.

Now repose, or rest, is an idea directly connected with the Stone of Foundation, for since that Stone is said to be identical with the stone

[4]*Seventeenth Clementine Homily,* paraphrased by Frederick Bligh Bond and Thomas S. Lea, in *The Apostolic Gnosis,* vol. 2, section II (Oxford: B.H. Blackwell, 1919).

rejected by the builders, we may profit by recalling exactly what is said of it by Isaiah: "Behold, I lay in Zion for a foundation a stone, a tried stone, a precious corner stone, a sure foundation: he that believeth shall not make haste." (Isaiah 28:16) That is to say, he who builds on this foundation shall enjoy security and repose. This is perfectly true. He who has the state of conscious union with the Originating Spirit is never in a hurry. He is absolutely confident and sure of his security. His inner self is at rest, even though his outer personality may be engaged in the most intense activity.

Freemasonry preserves a shadow of this same esoteric doctrine of the cube in its many references to the cubical stone. The practical meaning of the doctrine is simple. When we find the place of repose at the center, we have entered the *sanctum sanctorum*. There the Son, man, is one with the Father, God. The central point, then, is the point of identification with the Originating Spirit. That point is a definite location in the brain, the Zion mentioned by the prophet.

The cube opened out forms the cross of six squares and is therefore a symbol of the pattern of cosmic manifestation. The perimeter of this cross is fourteen units, and 14 is the number of the Hebrew noun ZHB, *Zahab* (gold). Hence, we may look for some indication in Rosicrucian tradition that the cross symbolizes that "gold" of the Sages that has been so beautifully described by Eliphas Levi: "The gold of the philosophers is, in religion, the absolute and supreme reason; in philosophy it is truth; in visible nature it is the sun, which is the emblem of the sun of truth, as that is itself the shadow of the First Source whence all splendours spring; in the subterranean and mineral world it is the purest and most perfect gold. For this reason the search after the *magnum opus* is called the search after the Absolute, and the great work is itself called the work of the sun."[5]

The Secret Symbols of the Rosicrucians, published at Altona in 1785, includes a plate showing the golden cross of the Order, with the explanatory text: "That is the golden Rosy Cross, of fine gold, which every Brother carries on his breast." The cross itself bears the Latin inscription, *Frater Rosae et Aurae Crucis*, "Brother of the Rosy and Golden Cross."

Sincerus Renatus (Sigmund Richter) also published the Rules of the Order in 1710, and among them we find that a Brother meeting another said, *"Ave Frater!"* to which the other responded *"Rosae et Aurae,"* and the first concluded with *"Crucis."* After this they said to one another, *"Benedictus Dominus Deus noster qui dedit nobis signum"* ("Blessed be our Lord God who gave us this sign"). These words are also written on the cross shown in the plate in *The Secret Symbols*.

Thus, there is established a definite connection between the cross and the metal gold. The same metal, it will be remembered, is mentioned in connection with the New Jerusalem, described in the twenty-first chapter of Revelation as being a perfect cube of pure gold, like pure glass (Rev. 21:18).

---

[5]Eliphas Levi, *The Mysteries of Magic* (London: Kegan, Paul, Trench, Trubner & Co., 1897), 292.

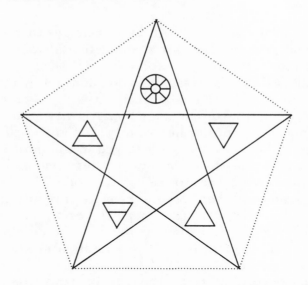

Figure 5. The Pentagram with 4 Elements and Quintessence

The number 14, besides being the number of the noun ZHB, *Zahab* (gold), is also the number of the Chaldaic noun DBCh, *debakh*, meaning "a sacrifice," and there is little need to enlarge on the significance of the cross as a symbol of sacrifice. Furthermore, 14 is the number of DVD, *Dawveed*, the proper name David.

The root of this name is a Hebrew verb spelled with the same letters, meaning primarily "to boil, to cook." Figuratively, it signifies "to love," and is fundamentally a verb designating love between the sexes. Thus, "David" means "Love" or "Beloved." Students of Hermetic Science will take this hint, I trust, as readily as it must have been taken by the wise readers of the *Fama* and the *Confessio*, for they will remember how often the alchemical books assure us that the Great Work, or operation of the Sun, is nothing other than "coction," that is, cooking or boiling. What the alchemists are hiding behind this veil of language is the simple truth that love is the fulfilling of the law, that the pure gold of the Absolute is found through the working of the gentle heat of love, that the sacrifice of sacrifices is a broken and contrite heart purified in the fires of love, that only through love can the true pattern of that perfect golden cube, the New Jerusalem, be rightly perceived and understood.

The rose too is a symbol of love, for it was the flower of Venus from a period long antedating the Christian Era. Thus, it adds its testimony to all the other references to Venus that we find in the *Fama* allegory. Furthermore, the rose is a symbol of secrecy, because it was the flower of Harpocrates, the younger Horus, the god of silence. Thus, it is an emblem of one of those mystical personalities we considered in Chapter V.

We have seen that the number 5 is connected with Harpocrates, or Horus, through the connection between Horus and the hypotenuse of the

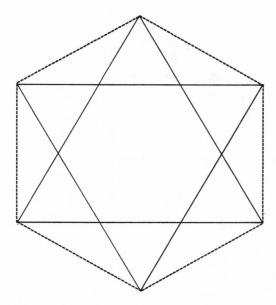

Figure 6. The Hexagram and Hexagon

Pythagorean triangle, which consists of five units. The same number is represented by the rose, because wild roses have five petals, and all roses have their petals grouped in multiples of five.

Thus, the geometrical pattern of the rose is the pentagram, as shown in Figure 5. This leads us at once to another occult diagram, shown in Figure 6. In other words, the mystery symbolized by the rose is the mystery of the Pentagram, as the mystery symbolized by the cross of six squares, opened from the cube, is related through the number 6 to the mystery of the Hexagram.

The Hexagram is the geometrical symbol of the manifested universe, from its connection with the wheel of the zodiac; for if a hexagram is circumscribed by a circle, then lines drawn through all the points and intersections of the Hexagram—from the center of the circle to its circumference—will divide the circle into exactly twelve equal parts and form the familiar zodiacal wheel used for horoscopes. The interlacing triangles of the Hexagram, moreover, represent the Law of Love and the union of all polar opposites throughout the universe. Thus, the Hexagram is a symbol of the cosmic order as conceived in the Universal Mind prior to the manifestation of man upon earth. It is therefore the proper symbol of the dispensation represented by the Old Testament and the chief symbol of Judaism.

The Pentagram, or Pentalpha (so called because it presents the form of the Greek letter Alpha, or *A*, in five different positions), was employed by the disciples of Pythagoras as a symbol of health. Throughout the East the same figure has been used from time immemorial as a charm to resist evil spirits. Henry Cornelius Agrippa says of it: "A Pentangle, also, as with the virtue of the number five hath a very great command over evil spirits, so by its lineature, by which it hath within five obtuse angles, and without five acutes, five double triangles by which it is surrounded. The interior pentangle contains in it great mysteries, which is also so to be enquired after, and understood."[6]

Eliphas Levi says:

> The Pentagram expresses the mind's domination over the elements and it is by this sign that we bind the demons of the air, the spirits of fire, the spectres of water, and the ghosts of earth. It is the Star of the Magi, the burning star of the Gnostic schools, the sign of intellectual omnipotence and autocracy. It is the symbol of the Word made Flesh.... The sign of the Pentagram is called also the sign of the Microcosm, and it represents what the Kabbalists of the Zohar term the Microprosopus. Its complete comprehension is the key of the two worlds—it is absolute natural philosophy and natural science. Its use, however, is most dangerous to operators who do not perfectly and completely understand it....All mysteries of magic, all symbols of the gnosis, all figures of occultism, all kabbalistic keys of prophecy, are resumed in the sign of the Pentagram, which Paracelsus proclaims to be the greatest and most potent of all. It is indeed the sign of the absolute and universal synthesis.[7]

Summing up, then, what has been explained thus far, we may say that the cross of the Rosicrucians symbolizes alchemical gold, that fundamental truth on which all occult practice is founded. This basic truth is revealed in the name David, which signifies "Love" and which also has a profound alchemical sense, having to do with the fundamental process of the Great Work. As the pattern of the cube, the cross of six squares has a correspondence in geometrical symbolism with the Hexagram, or great symbol of the Macrocosm. Its meaning may be summed briefly by the statement that the Rosicrucian cross is a representation of the One Law underlying all modes of the Life Power's cosmic manifestation.

On the central square of this cross, which would be the bottom of the cube if the cross were folded up, is fixed a rose of five petals. This is the symbol of the Microcosm, Man, because it is really a Pentagram. Its five petals represent the five senses, as do the five points of the Pentagram. As

---

[6]Henry Cornelius Agrippa, *Of Occult Philosophy* (London: Gregory Moule, 1651), 253.
[7]Eliphas Levi, *The Mysteries of Magic* (London: Kegan, Paul, Trench, Trubner & Co., 1897), 189, 191.

the flower of Venus it represents the desire nature and the secret force of which Venus and the metal copper (or brass) are symbols.

When the rose is fastened to the fundamental and central square of the cross, the meaning is that the desire nature of man has been unified with the One Law that is the basis of all manifestation. Close up the cross so that it forms a cube, and the rose will be hidden within it. The center of the rose and the center of the foundation square are the same. Here is the great practical principle of true Rosicrucianism. All the work of the Invisible Order and all the practices of those who become Rosicrucians are directed to this one end—the discovery of Reality and the conformation of man's life to that Reality. To know what really is and to make one's life a daily expression of that knowledge is true Rosicrucianism.

Among the wise men of Europe who read the *Fama* were some who had knowledge of Greek, for the books written in favor of the Rosicrucians include *Prodromus Rhodo-Stauroticus,* published in 1620, and *Colloquim Rhodo-Stauroticum,* published in 1621. The titles of these books show that their authors thought of the rose as *rhodon* and of the cross as *stauros.*

By Greek Gematria, the values of the letters in *rhodon* (rose) add to 294, which is also the number of the Greek noun *ekklesia,* literally "a calling out," an assembly for oral instruction. This was the original meaning of the word as used in the New Testament, although it is now applied to the external organization of the Church. Erudite readers of the *Fama* would have known this, and they would have known too that 294 is the number of the Hebrew noun ARGMN, *argaman,* a reddish purple color like that of the traditional Venusian rose. They also would have known that 294 is the number of ALHI ABRHM, *Alhi Abraham,* or God of Abraham; of NMRD, *Nimrod,* celebrated in Masonic tradition as one of the founders of the Craft; and of MLKITzDQ, *Melchizedek,* the mysterious King of Salem around whose name there have been woven so many esoteric doctrines. Thus, for such a reader the rose would be the symbol of the Secret Church, cherishing the true priesthood "after the order of Melchizedek" and possessed of the traditional wisdom relating to AL ShDI, *El Shaddai,* the God of Abraham.

Applying Greek Gematria to the word *stauros,* we find that its letters add to 1,271, which is the value of the phrase *He kleronomia hagion,* meaning "the sacred inheritance," and the words *He Gnosis,* meaning "the Gnosis." For a properly instructed reader of the *Fama,* therefore, the cross would be a verbal symbol of a treasure of wisdom, handed down from the wise men of other days, a Gnosis having to do with the secrets of time and space, summed up in the symbolism of the Cubic Stone of which the cross of six squares is a pattern.

It is impossible to believe that hundreds of well-read men in Europe would have interpreted the hints of the *Fama* in any other way. Such men were perfectly familiar with Gematria. They used it daily in their studies of the Qabalah. Not a few of them had penetrated deeply into the secrets of Hermetic philosophy, as the literature of that period abundantly testifies.

Some of them, no doubt, were already consciously in touch with the Invisible Order that announced itself to the world through the manifestoes. Yet there must have been many others who welcomed the good news that the hints to be found in the Hermetic and Qabalistic books, intimating the actual existence of a secret order of Sons of the Doctrine, were not without foundation. Let me repeat: The assertion, so often made that nobody ever got in touch with the authors of the *Fama*, is, on the face of it, no more than a miserable confession of ignorance.

In that day as in every generation since, those who knew how to interpret the manifestoes found therein clear indications of the only way in which one may come in touch with the Hidden Brethren. From earnest consideration of the symbols of the rose and cross, such readers would know not only *what* the Invisible Order is but exactly *where* entrance to it may be found.

They would know—even if they had no more than the information give in this chapter, meager and fantastic as that information may seem to some who may chance upon this book. For such as they, these words are written. It is not expected that these intimations of the nature of our sacred inheritance will move gross wits today, any more than they did in 1614. To those who have ears to hear and some degree of skill in comtemplation, what has been set down here concerning the meaning of the Rosy Cross should be more than sufficient to point out the shortest and easiest way to participation in the treasure of the Gnosis.

CHAPTER X

ROSICRUCIAN RELIGION
AND POLITICS

F THE "FAMA" AND "CONFESSIO Fraternitatis" are to be taken in their literal sense, the publication of these documents will not add new lustre to Rosicrucian reputations. We are accustomed to regard the adepts of the Rose-Cross as beings of sublime elevation and preternatural physical powers, masters of Nature, monarchs of the intellectual world, illuminated by a relative omniscience, and absolutely exalted above all weakness and all prejudice. We imagine them to be "holding no form of creed, but contemplating all" from the solitary grandeur of the Absolute, and invested with the "sublime sorrow of the ages as of the lone ocean." But here in their own acknowledged manifestoes they avow themselves a mere theosophical offshoot of the Lutheran heresy, acknowledging the spiritual supremacy of a temporal prince, and calling the pope Antichrist....All persons possessed of such positive convictions we justifiably regard as fanatics, and after due and deliberate consideration of the Rosicrucian manifestoes, we do not feel able to make an exception in favour of this Fraternity.... In other words, we find them intemperate in their language, rabid in their religious prejudices, and, instead of towering giant-like above the intellectual average of their age, we see them buffeted by the same passions and identified with all the opinions of the men by whom they were environed. The voice which addresses us behind the mystical mask of the Rose-Cross does not come from an intellectual throne, erected on the pinnacles of high thinking and surrounded by the serene and sunny atmosphere of a far-sighted tolerance; it comes from the very heart of the vexation and unprofitable strife of sects, and it utters the war-cry of extermination. The scales fall from our eyes, the romance vanishes; we find ourselves in the presence of some Germans of the period, not of "the mystic citizens of the eternal kingdom."[1]

---

[1]Arthur Edward Waite, *The Real History of the Rosicrucians.*

Thus, did Arthur Edward Waite write of the manifestoes in his *Real History of the Rosicrucians*. Thirty-seven years after this was written, Mr. Waite elaborated the same theme in *The Brotherhood of the Rosy Cross*, saying:

> The *Confessio* is a scurrilous and blatant document on the subject of Latin Christianity. One would think that its author had reflected on a remark of the *Fama* concerning the original "Brethren and Fathers," who if they had lived in the "clear light" of the post-Lutheran period would have handled the Pope more roughly. And thus reflecting it was concluded, one might think also, that the time was ripe for *illuminati* of the third circle to give samples of their mettle, seeing that—according to the Advertisement—it was now quite safe to call the Pope Antichrist, and to say what they would do with him, if only he came into their hands. The valour of Alsatia and Whitefriars broke out accordingly in the terminology of Colonel Blood. The Pope was found guilty of blasphemies against Jesus Christ; it was proclaimed, in hot-gospel derision of merely historical fact, that—"after many chafings in secret of pious persons"—he had been "cast down from his seat by a great onset" and nobly "trodden under foot." But as he was enthroned actually at St. Peter's, or holding royal court in the Vatican, hearing nothing of these gutter-born ravings, the aspirations of the *adepti* went further, and they expressed three hopes for the future: (*a*) that his utter destruction was in reserve; (*b*) that he would be "torn in pieces with nails"; and (*c*) that a "final groan" would end his "asinine braying." It may have been the manner born of the Holy Mysteries, as understood by the German mind in the early seventeenth century, and it may have breathed all the loving spirit of our highly "illuminated," "loving" and "Christian Father"; but to us at the present day it seems redolent of stables which have not been built in Bethlehem and in which Christ was never born.[2]

So, without explaining how with such an opinion of its beginnings he still believes in a valid mystery of the Rosy Cross, concerning which he throws out dark hints in the manner of one who might say much if only he dared, Mr. Waite states his case. But with the actual texts before us, and remembering that Mr. Waite himself asserts that these manifestoes can yield nothing of value if taken literally, let us consider the matter.

---

[2]Arthur Edward Waite, *The Brotherhood of the Rosy Cross* (London: William Rider & Son, 1924).

It may seem to some readers of these pages that Mr. Waite's own choice of language is not beyond reproach, and if so, the reproach is the more merited in these days than in those when the manifestoes appeared. It was a time of plain speaking, and in polemical writing authors permitted themselves liberties that today would offend good taste.

Yet on the hypothesis I have advanced, that the mysteries of the Rosy Cross were and are survivals of Christian Gnosticism combined with Hermeticism, is there much to excite surprise if some bitterness of expression found its way into the manifestoes? Should we expect fair words from the spiritual and perhaps lineal descendents of the Waldenses and Albigenses? With the memory of the wholesale massacres ordered by Innocent III and the relentless hounding of the Albigenses by the Inquisition, could one expect tolerance for Rome and its representatives?

The manifestoes make the issue clear enough. There is a great gulf fixed between the fundamental stand of the Roman Church and that taken by all who rely on the Inner Light. The Roman Church stands for an outer and traditional authority. It concentrates the power to express the mind of Christ into a single man, the Pope, whereas those who are responsible for the *Fama* and *Confessio* found the Christ Consciousness to be a potential for every member of humanity.

On the other hand, we must admit that the *Confessio* specifically says: "We execrate the pope." This, however, is by no means the same as declaring enmity against the Christian Church, even though Rome may so interpret it. The papacy is the outward and visible sign of an attitude of mind that Jesus himself vigorously condemned. This attitude is one of reliance on human traditions and authority, claiming for themselves the right to speak in the name of God. It is the attitude of mind that led to the Inquisition, to the burning of Savonarola, to the horror of St. Bartholomew's. Let me hasten to add that it is the attitude that led to the burning of Servetus by Calvin, to the witchcraft persecutions in Protestant New England, and to the intolerance shown toward Quakers and Baptists by the Puritans and Pilgrims of Massachusetts. The papacy is merely the oldest and strongest manifestation of this attitude, which encourages priestcraft and feeds the fires of intolerance.

Perhaps the strongest words on this subject were written by one whom thousands look upon as a great master of wisdom. In a letter to A.P. Sinnett, written in 1851 by Khoot Hoomi Lal Singh (the Master K.H.), we read:

> And now, after making due allowance for evils that are natural and cannot be avoided—and so few are they that I challenge the whole host of Western metaphysicians to call them evils or to trace them directly to an independent cause—I will point out the greatest, the chief cause of nearly two-thirds of the evils that pursue humanity

ever since that cause became a power. It is religion under whatever form and in whatever nation. It is the sacerdotal caste, the priesthood and the churches. It is in those illusions that man looks upon as sacred, that he has to search out the source of that multitude of evils which is the great curse of humanity and that almost overwhelms mankind. Ignorance created Gods and cunning took advantage of opportunity. Look at India and look at Christendom and Islam, at Judaism and Fetichism. It is priestly imposture that rendered these Gods so terrible to man; it is religion that makes of him the selfish bigot, the fanatic that hates all mankind out of his own sect without rendering him any better or more moral for it. It is belief in God and Gods that makes two-thirds of humanity the slaves of a handful of those who deceive them under the false pretence of saving them. Is not man ever ready to commit any kind of evil if told that his God or gods demand the crime?; voluntary victim of an illusionary God, the abject slave of his crafty ministers. The Irish, Italian and Slavonian peasant will starve himself and see his family starving and naked to feed and clothe his padre and pope. For two thousand years India groaned under the weight of caste, Brahmins alone feeding on the fat of the land, and to-day the followers of Christ and those of Mahomet are cutting each other's throats in the names of and for the greater glory of their respective myths. Remember the sum of human misery will never be diminished unto that day when the better portion of humanity destroys in the name of Truth, morality, and universal charity, the altars of these false gods.[3]

I do not offer this because of any supposed authority possessed by its writer. It does clearly set forth the attitude of one who is regarded by many as being high in the councils of the True and Invisible Rosicrucian Order. Furthermore, it likewise expresses an idea that the Roman Church invariably brands as heresy. This idea is that religious creeds and beliefs are, after all, confessions of ignorance. The Roman Church demands belief and proclaims itself the custodian of sacred mysteries. So do all other exoteric religions, with the exception of Buddhism.

Gnostic Christianity opposes itself to this false notion. It declares that man may *know* the Supreme Reality. Thus, we find the *Fama* saying, "We confess to have the knowledge of Jesus Christ (as the same now in

---

[3] *The Mahatma Letters to A.P. Sinnett* (New York: Frederick A. Stokes, Co., 1924).

these last days, and chiefly in Germany, most pure and clear is professed.)" A careless reader, like Mr. Waite, may interpret this as being a confession of Lutheran Christianity, if he will, but that one word "knowledge," in a cryptic and Gnostic text like this, is our clue to the real meaning.

Remember, these manifestoes were written by persons adept in cryptic writing and were addressed to others like them. Thus, they are "never so much to be suspected as when they speak most openly." The Lutheran Church in 1614 was just as bigoted and domineering as its Roman predecessor. Through the agency of one of its pastors at Gorlitz, it had actively persecuted Jacob Boehme for publishing his *Aurora*, and Boehme had been forbidden to write anything else. But to discerning eyes that word *knowledge* must have conveyed volumes. The exoteric Church has always demanded belief, has always imposed creeds. The true Gnostic Church has always pointed out the Way to Knowledge.

The very first paragraph of the *Fama* speaks of this knowledge of Jesus Christ as something to be perfected by a series of stages of unfoldment. The *Confessio* also says: "It must not be expected that new comers shall attain all at once all our weighty secrets. They must proceed step by step from the smaller to the greater, and must not be retarded by difficulties." In speaking of the Rosicrucian philosophy the *Fama* expressly states that "truth is peaceable, brief, and always like herself in all things, and especially accorded by with *Jesus in omni parte* and all members." So the great Rosicrucian secret is seen to be nothing other than knowledge of Christ.

Now the opposite of this is the Scarlet Woman described in the Apocalypse, the great harlot who sits on many waters. Fanatic Protestantism of the kind Mr. Waite decries has erred in supposing that the Scarlet Woman is a symbol to be applied to no church but that of Rome. The Beast and the Woman were, in the minds of the early Christians, symbols of pagan Rome, the oppressor, but the meaning of the symbols must now be extended. The Beast is materialism, and the Woman is what may be called "Churchianity." The harlot sits on many waters because water represents the psychic element in human nature and particularly the subconscious storehouse of traditions, superstitions, and other holdovers from the ignorance of the past. The scarlet beast on which she sits is the uncontrolled animal nature. The many waters are the appearance of multiplicity, which seems to deny the fundamental unity of Being. They refer also to the conflicting opinions that are the causes of all the cruelties we may trace to man's insane religious beliefs. Thus, the woman is called Babylon, and this gives us a sure clue to the underlying meaning of the symbol. It takes us back to the Old Testament story of the building of the Tower of Babel and the confusion of tongues. The essence of this Babylonian confusion is the error that anything sound in the way of philosophy or religion can be built on the foundation of the unregenerate human being's ordinary sense experience. So long as man accepts the uncorrected evidence of his physical senses as the final evidence, he is at the mercy of the fashioners of creeds.

Therefore the word *Mystery* is written on the woman's forehead; for priestcraft, pagan or Christian, Roman or Protestant, depends for its continuance upon the lie that the mysteries of the heavenly kingdom may not be known. Wherever we find the emphasis on creeds, wherever we find the laity misled into the belief that the arcana of the heavenly wisdom are beyond the limits of human knowledge, there we have the Scarlet Woman. The Church of Rome is, as I have said, the oldest and most powerful institution claiming final authority over the lives, consciences, and future destiny of human beings; but wherever a church organization imposes creeds and conceals from man his essential divinity and his power to advance step by step in the *knowledge* of Jesus Christ, that organization must be regarded as partaking of the nature of Babylon.

Opposed to the Beast and the Woman, according to Revelation 17:14 is the Lamb, and we have seen that the central figure of the *Fama* allegory is also the Lamb. The Lamb is destined to conquer, because he is Lord of Lords, and King of Kings. The Christos is eternally the ruling principle, which because of its omnipotence must ultimately overcome all that seems to oppose it.

This victory of the Christos over the forces of mystery and confusion is to be brought about by the awakening of a higher consciousness in man. It is what George Fox called the Inner Light. It is what the *Confessio* means when it asks: "Wherefore should we not freely acquiesce in the only truth than seek through so many windings and labyrinths, if only it had pleased God to lighten unto us the Sixth Candelabrum?" This Sixth Candelabrum is direct interior perception of the indwelling presence of the Christ. The perception itself is arrived at by the function of a center in the brain, called sometimes the Third Eye, sometimes the Transparent Jewel, and sometimes the Philosophers' Stone.

When this organ puts us in touch with the true Self, the Christos, then we are freed from fear of hunger, poverty, diseases, and age. When it gives us the knowledge that was in the mind of Christ Jesus, it makes us, like the writers of the *Fama* and *Confessio*, consciously immortal, so that we live as if we had lived from the beginning of the world and should continue to live to the end thereof. At the same time it releases us from the fear and uncertainty concerning after-death states, which is the stock-in-trade of those who seek to control humanity by the wiles of priestcraft. By the functioning of the Third Eye we are brought into communication with other centers of the Life Power, no matter how distant their bodies may be from ours. By it we see into the *Liber Mundi*, the Book of the World, and learn from it the simple truth, agreeing always with itself.

This higher consciousness is called the Sixth Candelabrum, partly because it is a stage of the unfoldment of human consciousness taking us beyond the limits of ordinary sensation, which is represented by the number 5, because of the usual rough classification of the senses. Yet there is another reason for this particular term. The number 6 in the Qabalah, is particularly connected with the idea of the Christos, or Divine Son, sometimes called the King; that is, the Anointed One, or Messiah. And as the number 6 is also the number of the letter Vav in the Hebrew alphabet, this letter, which is the third letter of IHVH, Jehovah, is also identified with the Royal Son.

Now the name of this letter means "nail," and we have seen that in the allegory of the vault of Brother C.R., the nail stands for the revelation of truth through intuition. Thus, we have no difficulty with what the *Confessio* has to say about the pope's being torn to pieces with nails. One would think the strange terminology might have struck a spark of understanding in the mind of one so well versed in the letter of the Qabalah as is Mr. Waite. What is meant is simply that the domination of man's thought by "Churchianity" will come to an end when intuitive knowledge of the One Reality takes the place of creedal bondage. Even the phrase "ass's braying," crude as it seems, refers to something more esoteric. It will be remembered that Apuleius wrote of one transformed into an ass, who was restored to human form by eating roses. The ass is an ancient symbol of the bondage of materialism and of the ignorance of those who try to build their house of life on judgments from outward appearances. The Church of Rome and all the other forms of exoteric religion condemned in the passage I have quoted from K.H.'s letter keep man in bondage by frightening him, by denying the possibility of the interior illumination, by taking away the keys of knowledge. Thus, all such exoteric religious formalism (including the falsest of all false religions, materialistic agnosticism), whatever names it takes or whatever claims it makes to ancient authority, is actually the embodiment of the spirit of Antichrist, if the plain meaning of the New Testament is not utterly ignored.

Fanatic I may be, by Mr. Waite's definition, but I trust it has been made clear that I have no special antagonism to Rome and none at all toward the members of the Roman communion. I do not forget that even the Pope was once a lay member of that communion. I do not doubt that many a Pope and many a priest believes sincerely enough in all the doctrines of the church he serves. These men are victims of an idea, of a system, and the idea and system have just as poisonous an influence on persons outside the Roman communion. It is against the system that the *Fama* and the *Confessio* direct their shafts of satire. An authoritarian Church or an authoritarian "science" cannot permit freedom of conscience and uses force when it can, or whatever other weapons offer when brute force cannot be employed, to suppress that freedom. Thus, among the enemies of Rosicrucianism and Freemasonry today, we find exoteric materialism not less active than exoteric "Churchianity," and for the same reasons.

Turning now to the political aspect of Rosicrucianism, we find the *Fama* saying: "In *Politia* we acknowledge the Roman Empire and *Quartam Monarchium* for our Christian head, albeit we know what alterations be at hand, and would fain impart the same with all our hearts to other godly learned men." Similarly, the *Confessio* says: "We offer to the chief head of the Roman Empire our prayers, secrets, and great treasures of gold."

The choice of words is significant. The Invisible Order, writing in 1614, *acknowledges* the existing political order. So might one today *acknowledge* the undoubted fact of the present Republican or Democratic administration in the United States and *acknowledge* the particular forms of social and economic procedure now in use. Acknowledge too the necessity of good citizenship and obedience to laws that are actually in operation, for he who understands the spirit of true Rosicrucianism must ever be a good citizen.

Yet with all this, such a person (like the Brethren who wrote the manifestoes we are considering) may know very definitely what alterations are at hand. Like Abraham Lincoln, who would not help a slave to escape while the institution of slavery continued to have legal sanction but who worked steadily toward the destruction of the institution itself, those who acknowledged the Roman Empire and the *Quartam Monarchium* foresaw the coming of the "strong child of Europe." They knew, long before the Pilgrims had landed at Plymouth, what changes were at hand, and they were active in bringing about those changes. Thus, when the "strong child of Europe" had attained his growth on the American Continent, it was through the channel of Freemasonry that essentially Rosicrucian ideas were made the first principles of the "New Order of the Ages" begun by the American Declaration of Independence. Thus, it is not surprising to find that the symbolism of the Great Seal of the United States includes one detail that any Qabalist would represent by the letters ABRC, of which the first two, AB, spell the Hebrew noun meaning "father"; so that ABRC may be read in English, "Father R.C."[4]

The first paragraph of the *Confessio* makes it evident that the authors of the manifestoes observed prudent reserve. It says: "We know certainly that what we here keep secret we shall in the future thunder forth with uplifted voice." One hundred and sixty years later this promise was fulfilled by the Declaration of Independence, in which many of the Rosicrucian principles veiled by the careful phrases of the *Fama* and *Confessio* were set forth as self-evident truths. And as has been said, the manifestoes make it perfectly clear that their authors recognized that there is sometimes the need for the use of force in establishing a better social order.

A man who knows truth is willing to lay down his life for it. Revolution is deplorable, but there are times when it is necessary. If ballots fail, bullets must sometimes be employed. When those who, like the learned of Spain mentioned in the *Fama*, have profited personally by error and injustice, refuse to permit the establishment of better conditions and use their political power and wealth to keep their fellowmen in bondage, it is the right and duty of the oppressed to use force to overthrow tyranny. Yet all who feel impelled to employ force to gain their ends must be willing to

---

[4]See Paul Foster Case, *The Great Seal of the United States* for further details.

accept the consequences of defeat. As Benjamin Franklin said: "Gentlemen, we must all hang together, or we shall all hang separately." The spectacle of a person who advocates revolution endeavoring to evade punishment by appealing to technicalities of laws he is trying to destroy is one we see from time to time. Such persons have no cause for complaint. Revolution is always treason, unless it succeeds, and they who choose this dangerous weapon hastily, when peaceful means seem to them too slow, have little claim on our sympathy.

That pope who asserted that Rosicrucians and Freemasons are enemies of religious and legitimate authority was not altogether in the wrong. His was the voice of traditional order, always raised against those who believe in man's essential freedom. Today the world as a whole has little respect for religious authority. Yet there are many otherwise reasonable people who have too much respect for social authority merely because it happens to be legitimate. Few would now maintain the thesis that slavery is anything but an evil, yet for thousands of years human slavery was perfectly legitimate, and a man's control of his human "property" was maintained by the laws of so-called "civilized" countries.

Today there are other kinds of slavery, just as evil and just as "legitimate" as was chattel slavery in Georgia in 1850. If the persons whom the laws of the land place in positions of unjust, though perfectly legal, mastery over the lives and destinies of thousands of their fellow creatures will not themselves give up that mastery, it must be taken away from them—peaceably, if possible. The New Order of the Ages is imminent, and nothing can prevent its complete external expression. Because it is true now, as it was in 1614, that the Rosicrucian philosophy that proclaims the essential principles of that New Order has in it "much of Theology and Medicine, but little of Jurisprudence," it becomes more and more evident that jurisprudence, as it affects the constitution of the social and economic order, must be thoroughly reformed.

The True and Invisible Rosicrucian Order foresaw that reformation and proclaimed it, under prudent reserves, in 1614. Today, as in 1776, its "Trumpet shall resound with full voice and no prevarications of meaning." Behind the outer veil of human governments there is at work a force that is rapidly bringing to a crisis a great movement for the liberation of humanity. The first principle of that movement is the spiritual value and the spiritual equality of *all* human beings. This being perceived, it becomes evident that neither superior mentality nor wealth nor social position nor anything else gives any person the right to control the life and destiny of even the least of his fellowmen.

Does this mean that all men shall be permitted to do just as they please? Certainly not. It will be, also, many a long year before disease and crime are wiped out. For generations to come, in all probability, society must protect itself against evils that are largely of its own making. But there is a tremendous difference between social control of dangerous nonconformists and the purely personal power, extending even to the power of life and death, that our present faulty jurisprudence confers on private individuals. It is a hopeful sign of the times that many thoughtful persons are beginning to realize that even criminals are people, so that the emphasis is shifting from punishment to reformation and from the consideration of ways and means to fight the criminal classes to the search for remedies for the social maladjustments of which crime and criminals are but symptoms.

Rosicrucian religion, then, is Christian Gnosticism. It is opposed to organized religious authority because that authority imposes creeds, plays on the fears and hopes of believers, and in Christendom founds itself on the essential ignobility and worthlessness of man. Rosicrucian religion begins by proclaiming man's nobleness and worth and proceeds to declare its knowledge of the Christos. It describes that knowledge as being progressive and as leading eventually to conscious immortality. It offers no creed, establishes no set proceeding. "None of the posterity shall be constrained to wear one certain kind of habit." It sums itself up in the word R.C., that is, in compassion and tenderness for all mankind; and it says that its religious philosophy agrees in all parts with "Jesus," that is, with "The nature of Reality is to liberate," which is the literal significance of the name Jesus.

In full agreement with this religious basis, the political philosophy of Rosicrucianism has always been on the side of freedom. It acknowledges the existing social order and offers to it its prayers, secrets, and treasures. That the offer is usually rejected is beside the point, for it should be understood that the Invisible Order is not less compassionate in its attitude toward those whose lot it is to be the instruments of oppression than it is to those who are cast for the role of the oppressed. The Pope it execrates is not the man who sits in Peter's seat. It is the office—of which the man is certainly as much a victim as the most ignorant peasant who lets his family starve that he may contribute his quota of Peter's pence. Similarly, a true Rosicrucian can feel no hatred for a political tyrant. For when "R.C." is truly one's mark and character, one has insight enough to perceive that the political tyrants of this world are among its most tragic and pitiable figures.

Thus, in politics, we find the Invisible Order lending all of its influence to promote the cause of human liberty. Sometimes that influence works through revolutionary channels, as it did in the United States in 1776 and a little later in France and South America. Whenever possible, however, the Order seeks to gain its objectives by peaceful means, and in our times it is actively engaged in an endeavor to end war altogether.

In a word, the religion of Rosicrucianism is a quest for the Inner Light of the indwelling Christos, and its political aspiration is an extension to society of the words of Aristotle: "Freedom is obedience to self-formulated rules."

PART TWO

THE TEN ROSICRUCIAN GRADES

CHAPTER XI

THE GRADES OF THE ORDER

HE *CONFESSIO* SAYS: "This Fraternity . . . is divided into degrees," but neither of the original Rosicrucian manifestoes gives any details as to the system of Grades. Tradition, however, has it that the Grades are ten in number. Every Grade corresponds to one of the Sephiroth, or numeral emanations, represented by the circles on the Qabalistic Tree of Life.

The Grades ascend the Tree from the tenth circle to the first. Hence, progress in the Invisible Order is approach to Unity, and this is also approach to true self-knowledge, inasmuch as the highest Grade corresponds to the first circle, *Kether* (the Crown), the seat of *Yekhidah* (the Indivisible), or the macrocosmic I AM, which is the same as the Hindu *Atman* and is probably closely related to the *Khu*, or spiritual soul, of the ancient Egyptians. *Yekhidah*, in other words, is the essential Man whose true nobleness and worth it is the purpose of Rosicrucianism to reveal.

The ten Grades are divided into three classes or Orders. The First Order comprises the Grades corresponding to the circles from 10 to 7 inclusive. The Second Order has three Grades, corresponding to circles 6, 5, and 4. The Third Order includes the Grades corresponding to circles 3, 2, and 1.

Every Grade has a number, represented by an equation, in which the first figure represents the number of steps taken by the aspirant in his journey toward Unity, and the second number of the equation indicates the Sephirah to which the Grade corresponds. Thus, the Grade of Zelator is represented by the equation 1 = 10, because it is the *first* Grade of the Order, and corresponds to the *tenth* circle on the Tree of Life. Tradition gives these Grades the Latin names shown in Table 4 on page 156.

Besides these ten Grades attributed to the Tree of Life, some societies working according to the Rosicrucian tradition include a preparatory Grade, that of Neophyte, 0 = 0. In this Grade are given certain

Table 4. Rosicrucian Grades

Number	Latin Names	Equation	Correspondence
FIRST ORDER			
1	Zelator	1 = 10	Kingdom
2	Theoricus	2 = 9	Foundation
3	Practicus	3 = 8	Splendor
4	Philosophus	4 = 7	Victory
SECOND ORDER			
5	Adeptus Minor	5 = 6	Beauty
6	Adeptus Major	6 = 5	Strength
7	Adeptus Exemptus	7 = 4	Mercy
THIRD ORDER			
8	Magister Templi	8 = 3	Understanding
9	Magus	9 = 2	Wisdom
10	Ipsissimus	10 = 1	The Crown

preliminary obligations, together with practical work that prepares the Neophyte to enter the progressive training represented by the ten Grades corresponding to the ten circles on the Tree.

This entire scheme will be understood better by reference to the frontispiece. There it will be seen that from each circle certain paths of the Tree of Life lead upward to the circles above. In the ceremonial work of societies following this pattern and in the actual work of physical and spiritual transformation corresponding to these ceremonies the paths of the Tree are traversed in reverse order.

Thus, it happens that entry into a given Grade does not always give one access to all the paths proceeding upward from that Grade. This will be understood better by reference to Figure 7. There it will be seen that the paths numbered 32, 31, and 29 all lead upward from the tenth circle. But when one has become a Zelator, the only one of these three that is open is the 32d path, because that is the path leading to the next Grade, the Grade of Theoricus.

When the Grade of Theoricus has been reached, the 31st path, from Kingdom to Splendor, is open, and also the 30th path, from Foundation to Splendor. Not until these two have been traversed, however, is the 29th path, that leading from Kingdom to Victory, open to the advancing aspirant, but when he has traversed this, he may pass through the 28th path, from Foundation to Victory, and through the 27th, from Splendor to Victory.

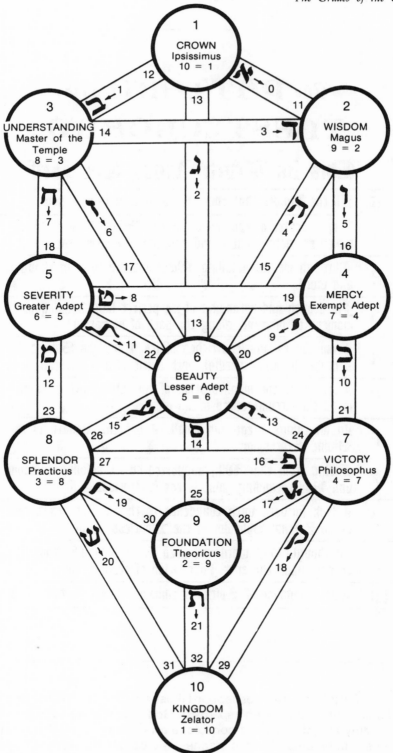

Figure 7. Tree of Life Diagram showing the Grades of Initiation

The PATTERN *on the* TRESTLEBOARD

This Is Truth About The Self

0	All the Power that ever was or will be is here now.
1	I am a center of expression for the Primal Will to Good. which eternally creates and sustains the Universe.
2	Through me its unfailing Wisdom takes form in thought and word.
3	Filled with understanding of its perfect law, I am guided, moment by moment, along the path of liberation.
4	From the exhaustless riches of its Limitless Substance, I draw all things needful, both spiritual and material.
5	I recognize the manifestation of the Undeviating Justice in all the circumstances of my life.
6	In all things great and small, I see the Beauty of the Divine Expression.
7	Living from that Will, supported by its unfailing wisdom and Understanding, mine is the Victorious Life.
8	I look forward with confidence to the perfect realization of the Eternal Splendor of the Limitless Light.
9	In thought and word and deed, I rest my life, from day to day, upon the sure Foundation of eternal being.
10	The Kingdom of Spirit is embodied in my flesh.

Figure 8. The Pattern on the Trestleboard illustrates the Ten Divine Emanations of the Qabalistic Tree of Life or ten aspects of God. It is also an evolutionary picture of man's destiny in unfolding his conscious awareness of the creator. Paul Case received these statements from the teacher who guides the work of Builders of the Adytum. The term *trestleboard* is used in Freemasonry to illustrate the plans of the Great Architect of the Universe, who is God. The term *pattern* indicates that ordered plan.

What this means is that although one enters the tenth Sephirah at the beginning of his Rosicrucian experience, he must have had the knowledge conferred in the Grade of Theoricus before he may enter either of the two paths leading upward to the Grade of Practicus. It is as if the doors to these paths were locked, and as if the keys were kept in rooms represented by circles 9 and 8. The keys to paths 31 and 30 are kept in circle 9; those to paths 29 and 28 are kept in circles 8 and 7, respectively; and the keys to paths 27 and 26 are also kept in circle 7, but the latter may not be used until the aspirant is ready to advance into the Second Order.

According to Qabalistic doctrine, the root of the Tree of Life is in *Kether*, and its fruit is in *Malkuth*, the Kingdom; that is, the Tree hangs upside down, like the Yggdrasil of Norse mythology and the sacred tree mentioned in the Bhagavad-Gita. The tenth Sephirah, the Kingdom, is the lowest or outermost manifestation of the Life Power and corresponds to the physical plane.

Consequently, the Rosicrucian scheme of initiation begins with this Sephirah and works upward toward *Kether*, the Crown, in the reverse order of the paths on the Tree of Life. This is in accordance with the notion that we must begin where we are, and that the path of initiation is a Way of Return. Hence, the Rosicrucian manifestoes speak of the amendment of philosophy as being a restoration rather than an innovation.

Every one of the circles on the Tree of Life has many occult meanings; so has every one of the connecting paths. The meanings of the circles are all developed from the abstract ideas of number. The meanings of the connecting paths are related to the occult significance of the twenty-two letters of the Hebrew alphabet. In the diagram the Hebrew letter in each path is the one pertaining to that path, and near each letter is a small arrow pointing to a number. This number is that of the Tarot Key corresponding to the letter. The other number in each path is its number in the scheme of the Thirty-two Paths of Wisdom. Of these thirty-two paths, the first ten are the circles on the Tree of Life. The eleventh to the thirty-second are the channels connecting the circles. Thus, the eleventh path is that of Aleph and of Key 0 in Tarot, and the thirty-second path is that of the letter Tav and Key 21.

In this book it is impossible to enter into a detailed analysis of the Tarot Keys. I have dealt with these at greater length in my book *The Tarot: A Key to the Wisdom of the Ages* and in courses on Tarot. Figure 8, The Pattern on the Trestleboard, should be studied as it will be referred to in connection with the Tarot Keys. The reproduction of the major trumps of Tarot used in this book are from the designs used by the Builders of the Adytum, one of the several societies working ceremonially according to the scheme of Grades explained hereafter.[1]

---

[1]Courses on Tarot form part of the curriculum of instruction issued by Builders of the Adytum (B.O.T.A.), 5101 North Figueroa Street, Los Angeles, California 90042. The Tarot Keys used in this book may be obtained through Builders of the Adytum at the above address.

The main thing to bear in mind in approaching this explanation of the Rosicrucian Grades is that every path on the Tree of Life corresponds to some particular mode of human consciousness. In the old Qabalistic books, the descriptions of these paths are very brief and are couched in language intentionally cryptic. Yet these descriptions are of vital importance, because they refer to mental states that are present in the life of every human being. Sometimes they are latent, sometimes active, but they are always part of the makeup of every man and woman.

The old Rosicrucian and Qabalistic training, therefore, is of immediate interest to you, because it not only deals with all the elements of your consciousness but also aims to bring each element into the best possible manifestation and into harmonious combination with all the others. No single book can exhaust this tremendous subject, but it is hoped that the following chapters will shed light on the Path of Return that leads to that priceless attainment, true self-knowledge.

CHAPTER XII

THE GRADE OF ZELATOR, 1 = 10

CCORDING TO SOME AUTHORITIES, Zelator means "zealous student." Others say it was a name applied to the assistant of an alchemist, whose duty it was to keep the fire burning in the *athanor*, or alchemical furnace. These are really two expressions of a single idea, because the principal object of the Grade of Zelator is to arouse the zeal and aspiration of the initiate. Zealous aspiration is what keeps the fire burning in the *athanor*, which is none other than the physical vehicle of human personality.

Hence, this Grade is assigned to the tenth Sephirah of the Tree of Life, to which Qabalists assign the physical body and its sensations. The Grade of Zelator is the only grade of *initiation*, because *to initiate* means "to introduce, to begin." The Grades following are Grades of advancement.

The actual beginning of progress toward adeptship and beyond is made here in the physical plane, in the field of sensation. The physical body and its environment concern us first of all. These are the initial objects for occult study. Initiation is not entrance into other planes of existence, and it is not the study of other worlds than ours. It is an introduction to the hidden laws behind the veil of familiar things.

Everything of which we are aware in physical life is, so far as our knowledge is concerned, basically a sense experience. Even our own bodies are known to us only as mental impressions of sensations. Thus, whatever we may know of the laws of life, quaintly described in the *Confessio* as being written in "those great characters which the Lord God hath inscribed upon the world's mechanism, and which he repeats through the mutations of empires," we must learn at first through sense experience.

What the Zelator learns primarily is that the realm he contacts through the various channels of sensation is a realm of order, a realm of cause and effect. The doctrine of the reign of law is primary in Rosicrucian teaching. The "great characters" are certain fundamental signs, which may be read by any human mind that has been trained in the art of accurate observation. They are repeated through the mutations of empires, because the same signs that can be read in the mineral kingdom can be read in the kingdom of plant life, the kingdom of animal life, and the kingdom of human nature. The number of these characters is not so very large, but their combinations are practically infinite. One and all, they declare plainly that everything reported to us by our senses is part of an order, the expression of a rational and mathematical series, and the manifestation of discernible and dependable sequences of cause and effect.

Thus, the Grade of Zelator is assigned to the Sephirah named *Malkuth,* the Kingdom. In Roman letters corresponding to Hebrew, *Malkuth* is spelled MLKVTh and represented by the following Tarot sequence: The Hanged Man (M); Justice (L); The Wheel of Fortune (K); The Hierophant (V); The World (Th). This sequence of Tarot Keys gives clear indications as to the doctrine of the first Rosicrucian Grade.

First comes The Hanged Man, intimating that initiation is a reversal of ordinary conceptions of the meaning of sense experience, a reversal that includes recognition of man's utter dependence on the operations of fixed and unchanging laws. Then comes Justice, with its symbolic declaration of that great law of equilibrium that has excited the admiration of sages in every period of human history. Justice is followed by the picture of a turning wheel, one of the most ancient representations of the mechanism of nature and symbolic expression of that great doctrine of cycles that is one of the fundamentals of practical occultism. After The Wheel of Fortune comes The Hierophant, suggesting that although the reign of law presents itself to our outer senses in mechanistic terms, the essence of that law is identical with the essence of ourselves and has within it always a tendency toward the revelation of hidden things, the unraveling of mysteries, the extension of light. At the end of the series of Keys is The World, testifying that, although there be few who see it, the Rosicrucian presentation of the reign of law declares that form follows form in rhythmic sequence, that life understood is a thing of joy, that the universe is truly a dance of life and not a dance of death. None of these initiatory doctrines of Rosicrucian teaching is one that requires us to possess knowledge beyond the reports of our physical senses.

Any reasonable person who reads these pages may see for himself that whatever he does, whether the outcome accords with his ideas of success or not, is conditioned, if not absolutely determined, by mental and physical laws that he did not make and that he must perforce obey. The better he obeys, the better he succeeds. All applied science is witness to this, and the wonders of our inventive age are so many demonstrations that our success in any field of endeavor depends on the accuracy with which we measure the forces operating in that field.

It is also obvious that action and reaction are equal. Throughout nature there is compensation. What Emerson wrote concerning this is merely the philosophic essence of a principle on which all the practical works of man depend. What we sow, that we reap. What we put into any endeavor, that we get out of it. Thus, the Zelator is made to understand at the very beginning of his work that it is only by devotion to the highest that he can expect to receive the highest. Therefore, the *Confessio* solemnly warns all of its readers that none are acceptable to the Fraternity who seek other things than wisdom, and this is fitting in an Order that proclaims Solomon as one who excelled in its philosophy.

Modern science has verified the old occult doctrine of cycles. The scientist relies on that law when he makes predictions as to future events. Careful observation reveals these cycles. Some are of long duration; some are short. But he who knows them knows, as others do not, the full significance of the signs of the times and is freed by that knowledge from the disasters that befall him who remains in ignorance.

Without going beyond the range of the physical senses, it also may be seen that whatever may be the ultimate explanation of the mystery called "life," it indubitably works eternally to make itself known to man. On every hand it leaves its records on the pages of what the *Fama* calls Book M, or the Book of the World. Life explains itself to us. It appeals directly to our physical senses and teaches us its lessons through our mental response to sense experience.

By this means it has become evident that although there seem to be many breaks in that part of the cosmic rhythms that manifests through the complex life of man, in reality no human ill is uncaused, none the result of the capricious ill will of either Deity or demon. When the causes of those ills are found, it always follows that remedies are discovered or invented. In no period of human history has it been easier to perceive this truth than it is today. Pestilences that our ancestors sought to avert by ineffectual prayers to a God supposed to be immediately responsible for them are well nigh banished from the earth—and in no other manner than by man's obedience to what he has learned by accurate observation and exact measurement.

In one Rosicrucian scheme of correlating the vibrations of color and sound, four colors are assigned to the tenth circle of the Tree of Life. In diagrams that show this attribution, the tenth circle is divided into four segments (see frontispiece). The lower segment is a deep blue-violet, so dark that in color printing it is practically equivalent to black. It is produced by the mixture of the three primary pigments; red, yellow, and blue. In sound this is the chord consisting of the notes C, E, and G-sharp. The right-hand segment is slate, produced by the mixture of green and violet. In sound it is the chord consisting of the notes F-sharp and A-sharp. The left-hand segment is russet, produced by the mixture of orange and violet. In sound its chord consists of A-sharp and D. The upper segment is citrine, the mixture of orange and green. Its chord is composed of the notes D and F-sharp.

In Rosicrucian tradition these four segments are attributed to the four elements of ancient physics. The blue-violet is the segment of earth, the russet of fire, the slate of water, and the citrine of air. These elements are indicated by their respective alchemical symbols. Their symbolic meaning is as follows:

1. *The blue-violet segment* of earth represents the darkness of ignorance. It is typified in initiatory ceremonies by a hoodwink or blindfold placed over the eyes of the candidate. Humble confession of ignorance is the first step toward discovery of truth. He who would be initiated into the inner secrets of the Invisible Rosicrucian Order must begin by realizing that he is more or less in the dark as to the real meaning of his sense experience. By adopting this attitude he intensifies his zeal for right knowledge and becomes adequately receptive.

2. *The slate segment* attributed to water typifies purification. This should be understood in the strict sense of the word *pure,* which means "free from mixture." Pure sense experience, unmixed with emotional coloring, unclouded by prejudice, is what is to be sought. Most persons never really *see.* They look at things, but what they *think* they see is modified by what they *think* they know and by what they *suppose* they want. A practical occultist trains himself to see what actually is, whether or not it agrees with his suppositions or his desires. He learns to welcome exceptions to previous experience, because he knows that whenever his senses report a seeming contradiction to the cosmic order (or rather, to his conception of it), they are really bringing to his attention a fresh instance of that very order.

3. *The fire segment* typifies consecration. This means wholehearted devotion to the discovery and practice of truth. In ceremonials that exemplify these ideas, fire or incense is used in consecration, and an obligation taken by the candidate completes his dedication of his life to the pursuit and practice of knowledge of the cosmic order.

4. *The air segment* represents the illumination that follows the three preceding steps. He who admits ignorance, works faithfully to purify his sensations, and devotes himself earnestly to the discovery of truth has united himself to an inherent tendency of the One Reality that was, is, and will be. In ceremonial exemplification of this

stage of initiation, the hoodwink is removed and the candidate is brought to light. Then various details of the meaning of the work are explained to him.

Among these details in the Rosicrucian system are those indicated by the name of the mode of consciousness attributed by Qabalists to the tenth Sephirah. They say that *Malkuth* is the Resplendent Intelligence, and the adjective *resplendent* is written MThNVTzO in Hebrew. The numbers of these letters add to 656; hence, the word shows numerically the characteristic figure of initiation. Represented geometrically, 656 shows the pentagram, symbol of Man, between two hexagrams, symbols of the forces of the universe, thus: ✡ ✭ ✡. Therefore, 656 represents the idea that man is the mediator and adapter, set between the infinite and eternal cosmic Past and the infinite and eternal cosmic Future. Moreover, 656, is the number of the Hebrew noun ThNVR, *thanoor* (furnace), which is the derivation of the alchemical term *athanor*, defined as "a self-feeding, digesting furnace, wherein the fire burns at an even heat." This *athanor* is the human body. Its fire is the fire of life, and this is the fire that the Zelator, or alchemist's assistant, must learn to control and regulate.

DOCTRINES OF THE GRADE

In Tarot, MThNVTzO (Resplendent), is the sequence: The Hanged Man (M); The World (Th); Death (N); The Hierophant (V); The Star (Tz); The Devil (O). From these Keys of the Rosicrucian *Rota* are derived the six initiatory truths, which are as follows:

1. THE HANGED MAN
Key 12 (M)

12 | HANGED MAN | ☐

Every human personality is absolutely and unqualifiedly dependent on the universal existence.

The Universal Existence is represented in Key 12 by the Tree from which the Hanged Man is suspended. In the version of Tarot issued under the supervision of A.E. Waite, this tree is in the form of an English letter *T*. In other versions it resembles a Hebrew Tav. Nowadays this doctrine of dependence is more generally recognized, especially in the various fields of science; but when Tarot was invented and when the Rosicrucian manifestoes were published, it was a revolutionary idea. Even now it is a reversal of common opinion, for although scientists have demonstrated the correlation of all physical forces, popular belief still holds that the mental life of human personality is "on its own." This idea has always been rejected by occultists, who have understood always that the whole personality, mental as well as physical, does nothing of itself; it expresses the sequence of unchanging law in every single activity.

2. THE WORLD
Key 21 (Th)

The Universe is an orderly, rhythmic manifestation of life, determined by fixed laws.

These fixed laws are represented in Key 21 by the four symbols in the corners of the picture. They correspond to the four fixed signs of the zodiac, which are attributed by Qabalists to the four letters of the Hebrew Divine Name IHVH, Jehovah. As signs of the zodiac, they suggest time and convey the idea that time is the fixed condition accompanying all manifestation. The wreath surrounding the central figure in the Key is made of leaves—that is, of something spontaneously provided by nature but suggesting also the intervention of the human factor, since wreaths are woven by human hands. Here is the idea of the human adaptation of laws and forces of nature that came into cosmic manifestation before man appeared. The dancing figure at the center of the design is a type of truth and of the powers of subconsciousness. These powers are in human form, but a veil partly covers the figure, and the veil is in the form of the Hebrew letter Kaph, the letter printed on Key 10, The Wheel of Fortune. What is meant is that the mechanical appearance of the laws of nature hides the truth that the universe is not a mechanism but an organism. Hence, this veil covers the reproductive organs of the dancer and, according to an ancient tradition, conceals also the fact that the dancer is an Hermaphrodite. Spirals in the hands of the dancer recall the words of the *Chaldean Oracles:* "The god energizes a spiral force." This emphasizes a fact always known to occultists and brought to light by exoteric science, viz., the form-building forces of the universe actually work in spirals. Key 21, moreover, is associated with the letter Tav, and to this letter is attributed the planet Saturn, the astrological symbol of all that makes things solid, definite and concrete. Saturn is the form-giving power. All forms whatever are manifestations of spiral activity.

3. DEATH
Key 13 (N)

The dissolution of physical bodies is a necessary and beneficent manifestation of life, but is not the cessation of self-conscious existence.

This is the truth that the death of the physical body is not really an evil. "Death is the last enemy to be overcome," understood from the Rosicrucian point of view, means: "Death is misunderstood by the unenlightened, who regard it as an enemy. This mistaken conception is the last to be overcome. When it is conquered by the true conception, the processes that lead to physical death will be understood correctly. So understood they may be adapted, and by means of this adaptation the very forces that make our bodies die will bring us into consciousness of eternal life." Of this more will be said at another point in this discussion of the Grades.

4. THE HIEROPHANT
Key 5 (V)

The Self of Man is a life that includes a consciousness above Man's personal intellectual level; and guidance from this higher level of consciousness is the birthright of every human being.

When this superconscious life is expressed in personal experience, mysteries are revealed, and intuitions of reality are added to the lower forms of personal consciousness. The presence of the Superconscious Life as an integral component of human personality is a cardinal tenet of Rosicrucianism. That indwelling presence is held to be the fact that makes possible for man a direct cognition of what Jacob Boehme called "the supersensual life." It is to this the *Confessio* refers when it speaks of the Sixth Candelabrum. Seers have this sixth sense in active operation, and the Rosicrucian training provides a method by which it may be awakened into full activity.

5. THE STAR
Key 17 (Tz)

Nature unveils herself to man when man practices right meditation.

Nature unveils herself; we do not unveil her. It is not so much that we learn to meditate as that we arrive at a degree of ripeness wherein meditation becomes possible. Thus, Eckhartshausen, who was a true Rosicrucian, describes the Invisible Order as the Interior Church, and says:

> Worldly intelligence seeks this Sanctuary in vain; in vain also do the efforts of malice strive to penetrate these great mysteries; all is undecipherable to him who is not prepared; he can see nothing, read nothing in the interior. He who is ripe is joined to the chain, perhaps often where he thought least likely, and at a point of which he knew nothing himself. Seeking to become ripe should be the effort of him who loves wisdom.
>
> But there are methods by which ripeness is attained, for in this holy communion is the primitive storehouse of the most ancient and original science of the human race, with the primitive mysteries also of all science. It is the unique and really illuminated community which is in possession of the key to all mystery, which knows the centre and source of nature and creation. It is a society which unites superior power to its own, and includes members of more than one world. It is the society whose members form a theocratic republic, which one day will be the Regent Mother of the whole world.[1]

---

[1]Karl von Eckhartshausen, *The Cloud Upon the Sanctuary* (London: George Redway, 1896), 28, 29.

6. THE DEVIL
Key 15 (O)

Evil is the appearance presented to us by natural processes that we do not understand. It is the veil of terror hiding the beautiful countenance of truth.

Human definitions of "good" and "evil" are, for the most part, extremely faulty. Thus, the occult comment on the Tarot Key illustrating this truth is "The devil is God, as He is misunderstood by the wicked." Compare this with the words of Jacob Boehme: "The Deity is wholly everywhere, all in all; but he is only called God according to the light of love, and according to the proceeding spirit of joy; but according to the dark impression he is called God's anger and the dark world; and according to the eternal fire-spirit he is called a consuming fire."[2]

Consider also these Old Testament passages, for it must be remembered that the true Rosicrucian philosophy is that which finds confimation in the Bible. "I am the Lord, and there is nothing else; beside me there is no God: I will gird thee, though thou hast not known me: that they may know from the rising of the sun, and from the west, that there is none beside me: I am the Lord, and there is nothing else. I form the light, and create darkness; I make peace, and create evil; I am the Lord, that doeth all these things." (Isaiah 45:5,6,7). Again, we read in Amos 3:6, "Shall there be evil in a city, and the Lord hath not done it?"

Seers are always courageous. That is one reason for their careful observation of the rule of silence. Seeing things as they really are and knowing how mistaken are popular notions, they wisely veil their knowledge in glyph and symbol. Occasionally, like Boehme, Isaiah, and Amos, they speak straight out and boldly declare that not only the physical and natural evils—like pestilence, famine, or earthquakes—but also the various evils that we call "wickedness" are orderly phases of the cosmic manifestation of the One Life, or Lord.

That Life, being the source of all activity, is necessarily the cause of the phenomena we dislike, those that inspire us with terror, those we dread and misunderstand. Step by step, however, man's understanding ripens, and activities that in former times were supposed to be results of the malice of a personal adversary of mankind, personified as "the Devil," are now understood to be the workings of natural laws that are purely beneficent when their operation is understood.

---

[2]Jacob Boehme, *The Signature of All Things* (Cambridge and London: Thomas Clarke & Co., Ltd., by arrangement with J.M. Dent & Sons, Ltd., 1969).

Of this, perhaps the most obvious example is lightning. For millenia the thunderbolt was a symbol of divine wrath or else regarded as a weapon of "the Enemy." Now we understand it better, and it serves us in countless ways. Even so, in times to come, the subtle causes of what we term "moral evil" will be better understood, and with that understanding will come man's ability to transmute into forms of beauty and joy the forces that now produce nothing but suffering. This process of transmutation begins with courageous acceptance of the truth that since there is only One Power, the sole cause of all activities, then even those events we classify as evils must proceed from it. Seeing this, one shifts the burden from the place where it does not belong to the place where it does. One learns that whatever seems inimical to his welfare has that appearance because of his own ignorance and lack of understanding. The trouble is not in the scheme of things but in ourselves; and the name of it is *ignorance*.

Such are the teachings of the first Grade. From this Grade three paths lead: the thirty-second path of the letter Tav; the thirty-first path of the letter Shin; and the twenty-ninth path of the letter Qoph. Only the thirty-second path is open at this point. It leads upward to the ninth Sephirah, *Yesod*, and to the Grade of Theoricus, 2 = 9.

THE THIRTY-SECOND PATH

The thirty-second path is called the Administrative, or Assisting Intelligence, because it directs all the operations of the seven planets, with their divisions, and concurs therein.

Book of Formation

The Hebrew for "Administrative" or "Assisting" is NOBD, and the corresponding Tarot sequence is: Death, Key 13 (N); The Devil, Key 15 (O); The Magician, Key 1 (B); The Empress, Key 3 (D). We are faced with the fact of death and with a multitude of conditions that we classify as evils. Yet as Zelatores we are taught that the fact of death has a useful purpose in the cosmic order and that the various evils appear as such because they are misunderstood. What may we do to verify this doctrine? How may we for ourselves gather evidence of its validity? For Rosicrucianism bids us to take nothing on authority and counsels us to test everything in the light of experience and reason. Thus N and O, the first two letters of NOBD, with their corresponding Tarot Keys, pose our problem.

B and D, the last two letters of the same word, give the key to the solution. B, attributed to Key 1, The Magician, indicates that the first thing to do is to watch. Man is ignorant because, having eyes, he sees not, and ears, he hears not. His notions of his environment and of himself are erroneous because they are superficial, because he finds it easier to accept a ready-made opinion than to get accurate information for himself. Therefore, we find all great teachers saying, with Jesus, "Watch!" The original Greek means "Keep awake! Be vigilant! Use your eyes! See what is really going on! Pay close attention to your surroundings!" In one word, "Concentrate!" This is exactly what The Magician symbolizes.

In the last two hundred years man has made great progress in the various arts whereby he controls his environment and its forces. Every bit of this control can be traced to some one man's unusual watchfulness. There is that in us which can see through the surfaces of nature to the hidden working of the laws within, if only we concentrate this power by acts of attention. The world is transparent to the attentive watcher. Nor does anyone long devote himself to such vigorous wakefulness without perceiving clearly that every slightest human thought, word, and action is part of the administration of cosmic law. There are no unimportant thoughts, no unimportant feelings, no unimportant words, no unimportant deeds or events. Whatever occurs is a specific manifestation in time and space of the limitless forces and the changeless laws of the One Life. Mere watchfulness will soon convince you of this, for watchfulness makes you see the Law at work, and the place where it is easiest to see is in your own immediate experience.

In consequence of this watching, typified by The Magician, there comes about a subconscious development, typified by The Empress, and the letter Daleth. In Key 3 one sees all the symbols of rich growth: a pregnant woman in the midst of a garden ripe to harvest. What could be more definite? But consider the title. "Empress" means literally "she who sets in order"—again the intimation of law.

One of the functions of subconsciousness is to reproduce whatever is planted in it by acts of conscious attention. If the acts of attention are superficial, the reports of the senses are not clear. False notions are thus implanted in subconsciousness, and the seeds of error multiply with a deceptive orderliness that leads many persons to mistake this false growth for truth.

It must be remembered that subconsciousness works wholly by deduction. Give it a premise, and if the premise is false, it will work out so orderly a sequence of consequences from the initial false statement that only the keenest critics can detect the error. On the other hand, subconsciousness is just as orderly in its development of the seeds of right knowledge. Thus, invention ever follows close on the heels of observation. No sooner do we perceive, for example, that our thoughts, words, and deeds are integrated with and inseparable from the whole cosmic process than subconsciousness begins to elaborate the consequences of this perception.

She does this in two ways: first, by developing a philosophy of life; second, by helping us to invent means for better expression of our relation to the whole. These means include methods and instruments for dealing with the forces of our inner life, as well as for controlling the forces and conditions in our environment.

It is with his inner life that the practical occultist is most concerned. He may safely delegate the invention of machinery for manipulating environment to the specialists who are called to that kind of work. When it comes to dealing with the forces of his own inner life, he must work out his own methods and build his own instruments. This is the real secret veiled in the words describing the thirty-second path.

"The operations of the seven planets" are the operations of the seven "interior stars." These are centers in the human nervous system. They are named after the seven heavenly bodies used in ancient astrology. They are also identical with the seven metals of the alchemists. These interior stars are centers of force active in the finer vehicles of human personality. In man's physical body their activities are manifest in the following centers:

- Saturn, or Lead. Sacral plexus, at the base of spine;
- Mars, or Iron. A ganglion a little below the navel;
- Jupiter, or Tin. The "solar" plexus, so-called;
- Sun, or Gold. The cardiac plexus;
- Venus, or Copper. A nerve-center in the throat;
- Moon, or Silver. The pituitary body;
- Mercury, or Quicksilver. The cerebrum, and particularly the pineal gland.

By watchfulness and subconscious response thereto, we find that our lives are actually *assisting* in the evolution of the Great Plan. We see that we have actually some share in the administration of the Great Work. When we find this out and begin to see into things as well as to look at them, our bodies begin to undergo subtle changes. The seven centers enumerated above begin to be brought into better adjustment with each other. The alchemical process of sublimation and transmutation has begun.

The Tarot attribution to this path is Key 21, and this Key also represents the pair of opposites, "Dominion and Slavery." When we are assisting in the cosmic administration with our eyes open, so that we know what is going on, we share consciously in the One Life Power's dominion over all things. While we are still blind, still asleep, still part of the herd of men-animals who hardly know they're alive, we are in a state of servitude.

In that state, to be sure, our lives are not one whit less integrated with the All. In that state, too, we are assisting in the cosmic administration, but we have no vision of the Great Business. We are like the man who screws on the 647th nut in an automobile assembly. We may get our day's pay, but we have little or no share in the joy of the work.

Finally, to this path the planet Saturn is attributed. Some astrologers call it malefic, but more enlightened astrological practice is beginning to abandon this interpretation. Occultists know that Saturn and Satan are closely connected in the typology of Ageless Wisdom. Perhaps the most illuminating sentences that can be offered in this connection are from Kingsford and Maitland's *The Perfect Way:*

> And on the seventh day there went forth from the presence of God a mighty Angel, full of wrath and consuming fire, and God gave unto him the dominion of the outermost sphere. Eternity brought forth Time; the Boundless gave birth to Limit; Being descended into Generation. As lightning I beheld Satan fall from heaven, splendid in strength and fury. Among the Gods is none like unto him, into whose hand are committed the kingdoms, the power and the glory of the worlds....
>
> Blessed are they who shall withstand his subtlety: they shall be called the sons of God, and shall enter in at the beautiful gates. For Satan is the doorkeeper of the Temple of the King: he standeth in Solomon's porch; he holdeth the Keys of the Sanctuary; that no man may enter therein save the anointed, having the arcanum of Hermes.[3]

Of the same import is the fact that in the Old Testament the word *Nachash*, NChSh, indicating the serpent who tempted Eve, is identical in numeration with *Messiach*, MShICh, the Redeemer. *Nachash* also is one of the Hebrew words for copper, the metal of Venus, and you will remember that the door of the Vault of Brother C. R. is attributed to Venus. Compare this with what *The Perfect Way* says about Satan being the keeper of the Keys of the Sanctuary. The number common to *Nachash* and *Messiach* is 358, whose digits are the fourth, fifth, and sixth numbers of the occult series 0, 1, 2, 3, 5, 8, 13, 21, 34, 55. In this series each number is the sum of the two preceding numbers (2 is the sum of 0, the symbol of absolute unity, and 1 is the symbol of relative unity.) The number 358 is also the number of *Iba Shiloh*, IBA ShILH (Peace shall come). Out of the fury and bondage of the Great Work, which has Time (Saturn) for its primary condition, shall come peace and rest. Observe in this connection that in the corners of Key 21 are the symbols of the four fixed signs of the zodiac, indicating Time.

The Fall into manifestation is to be followed by the Redemption from the misery that our misunderstanding now brings. The power that brought about the Fall is *identical* with that which is to bring about the

---

[3]Kingsford and Maitland, *The Perfect Way*, Appendix XV (New York: Macoy Publishing & Masonic Supply Co., 1912), 359-60.

Redemption. This, in very truth, is the mystery of mysteries that Jesus revealed in his parable of the Prodigal Son.

As you consider this, do you wonder that Rosicrucianism is occult? Do you wonder that arrayed against it are all the forces of priestcraft? Do you wonder that its inner teaching is reserved for those who have demonstrated their readiness to receive it? Do you wonder that it is suspect, even to this day, and an anathema to those who, like the men C.R. encountered in Spain, are content with what they have gained by imposing their errors on the credulous minds of those who support their ridiculous doctrines? There is no need to say more. If you have eyes to see and ears to hear, you know already. If not, may God ripen you speedily into clearer perception.

CHAPTER XIII

THE GRADE OF THEORICUS, 2 = 9

HEORICUS IS THE SECOND GRADE of the Rosicrucian Order. The aspirant advances into it through the thirty-second path of the letter Tav, explained at the end of the preceding chapter. As its name implies, the Grade of Theoricus is that in which one learns the underlying theory that will be applied in subsequent practice.

It is attributed to the ninth Sephirah, *Yesod*, the Foundation or Basis. In Qabalistic psychology, *Yesod* is the sphere of the automatic consciousness, or subconscious mind. Nearly every detail of the work of the Grade of Theoricus has to do with the occult theory of the operation of the forces of subconsciousness.

Symbolically, *Yesod* is said to represent the generative organs of the archetypal man. This symbology is based on the fact that it is through the agency of what we now term subconsciousness that the Life Power continually reproduces itself in a series of living forms.

In Qabalistic writings the mode of consciousness attributed to *Yesod* is thus described: "The ninth path is called the Purified Intelligence. It purifies the emanations, prevents the fracture and corrects the design of their images, for it establishes their unity to preserve them from destruction and division by their union with itself."

In Hebrew, "purified" is THVR, *Tahoor*, which adds up to 220, like the initials C.R., who is the Foundation of the Invisible Order. As *Yesod*, the Purified Intelligence, is the basis of the cosmic order, so is C.R., also a type of purified consciousness, the foundation of the Fraternity. Furthermore, 220 is the numeration of the letters R.C., which stand for tenderness and compassion. Similarly, when consciousness is purified, its quality is distinguished by this noun *compassion*. Hence, we have here also a hint that the fundamental nature of things is itself marked by that same quality.

Doctrines of the Grade

The letters of THVR give the four doctrines of the Grade. They correspond to the following Tarot sequence: Strength, Key 8 (T); The Emperor, Key 4 (H); The Hierophant, Key 5 (V); The Sun, Key 19 (R). The four doctrines are as follows:

1. STRENGTH
Key 8 (T)

Whatever exists is a form of spiritual energy. Every form of spiritual energy is subject to the control and direction of the form above it. The conscious imagery of Man is a form of spiritual energy. All forms of energy below this level are subject its control. It, in turn, is subject to the direction of superconscious levels of energy. These flow down into subconscious levels through the agency of the conscious mind of Man, which is the mediator between that which is above and that which is below.

The various distinctions between "causal," "mental," "astral," and "physical" are merely for the sake of convenience in classification. It is wholly erroneous to speak of material forces as being opposed to spiritual ones. On the contrary, as science abundantly proves, there is no separate entity called "matter." "Matter" is merely the way spiritual energy behaves within the range of the human senses and of the instruments man has invented to supplement those senses. This doctrine of the essential spirituality of all activities whatsoever is fundamental in Rosicrucian philosophy, as it is fundamental in the Qabalah.

It is the logical consequence of the doctrine of Hermes that all things are from One. Sometimes it is objected that this doctrine materializes spiritual things. On the contrary, it spiritualizes all things. So long as we continue to think of matter as being real, as having an independent existence and forces of its own, so long are we in danger from the limiting consequences of that error.

Yet the truth that opposes the error does not consist in saying that physical forms and forces have no actual existence. The liberating truth is that physical forces, and all other forces, are essentially spiritual, because their root is the Divine Life behind all things.

Our bodies and houses are spiritual facts. The solid earth is another spiritual fact. So are the sun, moon, and stars. When this is understood, the greatest barrier to success in practical occultism has been removed.

So long as we suppose spiritual forces to be antagonized by material forces, we never can be sure of anything; for it is perfectly evident that we do not understand the full extent of the physical world and its laws and forces. If we suppose this to be our adversary, we are defeated before we begin to fight, because we cannot possibly expect to overcome an adversary that is immeasurably greater in resources than ourselves. But if we see that what *seems* to be an adversary is really a manifestation of the very same order that is the basis of our own existence, if we grasp the truth that all forces are spiritual, if we see that the law of our own lives is the law of the universe, then we perceive that the only adversary is our own want of knowledge of the inner and single spiritual Reality. We may then begin our work with a reasonable prospect of success, because we approach it in the right mood.

The doctrine taught the Theoricus, however, says more than that all forces are essentially spiritual. In the symbolic language of Key 8 it declares that all the forces of the cosmos are under the control of the attentive, watchful, vigilant self-consciousness of man. It shows human subconsciousness as the mistress of the king of beasts, thus implying that modifications of the human levels of subconsciousness are transferable to the animal kingdom. It further intimates that the reign of subconsciousness extends itself to the vegetable kingdom, by showing verdure and trees that are evidently the results of cultivation. In the background looms a mountain peak, which is a symbol used again and again in Rosicrucianism and alchemy to represent the completion of the Great Work. That Work is finished when man masters the forms and forces of the mineral kingdom as completely as he masters the forms and forces of the vegetable and animal kingdoms. Nothing less than complete dominion is the objective.

That objective may be attained because what we now term subconsciousness is actually the substance of every form in all the kingdoms of nature below man. The Life Power, working at various levels or in various octaves of subconsciousness, *is all there is to anything that lies within the range of human experience.* Every single thing in the universe may be correctly described as a concourse of forces, temporarily presenting themselves as an object, by reason of the operation of laws of the Life Power working at subconscious levels.

Theoretically, then, it is perfectly reasonable to say that anyone who can modify the operation of subconsciousness at the point where he makes contact with it in his own personality may to some degree modify the forms that same operation takes in localities not so intimately connected with his personal life. Practical occultism rests on this theory *and verifies it by practice.* In brief, because you can control subconsciousness from the level of your self-conscious mental states, you may increase the extent of that control indefinitely. To this end the practical work of Rosicrucianism is directed.

2. THE EMPEROR
Key 4 (H)

The Universe is rational. It is composed according to a pattern intelligible to the mind of Man. That pattern may be seen, provided we train ourselves to look for it. Its characters are written on the mechanism of Nature, and we may read them.

From this it follows that nothing inherently unreasonable can possibly be an integral part of the cosmic order. What seems against reason is either false or else misunderstood. Whatever appears to contradict reason calls, therefore, for close examination. It must never be hastily rejected, since the appearance of unreason is frequently an appearance only, because of superficial observation. But on whatever authority any statement purporting to be truth rests its claims, if it runs counter to established principles that have the support of reason, we ought to reject it, or at least refuse to let our actions be governed by it until evidence is forthcoming that does away with the appearance of unreason. This is a cardinal tenet of true Rosicrucianism.

3. THE HIEROPHANT
Key 5 (V)

There are means of cognition beyond the ordinary forms of human experience. The Life Power immanent in every human personality can and does give that personality direct perceptions of reality transcending sense experience. These perceptions go beyond reasoning, but they are never contrary to reason. They provide us with correct solutions to particular problems, but every solution is also the revelation of an eternal principle.

The Hierophant was used in Chapter XII to illustrate one of the six truths taught to Zelators, but now another aspect of its meaning is emphasized. It still assures us that there are means of cognition beyond the ordinary forms of experience. It tells us that the Life Power, or Christos, can communicate to every one of us direct perceptions of reality that go far beyond the limits of sensation. But its chief meaning in the

Grade of Theoricus is to prevent the advancing pupil from supposing that reasoning is the only possible source of enlightenment.

The Hierophant is really identical with The Emperor, but he is a symbol of the Cosmic Reasoning beyond the levels at present attained by man. In the Qabalah the direct cognition this Key symbolizes is called the Triumphant and Eternal Intelligence—*Triumphant,* because it is a mode of consciousness that provides the "winning solution" to every problem; *Eternal,* because although the solutions are specific and adapted to every man's particular needs, they invariably come to us as perceptions of universal principles. The perception of these eternal principles is beyond the present scope of our reasoning power. The principles themselves, however, are always consonant with, and never contradictory to, whatever we have been able to establish on a solid foundation of reason. They supplement and complete the understanding we gain by reasoning.

4. THE SUN
Key 19 (R)

Man is the synthesis of all cosmic activities. Human intelligence gathers together all the various threads of the Life Power's self-manifestation and carries that manifestation beyond anything that could come into existence apart from Man and human intelligence.

This doctrine is based on the Qabalistic meaning of the Hebrew letter Resh, to which is attributed the "Collective Intelligence." It may also be noted that *Resh* means "the head, or face, of man," and it is in the human head and countenance that the controlling elements of the Life Power are concentrated.

This fourth doctrine of the Grade of Theoricus has been paraphrased by Judge Troward in what he calls the doctrine of the Personal Factor.[1] It means that man has been brought into existence for a particular purpose. That purpose is to carry the Great Work to completion.

Man's first share in the Great Work has to do with the regeneration of his own personality. Key 19 is a symbol of that regeneration. The two children in the picture are shown as being equal in age and stature and

---

[1]Thomas Troward, *The Creative Process in the Individual* (New York: Dodd, Mead & Co., 1915), 60-76. Used by permission.

standing on the same level. In the natural man, subconsciousness, typified as feminine, is subordinate to self-consciousness. In the regenerated man, subconsciousness is released for a higher purpose and becomes the equal of her mate, self-consciousness. But of this we shall learn more in a higher Grade.

Four other doctrines of the Grade of Theoricus are related to the four letters of the word ISVD, *Yesod,* and to the Tarot Keys corresponding to those letters. They are the following:

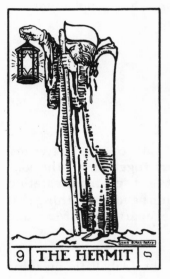

5. THE HERMIT
Key 9 (I)

The power that enables Man to contact the super-conscious levels when enlightenment comes is a form of energy derived from physical activities that are under the astrological domination of the sign Virgo.

This is why the *Fama*, in speaking of the Brethren who established the Order, says: "They were all bachelors, of vowed virginity." On the surface this seems to be a reference to celibacy. Really it alludes to the occult fact that the actual physical energy that leads to illumination is drawn primarily from the assimilative functions of the intestines and organs connected with those functions, all ruled by Virgo.

The Law of Response, represented by Key 9, is also involved in this. The mental attitude of intentional responsiveness or receptivity to the influx of the "Light from above" (represented by The Hermit's lantern) has a direct effect on subconscious processes controlling assimilation. What happens is that more solar energy is extracted from chyle, the Virgin's Milk of the alchemists. This additional energy cannot be received unless one is sincerely and wholly devoted to its right use. There is no way to evade this fundamental necessity. The psychic makeup of human beings is such that unless one devotedly intends to use this extra power correctly, he never gets it. The judge of the intention is by no means the personal consciousness of the aspirant but none other than the One Self, which can never be deceived. One may fool himself as to his motives for gaining occult powers, but nobody can fool the Self. Thus, none but those who are truly devoted ever find this power at their disposal.

6. TEMPERANCE
Key 14 (S)

Daily practice of the thought that the personal life is directly guided by a higher intelligence, daily remembrance of the truth that nobody can ever do anything of himself, daily endeavor to approach all circumstances and activities from this point of view are fundamental exercises in the Grade of Theoricus.

Little needs to be added to this, but the aspirant should consider carefully every detail of Key 14, which sums up symbolically what is stated here. The thought that one is under momentary guidance is one that the greater number of persons have to practice. It does not enter the mind spontaneously. Over and over again one must bring to mind the idea that one's personal activities are expressions of universal forces and laws. These practices include intense watchfulness and oft-repeated recollection.

7. THE HIEROPHANT
Key 5 (V)

The subtlest and most important knowledge of the fundamental theory is not gained by reading nor by listening to the instruction of a human teacher. It is gained by listening with profound attention for the instruction of the Inner Voice. This listening is an active state of consciousness, a throwing of the whole personal consciousness into the form of expectant receptivity.

This intent listening can be practiced many times a day. It should be resorted to whenever one has to make a decision or solve a problem. What is required is the establishment of the habit of turning to the Inner Teacher for light on all daily needs of this sort. The Voice that instructs us is a "still, small Voice," and we do not hear its counsel unless we listen for its message. So fixed are most persons in the delusion that they act of themselves that this inner monitor is seldom heard. It is not the voice of conscience, in the ordinary meaning of that term, but something very much higher.

Many students of occultism keep their studies in a compartment of their minds that seems to be hermetically sealed from the rest of their lives. They think they are studying when they read occult books, attend classes and lectures, or sit in silence at set periods of the day. This is a grave mistake. Practical occultism makes use of books and lectures and classes, to be sure, but its really successful practitioners utilize it during all of their waking hours. More than this, they learn to carry it over into the time when the physical body is asleep. All this comes only by the most attentive practice.

8. THE EMPRESS
Key 3 (D)

Mental imagery is the door to the Higher Knowledge.

This one sentence is a key to the whole occult theory. Remember that the Tarot picture used in this connection is that representing the planet Venus. Hence, it is connected with all the Venus and copper symbolism of the *Fama*. The reader will do well to devote days to developing his consciousness of the inner meaning of this sentence.

Such are the outlines of the occult theory developed in this Grade. When they are firmly fixed in mind, the advancing aspirant is ready to traverse two paths that lead still higher. Of these, one leads from *Yesod* to *Hod*, from the ninth circle to the eighth. This is the thirtieth path, attributed to the letter Resh and to Key 19 in Tarot.

Two other paths lead from the ninth circle. The first is the twenty-eighth path of *Tzaddi*, and the second is the twenty-fifth path of *Samekh*. Neither of these is open to the Theoricus.

His advancement to this Grade, however, entitles the Theoricus to traverse a path leading from the tenth circle to the eighth circle, which was not open to him while he was merely a Zelator. This is the path attributed to the letter Shin and connected with Key 20 of Tarot.

THE THIRTY-FIRST PATH

The thirty-first path is called the Perpetual Intelligence. Why is it so called? Because it rules the movement of the sun and the moon according to their constitution, and causes each to gravitate in its respective orb.

Book of Formation

This is the path of Shin, called the "holy letter" because its number, 300, is that of the words RVCh ALHIM, *Ruach Elohim,* "The Life-breath of the Creative Powers." This Life-breath is what Hindus call *Prana,* the basic energy of the cosmos. It is fiery and electric in its nature, and therefore this path is associated by Qabalists with the element of fire. *The Book of Formation* says: "He caused the letter *Shin* to reign in fire."

This electric fire, the source of all activities in both the macrocosm and the microcosm, is a conscious energy. Its activity subsides, we are told, at the end of a particular cosmic cycle, but although it then passes from its active to its latent state, it does not cease to be. It is perpetual, eternal, without beginning or end. This is the reason for the designation "Perpetual Intelligence."

According to occult teaching illustrated by Key 20 of Tarot, this Perpetual Fiery Life-breath works not only on the plane of the three dimensions we know and within the limits of time that we are now able to grasp but also in a fourth dimension that is likewise an Eternal Now. This fourth dimension of the Life Power, according to Rosicrucian philosophy, now *Is.* Therefore, the Perpetual Intelligence is now an integral part of every human being.

We are not aware of it, but it is here in our lives, just the same. And even as mathematicians are being impressed with the necessity of taking this higher dimension into consideration, so must the aspirant to advancement on the Way of Return do all that he can to build up his conception of this aspect of his own nature. It may as yet have made almost no impression on his personal consciousness, but if he bears in mind the eighth doctrine of the Grade of Theoricus, he will learn how to become intensely aware of this important element of his makeup.

Tarot Key 20 was designed to help the aspirant build up this perception. In accordance with the biological law that subconsciousness builds organisms in response to desire and demand, the daily use of this picture will gradually build into the aspirant's brain the cells that must function before the experience the Key symbolizes can become a vivid, actual element of the seeker's personal consciousness.

The statement that this path rules the movement of the sun and moon is true in two ways. It is true in the macrocosm, because the currents of the cosmic Life-breath are the determiners of the motions of all heavenly bodies. The second application of this truth has to do with the microcosm and is taught in alchemical writings of the Western school of occultists, as well as in the Yoga philosophy of the Eastern school.

The currents of *Prana* are distinguished by the yogis as being solar and lunar, and these currents are actual forces at work within the vehicles of human personality. In alchemy these two are sometimes called gold and silver, and sometimes *our* sun and *our* moon. Furthermore, the sun center in the human body is the cardiac plexus, and the moon center is the pituitary body. When one knows that a current of the Life-breath flows between these two centers and regulates their activity, it is easy to understand why so many important occult practices have to do with the control of this current.

So far as readers of this work are concerned, the only safe practice is that which has to do with impressing subconsciousness with the pattern given in the symbolism of Key 20. Without any other technical practice whatever, daily use of this Key will begin subtle changes in the aspirant's organism. Eventually, these changes will make possible a firsthand experience of the higher state of consciousness termed the Perpetual Intelligence.

In addition to working with Key 20, one should often bring to mind the idea that fourth-dimensional existence is even now part of one's real makeup. Perhaps the simplest way to do this is to think of oneself as having eternal life here and now. The consequences of the repetition of this idea until subconsciousness takes hold of it and elaborates it are extraordinary. It is a seed idea whose fruit is complete release from three-dimensional limitations.

It must be understood that those who make contact with the true Rosicrucian Order will eventually receive more detailed and specific instruction than is to be found in these pages. But it is true as ever that newcomers are not admitted all at once to all our weighty secrets. What is set down here is the rule and pattern for beginners on the path, and here it may be said that the surest sign that one is just a beginner is the feeling that one is so very advanced that exercises like this one with Key 20 are dismissed as being too simple.

The simple truth is that precisely this kind of practice is used by members of the very highest Grades of the Invisible Order. No matter how far advanced one may be toward adeptship, the practice of symbolic mental imagery is a daily and indispensable mental exercise. Thus, the farther advanced one really is, the better does he understand the value of this practice and the reasons for its value. It is the mark of the tyro to underestimate the very things that are the chief treasures of the adept.

THE THIRTIETH PATH

The thirtieth path is called the Collective Intelligence, for thence astrologers, by the judgment of the stars and the heavenly signs, derive their speculations and the perfection of their science according to the motions of the stars.

Book of Formation

It is because man is a synthesis of the cosmic forces, a summary of the powers of the One Life, that any science is possible, and particularly true astrology. The meaning of life is wrapped up in man, the microcosm. This is by no means the idea that the universe was made for man. It is the doctrine that man came into existence for the completion of the Great Work in which the One Life is engaged.

By right judgment of the movement of the stars, certain basic patterns are revealed. The orbits of the planets have relations to each other that are also the relations of musical tones, the relations revealed by the crystallization of minerals, the relations developed in the production of all forms.

Man is the only being on earth who can recognize these patterns and apply them consciously. Astrology, essentially a mathematical and geometrical science, is brought to perfection when these key patterns are perceived. This science, by no means perfect as now practiced, has within it the germ of a great development. The key to that development is the fact that human life is the expression of the same forces and laws that are manifested in the visible changes of position and relationship written in the language of the stars.

Until man perceives and applies these patterns, he is a slave of the forces whose ebb and flow are indicated by the stars. When he knows and uses these patterns, he shares consciously in the reign of cosmic law. Apart from this knowledge, astrology leads to an arid, sterile fatalism. Perfected by this knowledge, the same science adds immeasurably to the richness and resources of human personality. This may be one of the reasons that the pair of opposites, "Fruitfulness and Sterility," are among the various attributions of the letter Resh.

These two paths lead from the Grades of Zelator and Theoricus to the next Grade. The thirty-first path begins in the Grade of Zelator because it is an elaboration of the six doctrines of that Grade. Hence, Key 19 should be considered with special reference to those doctrines, which shed much light on the inner meaning of its symbols. Furthermore, what is represented by Key 19 demands the refinement of physical sensation that is a main object of the work of the Zelator.

The thirtieth path begins in the Grade of Theoricus, because in traversing it one has continually to return to the underlying elements of the theory taught in the second Grade. The idea that human life is a synthesis of the whole range of cosmic powers is, for persons below the highest Grades of the Invisible Order, as yet little more than theory, and in traversing the thirtieth path one elaborates and rounds out that theory.

CHAPTER XIV

THE GRADE OF PRACTICUS, 3 = 8

HE GRADE OF PRACTICUS CORRESPONDS to the eighth circle of the Tree of Life, named HVD, *Hod*, "Splendor." *Hod* is the Sphere of Mercury; hence, the activities of this Grade are dominated by the mode of consciousness represented in Tarot by Key 1, The Magician. It is the Grade of those who have passed from the study of theory to the experimental work that establishes the correctness of that theory.

This work consists largely in mental practices carried on at the level of self-consciousness. It is practice in the art of inductive reasoning, in the drawing of logical inferences from experience, in the development by induction of the general truths to be ascertained from examining a controlled series of events.

This experimental work is indicated by the eighth statement in the *Pattern on the Trestleboard:* "I look forward with confidence to the perfect realization of the Eternal Splendor of the Limitless Light." The Practicus works with the tools on the Magician's table: the Wand of will, the Cup of mental imagery, the Sword of action, and the Pentacle of actual physical conditions.

This Grade corresponds also to the eighth of the Thirty-two Paths of Wisdom, termed the Perfect or Absolute Intelligence, concerning which it is written: "The preparation of principles emanates therefrom." It is furthermore said that the roots to which the eighth path adheres are in the depths of the Sphere Magnificence, that is, in the depths of *Chesed*, the fourth circle of the Tree of Life, corresponding to the Grade of Exempt Adept, the highest Grade of the Second Order.

The work of the Practicus is concerned with the preparation of principles, that is, with the combination of principles so as to produce predetermined effects. Yet the roots of this work go still higher and are to be found in the depths of the sphere named *Chesed*, or Mercy. *Chesed* represents the Divine Beneficence, and the essential idea connected with *Chesed*, as we shall see more definitely in Chapter XVIII, is that of *receptivity*. This same receptivity is clearly symbolized in Key 1 of Tarot, for The Magician holds his right hand aloft, to show that the primary and most important function of self-consciousness and its power of inductive reasoning is to maintain man's contact with the superconscious level of the Life Power's action. In other words, the logical inference to be drawn from human experience, rightly understood, is that personality and self-consciousness are but the instruments and vehicles of something higher. Hence, the first work of occult practice is to maintain consciously the attitude of voluntary receptivity to direction recognized as coming from above.

DOCTRINES OF THE GRADE

The adjective translated "Perfect" in the title of the eighth path is ShLM, *Shalom*, in Hebrew. It also means "well, peaceful, happy," and it is the root of the Hebrew proper name ShLMH, *Shelomoh*, or Solomon. The three primary doctrines of the Grade of Practicus correspond to the three letters of ShLM and to the Tarot Keys representing those letters, as follows:

20 JUDGEMENT

1. JUDGMENT
Key 20 (Sh)

Human life, even now, extends beyond the limits of the physical world.

Even now we live in what is known to some as the Fourth Dimension. Relatively few human beings have even the slightest intellectual realization of this fact, but it is a fact, and it applies to every man and woman on earth. Even now we are immortals, though our misunderstanding of the meaning of death and the imperfect organization of certain centers in our brains prevent us from knowing that we were never born and will never, never, never die.

2. JUSTICE
Key 11 (L)

All the activities of the universe are held in equilibrium.

For many persons this is hard to understand. Inequality and injustice are *apparent* everywhere, but the esoteric doctrine states plainly that this appearance is untrue. It does not say, you will observe, that justice will prevail in some distant future. It declares emphatically that perfect balance is maintained continually. The doctrine is that for every action there is an immediate reaction; that the Law of Compensation is always in operation; that if we could see the whole past, we should find not one least deviation from strict justice in all the events that have culminated in the present moment.

3. THE HANGED MAN
Key 12 (M)

The personal man is never the thinker, the speaker, nor the actor. Any thought, any word, any deed is the operation of the sum total of cosmic forces and laws, taking particular form in time and space, through the instrumentality of a human being (or other vehicle of the Cosmic Life).

This third truth, until its import is grasped, seems like fatalism. It appears to make man a mere puppet. Yet it is a truth reiterated by all wise men, who all insist, furthermore, that it is not in the least fatalistic. They tell us that the reason it seems to be so is that human beings do not really know what they mean when they say "I." When this ignorance is corrected by right knowledge, the center of consciousness is no longer located in personality. It is shifted to the Real Self, and that Self is perceived as being identical with the Originating Principle of the universe. The personal life is lost, but the Cosmic Life is found. An illusion is exchanged for a reality. A counterfeit freedom is renounced in order that real freedom may be enjoyed.

What the Practicus endeavors to perfect is the mental attitude expressed in these three truths. To achieve this result he must be continually on the watch. Such watchfulness is distinctly an operation of the self-consciousness and is therefore properly related to the Sphere of Mercury.

What is aimed at here is the formation of new habits of thought. Nobody ever truly realizes that his personality is a vehicle for universal life unless he affirms and reaffirms the idea and exercises all the ingenuity he can muster to find new ways of reminding himself that this is true.

Actual dependence on cosmic law and perfect self-surrender to its operation requires as much practice as one needs to learn to sing, or write, or dance. Just saying, "I surrender," now and then, will not produce the desired result. Many gentle, suave repetitions are required before we succeed in "separating the earth from the fire, the subtle from the gross," i.e., before we make a conscious distinction between the physical vehicle of life and Life itself. Above all things, we must take care too that none of these are *vain* repetitions. Spirit and intention must be in our efforts. We must not go mechanically through any words or formulas. All of this, as has been said, demands intense watchfulness.

Poise is one of the meanings of Justice in Tarot, and to gain poise takes practice. A few perfunctory relaxation exercises will never build a poised personality. We must, to be sure, relax at regular periods; but what brings the best results is the habit of perpetual watchfulness, which makes us aware of the *beginnings* of tensions and anxieties. Repeated reflection on the teaching of Ageless Wisdom that all events are ordered according to a law of undeviating justice is an important feature of the practice that leads to personal poise. Beginners often have great difficulty with this teaching, but none is more emphatically insisted on by the Teachers. Meditation on it and continual endeavor to see the law of equilibrium at work in every experience is enjoined on the Practicus.

He also devotes himself to becoming familiar with the idea that even now part of his consciouness is having what we call "fourth-dimensional experience." This is easier to grasp when we understand that every human being has bodies of finer texture than the physical. The physical body is the outermost of the vehicles of the I AM. It is composed of vibrations of energy that are slower and grosser than those of higher vehicles. It is, moreover, corrupted by errors of race thought, and it is far from being perfectly adapted to the transmission of the finer modes of the Life Power's activity.

The physical body needs tuning; and part of the Rosicrucian work is a method of attunement that puts us in a proper position to receive the finer, higher vibrations of our subtle bodies, which already experience the phenomena of the higher planes of existence. Every human being, even the lowest savage, has fourth-dimensional consciousness; but awareness of that consciousness on the physical plane requires a special kind of physiological development. It is to this that Brother C.R.'s sojourn at Damascus and his subsequent training in the Temple at Damcar, as described in the *Fama*, allude. As is hinted there, the training brings about subtle chemical changes in the bloodstream and microscopic alterations of cell structure, chiefly in the brain and the sympathetic nervous system.

Perhaps a simple comparison will make this clearer. In the room where you are reading, a great many different etheric vibrations are doubtless being set up at this moment by impulses sent out from various broadcasting stations. Unless you have a radio set, properly built and correctly tuned, you hear none of these vibrations. Yet they are actually present, and you can hear them whenever you tune in. Your physical body is a much finer receiving set than any radio built by man. At present, however, some of the parts essential to reception may not be, in media parlance, "hooked up." These parts of your physical organism may be correctly adjusted by occult practice. When this is accomplished, you will be able to tune in so as to become aware of rates of vibration that now seem to be nonexistent.

All that has just been outlined is part of the "vision of possibility" the Practicus works to perfect. "Where there is no vision," says the Bible, "the people perish." Vision may be strengthened. Just as plants are cultivated by a gardener, so may the functions of foresight and confident expectation be developed by intelligent practice directed to that end. The grossest of errors is the notion that the gift of vision is an accident of birth. Every human being has the seeds of genuine seership. We are all potential prophets.

In no essential particular does the development of these functions differ from the development of such functions as walking or speaking. First comes the attempt to perform the required action—and these attempts fail again and again, at first. Yet every trial brings one nearer to success.

How often, do you suppose, did you fall while you were learning to walk? If you swim, how many failures preceded your first successful stroke? Countless apparently fruitless endeavors precede every successful attempt to gain skill in the most ordinary physical activities. With practice, the manuscript for a page like this may be written in fifteen minutes; but when one begins to learn typewriting, it takes longer to write a few imperfect lines. Yet not a few persons who profess interest in occult training are ready to give up the work and to condemn esoteric teaching as nonsensical just because their first ten or twenty attempts to concentrate do not put them immediately in touch with the Inner School.

Many a student has sat working at concentration for more than ten months, in half-hour periods twice daily, before perceiving the slightest indication of a result. Among the Brethren of the True and Invisible Order are some who have devoted lifetimes to developing the skill they now exercise. Some of the best work that ever has been done has been accomplished by persons in the midst of a hard struggle for daily bread, by persons having little or no leisure for special occult practice.

Hence the excuse "I haven't time for study or practice," fails to convince one who knows what occult work really is. We all have plenty of time, but the lazy habits of the race mind lead us astray. If we don't practice, it is not because we are too busy. It is because we really prefer to do something else.

The only failure is failure to try, and try again and again. Our attempts, however, are more likely to succeed if we have some clear notion of what we are aiming to accomplish, and some knowledge of the laws and forces we seek to utilize. This is why the Grade of Practicus comes third in the Rosicrucian series, following a Grade devoted to theory.

In all this mental practice it is well to remember that one is dealing with an actual force. Eliphas Levi called it "Astral Light," and described it as follows:

> There exists a force in nature which is far more powerful than steam, by means of which a single man, who can master it, and knows how to direct it, might throw the world into confusion and transform its face. It is diffused throughout infinity; it is the substance of heaven and earth. When it produces radiance it is called light. It is substance and motion at one and the same time; it is a fluid and a perpetual vibration. In infinite space, it is ether, or etherized light; it becomes astral light in the stars which it magnetizes, while in organized beings it becomes magnetic light or fluid. The will of intelligent beings acts directly on this light, and by means thereof, upon all nature, which is made subject to the modifications of intelligence.[1]

The same writer gives a valuable suggestion in relation to the work undertaken in the Grade of Practicus when he says: "Every individuality is indefinitely perfectible, since the moral order is analogous to the physical, and in the physical order we cannot conceive a point which is unable to dilate or enlarge itself, and radiate in a philosophically infinite circle. What can be said of the entire soul must also be predicated of each faculty thereof. The understanding and the will of man are instruments which are incalculable in their power and capacity."[2]

---

[1]Eliphas Levi, *The Mysteries of Magic* (London: Kegan, Paul, Trench, Trubner & Co., 1897), 68, 69.
[2]Eliphas Levi, *The Mysteries of Magic*, 66.

The same thought is contained in a passage in the *Book of Formation* that speaks of restoring the Creator to his throne. Human understanding, human examination and research, human knowledge and calculation and writing—these are means by which the Creator may be restored to his throne. Has He ever been dethroned? Not really; but human error has placed Him on a mythical seat in the sky instead of on the true throne at the center of human existence. Study of the ten aspects of the One Reality, which is the real purpose of our examination of these Rosicrucian Grades, corrects this error. It restores to man his knowledge that the creative, controlling power of the universe is a real presence within the heart of man.

Because of that real presence, because "All the power that ever was or will be, is here now," the vehicles through which that power manifests its omnipotence must be indefinitely perfectible. These words fall under your eyes because the time has arrived in the course of your development when you are ready to be awakened to the truth they set before you. Nobody who is not ready will ever read these lines.

This does not mean that every reader will instantly accept the ideas set forth in this book. On the contrary, some will scoff and reject this teaching utterly. Nevertheless, even the scoffer will not read until he is ready. The mental attitude of self-consciousness is by no means the final arbiter.

You, whoever you may be, who read these words, know this. Henceforth you will never be quite the same. You have touched something more potent, more lasting, more far-reaching than you dream. It stirs in you an activity that eventually will ripen into realization. If now you scoff, the Masters of Compassion grieve for you, because they know life has in store for you bitter lessons of pain, which will break the shell of selfish unbelief that now limits the expression of your higher powers. But if when you read these words an echo seems to stir in you, as of things long forgotten reviving in the depths of your soul, They rejoice with you, knowing that for you the happiness of release is near at hand.

From the Grade of Practicus three paths lead to higher Grades, but of these only the twenty-seventh path of the letter Peh is open, leading to the Grade of Philosophus. Before this path may be entered, the twenty-ninth and twenty-eighth paths must be traversed.

The twenty-sixth path of Ayin remains closed until the aspirant's advancement to the Grade of Philosophus is completed. The twenty-third path of Mem is not open until the Grade of Lesser Adept has been attained. Yet both these paths begin in the Grade of Practicus, because the skill gained in that Grade is what enables the aspirant to pass through them. That skill, remember, is developed by continually practicing the intellectual perception of what may be confidently expected as the outcome of the creative process. This is expressed by the eighth statement of the *Pattern on the Trestleboard:* "I look forward with confidence to the perfect realization of the Eternal Splendor of the Limitless Light."

Three other truths, based on the esoteric meaning of the letters in the word *Hod* (HVD) are taught in the Grade of Practicus. They are as follows:

THE EMPEROR
Key 4 (H)

The original Creative Power, the rational Life that makes, frames, and composes the Universe, directs every detail of cosmic manifestation; hence there are no accidents. Nothing happens by chance. Consequently, every detail of any person's experience is a particular manifestation of this directing Power, a particular note in the universal symphony. That directing Power is the true Seer of all we see, the true Knower of all we know, the supreme Authority over all creation. It only is the Indivisible self.

Here again is a doctrine that may easily be mistaken for fatalism, and when it is so mistaken it paralyzes initiative. But the key to right understanding is the Rosicrucian teaching that the Supreme Authority is not something external to human personality but rather a reality enthroned within the personality. At one and the same moment it is present in all persons, and is that to which all refer when they think or speak of Self. That the majority have no adequate notion of the Self does not change the fact.

5. THE HIEROPHANT
Key 5 (V)

The Self is enthroned above the level of personal consciousness, and from that superior station directs by its infallible Word those who have ears to hear.

Thus the Book of Proverbs puts these words into the mouth of Wisdom: "Unto you, O men, I call; and my voice is to the sons of man.... Hear; for I will speak of excellent things; and the opening of my lips shall be right things" (Prov. 8:4,6). Of similar import is this promise: "And though Jehovah give you the bread of adversity, and the water of affliction, yet shall not thy teachers be removed into a corner any more, but thine eyes shall see thy teachers: And thine ears shall hear a word behind thee, saying, This is the way, walk ye in it, when ye turn to the right hand, and when ye turn to the left" (Isaiah 30:20,21). Direct vision of the teachers, the Brothers of the Invisible Order, is an experience shared by many in these days, and many more have learned that the Voice or Word of the Indivisible Self is always ready with counsel in season.

6. THE EMPRESS
Key 3 (D)

All substance is mental substance, hence all forms are mental images. The production of mental images is the function of the Universal Subconsciousness, and from that function all forms, on all planes, have their immediate origin.

The doctrine here is identical with Oriental teachings. Man has dominion over nature because what appears to be "material" is really mental. The stuff from which a rock is made is not different in substance from that which takes form in our thoughts. Here we come very close to the alchemical doctrine of the First Matter, declared in the axiom of Hermes: "All things are from one, by the mediation of one, and all things have their birth from this one thing, by adaptation."

CHAPTER XV

THE GRADE OF PHILOSOPHUS, 4 = 7

THREE PATHS LEAD TO THE Grade of Philosophus. The twenty-ninth path of the letter Qoph, beginning in the Grade of Zelator, is the first. The second is the Twenty-eighth path of the letter Tzaddi, which commences in the Grade of Theoricus. The third is the twenty-seventh path of the letter Peh, beginning in the Grade of Practicus.

Here is a plain intimation that in order to be able to grasp the Rosicrucian philosophy one must first have developed the perception that he lives in a cosmic order, then he must have received sound instruction in the fundamentals of Rosicrucian theory, and finally he must have worked at training himself in confident expectation that the Great Work will be brought to a gloriously splendid completion.

THE TWENTY-NINTH PATH

The twenty-ninth path is called the Corporeal Intelligence. It informs every body which is incorporated under all orbs, and it is the growth thereof.

Book of Formation

This is the path of body consciousness, the path of the coordinated working together of the thirty trillion cells of the physical organism. Knut

Stenring says that in black magic this path enables the operator to become *en rapport* with his victim. Pay no attention to this pseudo-occult bugaboo; for though it is perfectly true that black magic depends on some sort of physical connection between the operator and the victim, it is equally true that the same law works in the opposite direction. In white magic this same path is the one that enables the operator to establish the connection whereby he heals and helps a sufferer. It is by the vibrations of physical cells in a physical body that any magician, white or black, is able to "step down" the subtle currents of energy operating on higher levels so as to make them available for the modification of physical forms. Remember always that the black magician uses the same forces and operates by the same fundamental laws as the operator engaged in white magic. What distinguishes black from white in magic is the intention of the operator, and the purposes for which the subtle forces are applied. In physical science we may find a good analogy. It is white magic to use explosives to clear a field, and black magic to use the same explosives to shatter human bodies in warfare.

When the text says this path "informs" bodies, it uses the verb in a sense now almost obsolete, meaning "to give form to; to mold; to arrange." Corporeal Intelligence is therefore the consciousness that shapes bodies. It is associated through the letter Qoph with the back of the head, because in the back of the head is located the specific organ of the body-building intelligence. This organ is the medulla oblongata, and it is what responds to our endeavors to take control of our bodies, to change their chemistry, and to rearrange their structure.

When we use occult methods for controlling the astral light and the forces of subconsciousness, activities are set in motion that eventually result in actual cell adaptation. We cannot do this until we are informed of the theory developed in the second Rosicrucian Grade. Nor shall we succeed unless we have spent some time in the kind of practice associated with the third Grade. It is on this account that the twenty-ninth path cannot be traversed until the aspirant has become a Practicus.

As a Zelator he learns that his body is a vehicle of the cosmic life. As a Theoricus he learns that every function of that body is under the immediate control of subconsciousness. But it is only when he has learned to make clear, specific patterns of what he may expect in the future that he really begins to modify his body so that its chemistry and organization are such that he can grasp the Rosicrucian philosophy.

It is not enough to be willing to learn. One must have the right kind of brain cells and the right kind of body chemistry. The ordinary modes of human life do not build the brain cells, and they poison the body. As well expect a drunkard to grasp the finer significance of experience as to expect the average human being to do so—and for precisely the same reason. A poisoned body cannot grasp a true philosophy.

THE TWENTY-EIGHTH PATH

The twenty-eighth path is called the Natural Intelligence, whereby the nature of everything found in the orb of the sun is completed and perfected.

Book of Formation

One of the early lessons in true Rosicrucian philosophy is that everything is natural. Nothing is supernatural. Some planes of activity are superhuman, perhaps, if we apply the adjective *human* merely to personality. All events and phenomena, however, are part of nature; and if esoteric philosophy does show that the essence of that nature is Divinity itself, it by no means admits the existence of the supernatural.

The twenty-eighth path, represented in Tarot by Key 17, is the path of meditation. The picture on the Key shows a nude woman, symbolizing Truth unveiled. She pours water from two vases, and this part of the symbolism corresponds exactly to the definition of meditation given generations ago by the Hindu psychologist, Patanjali: "Meditation is an unbroken flow of knowledge in a particular object."

The aspirant to advancement in the Way of Return seems to himself to be meditating. Esoteric doctrine, however, distinctly declares that the personality of the aspirant is merely an agency through which the natural process of an unbroken flow of knowledge in a particular object finds expression. From this point of view human personality is an instrument that Nature herself has devised and perfected. Human bodies and brains are the means the One Life has invented, so to speak, in order to carry on the natural process of meditation. This instrument enables the universal consciousness to take forms it could not assume without such a vehicle of expression.

Taking such forms, the Life Power brings the nature of everything found in the "orb of the sun" to completeness and perfection. The "orb of the sun" is the sphere of influence of solar activity, i.e., the solar system. The cosmic process of Involution-Evolution works through all the kingdoms of nature to perfect the instrument named "man." When this instrument is ripened to a certain point, the natural process of meditation makes the instrument of human consciousness the means of expressing the Life Power's knowledge of its own nature and the possibilities of that nature. Thus, human thought and action become the means by which the forces of the cosmos take forms that could not otherwise be brought into manifestation.

The introduction of human personality as an integral part of the cosmic process is what Judge Troward, himself under the direct guidance of the Invisible Order, as his works on Mental Science make evident to a discerning reader, designated as the "Personal Factor." In *The Creative Process in the Individual*, he said:

> The function, then, of the Personal Factor in the Creative Order is to provide specialized conditions by the use of the powers of Selection and Initiative, a truth indicated by the maxim "Nature unaided fails"; but the difficulty is that if enhanced powers were attained by the whole population of the world without any common basis for their use, their promiscuous exercise could only result in chaotic confusion and the destruction of the entire race. To introduce the creative power of the Individual and at the same time avoid converting it into a devastating flood is the great problem of the transition from the Fourth Kingdom into the Fifth. For this purpose it becomes necessary to have a Standard of the Personal Factor independent of any individual conceptions, just as we found that in order for us to attain self-consciousness at all it was a necessity that there should be a Universal Mind as the *generic* basis of all individual mentality; only in regard to the generic build of mind the conformity is necessarily automatic, while in regard to the specializing process the fact that the essence of the process is Selection and Initiative renders it impossible for the conformity to the Standard of Personality to be automatic—the very nature of the thing makes it a matter of individual choice.
>
> Now a Standard of Personality independent of individual conceptions must be the *essence* of Personality as distinguished from individual idiosyncrasies, and can therefore be nothing else than the Creative Life, Love, Beauty, etc., viewed as a Divine Individuality, which, by identifying ourselves with, we eliminate all possiblity of conflict with other personalities based on the same fundamental recognition; and the very universality of this Standard allows free play to all our particular idiosyncrasies while at the same time preventing them from antagonizing the fundamental principles to which we have found that the Self-contemplation of the Originating Spirit must necessarily give rise. In this way we attain a Standard of Measurement for our own powers. If we recognize no such Standard, our development of spiritual powers, our discovery of the immense possibilities hidden in the inner laws of Nature and of our own being, can only become a scourge to ourselves and others, and it is for this reason that these secrets are so

jealously guarded by those who know them, and that over the entrance to the temple are written the words "Eskato Bebeloi"—"Hence ye Profane."

But if we recognize and accept this Standard of Measurement then we need never fear our discovery of hidden powers either in ourselves or in Nature, for on this basis it becomes impossible for us to misuse them. Therefore it is that all systematic teaching on these subjects begins with instruction regarding the Creative Order of the Cosmos, and then proceeds to exhibit the same Order as reproduced on the plane of Personality and so affording a fresh starting point for the Creative Process by the introduction of Individual Initiative and Selection. This is the doctrine of the Macrocosm and the Microcosm; and the transition from the generic working of the Creative Spirit in the Cosmos to its specific working in the Individual is what is meant by the doctrine of the Octave.[1]

When the Personal Factor is correctly understood as the agency for the One Life, nothing but good results from its activity. When it is erroneously supposed to be an independent existence having power and will of its own, all sorts of pain-bringing conditions arise from what it thinks, says, and does. The ignorant think of these pain-bringing conditions as being "evils." Occult doctrine, however, declares that because pain drives man to seek relief, and this search leads ultimately to the discovery of truth, even the seeming evils of human life are the raw material for beautiful results. Thus, the *Confessio* says: "But as commonly even in the same place where there breaketh forth a new disease, nature discovereth a remedy for the same, so amidst so many infirmities of philosophy there do appear the right means, and unto our Fatherland sufficiently offered, whereby she may become sound again, and new or renovated may appear to a renovated world."

THE TWENTY-SEVENTH PATH

The twenty-seventh path is called the Exciting Intelligence, for thence is created the spirit of every creature of the supreme orb, and the activity, that is to say, the motion, to which they are subject.
Book of Formation

This path, typified in Tarot by Key 16, corresponds to the Hebrew letter whose name means "the mouth of man as the organ of speech." In the

---

[1]Thomas Troward, *The Creative Process in the Individual* (New York: Dodd, Mead & Co., 1915), 73-75. Used by permission of the publisher.

Tarot picture the flash of lightning that destroys the building is a reference to that passage in the *Book of Formation* that says: "Ten ineffable Sephiroth: their appearance is like that of a flash of lightning, their goal is infinite. His word is in them when they emanate and when they return; at His bidding do they haste like a whirlwind."

Note well the imagery. Instantaneous and simultaneous manifestation of the ten fundamental aspects of the Life Power is suggested by the flash of lightning. As soon as the Life Power manifests itself at all, the sum total of its ten aspects comes at once into existence. The idea of speech, or the Creative Word, is bound up with this lightning-flash symbol by the phrase "His word is in them"; and the idea that the whole cosmic activity is a continuous expression of that Word, from beginning to end, is conveyed by the phrase "when they emanate and when they return." Furthermore, this emanation and return is compared to a whirlwind, that is, to a *whirling breath*. This last is particularly interesting, since it has been demonstrated by modern science that a lightning flash is really a whirling, spiral motion. It will yet be shown that this whirling motion is double, consisting of an outgoing and a returning current.

When the Bible says again and again, "The mouth of Jehovah has spoken it," and when the same book tells us, in Genesis, "The Elohim said," this same idea of the creative power expressed in the Word is implied.

Thus, the third path leading to the Grade of Philosophus suggests to an occultist that there is a definite connection between consciousness that forms itself into speech and the electric energy that is the substance of every physical form. The occultist accepts all that the physicist has learned concerning the electrical constitution of the physical universe but adds that the real nature of that mysterious energy the physicist labels "electromagnetism" is *consciousness*. Occult philosophy maintains that all activity, all motion, all energy is basically the activity, motion, and energy of consciousness. It sees in the universe a continuous utterance of the Word of Life.

This interpretation of experience runs counter to generally accepted opinions. Thus, in Key 16 the lightning flash is shown destroying a tower that typifies false science. The basis of this false science is the notion that forms are built from a separate substance called "matter," which is moved by "force" and perceived by "mind." Occult science says that the "matter" or substance of all things is the motion of an energy that is essentially mental, or conscious. That energy, working on itself, produces all things out of itself—or rather, *within* itself. "Matter," "force," and "mind" are three aspects of One Reality.

This One Reality is the exciting cause of all manifestation throughout the universe. From it is formed the spirit or inner essence of every creature. From it proceeds the motion or activity to which they are subject. Here is a definite statement that nowhere in the universe is there any form of existence, or creature, that is not dependent on the activity of the

Originating Principle. The spirit of every creature is a particular expression of this one Activity. The varied functions of all the different species of creatures depend absolutely on the One Motion that runs and returns, like a whirling breath, though the whole cosmos.

The doctrines of the Grade of Philosophus are six in number and are derived from the letters of the words NTzCh, *Netzach,* or Victory, the name of the seventh circle on the Tree of Life, and *NSThR, Nesether,* meaning "Occult," which designates the special mode of consciousness associated by Qabalists with that seventh circle. There are only six doctrines, although the two words comprise seven letters, because both *Netzach* and *Nesether* begin with the same letter, Nun.

The letters of NTzCh, *Netzach,* correspond to three great truths of occult philosophy. The word *Netzach* itself clearly shows that this is a success philosophy, an interpretation of experience having for its fundamental postulate the idea that the cosmic undertaking is a success.

Observe that the preceding sentence is written in the present tense. Occult philosophy holds that at every stage of the Great Work that Work is free from any trace of failure. It is at this moment as certainly a success as it ever will be. Whatever seems to be an appearance of failure is the result of our mistaken interpretations and partial knowledge.

First of all, the cosmic undertaking itself is eternal. It has neither beginning nor end. Yet it has also certain definite cycles of activity, directed toward the realization of specific ends. We are in the midst of such a cycle, and few persons know toward what end this present stage of the Great Work is moving. We are in the midst of an operation that is going on. The final result has not yet been brought about.

Yet the present stage of the work proceeds in perfect, orderly sequence from all that has gone before and prepares the way for all that is yet to come. The Grand Artificer of the universe is Omnipotence itself, and the idea that Omnipotence can possibly fail, at any point or in the least degree is a contradiction of the very meaning of Omnipotence. Lacking knowledge of the design and misunderstanding the processes whereby that design is being brought to completion, the undeveloped human mind interprets these processes incorrectly and bewails as "failure" what better vision perceives as being an aspect of success.

DOCTRINES OF THE GRADE

Bearing this in mind, let us now consider the doctrines of the Grade of Philosophus. They are as follows:

1. DEATH
Key 13 (N)

The dissolution of form is a fundamental tendency of the Cosmic process. All things change. All conditions pass away. No form ever remains fixed. Existence is a stream, a series of waves, an eternal movement.

Hence, he who would know the Rosicrucian philosophy must rid himself of the irrational desire for fixity, must eliminate the wish for crystallization. We are in the midst of a flowing universe, and in order to bring to completion the Great Work to which we are called, we must grasp the truth expressed in the alchemical maxim: "Dissolution is the secret of the Great Work."

The fact of physical death is a recurrent phenomenon of our experience, yet most persons grossly misinterpret the fact. The decay of physical powers with advancing years and the death of the body, often at a time when it seems that one has most to expect from life, appear to many to be unmitigated evils. The desire for life is strong in us. The instinct of self-preservation is fundamental. Small wonder, then, that death is commonly regarded as man's enemy. Small wonder that death seems to give the lie to all the promises of life. Small wonder that after thinking of death so many persons are ready to agree with the author of *Ecclesiastes* that "All is vanity and vexation of spirit."

The greater number of persons in the world do their best to ignore death. They put the thought of death out of their minds. They refuse to think about it. If they must speak of it, they resort to euphemisms. Yet all the while the shadow of approaching dissolution is upon them, influencing their subconscious life in innumerable ways.

Others, more courageous, face the fact. They perceive the common lot and train themselves to the thought that it will sooner or later be their turn to pass through the dark portal. In these days few among the so-called "educated" classes have any confident expectation of life beyond physical existence. What passes for education in our times tends very definitely to giving a negative answer to the question, "If a man die, shall he live again?" One cannot help admiring the fine courage with which so many of our modern men and women face extinction. To live and work as they do for no other reason than that the conditions of life in future generations may be more tolerable is one of the most inspiring evidences of the essential worth of the human spirit.

Such a spirit seems to deserve something better than hopelessness. Yet, paradoxically, it is not hope that is offered in the Rosicrucian philosophy. The Hindu *Vairagyastaka* says: "There is the greatest misery in hope, in hopelessness is the height of bliss." Hope has in it an element of uncertainty, a tinge of doubt. Millions of human beings *hope* for survival. They receive religious training that boldly affirms a state of existence after death. They are told that life beyond the grave is inexpressibly better than this life, but their hope does not prevent them from doing everything they can to stay right here. Nor does the teaching that death is a door to eternal bliss make the bystanders at a deathbed sing praises or turn funerals into festivals of rejoicing.

No, the Rosicrucian philosophy does not offer hope. It brings about the state of mind that the Hindu writer subtly terms "hopelessness." That is a state in which there is no hope, because hope has given place to certainty. The Roscrucian teaching specifically declares that man may have definite, firsthand knowledge that his conscious existence is not limited to life in a physical body. It does not bid us hope. It shows us how to *learn*.

It bids us learn, first of all, that the natural processes that result in death are not inimical to man. It says to us: "Learn to think of physical dissolution as being a process that has positive advantages for the race and for the individual. You are mistaken when you think death is your enemy. Learn what death really is, and you will find that it is a friend."

This departure from common ways of thought is so radical that many immediately reject it. In their opinion such doctrine is too absurd for even a moment's consideration. Nothing can be done with such determined prejudice. For minds more open, however, the Rosicrucian philosophy continues as follows:

"We say that the fact of physical death is advantageous to man. Death, indeed, is what makes room for human life on earth." Unchecked by death, the offspring of a single pair of codfish would soon choke the seas. At one American university there is a culture of a low form of life, the Paramecium, which multiplies so rapidly that if death did not balance the reproductive power of this little creature, the bodies of Paramecia sprung from this one culture would fill all the space between the earth and the orbit of the planet Neptune in less than twenty-five years. The death of countless organisms is required to support a single human life. Furthermore, our own organic processes are death processes, for we can do nothing that does not cause the dissolution of our body cells. Wisely is it written in one of the Oriental books: "Death is the law of being. The wise describe it as 'Life'."

The death of human beings also has positive advantages to the race. The earth cannot support too large a population. The health of the race depends on the elimination of weaklings. Men and women, when they grow too old to change their ideas and habits, are a serious hindrance to humanity's progress.

Rosicrucian philosophy goes further than this. It says that the same forces that bring about physical death are those that, when they are understood and rightly directed, produce two important results:

1. A change in the human body that enables the person who experiences it to know that his physical body is only one among several vehicles or instruments of his self-conscious existence. This change consists in the development of certain brain cells not functioning in the average human being. The work of these cells is to give the person a memory record of his personal experiences while "out of the body." From these experiences one gains firsthand knowledge that the continuance of his self-consciousness is not dependent on physical life. Thus, he learns that *he* does not die, whatever happens to his physical body.

2. A gradually increasing command of certain subtle forces of the physical plane, which enables the adept to establish a state of perfect balance between those activities that tear down the body and those that build it up. By this means physical existence may be prolonged far beyond the average period of human life. It is fairly well known to occultists that in both the Orient and the Occident men and women are now living who were alive when the Rosicrucian manifestoes were first published. Exoteric science knows nothing of them and derides the notion that there are methods for so prolonging the existence of the physical body. Hence, the world doubts either the sanity or the sincerity of a person who speaks seriously of the possibility of such longevity; but as in other instances, the world is wrong, and the occultists are right.

One of the first fruits of Rosicrucian practice is that the aspirant comes to know that he does not and *cannot* die. The ability to remember what happens to personality while one is "out of the body" is by no means a mark of adeptship, by no means evidence of mastery. It is fairly early in the course of rightly directed practice that one builds brain cells that record this type of experience. For such persons the sting of death is removed, inasmuch as they know that death is no more than the laying aside of the outermost vesture of personality. Their "out of the body" experiences enable them to answer to themselves the question "What happens when we die?" Thenceforth, for them, not only the fear of dying but also the thought of death as an enemy comes to an end.

2. THE STAR
Key 17 (Tz)

The Cosmic process is a meditation. The Life Power is conscious energy, flowing through a succession of forms related to a particular object. Each cycle of the Life Power's self-expression has some definite objective, and from the beginning of a cycle to its completion, there is no moment in which that objective is forgotten or otherwise obscured.

The One Life maintains an "unbroken flow of knowledge" in the "particular object" we call the universe. From the initiation of the cycle of self-expression to its completion there is not a moment of forgetfulness. Thus, various Scriptures tell us that God never sleeps.

It is precisely because meditation is the supporting or maintaining condition of all existence that the practice of meditation leads to such wonderful results in the life of an aspirant. When one really meditates (and not many really do), he shares in the activity by which the cosmos is kept going. In right meditation, moreover, he perceives that the Great Work is always a success, in its least details as well as in its greater operations. Hence, he knows, as a corollary, that no matter what appearances may be, the exact situation at any given moment is precisely the right and necessary one.

3. THE CHARIOT
Key 7 (Ch)

The Life Power is perfectly successful at every stage of the Cosmic process. All appearances of failure are illusive. The One Identity is the victor before ever the battle is joined.

The real I AM is now in a state of perfect rest, enjoying the bliss of perfect peace. So is it pictured in Key 7 of Tarot. The same doctrine is stated clearly in the Hindu *Bhagavad-Gita* and in many another Scripture.

This third element in Rosicrucian philosophy is the logical consequence of the first two truths delivered to members of this Grade. For the Philosophus, there is no battle to be won, no victory to be achieved. He knows the Self as victor already. He knows that all appearances of failure are illusive. He begins to understand that the Great Work does not contribute to this cosmic success but does rather make that success openly manifest.

4. TEMPERANCE
Key 14 (S)

Every human being is under the direct guidance of the One Identity. Every personal action is a special and particular expression of that One Identity's overshadowing activity. Knowledge of this is the secret of the perfect freedom of the truly wise.

This guidance becomes a matter of daily personal experience. It should by no means be accepted as a mere article of faith. The aspirant to the Grade of Philosophus must deliberately practice receptivity. Again and again he must adopt and endeavor to maintain the attitude of response to this guidance. He must train himself to think of human personality as a vehicle and instrument for the One Identity. This kind of active submission will eventually lead to full conscious awareness of the truth of this fourth doctrine.

5. THE WORLD
Key 21 (Th)

All form is a limitation of the infinite energy of the Life Power. The primary cause of limitation is the image-making power of the Universal Mind. Every act of human imagination is really a particular expression, through a personal center, of this image-making power. Hence, human imagination is, in kind though not in degree, the same as the Imagination that forms the Universe.

When the implications of this doctrine are understood, we see that we are the administrators of the laws of the Life Power and the wielders of the formative force of the universe. This is what Eliphas Levi means by saying that the man who learns to control and direct the currents of the Astral Light, which Levi calls also the "Imagination of Nature," becomes the depository of the power of God. Through human beings the forces and laws of nature may be applied in ways impossible without the instrumentality of human personality. The Dance of Life is incomplete without our participation. We were made, as the eighth Psalm tells us, to have dominion; and in the Qabalah the idea of dominion is specifically attached to the letter Tav, illustrated in Tarot by Key 21.

6. THE SUN
Key 19 (R)

Human personality is a synthesis of all cosmic processes. Man summarizes all that precedes him and is the point of departure for the manifestation of a New Creature. The natural man is the seed of the spiritual man.

This is what Judge Troward had in mind when he wrote of the Fifth Kingdom. The First Kingdom is that of the mineral; the Second Kingdom is that of vegetable; the Third Kingdom is that of the animal; the Fourth Kingdom is that of the natural man; the Fifth Kingdom that of the spiritual man. These five kingdoms are symbolized by the five divisions in the ascending hypotenuse of the Pythagorean triangle.

When the natural man, under the influence of Those who have preceded him on the Way of Return, begins to understand the processes that brought life out of the Third Kingdom into the Fourth, he begins to be able to utilize those processes consciously and intentionally in order to take him farther. This has been going on in the human race since thousands of years before the beginnings of recorded history. Those who have succeeded in passing into the Fifth Kingdom are the "regenerated" or "twice born." For the natural man this regeneration is the next step toward the Great Objective. That objective, of course, is the union of the Son with the Father, the linking of the final point of the hypotenuse of the Pythagorean triangle with the initial point of the line of Osiris, the Father. And this is the Stone, or ABN, *Ehben,* whose number, 53, is the number also of the degrees in the angle of the Pythagorean Triangle where the hypotenuse joins the vertical line.

From these statements it must not be concluded that the Philosophus has arrived at a stage where he abandons all personal effort. Neither has he gained release from the illusion of separate existence.

He still finds plenty of work to do. He still sees evidences of apparent failure. He still feels the urge of desire. All that has been attained in the Grade of Philosophus is an intellectual grasp somewhat beyond the average. The Philosophus has clearer vision. He has a better understanding of the meaning of human existence. He might be compared to a man who has learned to read an architect's plans. The house is yet to build.

This Grade of Philosophus, finally, is associated with the desire nature of man, which Qabalistic psychology assigns to the seventh circle on the Tree of Life. The implication is that all philosophy springs from desire. In the last analysis we interpret life in accordance with what we want. Our philosophy is what we want it to be. This is as true of Rosicrucian philosophy as of any other. It formulates the heart's desire of every member of the True and Invisible Order.

In other words, Rosicrucians have grasped the philosophic truth that man explains life always in accordance with what he *wants* to be true. Hence, they say, "If a man's desires are actually in harmony with the real tendencies of the cosmic process, *what he wants to be true will be true.*" This is one secret of the symbol of the Rosy Cross.

The cross itself, as has been explained, is the pattern of a cube. Thus, it represents the pattern of the cosmos, because from time immemorial the cube has been a symbol of that which actually exists.

The five-petaled rose in the center of the cross, as the flower of Venus, is typical of desire. When human desires, like the rose, are fixed on the central point of the pattern of existence, those desires are completely unified with the actual laws and tendencies of the cosmos. In simple language, a true Rosicrucian wants what the Life Power wants. He has no desire other than those that are expressed throughout the cosmic order. A philosophy grounded in such desires must therefore be a correct explanation of experience.

The foundation of the Rosicrucian philosophy is the doctrine that all things are in a state of flux. Nothing in this universe can be understood unless one understands first that all things are in process of transformation. This is of primary importance in learning how to formulate desires.

When we set our hearts on things, we are sowing seeds of misery. This was the mistake of the builders of the Tower of Babel, as it has been the mistake of many since that day. Permanence in form is an impossibility in this universe. Hence, all desire for that kind of permanence is vanity of vanities. Here is another clue to the meaning of the Rosicrucian agreement that none of the posterity should be constrained to wear one special kind of habit.

What is possible for us is identification with the stream of the Life Power as it flows from one form to another. We may share in the Great Meditation that creates and sustains the universe. We may become conscious vehicles of the One Will that moves irresistibly toward its determined objective. Our lives are not only under guidance, but we may also be keenly aware of that guidance. Thus, our daily activities may become for us experiences of joyous participation in the administration of cosmic law. The meaning of life, for Rosicrucians, is that man is a synthesis of all the powers of the Limitless Light, destined to advance in consciousness and also in organism beyond the level of the natural man to that of the spiritual man who, though he says: "Of myself I can do nothing," says also: "All power is given unto me: all that my Father hath is mine."

Two paths lead upward from the Grade of Philosophus to higher Grades; but only one is open, that of the letter Nun, and it may not be traversed until the Philosophus has passed through the paths immediately preceding it, those of Ayin and Samekh. Of these, the first leads upward from the Grade of Practicus, and the second leads upward from the Grade of Theoricus.

This Grade of Philosophus completes the Grades of the First or Outer Order of the Rosicrucian Fraternity. It is followed by the three Grades of the Second or Inner Order. These are the three Grades of adeptship: (1) Adeptus Minor, or Lesser Adept, 5 = 6; (2) Adeptus Major, or Greater Adept, 6 = 5; (3) Adeptus Exemptus, or Exempt Adept, 7 = 4.

Before reading the chapters devoted to these Grades, the student will do well to review carefully what has been said up to this point. He should also make himself familiar with the story of the Vault, as given in the *Fama*, and review the chapter explaining it.

Do not neglect this precaution. Skimming this book will do little for you. But if you read it carefully you will, in a measure, receive real initiation and advancement. Remember that what is written here comes to you from the same root sources that first published the *Fama* and the *Confessio*. In accordance with the promise made three hundred years ago, the trumpet of the Invisible Order now sounds without prevarications of meaning. Full explanation of the practical mysteries cannot be put in print as yet; but what is here printed openly was once jealously guarded from all but vowed initiates of societies working according to the Rosicrucian pattern, whose guiding spirits were men who had actually made contact with the Invisible Order.

Such societies still work in the world today. None of them, it may be said once more, makes any claim to historic connection with the "original" Rosicrucians. The presence of such a claim in any document issued by a society calling itself Rosicrucian is sufficient evidence that the leaders of the organization are either themselves misled or else deliberately trading on the word "Rosicrucian" for the sake of monetary advantage.

CHAPTER XVI

THE GRADE OF LESSER ADEPT, 5 = 6

HE GRADE OF LESSER ADEPT corresponds to the sixth circle on the Tree of Life, named ThPARTh, *Tiphareth,* Beauty. To it corresponds the sentence in the *Pattern on the Trestleboard:* "In all things, great and small, I see the Beauty of the Divine Expression." In Qabalistic psychology, imagination is attributed to Tiphareth, and the work of the Lesser Adept has much to do with controlled mental imagery.

The sixth Sephirah is also termed "Intelligence of Mediating Influence." It is likewise known as BN, *Ben,* the Son, as MLK, *Melek,* the King, as ADM, *Adam,* Man (in the generic sense), and as AISh, *Ish,* man (the personal man). But the greatest secrets of this Sephirah have to do with what is termed in Hebrew ZOIR ANPIN, *Zauir Anpin,* the Lesser Countenance, or Microprosopus.

In the Qabalah *Ben,* the Son, is said to be the husband of the Bride, *Kallah* (KLH). This Bride is the Kingdom, or tenth Sephirah. *Ben,* the Son is called also the child of AIMA, *Aima,* the Mother, and this Mother is represented on the Tree of Life by Understanding, the third circle. The Son's Father (in Hebrew AB, *Ab)* is Wisdom, the second circle of the Tree. In Qabalistic number occultism, therefore, 6 is the Son of 2 and 3, and the Husband or Bridegroom of 10.

Tiphareth is the seat of the mediating influence of the incarnate Christos. Hence, the Qabalists tell us that the Lesser Countenance, or Microprosopus, is the reflection of the Greater Countenance, or Macroprosopus. That Greater Countenance is *Kether,* or Crown, or the number 1, wherein is seated the cosmic Self, named IChIDH, *Yekhidah,* the Indivisible. *Yekhidah* is the universal I AM, but the Lesser Countenance is the Self seated, as the *Bhagavad-Gita* puts it, in the heart of man. Hence, we find that *Tiphareth* is also attributed to the heart.

The meaning ought to be evident to the thoughtful reader. *Tiphareth* is the central point on the Tree of Life, standing halfway between *Kether* and *Malkuth.* Thus, its very position suggests mediation, adaptation, equilibration, and the like. It is the center of balance in the cosmic order represented by the Tree.

It is called King because it actually does exercise a royal authority. It has the names of generic man, *Adam*, and of personal man, *Ish*, because the essential reality of both of these is one and the same. It was by identifying himself completely with this one reality that Jesus was able to say, "I and the Father are One," and it was for the same reason that Jesus called himself the Son of Man. Strangely enough, the New Testament records this title, Son of Man exactly 37 times, and 37 is the number of IChIDH, *Yekhidah*, the Hebrew name for the cosmic I AM of which *Adam* and *Ish*, the two aspects of the Royal Son, are the reflection.

In ceremonial versions of Rosicrucian instruction, this Grade of Lesser Adept is the one in which the allegory of Brother C. R. is rehearsed and explained. In it one enters ceremonially into the Vault described in the *Fama*. In it the advancing aspirant is identified with Brother C. R. and also with the Egyptian Osiris, "slain and risen." Thus, there are points of correspondence between this Grade and the Third Degree in Craft Masonry, which has to do with the death and raising of Hiram Abiff.

You will better understand the meaning of this Grade if you bear in mind the truth that real beauty is always related to fitness and strength. Whatever is truly adapted to its uses is always beautiful in the eyes of those who perceive its fitness. Beauty is not necessarily prettiness. Often the untrained eye rejects what is profoundly admired by those who have had right instruction.

In Central America, some years ago, an aqueduct was built to carry water through miles of jungle. The engineer took an artist friend to see it, and the eye of the artist was ravished by the beautiful symmetry of the arches supporting the structure.

"What a pity," he exclaimed, "to waste such perfection in a place where nobody will see it! However did you come to choose such beautiful arches?"

"Beautiful, are they?" responded the engineer. "Well, we never thought of that. We used the type of arch that our calculations demonstrated to be the strongest and best adapted to this particular kind of load."

Compare a racing yacht with a dugout, a modern locomotive with the engines of 1860, modern setback buildings with early skyscrapers, an athlete's body with that of the average man. Beauty is a direct consequence of increased efficiency. "The more correct the measurement," said Albrecht Dürer, "the better the composition." And Eliphas Levi tells us, "The beautiful lives are the accurate ones, and the magnificences of Nature are an algebra of graces and splendors."

Here is no namby-pamby estheticism, such as Gilbert and Sullivan delighted to burlesque. The beauty that the Lesser Adept learns to see is rooted in strength and balance.

THE TWENTY-SIXTH PATH

The twenty-sixth path is called the Renewing or Renovating Intelligence, because by it the Holy God renews all that is begun afresh in the creation of the world.

Book of Formation

This is the first of the three paths leading to the Grade of Lesser Adept. It begins in the Grade of Practicus and is assigned to Tarot Key 15, named *The Devil.*

The adjective *renewing* is MChVDSh, *mahkodesh,* from a Hebrew root meaning "to be fresh, new, young; to renew, to erect anew." The number of this adjective is 358, which is also the number of GShNH, *gashenah,* "shame"; IBA ShILH, *Iba Shiloh,* "tranquillity shall come"; MShICh, *Messiah;* NChSh, *Nachash,* "the serpent of temptation" (also, with the same letters but differently pointed, "copper"); and ChShN, *khoshen,* "the breastplate of the High Priest."

Shame has more to do with the renewal of consciousness than may appear at first. It was with some understanding of this that evangelical churches put so much stress on "conviction of sin." When one is thoroughly disgusted with one's own state or with one's circumstances, it seems to be easier to make the required effort to begin afresh.

The other words in this series are also important. *Iba Shiloh* has been traditionally associated with the Hebrew Messianic expectation. In this connection it is interesting to note that the name of the serpent that intiated Eve into the mystery of good and evil is numerically the same as Messiah, and that the name of this serpent is also spelled with the same letters as those used to spell the Hebrew noun sometimes used for "copper," the metal of Venus.

Finally, the word ChShN, *khoshen,* the name of the High Priest's breastplate, brings in another mathematical element. For the breastplate was a perfect square, subdivided into twelve parts, so that each of its divisions was a rectangle of three by four units. In this arrangement is concealed a geometrical formula having to do with the series of numbers 0, 1, 2, 3, 5, 8, 13, 21, 34, 55. The number 358 is composed of the fourth, fifth, and sixth terms of this series. In what manner this is connected with the breastplate is too intricate for explanation here.

What is more important is that the series of words belonging to the number 358 includes *Nachash* (the serpent), which came to be personified during the Middle Ages as the ridiculous monster pictured by Key 15. The same number also represents the Messiah. There is no escape from the implication, which becomes the more emphatic when one remembers that the brazen serpent of Moses, lifted on a T-cross, was understood by the early Christians to be a foreshadowing of the crucifixion of Jesus.

This path is connected with the letter Ayin, and the name of this letter, besides signifying "the eye, as organ of sight," also means "the visible part of an object, the surface, the appearance." Thus, the word *Ayin* stands for the phenomenal as opposed to the noumenal, that which is given to sensation or impression as opposed to that which is subject to rational verification. The eye is therefore the natural symbol of those external shows that conceal Reality. It is the sign of man's finite experience of things as they seem, as opposed to the realities of the hidden essence veiled in form.

Through the function of the eye we become aware of the phantasmagoria of the phenomenal world, which Shakespeare called "this unsubstantial pageant." The untrained eye is the great deceiver. On this account the letter Ayin is attributed to the Tarot Key whose title means "The Slanderer."

Just as a slanderer's aim is to blacken the reputation of the person he lies about and thus to hinder him in the execution of his plans, so that which Key 15 personifies is what tells man falsehoods about his own nature and about his place in the scheme of things.

Nevertheless, Ageless Wisdom declares that this same power is what makes all things new. This brings us close to a profound occult doctrine. According to it, the world of appearances is not in itself a world of deception. The delusions arise from our own tendency to take things at their face value. Furthermore, the world of appearances excites attention. However much we may misunderstand it, it piques our interest. We wonder about it. We are made curious by what we see. Wherever we look there is something to challenge us, something to puzzle, some riddle to read, some problem to solve.

To the untrained eye and the udisciplined mind the marvels of the world strike terror. It is written that the fear of the One Reality is the beginning of wisdom. In every generation, however, there are a few persons whom wonder prods into investigating something that scares most of their contemporaries.

Thus, what men fear is what really instructs them and so leads finally to their liberation. Hence, it is written: "The Devil is God, as He is misunderstood by the wicked." (Here it may be noted that the number of the path we are studying is 26, the number of the Divine Name IHVH, *Jehovah*, and that the number of the corresponding Tarot Key is 15, the number of the Divine Name IH, *Yah*, the short form of *Jehovah*, used by Qabalists to designate Wisdom.)

The central figure of Key 15 symbolizes the ridiculous combination of false interpretations of nature that leads man to believe that all sorts of powers are arrayed against him in his progress toward the Light. It is a picture of what occult writers call "the Dweller on the Threshold."

For primitive man, everything unknown is an adversary. The savage lives surrounded by devils—demons in trees, stones, rivers, the clouds. Everything frightens him. Everything seems to thwart him.

As man progresses, he comes to learn, little by little, that the forces of nature will work with him when he learns their laws and obeys those laws. The conflict between man's inner feeling that he is born to command and the outward appearance that all sorts of forces are working against him is what goads the race on toward the discovery of the means through which man's seeming adversaries may be transformed into friends.

There is no adversary but ignorance, no antagonist but human misconception of the various ways in which the Life Power presents itself to us through the medium of sensation. When we take our sensations at face value, we suppose ourselves to be competing with our fellowmen. When we permit ourselves to be deceived by appearances, we suppose that our neighbor's real interests may clash with ours. When we look at the outsides of things only, we believe ourselves to be separated from other persons, physically and psychically. Under the spell of this delusion we entertain the notion that the universe holds two sets of antagonistic causes. We believe there is a fight between Spirit and Matter, an age-long warfare between God and the Devil in which the Devil, so far, seems to have won most of the battles.

An aspirant to the Grade of Lesser Adept must overcome this dualism. He begins to do so by taking up the work of the Grade of Practicus. When he has learned by experiment that confident expectation really does form patterns that actually are realized as physical forms and conditions, he has taken a long step toward freedom. He sees then that he may be master of circumstances to the degree that he is skillful in making mental patterns. Thus, he learns that nothing fights against him but his own ignorance and clumsiness.

It requires little practice to gain this knowledge. Some years ago a young woman in Toronto attended a public lecture in which the underlying principle of mental imagery was explained.

"Don't attempt elaborate things at first," the lecturer said, "because small successes will build up your confidence for greater undertakings. Begin with something easy, say, a hat. Pick out just the kind of hat you want. Draw a picture of it, if you can. Write a description of it and specify the material, the color, the shape, the size, the price—all the details. Expect to have it. Stand before a mirror and see yourself wearing it. You will surely get it, if you follow this procedure."

The young woman was impressed. Later she joined a class for further instruction from the same teacher. One evening just before class time she rushed up to the teacher, exclaiming:

"I've got the hat!"

"What hat?"

"Why, *the* hat—the one you told us to picture. I'll wear it to class tomorrow night."

And she did. She found that hat in a little out-of-the-way shop. None of the milliners she usually patronized had anything like it. Neither did any of the big department stores. Yet she kept on visualizing, and one day obeyed an impulse to turn down a street she was passing on her way home. Presently she found herself before a shabby little millinery shop. No such hat as she wanted was in the window. As she entered, nothing like it struck her eye. But when she asked if they had such a hat, the clerk opened a drawer and produced the exact duplicate of her mental image.

Their designer had finished it the day before. No such hat was in Toronto, or anywhere else, when she began to visualize. The milliner's hands did the cutting and sewing; but the visualizer really made that hat. The idea in her brain was executed through the activity of the milliner's body.

Note particularly that there was no coercion. The young woman did not try to influence some particular milliner to make such a hat. She simply created the mental pattern and kept it vividly in mind, in the mood of confident expectancy. The milliner found self-expression and self-satisfaction in making it. The shopkeeper's overhead was less than that of more expensive ships, so he made a fair profit on the transaction at the very price determined by the visualizer. All concerned shared in the benefit.

This one example is a whole lesson in the practical use of mental imagery. Such practice leads to the realization that the Life Power in us is really a "mediating influence," an adaptive, modifying force that can effect physical changes at a distance. The mind of man is creative; but its images must be confidently expected to materialize, in spite of all appearances to the contrary.

THE TWENTY-FIFTH PATH

The twenty-fifth path is called the Intelligence of Probation or Trial (or the Tentative Intelligence), and it is so called because it is the first test whereby the Creator tries the devout.

Book of Formation

This path is the second path leading to the Grade of Lesser Adept. It begins in the Grade of Theoricus, because in this path one puts the fundamental occult theory to the test of actual trial. In Tarot this path is represented by Key 14, Temperance.

The Hebrew adjective translated "tentative" is NSIVNI, *nahsahyuni*, and its number, 186, is that of ABN NGP, *Ehben nawgaf*, "a stone of stumbling" (Is. 8:14); MVSP, *mosaph*, "an increase"; MMVNIM, *mamonim*, "chiefs, prefects"; MQVM, *mahkom* (a place on which something stands or exists, a location); and QVP, *Qoph*, the back of the head, which is the name of the letter assigned to the twenty-ninth path.

The first of these number correspondences (see the passage in Isaiah) refers to the One Identity itself, indicating that those who approach that Identity in the right spirit find it a sanctuary, a place of safety, whereas those who misinterpret their relation to it look upon it as the cause of all their troubles. The same thought is found in David's Song of Victory (2 Samuel 22:27,28), and in Psalm 18:26,27. The Psalm is a slightly different version of the song recorded in 2 Samuel.

Judge Troward has developed this point at some length in *The Edinburgh Lectures.* He says:

> It becomes, therefore, the most important of all considerations with what character we invest the Universal Mind; for since our relation to it is *purely subjective* it will infallibly bear *to us* exactly that character which we impress upon it; in other words it will be to us exactly what we believe it to be....This is the meaning of that remarkable passage in the Bible, "With the pure thou wilt show thyself pure, and with the froward thou wilt show thyself froward," for the context makes it clear to us that these words are addressed to the Divine Being. The spiritual kingdom is *within* us, and as we realize it *there* so it becomes to us a reality.[1]

After we have overcome the fears and delusions represented by Key 15, we must do all that we can to deepen our realization that the One I AM is the real Actor and Knower in our personal lives. The angel in Key 14 represents that I AM.

The stumbling block to right thinking about this One Identity is to be sought in misinterpretations of sense experience. Until our senses are refined and their reports correctly correlated, they lead us to form wrong conclusions as to the nature of the governing powers of the world (MMVNIM, *mamonim*, "the prefects"). These wrong conclusions are usually misunderstandings of the real nature of the One Reality on which creation is established, and also of man's location or place in the cosmic order (MQVM, "place"). The cause of this misunderstanding is a defect in our own organization, which is not complete and so gives us only a partial experience of reality. This is the import of the correspondence of NSIVNI, the name of the twenty-fifth path, to QVP, *Qoph*, the letter name related to Corporeal Intelligence, or body consciousness. When we understand the Law of Growth or Evolution hinted at by the word MVSP, *mosaph*, meaning "increase," we begin to take our own evolution in hand and proceed step by

---

[1]Thomas Troward, *The Edinburgh Lectures on Mental Science* (New York: Dodd, Mead & Co., 1909), 99.

step along the path of liberation that leads to the perfection of the organism. Then we shall remedy our partial knowledge by our ability to make contact with the Universal Mind. This does not mean that we shall become omniscient ourselves, as persons. It does mean that we can bring the perfect knowledge of Omniscience itself to bear on any problem we may be called on to solve.

Understand that until the first test mentioned in the quotation from the *Book of Formation* has been passed, no other tests are given. There is a disposition among the romantically inclined to look on all their mishaps as "occult tests." Thus, the more miserable they are and the worse their circumstances, the more twisted satisfaction they derive from their foolish supposition that they are getting special attention from what they usually call "the Hierarchy." It is not at all uncommon to find this kind of inverted egotism.

The truth is that such conditions in our lives are always indications that we have failed in the first test. What that test is we learn from what Jesus said when he warned his disciples to be *doers* of the Word and not hearers only. In these days of many books, innumerable lectures, and classes, there is a temptation to rest content with the acquisition of esoteric information. Occult knowledge cannot be properly assimilated unless it is put into practice. We must live the life if we would know the doctrine.

It is not without significance that this twenty-fifth path is associated by Qabalists with the zodiacal sign Sagittarius, whose symbol is the arrow. We must aim at something and shoot at it. Even if we miss, we have done that much toward gaining the skill that will eventually enable us to make bull's-eyes every time. The most accurate instructions in archery will never make an archer. One must draw the bow and let fly the arrow.

This is the first test—the test of practical application. When things go wrong with us, it is because we are not aiming right. The power of increase is a rock of stumbling to us, because we have taken no steps to verify the fundamental doctrine of Ageless Wisdom, which is that every personal expression of the One Identity thinks, feels, speaks, and acts (consciously and subconsciously) through the operation of a single Life Power, which *flows through* the personal organism but does not originate therein.

The means by which the truth of this doctrine may be verified are perfectly simple and easy. Whatever difficulty there may seem to be arises from inertia and heedlessness. He who would become a Lesser Adept must be in dead earnest. He must consider the tremendous claims of the Invisible Order, as set forth in the *Fama* and the *Confessio* and in all other texts of Ageless Wisdom. If those claims be true, nothing can be more important than their verification. Nothing can be more worth one's utmost exertions than to find out for oneself that there is really available to every human being a power that he may so apply to the reconstruction of his personality that he may become a conscious instrument for the expression of the limitless potency of Omnipotence itself, a conscious channel for the expression of the inexhaustible knowledge of Omniscience.

This being understood, the actual work is comparatively easy, though at first it requires alert attention and a great deal of patience. One has simply to remind oneself again and again of the overshadowing presence of the One Identity. Again and again he has to recall the truth that he does *nothing* of himself. Over and over he has to bring to mind the thought that the appearance that he is engaged in this or that personal activity is *merely* an appearance.

In time these repetitions will make a deep impression on subconsciousness. Thus, one will form the habit of being continually receptive to the influx of the Life Power. At first one simply acts *as if* this were so. He assumes that the doctrine just stated *may* be true. In so doing he follows the method of science, which conducts all its experiments in verification on similar assumptions. But since this particular assumption is really true, the line of conduct here indicated invariably leads to firsthand knowledge of that truth. Faithful practice of this method always brings about such changes in personality that one finds out for himself the accuracy of what he has been taught. From then on the path of practical occultism becomes one of thrilling adventure.

Note that the text says this test is given by the Creator. It is not given by persons. It is in the nature of things. It is as inevitable as any other natural law. Just as we may not use electricity unless all our endeavors to do so conform to its nature, so we may not become depositories of the power of God unless we put ourselves in a position to receive the influx of power from higher levels of being.

"The devout" means, of course, those who are devoted. It must not be understood in any narrow sense as designating those who are outwardly religious. The Hebrew word is *Chasidim*, and this is the technical designation of all practical Qabalists, hence of all true Rosicrucians. The word comes from the noun ChSD, *Chesed*, "Mercy" or "Benevolence." This is the name of the fourth circle on the Tree of Life. It is the Sphere of Jupiter, and astrologically Jupiter represents comprehension of natural law, expansiveness, and hence, good fortune. *Chesed*, moreover, is said to be the seat of the Measuring Intelligence. Thus, we perceive that one of the Chasidim is one who rightly measures his position in the cosmic order, perceives that human personality rests on the eternal foundation of the Limitless Light, and looks upon himself as a channel for inexhaustible benevolence. On this account the "word" R. C. becomes his mark and character.

We are exhorted to love our neighbor as ourselves, because the Self of one is the Self of all. We are told that pure and undefiled religion is to visit the fatherless and widows in their affliction and to keep ourselves unspotted from the world. This last statement has been sadly misunderstood by those who have taken it to mean that one must withdraw from all the usual vocations of human beings and shut oneself up in monastic seclusion. What is meant is that we should not accept the half-knowledge of the worldly minded, that our measurements should be accurate and not mere rule-of-thumb. The emphasis, however, falls on the simple life of brotherliness, charity, and unstinted beneficence. This is really fundamental, and no amount of occult information is worth anything without it.

Since 1875 we have had in our midst abundant evidence of this. The Invisible Order, making one of its periodical endeavors to add to human knowledge of the Simple Way, established a society having for its first principle the recognition of human brotherhood and the practice of that principle. The few who understood the importance of this principle have had abundant evidence that all the other wonderful possibilities latent in human life may really be brought into manifestation. The many who were dazzled by phenomena and who sought to develop "powers," neglecting the first object of the society, became occult failures, as those responsible for the whole undertaking knew they would. Hence, the outer organization seems to have accomplished little and has split into many factions. Yet the inner movement has been a brilliant success, for through it enough persons have passed the "first test" to provide channels whereby the Invisible Order has been able to effect radical changes in the thought of the whole Western world.

He who would become a Lesser Adept, then, must devote himself to a life of giving. He must give freely of himself and of all of his possessions, spiritual and material. To be niggardly is to demonstrate one's want of comprehension. Thus, the Appendix to *The Sophic Hydrolith*, an alchemical text in *The Hermetic Museum*, warns us: "If, after obtaining this knowledge [of the Philosophers' Stone], you give way to pride or avarice (under the pretext of economy and prudence), and thus gradually turn away from God, the secret will most certainly fade out of your mind in a manner you do not understand. This has actually happened to many who would not be warned."[2]

On the other hand, one must not be prodigal. Our giving must be measured according to the requirements of those to whom we give. Too much light is dazzling, and if we are giving knowledge, the gift must be so measured as to fit the capacity of the recipient. The same principle holds good in all our giving.

Yet must we always give freely and royally. Never must we withhold anything because we are afraid that our own supply may be exhausted. The measuring is not of what we have but rather of the manner in which what we give is distributed, so that it may be best employed. By such giving we enlarge our capacity to receive and increase our power to transmit. The more we give intelligently, the more are we able to receive. The one source of supply, remember, is absolutely inexhaustible.

---

[2]Arthur Edward Waite, from "The Sophic Hydrolith" in *The Hermetic Museum* (reprinted in 1973 by Samuel Weiser, Inc., York Beach, ME), 117.

The Twenty-fourth Path

The twenty-fourth path is called the Imaginative Intelligence. It is so called because it bears fruit in the patterns of the images of created beings.

Book of Formation.

This path corresponds to Key 13 in Tarot. It is the last of the three paths leading to the Grade of Lesser Adept. It is the path attributed to the zodiacal sign Scorpio, and thus it has to do with the "secret force" utilized in practical occultism. For Scorpio, according to astrologers, rules the organs of generation, and Eliphas Levi tells us explicitly that the Great Magical Agent, whereby one who knows how to control and direct its currents may reduce the world to chaos and transform its face, is the instrument of life. He says: "God creates it eternally, and man, in the image of the Deity, modifies and apparently multiplies it in the reproduction of his species."

Similarly, in alchemical literature we find recurrent mention of the "seed of minerals." The Great Magical Agent is active in the generative organs of men and animals. It also governs the functions of flowers, the generative organs of plants, and here is another clue to the symbolism of the rose. The same force is active too in the processes by which cells reproduce themselves in our bodies.

Symbolists learn early in their studies that no occult emblems are so numerous as those that refer to reproduction. Shiva, the Hindu personification of transforming power, is represented by the image of a phallus. So was Osiris among the Egyptians. The serpent symbol means the same thing, and like the scorpion, it also corresponds to the eighth sign of the zodiac. The fish has precisely the same meaning, and that meaning was known to the early Christians and to the Gnostic sect called Ophites, who associated the Christos with the serpent.

Wherever Gnostic Christianity has penetrated, this identity of fish, serpent, and scorpion has been recognized. It is subtly woven into the doctrine of the *Fama* and the *Confessio*. These manifestoes give the age of Brother C. R. as 106 years, and 106 is the number of the letter name NVN, Nun. They speak of C. R. as being a reformer or transformer. They mention specifically the appearance of new stars in Serpentarius. Serpentarius, or Ophiucus as it is now called, is a constellation connected with the first decanate of the sign Scorpio. It is pictured as a man wrestling with a serpent and typifies that aspect of the Great Work that has to do with the transmutation of the reproductive force. The manifestoes say the Fraternity was established by eight persons, and they otherwise emphasize the magical number 8, which is the number of the sign Scorpio.

Persons who study symbolism without understanding its inner meaning are often horrified by the predominance of what they invariably term "sex symbols." Since the days of Godfrey Higgins, early in the nineteenth century, books written by these exoteric symbolists have rung the changes on the theme that religion and occultism are "nothing but veiled sex." A prominent ebullition of this periodic expression of total misunderstanding is the Freudian school of psychoanalysis.

Let it be said, then, that though the magic force is certainly what operates in the reproduction of plants, animals, and men, neither true religion nor the true occulism that religion veils is in any sense sex magic. Whenever one comes upon some "very secret teaching" that whispers mysteriously about the sex function or hints that some occult use or modification of that function is the way to illumination and power, one may know that perversion and insanity are the fruits, and the only fruits, of the practices taught. There is much of this sort of thing in the world, but it usually may be recognized by its pretensions to great secrecy, or else by its expressed intention to interfere in some way with the normal life of human beings.

True Rosicrucian doctrine makes no mystery of this important matter. Nor does it encourage any practice that will weaken, pervert, or aim at direct modification of the sex function in human beings. It states boldly and openly that the power used in practical work is the force that reproduces physical forms. It insists on healthy bodies and on absolute cleanliness of thought concerning this whole matter. Having said that the power it employs is the power that peoples the world, the true esoteric doctrine points to the fact that there is evidently very much more of this force available than is required for this one purpose.

It utilizes this power by drawing it off from the particular nerve center that energizes the sex organs and applying it to other kinds of work. The methods that accomplish this result have nothing to do with perpetual celibacy, on the one hand, nor with the quest for "soul mates," on the other. In fact, there is nothing in practical work of this sort to encourage the notions current in some of the cults and sects composing the "lunatic fringe" of occultism.

The adjective *imaginative*, describing the twenty-fourth path, and the position of the path itself on the Tree of Life show by what means true Rosicrucians control the Great Magical Agent. Mastery of the currents of this nervous energy in the physical body is achieved by mental imagery, but the images employed have nothing whatever to do with the sex function. All magic is accomplished by the mind's power of generating mental images. Imagination directed toward the formation of specific patterns for desirable conditions is the secret of this twenty-fourth path.

The higher technique of these exercises in creative imagination has to do with building the pattern of the deathless "solar body," which is symbolized by the rising sun in the background of Key 13. Few persons know that such a body can be built. Fewer still are aware that some human beings actually have built such a vehicle. The race thought runs counter to this idea. We mistakenly suppose that everyone must die.

This is not true, and one of the principal undertakings of the Invisible Order is to sow this seed idea in the race mind as a counteractive to the natural man's belief in the reality of death. Thus, in the Third Degree of Craft Masonry one hears, after witnessing a drama centering around the death and raising of Hiram Abiff, that there is something in man that will never die.

Few members of the Craft have any conscious understanding of the tremendous implications of this Third Degree. Yet every time a Master Mason is raised, the whole story of the alchemical work of transmutation is rehearsed in compact form. Thus, all who attend such ceremonies have the seed idea impressed on them over and over again. They do not share the benefits of the truth so expressed unless they become consciously aware of its meaning; but they do further the purpose of the Invisible Order in another way, *for every person who sees these rites and hears the accompanying words is a channel through which the great truths behind the symbols enter the race subconsciousness.*

It is on this account that every ceremonial representation of these mysteries includes a portion in which the candidate is obliged to undergo a simulated death. He must be killed and then raised. Whether it be Osiris slain and risen, Hiram murdered and raised from the grave, or Brother C. R. receiving initiation after the death of P. A. L., the intimation is ever the same. And the purpose of all of these ceremonies, from the mysteries of Eleusis down to this day, is to send into the race mind the seed thought that man as an immortal may build himself a deathless vehicle, a body that shall never die.

If in our patterns of desirable action we include that of building such a body, in which the balance between integration and disintegration shall be preserved indefinitely, we have taken a step in the right direction. This is the first step in that control of the secret serpent force that has enabled others in the past and will enable some in this present generation to complete the Great Work from "this side" of life.

Recognition that this is a reasonable expectation comes first. Even if this recognition is not actualized in the lives of some of us, by our practice we shall have planted a seed in subconsciousness that will survive the death of the physical body and that may be developed during our sojourn on the "other side of the veil of death."

One who does this learns to face death with equanimity. He really faces it and studies it in order to see what purposes it serves in the cosmic order. He goes *through* death mentally and symbolically. And on the other side of death he finds life eternal.

With such preparation he may go on, for the Lesser Adept must be released from the fear of death and the hatred of death that prevents one from understanding and overcoming it. He must be free too from all belief in luck, chance, fate, or limitations imposed by environment. He must know by experiment that the Great Magical Agent is indeed "the strong force of all forces, overcoming every subtle, and penetrating every solid thing." He must be free from egotism, because some of his labors will test his reliance on the All Power behind his personality. He must be willing to follow his path even to death and beyond, because none of the cringing compromises of the coward who preserves physical existence at all costs are possible for the person who has reached any degree of adeptship.

Yet the Grade we are now studying is that of the *Lesser* adeptship, because in it the aspirant trains himself in nothing but those things that give him skill in controlling his mental imagery. Throughout his work he knows that physically and psychically he is one with the other manifestations of the One Identity, whose particular center of expression for earth dwellers is the sun. A Lesser Adept accustoms himself to regard everything in his environment as being so much solidified sunlight. He sees all things and creatures as being special manifestations of the daystar's radiance. He perceives his own thoughts, words, and deeds as being inseparable from that one force. Thus, he comes in time to understand to the full the occult phrase "Light in extension" and the Master's admonition, "Let your light shine."

This does not mean that he sees no further. At this stage of his development, however, he pays particular attention to mental practices that substitute for the conception of "many-ness" held by most persons the fixed and permanent idea that all things and experiences are forms taken by the one radiant energy of the sun. The work of the Lesser Adept enables him to realize that the Great Work is indeed the "Operation of the Sun," as the *Emerald Tablet of Hermes* declares it to be. Thus, the Lesser Adept's practice results in a mental attitude that may be put thus: "One Reality, the same yesterday, today, and forever, enters my experience as the radiant energy of the sun. This is the real substance of my body and of all other things I know. It is the source of every mode of power, the origin of every force, known and unknown. It is also the source of whatever has been known in past ages, of all knowledge existing now, and of all knowledge destined to be brought to light in the future. For it is the *something* that takes form eternally in every manifestation of power and in every expression of knowledge."

Imagination is the direct application of this one power. It is the mental activity through which the will of intelligent beings acts directly on the Great Magical Agent. Just as the young woman actually made a hat by her mental imagery even though her idea expressed itself through the action of another person, so a Lesser Adept, working incessantly to perfect his skill, has experience after experience demonstrating that his mental pictures are molds or patterns that determine the physical forms taken by the One Force.

A Lesser Adept learns that the external world is like the screen in a cinema theater. The light is the universal Conscious Energy. The projection machine is the self-conscious mind. The lens is attention. The pictures on the film are the work of the Adept's imagination. What he sees with his mind's eye becomes actualized through the operation of nature's basic laws.

In his presence marvels take place, events occur that are inexplicable to the ordinary human being; but these are marvels of law, miracles of right adaptation, mighty works of his creative imagination.

A Lesser Adept, remember, employs no powers that are not used by all men. Every human being projects mental images on the screen of environment by the process outlined here. Most persons, however, make distorted images. Few have the least conception of the fact that they have this power. Their light shines dim. The lens of attention is poorly focused. The pictures are deformed and hideous. Thus, their experiences correspond to their want of skill in scientific imagination.

Hence, the work of the Lesser Adept is summed up in the statement: "In all things, great and small, I see the Beauty of the Divine Expression." To make this mental pattern as a suggestion to subconsciousness is to set in motion a whole train of subtle activities that result at last in actual perception of the order and beauty behind the surface appearances of this world. Because beauty and balance, symmetry and efficiency, loveliness and strength, are really inseparable, the cultivation of the eye for true beauty is the best possible way to make one's environment what he wants it to be.

The aspirant may lack technical training to do the actual work that will beautify his world. Yet his mental pattern, held steadily, will certainly realize itself through somebody's action if not through his own. Let anyone build up a definite, clear image of a beautiful world, and thousands of pairs of hands will set to work to give it physical shape and form.

In the Hebrew spelling of the aspect of Reality to which the Grade of Lesser Adept is attributed (THPARTh), the first letter is Tav, corresponding to Key 21 in Tarot and to the Administrative Intelligence. A Lesser Adept begins with the assumption that every man is a special manifestation of the powers of the whole universe—that a personal life is simply a particular expression of all the life there is. This is what is really meant when man is called *microcosm* or little cosmos. From this point of view, the life of any man, whether he knows it or not, is actually an administration of cosmic law.

No sooner is this assumption made with sufficient force to affect subconsciousness than what is suggested by the letter Peh and by Tarot Key 16 follows as a corollary. Since every man is an administrator of cosmic law, since every man's actions are special expressions in a particular time and place of the whole interplay of cosmic forces, then surely no man stands alone. The false philosophy of exoteric religion, the false proverbs of "common sense," and the false science that still dominate race thought assert that man does stand alone. Hence, the Lesser Adept must work assiduously to break down the delusion of separateness.

He identifies himself with the cosmic vision typified by Key 0, The Fool, and in so doing he accepts also the burden implied by the fact that this Key corresponds to the letter name *Aleph*, the Ox. A Lesser Adept comes to perceive that those who really know are aware that they are carrying the burden of manifestation, that on them is laid *Legis Jugum*, the yoke of the law. True, the yoke is easy and the burden is light, but it is a real responsibility nevertheless. When you know that to you is entrusted a share in the Great Undertaking, life will have new meaning for you. When you know that through the personality labeled with your name, the Eternal Pilgrim journeys onward toward the Great Beyond, you will find in the least of your daily experiences something unsuspected by most children of earth.

This knowledge a Lesser Adept has in perfection. He knows himself as the personified Sun. That is to say, he knows that all his personal activities are really transformations and transmutations of consciousness, as well as of force. Thus, he understands why in Key 19, corresponding to the letter Resh, the sun has a human face.

On the other hand, he knows that human personality is the form through which the One Force that manifests physically as solar energy is destined to perfect the Great Work. Thus, he sees why the open sunflowers behind the wall turn toward the two children instead of to the sun above. The children and the sun are not diverse and separate entities. They are different aspects of the One Thing. So are the flowers, the wall, and everything else in the Key.

The human aspect of the One Thing is the master and administrator of the laws and forces of all the other aspects of that same Reality. Human consciousness is truly the Collective Intelligence, the synthesis of all forms of consciousness. It is something more than *mere* synthesis too, for human life is that aspect of the One Thing whereby all the wonderful adaptations are made. "So thou *hast* the glory of the whole world," says the *Emerald Tablet*, "therefore let all obscurity flee before thee."

DOCTRINES OF THE GRADE

The Hebrew for "Intelligence of Mediating Influence," assigned to the sixth circle on the Tree of Life, is ShPO NBDL, *Shefah Nabadal*. Hence, there are ten doctrines in this Grade of Lesser Adept, derived from the ten different letters in the words ThPARTh, *Tiphareth*, and ShPO NBDL, *Shefah Nabadal*. The three words contain twelve letters, but since Tav and Peh each occur twice, the doctrines drawn from the letters are only ten. They are as follows:

1. THE WORLD
Key 21 (Th)

The world every man lives in is the world he forms by his mental imagery. The better he images, the better the world. "Better" in this instance means "more truly agreeing with the fundamental imagery of the Universal Mind."

All form is limitation of the infinite energy of the Life Power. The primary cause of such limitation is the image-making power of the Universal Mind. Every act of human imagination is really a particular expression through a personal center of this image-making power of the Universal Mind. Hence, human imagination is in kind, though not in degree, the same as the universal image-making power. By schooling himself in the truth that all his personal activities are aspects of the cosmic process, a Lesser Adept overcomes the illusion of separateness that interferes with his personal transmission of the images of the Universal Mind.

2. THE TOWER
Key 16 (P)

To image truly, one must first overthrow erroneous conceptions. The various forms of the error of separateness must be corrected. This practice leads to the perception that all activity within the range of personal experience is really a series of transformations of the One spiritual energy.

A Lesser Adept refuses to think of any act of his as being separate from the activity of the One Life Power. By as many ingenious devices as he can think of, he trains himself to see that all that occurs within the range of his personal experience is a transformation of the single energy at work throughout the universe.

3. THE FOOL
Key 0 (A)

The peak of present realization is the point of outlook from which we may perceive the vision of future possibility. Clear images of definite objectives are the seed ideas of future manifestations. Yet these must be seen as actual realities in the living present.

As the sixth circle on the Tree of Life is also related to the Life Breath, which is called *Ruach* in Hebrew, it is natural that the letter Aleph—the letter of The Fool—should be prominent in the name of this aspect of the Life Power. Aleph is the central letter in ThPARTh, *Tiphareth*, the heart of the word, so to speak, and to Aleph also is *Ruach* attributed in Qabalah.

A Lesser Adept seeks always to clarify his vision of what lies beyond the heights of present human attainment. Again and again he reminds himself that Principle is not bound by precedent. He works with specific imagery in relation to his personal share in the cosmic process. In so doing he occupies his imagination almost exclusively with the work of picturing definite objectives, giving practically no thought at this stage to the consideration of ways and means.

4. THE SUN
Key 19 (R)

Since natural man is the seed of the spiritual Man, he who would scale the heights of adeptship must resolve to become more than man. The New World Order is an Order composed of new creatures, who constitute a new species of organic life.

In the Grade of Lesser Adept the idea of regeneration is emphasized. In one ritualistic version of the ceremonies of this Grade the aspirant takes this vow: "With the Divine permission, I will from this day forward apply myself unto the Great Work, which is so to purify and exalt my spiritual nature that with the Divine Aid I may at length attain to be more than human, and thus gradually raise and unite myself to my higher and divine Genius."

He aims to become a new creature, actually a new species of organism on this planet. He knows that others have done this and seeks to do it himself. He makes himself familiar with the attainments of the Brethren who have preceded him on this Way of Return, and he devotes himself to bringing about like changes in his own organism. This is the New Birth.

5. JUDGMENT
Key 20 (Sh)

The New Creature is newborn. He rises from the limitations of time and space into a higher dimension. He is changed from mortality into immortality. The New World Order is an order of immortals, and its nucleus is now manifest on this planet.

This New Birth leads into a new life experience. This is dimly apprehended in modern exoteric teachings and speculations concerning the fourth dimension. It is even more clearly set forth in Oriental doctrines concerning the enlightenment that follows Yoga practice. Nobody can tell another what this experience is, but those who have enjoyed it are able to indicate the fact to each other by means of various symbols. These symbols, however, will be meaningless to persons who have not had the illumination. Thus, in the Grade of Lesser Adept emphasis is placed on the fact that only by firsthand knowledge, going beyond the limits of human speculative philosophy resting on ordinary sensation, may enlightenment be gained. This experience includes conscious immortality. Thus, throughout the *Fama* and the *Confessio*, the anonymous writers address the readers as mortals, as if to intimate that the Brethren themselves are consciously immortal.

6. THE DEVIL
Key 15 (O)

Every aspect of evil presenting itself to the human mind is the raw material for transmutation into a beautiful result. Behind all appearances, whatever they may be, is the operation of a perfect law having beauty for its foundation. Apparent evils are temporary and necessary phases of the Cosmic process.

If we see ugliness, it is because we do not see correctly. This does not mean that Rosicrucian doctrine denies the existence of relative evils. It does not mean that we should not do all we can to correct such evils. The Lesser Adept, however, instead of being frightened or paralyzed by appearances of evil, looks on them as necessary. He sees them as proceeding from the One Source, just as much as do those things that appear to be good. What he is taught and what he practices continually is the transmutation of apparent evils into evident goods by the operation of the power of mental imagery.

7. DEATH
Key 13 (N)

He who is master of the force of dissolution is master of all changes of form. Disintegration is the opposite and complement of integration. Only he who can dissolve form may master the art of constituting forms.

A Lesser Adept, having passed through the path of the letter Nun on his way to this Grade, knows very well that the fact of physical death is inevitable, necessary, and beneficent. He knows why physical bodies die. He knows that the death of the physical body is not the end of personal existence. He knows that the experience of physical death is necessary until man learns how to build the kind of organism that will retain its form on the physical plane just as long as he wishes to use that form. The Lesser Adept knows too that the knowledge and skill required to do this include the knowledge and ability to disintegrate the physical form instantly whenever it has served its purpose and to reintegrate it again whenever it may be required. He who can do this is master of death.

8. THE MAGICIAN
Key 1 (B)

Conscious transformation is an act of Self-consciousness. It is the use of mental imagery in the arrangement of patterns of form, by which forces are combined. The Self of man is master of all forms.

This mastery is exercised from the vantage ground of self-consciousness represented in Tarot by Key 1. A Lesser Adept is a conscious transformer of his environment by means of mental imagery. He deliberately plans his constructions. He arranges the various combinations of forces that make up his surroundings. He does so as an instrument of a power higher than himself, for in the Grade of Lesser Adept he has not yet completely identified himself with that power.

9. THE EMPRESS
Key 3 (D)

Due skill in the mental direction of the Life Power as it flows from superconscious levels, through self-conscious levels, enables one to control, modify and altogether alter the mental images generated by subconsciousness. Self-consciousness is the point of control.

In Qabalistic psychology the sixth circle on the Tree of Life is attributed to Imagination. Hence, it is natural to find a doctrine based on Key 3 and the letter Daleth receiving strong emphasis in this Grade. It will be remembered too that in ceremonials of this Grade the whole story of the finding of the Vault is rehearsed and dramatized, which means that all the Venusian symbolism is brought into prominence. A Lesser Adept deliberately manipulates his mental imagery. By applying the law that subconsciousness is always amenable to suggestion, he finds out for himself that no person need be dominated by subconscious imagery. This is not a matter for argument; it is a matter for experiment. The greater number of us are victims of subconscious generation of mental imagery. A Lesser Adept learns to control the products of that generation and thus frees himself gradually from every kind of bondage.

10. JUSTICE
Key 11 (L)

Any modification of the mind may be overcome by exercising its opposite. This is the secret of mental equilibrium and emotional poise. Every evil may be overcome by its corresponding good.

"Equilibrium is the basis of the Great Work." This ancient doctrine is reiterated in the Grade of Lesser Adept. He who is at work in this Grade never attempts to suppress a negative state of mind. Instead of this he uses intelligence to discover its positive opposite, and he cultivates the expression of that opposite state—the active expression, observe, not the passive contemplation of the opposite. Thus, the final work of a Lesser Adept has to do with the establishment of poise and balance in his own consciousness, and the manifestation of his highest conceptions of justice in every detail of his personal conduct.

Beginning with the assumption that he is really an administrator of cosmic law (Th, Key 21), a Lesser Adept works at first for some time at uprooting and destroying various forms of the error of separateness (P, Key 16). By the exercise of imagination he cultivates vision and mentally identifies himself with the One Life Power (A, Key 0). This practice clears away various mental, emotional, and physical obstructions and produces in him the change termed *regeneration* (R, Key 19). Thus, he arrives at last at a point where what was at first an assumption becomes an actual experience. By repeated experiments he has demonstrated to himself that he is actually sharing in the goverment of the cosmos, that through him are playing the forces that really determine the forms assumed by his environment (Th). After having made this demonstration he is ready to proceed to the next Grade.

CHAPTER XVII

THE GRADE OF GREATER ADEPT, 6 = 5

HE GRADE OF GREATER ADEPT corresponds to the ideas connected with the number 5 and with the fifth circle of the Tree of Life, which is named PChD, *Pachad* (Fear); GBVRH, Geburah (Strength); and DIN, *Deen* (Justice). The mode of consciousness corresponding to this Grade is the Radical Intelligence, in Hebrew NShRSh, *Nasharash*. The number of this word is 850, combining 0, the sign of Absolute Unity, with the digits 5 and 8, so important in Rosicrucian symbology.

As a preparation for the study of this Grade consider the meanings of the number 5, as summarized in *The Tarot: A Key to the Wisdom of the Ages.*

The number 5 stands for mediation (because 5 is the middle number between 1, Beginning, and 9, Completion), adaptation, means, agency, activity, process; the dynamic Law, proceeding from the abstract Order typified by the number 4; versatility, because it shows the changing aspects of the One Law, inspiring fear in the ignorant and presenting itself to the materialist as mere relentless strength but understood by the wise as undeviating Justice; the instrumentality that carries energy into manifestation as form.

The One Law represented by the number 5 is the root of all operations of the Life Power and is therefore called the Radical Intelligence. This root consciousness, expressed through human personality, is the agency of all works of mediation and adaptation. As the *Emerald Tablet* says, "All things have their birth from this One Thing by adaptation."

The ignorant see in the innumerable manifestations of the One Law the operation of forces greater than man—some of which help him, although most of them seem to be against him. These forces they propitiate by sacrifice (from which exoteric religion had its beginning), and the dominant emotional response to Law is that designated by the word PChD, *Pachad*, "Fear."

A little, but very little, further along are those who see in the One Law the operation of impersonal forces utterly disregarding man, who is conceived as being merely a cog in the cosmic mechanism. This was the predominant attitude of the "naturalism," which began with the writings of Francis Bacon. Latterly, it has been somewhat modified by those who deny that there is any real order in the universe and ascribe all events to accident. Either of these interpretations of the forces that surround man make of him only a puppet, helpless in the grip of forces that are adequately described by the Hebrew noun GBVRH, *Geburah*, meaning both "Strength" and "Severity."

The third and highest interpretation of the One Law is that which is given to us as a result of the experience of men and women who have attained the Rosicrucian objective of becoming "more than human." Unanimously, these seers report that the powers around us are working toward a beautifully symmetrical result, that balance is maintained in both the moral and the physical worlds, and that the true expression of the significance of the One Law is summed up in the Hebrew noun, DIN, *Deen*, "Justice."

The section of the *Pattern on the Trestleboard* corresponding to the fifth Sephirah and to the Grade of Greater Adept, says: "I recognize the manifestation of the undeviating Justice in all the circumstances of my life." Here the verb is very important. It indicates clearly that what happens in us is a *re*cognition, a knowing again. Rosicrucian doctrine does not bid us hope for the establishment of justice at some future date. It does not make an ideal or a goal of justice. It declares unequivocally that only our surrender to the illusions of appearance, our failure to estimate correctly the meaning of experience, and our want of insight make us believe in injustice. The Ageless Wisdom declares that the self-manifestation of the Life Power is perfectly just, accurate, and properly balanced at this moment, that it has always been so, and that it always will be. It calls us to recognition, to remembrance, to vision. Hence, in the Rosicrucian Grades, a Greater Adept is one who is fully awakened from the delusion of separateness and injustice into the full recognition described in the statement we have quoted.

He arrives at this recognition by passing through the paths of the letters Mem and Lamed, the twenty-third and twenty-second paths of the Tree of Life. He enters the path of Mem from the Grade of Practicus, but he cannot do so until he has become a Lesser Adept. The path of Lamed is entered directly from the Grade of Lesser Adept, but not until the path of Mem has been traversed.

THE TWENTY-THIRD PATH

*The twenty-third path is called the Stable Intelligence. It is so called
because it is the source of consistency among all the Sephiroth.*
Book of Formation

In Hebrew the adjective translated "Stable" is QIIM, *khayam.* The
spelling is a rabbinic form of the Aramaic QIM, meaning "firm, hard,
constant, lasting." Its numeration is 160, and words equivalent to this
include: KSP, *kesaph* (silver); NOM, *noam* (delight, suitableness, pleasure,
grace); NPL, *nawfal* (a word having many meanings, primarily "to fall" but
also to be born, to revive, to result, to happen, to befall) SLO, *sehla* (a
burden, weight, stone, rock); OTz, *autz* (tree); and TzLM, *tselem* (image).

Thus associated with QIIM by numeration are the ideas of value
(silver, money) and of the lunar current of the secret force, symbolized by
silver; of grace, pleasure, suitability; the descent of the cosmic energy into
form; the weight or ponderability of physical manifestation, typified as a
stone or rock; the organic expression of the potencies of the Life Power,
symbolized among all nations by the image of a tree; and the reflection of
the ideas of the Universal Mind in forms or images.

All of these ideas are indicated in one way or another in the subtle
symbolism of Key 12, The Hanged Man, one of the most important pages of
the Rosicrucian *Rota.* This Key is a summary of the whole Path of Return,
which the Chinese teacher, Lao-Tze, called Tao, concerning which he wrote:
"The path of Tao is backward. The characteristic of Tao is gentleness.
Everything in the universe comes from existence, and existence from nonexistence."

The name of this three-sentence chapter of the *Tao-Teh-King* is
"Resigning Work." It may seem strange to quote it after so much has been
said in these pages about the importance of action. To resign work,
however, is not to cease from action. Look closely at this verb *resign.* Most
persons sign their names to their work, and it frequently happens that the
signature is more prominent than the work itself. A Lesser Adept learns to
erase this flamboyant personal signature and lets his work become so
perfect an expression of the Will of the One Artist that it will, so to speak,
sign itself.

Since everything comes from existence, and existence comes from
nonexistence, the true source of all action must be the unmanifested Light.
If we would be in harmony with cosmic rhythms, then we must stop
scribbling our names on the masterpieces of life like travelers who scratch
their silly cognomens on the walls of some ancient temple.

This is the idea represented by the twenty-third path of the letter
Mem. Consider what is said of this letter in *The Book of Tokens:*

Absorb thyself in this Great Sea of the Waters of Life
Dive deep in it until thou hast lost thyself.
    And having lost thyself,
    Then shalt thou find thyself again,
    And shalt be one with me,
    Thy Lord and King.
Thus shalt thou learn the secret
Of the restoration of the King unto his throne.

    And in this path of Stability
Shall my knowledge of the Roots of Being
Be united to the glorious Splendor
Of the perfect Knowledge
Which is established in the mirror
Of the clear waters of HOD.
For when the surface of those waters
Is disturbed by no slightest ripple of thought
    Then shall the glory of my Self,
    Which is thy true Self,
    Be mirrored unto thee.

These words convey the secret of the path of Mem. It is the path of resigning the work done by the Self through personality. Thus, it is the path of the total extinction of the illusive personal self.

How we dread to enter this path! How reluctantly we set foot on it! Yet we fear to lose what is really nothing. A delusion like that described in an Eastern tale makes us believe that we are rich in personal possessions, when the truth is that the treasure chest holds nothing but a handful of withered leaves. A day comes when the truth flashes like lightning on the mind. Then it becomes evident that all this talk of sacrifice is meaningless noise. In truth, the aspirant is called on to give up *nothing*, yet most persons hold fast to this nonentity as if it were a pearl of great price.

Who is the King who must be restored to his throne? He is the true Self, standing patiently waiting at the door, knocking gently for admission. But the clamor of a multitude of anarchistic cells shouting madly, "The voice of the people is the voice of God!" drowns the still, small Voice, and the Stranger-King must wait outside. He could force his way in. He could still the mob. He could command their silence and even hush them forever, because His is the Life Power on which they depend for everything. Yet He stands and waits until they remember, until they wake from their insane dream of separateness.

The path of Mem leads upward from *Hod*, the eighth Sephirah, to *Geburah*, the fifth. It begins in expectation, in an eager, long look upward toward the Source of Life. This is expressed in the statement, "I look forward with confidence to the perfect realization of the Eternal Splendor of the Limitless Light." Our lips say it now. When our hearts begin to whisper it, we shall enter gladly on the path of surrender.

Now we have some doubts of the undeviating justice that is revealed at the upper end of this path, and so we stand hesitant at the portal. We ourselves are just. Yes, most of us are sure of that! But we doubt the justice of our neighbors. One of the main reasons we find it so hard to give up the illusion of personal free will, so difficult to overcome the sense of separate personality, is that we feel subconsciously that to do so is to remove even the shadow of an excuse for holding other persons responsible for the seeming evils that are done through them.

Yet this was the mind that was in the Master Jesus, as it has been the mind in every other Master of Wisdom. "Judge not" is the admonition of them all. It implies, "Do not presume to fix the measure of another's responsibility." All of the world's laws and customs, all of the habits of unnumbered lifetimes, pull against us when we try to stop judging our neighbors. But Jesus, like other great teachers, came with the message that human personality originates nothing, that the Primal Will is the only real Will, that men may become wide-open channels of that Will, once they rid themselves of the delusion of personal independence. The Masters live to show us what we are able to do. The way they took is open to us as soon as we find courage to brave its terrors.

This we may not do until we have become at least Lesser Adepts. The path of The Hanged Man is not for beginners on the Way of Return. Jesus was a mighty wonder-worker before he was called on to meet the test of the cross. This path of Mem is the path of what Hindus call *Samadhi*, the path of perfect concentration long continued, which brings one into conscious union with the essence of the Law of Life and makes one see everywhere the exquisite adjustments of that Law.

Such a man, having been faithful in the lighter tasks of the Inner School, now becomes a Greater Adept who knows himself as a channel for the operation of the unfailing Law of the cosmos. He ceases to regard his actions in any personal light. He not only feels the One Law working through him, but he also knows just how it works in every specific instance. He perceives both the seeds and the fruit of all that is done through him, and he becomes a reader of the hearts of men.

Samadhi is not merely going into a trance. So far as the lower personality is concerned it *is* a trance, but the trance of *Samadhi* is different from the trance of hypnosis; nor is it to be confounded with the unconsciousness of negative mediumship. As Vivekananda writes:

> Whenever we hear a man say "I am inspired," and then talk the most irrational nonsense, simply reject it. Why? Because these three states of mind—instinct, reason, and superconsciousness, or the unconscious, conscious, and superconscious states—belong to one and

the same mind. There are not three minds in one man, but one develops into the other. Instinct develops into reason, and reason into the transcendental consciousness; therefore one never contradicts the other. So, whenever you meet with wild statements which contradict human reason and common sense, reject them without any fear, because the real inspiration will never contradict, but will fulfil. Just as you find the great prophets saying, "I come not to destroy but to fulfil," so this inspiration always comes to fulfil reason, and is in direct harmony with reason, and whenever it contradicts reason you must know that it is not inspiration.[1]

It is just because superconsciousness does not contradict reason that so much is said by careful teachers about training the intellect, and about the truth that the only reasonable interpretation of modern scientific discoveries in the fields of biology and psychology is the doctrine of determinism—the denial of personal free will. The world's leading thinkers accept this doctrine. The occult wisdom perfects and fulfills the exoteric version of modern thought. From superconscious experience comes the knowledge that fulfills the rational doctrine of determinism by giving man direct experience of the true nature of the Will principle at work through his personality. The purpose of occult training is to free us from the bondage of a lie, and the essence of the lie is the notion that man has a personal will by which he can somehow circumvent the laws of the cosmos.

The path of *Samadhi* is difficult, but eventually it does away with the delusion that personality does anything whatever. Nobody can go through the path of Mem who has not passed the trials of the twenty-fourth path of Nun and so overcome death; for *Samadhi* has all the appearances of death, yet it is more than death. It is the extinction of the illusion that there are *two* in the sphere of being. It is the extinction of candlelight in the blaze of the sun. *Samadhi* is not of long duration, usually not more than half an hour. For the space of a half hour there was silence in heaven, we are told in Revelation. But the man who returns from *Samadhi* is changed forever. He has become what Will Levington Comfort called "one of those who know and cannot tell."

Such a one is a Greater Adept. Thenceforth he participates consciously in the administration of cosmic law. Having given up the delusion of separate personality, he has done what Lao-Tze advised: "Having emptied yourself, remain where you are." He is an open channel for the One Life, and because he takes care not to yield to the illusion of separateness—not to believe in it though it still surrounds him—when such a man says, "Be thou healed," healing follows, and when he says, "Thy sins

---

[1]Swami Vivekananda, *Raja Yoga* (New York: The Baker & Taylor Co., 1899), 80.

be forgiven thee," he voices the knowledge of the One Life that the one to whom he speaks has reached a stage of spiritual unfoldment where he is released from the consequences of his former failures to hit the mark. A Greater Adept seems to perform miracles, but he does them all by getting himself out of the way.

From this point on, as the Tarot pictures show, the nature of the paths changes. The terrors are past. The last illusion of "me and mine"— that great hindrance to love—is dissolved in the path of The Hanged Man. Thereafter the advancing adept identifies himself with an ascending scale of attainments one by one, represented by the remaining paths and Tarot Keys.

The Elder Brothers who have reached the Grade of Greater Adept are those who participate consciously in the administration of cosmic law. In this preliminary survey of the Way of Return, written as it is from a level of consciousness far below the Grade of Greater Adept, we can only dimly apprehend what this attainment means. Yet we should try as best we can to understand the instruction imparted to us by those who have reached these high Grades of the Invisible Order, for it is from them, of course, that all we know concerning these Grades has been received.

After traversing the path of Mem even a Greater Adept must pass through the twenty-second path of Lamed in order to complete his attainment of the Grade. It is not enough to be conscious of participation in the government of all things. One must know, but one must also be able to instruct. It is not enough to be consciously immortal, so as to say, "Before Abraham was, I am." One must recognize the truth that he is incarnate Law and must be able to impart that truth to others.

THE TWENTY-SECOND PATH

The twenty-second path is called the Faithful Intelligence, because by it the powers of the Life-Breath are caused to multiply, and all dwellers on earth are merely under its shadow.

Book of Formation

The name of the letter Lamed as a noun means "ox-goad," and as a verb signifies "to teach, to instruct." Greater Adepts learn to direct the Life-breath so as to cause its powers to multiply. That is to say, they master the currents of what Yoga philosophy calls *Prana* and develop the powers of this Great Magical Agent. Furthermore, they perfect their own knowledge and skill by becoming teachers, or rather, by becoming mouthpieces for the One Teacher.

They do not usually come before the public, although there are some exceptions to this rule. But certainly most public teachers of occultism are not Greater Adepts. A Greater Adept teaches by more subtle means than the spoken or written word. He reaches the minds of his selected pupils by means of their interior hearing. They hear his voice within and often confuse it with the One Voice of the Creative Word. Yet in a sense they are not wholly wrong, for though the instruction of the Greater Adept from whom they learn is colored to some extent by his personality, he is simply the vehicle through which the One Life relays its perfect knowledge to the mind of the learner.

But here is something for us, even though we are not yet eligible for actual advancement to the Grade of Greater Adept. We may begin now to prepare ourselves by remembering that each of us stands before the world as an image of the One Teacher. Somebody, somewhere, takes every one of us as an instructor now, whether we know it or not. Let us see to it that we are not taken as teachers of what not to be! By watching ourselves carefully we may accomplish at least one useful bit of instruction. Our daily behavior may serve to show others that one may be interested in occultism without being a freak, without neglecting the niceties of appearance and conduct, without trying to be different by doing and saying queer things, or by wearing outlandish apparel.

Some years ago I met a man who is regarded by many as being a Greater Adept. He himself made no such claim. Indeed, he made no claims at all. Yet like another Teacher, this man told me all the things that ever I did. He was in no sense a conspicuous personality. People never turned to look at him as he passed them on the street. He could sit unnoticed in a hotel lobby. His dress conformed to the ancient Rosicrucian rule and followed to perfection the current styles.

There are grounds for believing that the number of such men is considerably greater than is generally supposed, even among students of occultism. They conceal themselves in order to teach without interference. One may know them by this: that they are faithful in all things to the ideal of beauty. This man's dress was beautiful, his carriage was beautiful, his voice was beautiful, his choice of words and images was beautiful, his outlook on life was a perpetual recognition of beauty, and the lessons he taught me—lessons I shall never forget—were lessons of beauty too.

To return to the path of Lamed, we find that this path is called Faithful Intelligence. The original Hebrew is AMN, *Amen*, the same as the word meaning "so be it" used as a confirmatory ejaculation at the end of prayers. *Amen*, moreover, is one of the names of *Kether*, the Primal Will, so that it is related to the idea of the originating volitional impulse from which the universe proceeds.

The ordinary numeration of AMN is 91, the sum of the numbers from 0 to 13. So taken, AMN stands for the full expression of the concepts of unity and love (AChD, *Achad*, and AHBH, *Ahebah*), each of which is 13 in Hebrew. But sometimes a final Nun is understood to represent the number 700. By this reckoning AMN would be the number 741. This is also related to 13, for a 91 is 7 × 13, so 741 is 3 × 13 × 19. Thus, the factors of 741, written as Hebrew words, would be AB (3) × AChD (13) × ChVH (19), or Father *(Ab)* × Unity *(Achad)* × Mother *(Chavah,* Eve). The occult meaning of AMN as 741 is therefore the power of the Father, which is One Power, manifested through the agency of the Mother. Again, AMN taken as 91 is equivalent in numeration to the words IHVH ADNI, *Jehovah Adonai,* God the Lord.

All these Qabalisms serve a single purpose. They indicate that the quality of consciousness distinguished by the word AMN, *Amen* (Faithful), is fundamentally of the nature of the Primal Will, and is the actual power by which forms are brought into manifestation. Thus, St. Paul, trained by Rabbi Hillel, declared: "Faith is the *substance* of things hoped for."

In connection with the letter Lamed, moreover, faith is combined with the idea of action. Faith is not blind belief in the pronouncements of authority. The faith of the wise is based on their perception of the undeviating accuracy of cosmic law. Faith is associated with action because the perception of the working of the law of cause and effect in the inner life of man cannot be established by any other means than assiduous practice. This practice is facilitated by looking at Tarot Key 11, because this Key impresses on the subconsciousness of the observer pictorial symbols that evoke active faith. To look at this Key is to build faith, because looking at it is a kind of action, which modifies brain structure.

The text says of this path that "all dwellers on earth are merely under its shadow." Since this is the path of what Oriental teachers call Karma, to be under its shadow is to be a slave to the series of causes and effects. This does not mean that there is no escape. The phrase, "dwellers on earth," means more than it conveys to a hasty reader.

There are two kinds of human beings. By far the greater number do "dwell on earth." Their consciousness is limited to physical conditions, their judgment is based on physical sensation, and their expectations are determined by past experiences. On the other hand, in every generation there have been some (and in this age their number increases rapidly) who know that they live in "heaven" as well as on earth. They realize that the real Self of man is the controlling center of the world of causes and not merely one of the phenomena of the world of effects.

Because they have identified themselves with that controlling center and with the perfect freedom of its inner essence, they know that the reign of law is no chain that binds them fast to the working out of all their past mistakes.

Theirs, therefore, is a faith that really works, even to the least details of daily experience. They live in a reasonable expectation that their inner lives and outward environment will be always in a state of progressive improvement. They have the unshaken conviction that every condition that hampers the free, joyous expression of the Life Power can be eliminated. They understand that no circumstance can be a final boundary for infinite power, that no form can mark a point beyond which unfoldment of the Life Power's limitless potencies may not proceed. Thus, they know that adjustment is always possible. No matter how things look, no matter how twisted and abnormal any situation may appear to be, those who are called "citizens of heaven" in the manifestoes are sure that balance may be restored, that equilibrium may be regained.

DOCTRINES OF THE GRADE

The doctrines of the Grade of Greater Adept are ten in number, and are derived from and associated with the letters in the three names of the fifth Sephirah: *Pachad*, *Geburah*, and *Deen*. They are as follows:

1. THE TOWER
Key 16 (P)

No form is permanent, nor does any form separate a portion of the One Identity from the whole of that Identity. The Reality manifested at any point in space is identical with the Reality existing at all points in space. The Reality existing in the present is identical with the Reality that has continued unbroken through the past and will continue unbroken through the future.

It is to be noted in connection with this doctrine that the letter Peh is the letter of Mars and that the fifth circle on the Tree of Life is known as the Sphere of Mars. Mars is the planet of action, and thus the quality of the second of the two paths leading into this Grade of Greater Adept is tinged with the spirit of Mars, even though the letter Lamed is assigned astrologically to the zodiacal sign Libra, ruled by Venus. This is one of many indications in occult literature of the interplay of imagination (Venus) and action (Mars).

All action is disintegrative. An illusion that does not in the least deceive the wise makes the ignorant believe that something is brought into being when a form is made to appear. Those who know understand that whenever one type of form appears another type disappears. Apply cold to water. The liquid vanishes as the ice forms. Bring the ice into a warm room. As the ice melts, water makes its appearance again. So it is with every other production of form. The integration of any specific form is the disintegration of another form that is in complementary relation to it.

2. THE CHARIOT
Key 7 (Ch)

The One Reality is the field of its own manifestation, the vehicle of its own existence; and that One Reality is the directive principle in human beings, designated by the pronoun "I".

The name of the Hebrew letter Cheth, assigned to Key 7 in Tarot, means "field," or a fenced-in enclosure. This doctrine emphasizes the idea that the substance from which all forms are built is the Life Power's own nature. It is not that Spirit acts on Matter to build and disintegrate forms. Spirit acting on itself is the cause of all form production and disintegration. The pure consciousness of the Life Power, everywhere present, is that internal directive principle we recognize as the Self, manifested through the human form. That same Self is at once the substance and the integrating and disintegrating power that manifests itself as our environment, beginning with that aspect of our environment that we call mind, and continuing (as it appears) outward from mind to body, then from body to the various forms surrounding that body, and out to the most distant galaxies in the heavens.

3. THE EMPRESS
Key 3 (D)

Nature is the manifesting power of that One Identity. In all nature no force opposes itself to that One. All the forces of nature, with no exception, are instruments for expressing the free will of that One Identity. Whatever appears to the contrary is illusion, and the acceptance of that illusion for truth is the delusion that binds the ignorant.

The reader will do well to compare the central figures of Keys 3 and 7. The rider in The Chariot appears to be male, but he has the same yellow hair as The Empress, and like her wears a green wreath. His countenance too has more than traces of the femininity that appears in Key 3. Furthermore, the sign Cancer is attributed to Key 7, and this is a feminine sign, ruling the breast of woman, as a source of nutrition. The sign itself, moreover, is ruled by the Moon, represented in Tarot by Key 2, The High Priestess.

Observe also that in our explanation of the Vault of Brother C.R., we spoke of the number 7 as a Venusian number. The magic square of 7 has been for ages attributed to Venus. Again, the seventh circle on the Tree of Life, *Netzach*, is called the Sphere of Venus.

In the dualistic pseudophilosophy on which all exoteric "Churchianity" is based, Nature (or the Universe) is one and God is another. In occult and Rosicrucian philosophy, what men call Nature is none other than the *power* of God and is regarded throughout as the manifestation of the Holy Spirit. Therefore, in Key 7, the scene is one of peace. There is no battle—the victory is already won—and the essential meaning of the picture is precisely the same as the essential meaning of Key 3.

4. THE HIGH PRIESTESS
Key 2 (G)

The manifesting power of the One Identity is grounded in the Life Power's perfect remembrance of all it has ever done. Because that Life Power is the Central Reality of every personal existence, every human being has access to this imperishable and perfect record of the past. This perfect memory of the One Identity is the link that unites all personalities, as the characters of a drama are united in the consciousness of its Author.

The letter Gimel means "Camel." Thus, it is a symbol of transportation, commerce, that which unites one point in space with other points and carries news from one place to another. In the Qabalistic system this letter is attributed to the Uniting Intelligence of the thirteenth path on the Tree of Life, joining *Tiphareth*, the seat of the personal Ego consciousness, to *Kether*, the seat of *Yekhidah*, the universal Ego consciousness.

The letter Gimel and Key 2, The High Priestess, also are connected with memory. Thus, we read in the works of Philo Judaeus the following statement about Gimel:

> For the animal while eating its food ruminates, and when, having stooped down it has received a heavy burden, with exceedingly great vigour of muscle it rises up lightly; and in the same manner also, the soul of the man who is devoted to learning, when the burden of its speculations is placed upon it, becomes more lowly, and when it has risen up it rejoices; and from the mastication, and as it were the softening, of the first food that is

placed down before it, arises its memory of those speculations.[2]

5. THE MAGICIAN
Key 1 (B)

Human self-consciousness, seemingly poised between an infinity above and an infinity below, is really an aspect of the One Identity. That One sees through our eyes, hears through our ears, speaks through our lips. Appearances of unequal development arise from the law of progressive change in form. Since the Life Power at work in and through any given form perfectly knows itself and its powers, it also knows that even an incomplete or unperfected form is not a failure. Man judges by appearances and judges falsely because he sees only in part. The One Identity knows all truth because it is—and therefore knows— the beginning, middle, and end of all creatures.

Study carefully this doctrine, in connection with the symbols of Key 1. All of this is a development of the doctrine of absolute nonseparateness. All things are from One. All activities are functions of that One. Nothing for a moment divides the unbreakable unity of the Indivisible Identity.

6. THE HIEROPHANT
Key 5 (V)

The Life Power is ready to impart its higher knowledge to any man. Always it dwells at the center of the Temple of human personality. Always it is ready to speak. We have only to listen.

The Rosicrucian manifestoes say, "We do not seek after your goods with lying tinctures. We are ready, bountifully to impart." And it is written elsewhere that whosoever *will* may partake of the Water of Life, freely.

What then of those who refuse the gift? The Ageless Wisdom declares that they who refuse cannot do otherwise. They are not ready. By this it means that readiness to listen to the Voice of the

---

[2]Philo Judaeus, *Works,* ed. by Bohn (London: Henry G. Bohn, 1854), 1:321.

Teacher pictured in Tarot as The Hierophant is a definite stage in the evolution of human personality. To those who say, "But so much suffering might be avoided if only the Life Power compelled men to listen," the wise answer: "Not so. The essence of the joy of release is that the tears are wiped away, that suffering is transmuted into happiness."

As well ask, "Why can't apples be ripe all at once?" as "Why do not all men immediately turn to the instruction of the One Teacher?" Apples are sour before they are sweet, hard and bitter before they are tender and pleasant to the taste. Men are hard of heart and full of the acidity of ignorance at one stage of their growth. Yet they ripen eventually. In our shortsighted interpretation of experience, we may wish there were no green apples and may wonder why men have to be ignorant. Thus, we lose sight of what is, after all, the real marvel. Fruit does ripen under the laws of its development. So do men ripen under the laws of their development. To find those laws and to hasten the process of ripening, as a wise gardener hastens the ripening of fruit, is the real practical work of the occultist.

7. THE SUN
Key 19 (R)

The One Identity is the Sun of life and light, the spiritual Sun of which our daystar is the external manifestation and symbol. He who would know will understand eventually that his personality has no existence apart from the shining of the spiritual Sun.

In Key 19, the sun in the sky is the actual motive power that enters into all that is shown in the picture. Everything on earth is solidified sunlight. The sun dances in the fairy ring with the children. Solar energy formed the stones of which the wall is built. Sun power was transformed in the work of the stonecutters, the quarrymen, the builders of the wall. Solar energy caused the weather changes that made soil in which the sunflowers and the grass find root, and sun power is in the growth of every plant.

The physical sun in the sky is just a dynamo storing and radiating the universal energy, which is a spiritual energy, taking physical as well as metaphysical forms.

8. THE EMPEROR
Key 4 (H)

The highest manifestation of the spiritual solar energy is the Constituting Intelligence that makes, frames, and composes everything in the universe. That intelligence is an actual presence in every human personality. Every human personality is a center for the expression of that intelligence. This is the real truth about man. A Greater Adept is one who fully recognizes this truth.

He who said, "I and my Father are One" and declared also, "He who hath seen me hath seen the Father" was most explicit in proclaiming what is stated in this eighth doctrine of the Grade of Greater Adept. For he said also: "Indeed, I say unto you, That since you have done it unto one of These the least of my brethren, you have done it unto me." Read, in this connection, chapter 25 of the Gospel of Matthew, beginning at verse 31.

Note that the King James Version mistranslates the original when it speaks of "everlasting fire." What Jesus said would be the penalty for failing to understand and apply his doctrine is correctly translated in Wilson's *Emphatic Diaglott* as *aionian fire* and *aionian cutting-off.* The literal meaning of the Greek original is "age-lasting." And the implication is not at all difficult to understand. If one does not learn the lesson of the age, he has to be put back a grade in the cosmic school. This is painful, and it cuts one off from his natural companions on the Way of Life.

Just as those who neglect their studies and do not pass their examinations are separated from their classmates, so are those who misunderstand or misapply the laws of life required to take the same lessons over again. They fall behind in their classes, and that is punishment enough. There is no *everlasting* punishment nor any *everlasting* cutting-off.

But note particularly the emphasis on the *least* "of my brethren." This is in direct contradiction to all the world's popular estimates, in direct contradiction also to much occult nonsense about the "Hierarchy." When will occult students learn that the Hierarchy is actually no more or less than what might be described as a series of offices, which is to say, a series of positions of increasing responsibility and service? The highest position is that which entails the most extensive and arduous service. And a succession of persons pass through these stations, as men pass through the chairs of a lodge.

But Those who Know are fully aware that the least of the members of that great fraternity—humanity—is an incarnation of the actual ruling and constituting power of the universe, destined at some time or other to sit in the Master's seat and rule the whole Lodge. Thus, all worldly distinctions and honors are as nothing in comparison to the truth that the actual ruling principle of the universe is the central reality of every human life.

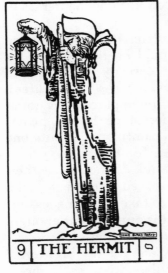

9. THE HERMIT
Key 9 (I)

Thus, the whole work of the Greater Adept is seen to consist in his conscious identification with the One True Will. He recognizes the nothingness of the false notion of separate personality. His clear perception of the nature of the true Self brings him perfect freedom, because he realizes that the One Identity, as master of all, acts freely, and never under compulsion.

The sense of bondage is part of the delusion that has its root in the illusion of separateness. All men are *essentially* free even when they seem to be most completely bound. Yet merely to say, "I am free" does not constitute release. Here is something extremely difficult to express in ordinary language. Yet the sages agree that it is true.

In Tarot, Key 9 suggests it by The Hermit. He who stands on this high eminence, looking down to those who are toiling up from below and holding up his lantern as a beacon for them, is the One Self. He knows their destiny and knows that his own life and light is the moving power that makes them climb. Sooner or later they will be one with him and stand where he stands. Or rather, the time will come when they will know that they are one with him and standing where he stands, as he knows it now.

10. DEATH
Key 13 (N)

Such a one recognizes the necessity for the continual transformation of the outer vehicles of the Life Power. He understands the real significance of the appearance that Man calls death. He is no longer the victim of that appearance, because he has become identified with the power that produces it. Thus, he maintains self-conscious identity through all transformations. He has overcome death.

Do not misunderstand this last statement. The Greater Adept has by no means arrived at the secret of physical immortality, for he is not yet Master of the Temple. What he has achieved is continuity of self-conscious awareness. This includes, of course, what is often termed memory of past lives.

Careful reading of the *Fama* and the *Confessio* will show that the authors of those documents made no claim to having the secret of physical immortality. On the contrary, the *Fama* distinctly states: "Although they were free from all diseases and pain, yet, notwithstanding, they could not live and pass their time appointed of God." The same paragraph says of Brother I.O. that he died in England, as Brother C. long before had foretold him. Mr. Waite, with his usual inconsequentiality, hits on this as a contradiction of the statement made a few lines further on concerning the Book M: "Although before our eyes we behold the image and pattern of all the world, yet are there not shewn unto us our misfortunes, nor hour of death, the which only is known to God Himself, who thereby would have us keep in continual readiness." We submit that there is no little difference between foretelling that one will die in a certain *place* and predicting the exact *time* of death, and readers of these pages who understand astrology will see how true this is.

What the Greater Adept does attain is the power alluded to by the *Confessio* when it asks, "Were it not an excellent thing to live always so as if you had lived from the beginning of the world, and should still live to the end thereof?" Continuity of consciousness is what a Greater Adept achieves. Masters of the Temple, as we shall see, greatly prolong their existence on this planet, but even they do not attain to the state imagined by foolish dreamers who seek the endless perpetuation of their present physical bodies. What a Master of the Temple does accomplish is something higher and better than this.

Both continuity of consciousness as attained by a Greater Adept and the higher attainment of a Master of the Temple depend on control of a force at work in that part of man's body governed astrologically by the sign Scorpio. It is of the control of this force that the *Confessio* speaks when it mentions the powers of an adept as being those of a person "to whom neither poverty, disease, nor danger can any longer reach, who, as one raised above all men, hath rule over that which doth anguish, afflict, and pain others."

What is mastered by an adept is something that the world fears and hates. Thus, an old Rosicrucian alchemical treatise tells us, speaking of the First Matter: "It is set up for the ruin of many and the salvation of some. To the crowd this matter is vile, exceedingly contemptible and odious, but to the philosophers it is more precious than gems or gold. It loves all, yet is well-nigh an enemy of all; it is to be found everywhere, yet scarcely any one has discovered it."

What a Greater Adept learns, by many experiments, is that all his personal activity, which most men suppose begins in themselves, is really a particular manifestation of an unbroken stream of consciousness that links all persons together and unites every person to the One Originating Principle. His first lesson is that his personal activity is at all times joined to the Primal Will by the Uniting Intelligence. He learns too that his waking, self-conscious mental activities are simply particular expressions of that same Originating Principle. He discovers that his brain is an instrument that, so to speak, steps down currents of conscious energy above and beyond his mental level. Day by day he surrenders his life to guidance from above. His organ of interior hearing is highly developed. As he hears he judges, and his judgment is just because it originates in the Eternal Intelligence typified by The Hierophant. Thus, he is one of that company who in China are called "Boys," or "Little Children," a name applied to Taoist sages who have discovered the secret of perpetual youth. He has found that secret, a secret having to do with control of solar energy (in a special form) so as to bring about regeneration. The "Little Boy," moreover, is one with the Father; thus, he is a vehicle for the Constituting Intelligence, which orders all things throughout the universe.

In short, a Greater Adept is a conscious adapter of the cosmic powers by which worlds are built. He works with more potent forces than those under the command of a Lesser Adept, and he is able to do so because in passing through the path corresponding to The Hanged Man he has overcome the illusion of separate personality; whereas in passing through the path corresponding to Justice he has learned the secret of equilibrium.

But the most important key to the meaning of this Grade is The Tower, the Tarot picture corresponding to the letter Peh. This is the Grade of the utter destruction, as by lightning, of the sense of separate personality, so that the adept perceives clearly that his personality is absolutely *nothing* apart from the One Life Power. This perception is the Great Awakening, and when that awakening is complete, one passes on to the next grade, Exempt Adept.

CHAPTER XVIII

THE GRADE OF EXEMPT ADEPT, 7 = 4

HE GRADE OF EXEMPT ADEPT corresponds to ideas connected with the number 4 and with the fourth circle of the Tree of Life, which is named ChSD, *Chesed,* a Hebrew noun variously translated as "Mercy," "Loving-kindness," and "Beneficence." Its literal meaning is "good-givingness," and this aspect of the Life Power is therefore associated with the power of the planet Jupiter. In Hebrew, Jupiter is named TzDQ, *Tzedek,* literally "righteousness."

This Grade is the highest of the three constituting the Second Order. Its name, Exempt Adept, is worth considering. Exempt from what? From the delusion of *personal* participation in anything or in any action—perfect freedom, without the least tinge of the error of separateness. He who has reached this Grade is more than an open channel for the Law that cannot be broken, more than a teacher of that Law. He is a distributor of the inexhaustible Mercy of the Life Power.

In Mercy there is a higher majesty than in Justice. Thus, in ancient law the judges had no recourse from the statutes and had to condemn offenders proved guilty. Only the king might exercise the higher prerogative, that of mercy. Justice keeps a balance, and where accounts are kept there is the shadow of separateness. Mercy gives without stint, even though the Hebrew Wisdom hints that this beneficence is in accordance with measured rhythms: The Qabalah says that *Chesed* (Mercy) is the path called QBVO, *Qavuah,* usually translated as "Measuring," "Arresting," or "Receptacular" (receptive). One English translator renders the doctrine concerning this path as follows: "The fourth path is called the Arresting or Receptacular Intelligence, because it arises like a boundary to receive the emanations of the higher intelligences which are sent down to it. Herefrom all spiritual virtues emanate by way of subtlety, which itself emanates from the Supreme Crown."[1]

---

[1]Arthur Edward Waite, *The Holy Kabbalah* (Hyde Park, N.Y.: University Books, 1960), 214.

The emphasis here is on the receptivity of *Chesed*. A Grade allocated to *Chesed* would therefore be distinguished by this quality of receptivity. The spiritual powers exercised by an Exempt Adept are received *from above*. He himself is a center for the radiation of these powers. The agency whereby he broadcasts them is called DQVTh, *dakkeoth*, literally, "smallness, thinness, fineness." This agency, we are told, itself emanates from the Supreme Crown, that is from *Kether*, the first aspect of the Life Power. *Kether* is the seat of *Yekhidah*, the Indivisible, or the cosmic Self.

Thus, it appears that the work of the Exempt Adept has to do with the outpouring of the powers of the higher intelligences. The medium by which these powers are communicated to those who are the recipients of this spiritual bounty is a subtle emanation from the cosmic Self; that is, the Exempt Adept uses this subtle emanation somewhat as a speaker in a broadcasting station uses the electric current. The energy employed comes from a higher source, as do the powers that are radiated.

In this connection it is noteworthy that the noun DQVTh, *dakkooth*, has the numeral value 510, which is also the value of the Hebrew letter name RISh, Resh, corresponding in astrology to the sun and in Tarot to Key 19. *Dakkeoth*, subtlety, is a technical name for a force used in practical occultism, and that force is actually a form of solar radiation. The word is from the root DQ, *dahk*, "fine, slender, lean." The same word means "dust." In modern Hebrew it signifies "minute, infinitesimal." Try to get a mental picture from these hints. Remember that the thing we are discussing is an actual reality. Metaphysically it is the radiant energy of *Kether*, represented in Key 0, The Fool, by the white sun. But this is not merely metaphysical. It is a real force, properly designated by a Hebrew term signifying "dust," because it is the fine-grained cosmic "dust" that eventually takes form in all things. The work of a Greater Adept is concerned with his control of this subtle something, which is substance and energy at one and the same time.

Three paths lead to this Grade. The first is the twenty-first path of Kaph, beginning in the Grade of Philosophus. The second is the twentieth path of Yod, beginning in the Grade of Lesser Adept. The third is the nineteenth path of Teth, beginning in the Grade of Greater Adept.

THE TWENTY-FIRST PATH

The twenty-first path is called the Intelligence of Desirous Quest. It is so called because it receives the divine influence which flows into it, and through it sends a benediction upon every mode of existence.
Book of Formation

This path is also called "The Rewarding Intelligence of Those who Seek" and "Intelligence of Conciliation." The longing desire that leads to earnest quest has its origin in dim memories of the true powers of the inner life of man. This longing inclines him to make inquiries that bring him the knowledge requisite to attain the heights of realization. The impulse that drives us out of the depths of ignorance and ineffectiveness is derived from the well-nigh forgotten knowledge of what the *Fama* calls "man's nobleness and worth." The intuitive conviction that man is not the slave of circumstances that he so often seems to be is the driving force behind all works leading to real supremacy.

The alternative titles of this path suggest the following:

1. The work leading to the heights is one of reconciliation with the true nature of things. The mass of mankind are estranged. Like the Prodigal Son, they have wandered far from home and heritage. Thus, Lao-Tze calls the work of Tao a "going home"—hence the title "Intelligence of Conciliation."

2. This work is for seekers only. It is not enough to hear the word of liberation. Active and assiduous inquiry and search are necessary.

The adept who passes through this path does not strive to acquire anything. Neither has he any wish to impose his personal will on any other person or even on the forces of nature; for he has learned thoroughly the utter illusiveness of *personal* will, and the knowledge cancels all such erroneous desires. What the Greater Adept seeks, as he moves on toward the Grade of Exempt Adept, is *increased receptivity.* He endeavors to open himself more and more to the divine influx of power. He strives, we might say, *not* to strive. Thus, Lao-Tze writes: "The greatest virtue is like water; it is good to all things. It attains the most inaccessible places without strife. Therefore it is like Tao. It has the virtue of adapting itself to its place."

No life is worth living unless it is a blessing to others. Happiness is not an objective; it is a byproduct of the life of benediction. Fame, fortune, success—these have no savor without happiness, and none are truly happy save those who are instruments of blessing.

This is not mere goody-goody talk. It is simple truth, rejected by many because it is free from all pretentiousness, also rejected because perversions of human opinion have made "goodness" stand for the repudiation of all wholesome joy in life. Misunderstanding of the subtle doctrine of renunciation is largely to blame for this.

Certainly the wise declare that we must renounce "this world" in order to find liberation. That renunciation, however, is not repudiation of our delight in sea and sky and earth, nor by any means a denial of any legitimate satisfaction of the senses. We are warned not to become *slaves* to our bodies, but nothing that comes to us from Those Who Know is any warrant for supposing that our bodies are to be ill-treated and our senses dulled.

What is required is renunciation of belief in the kind of world that is *imagined* as the result of inaccurate and superficial reasoning, based on faulty and imperfect sense experience. This is the world of popular proverbial philosophy. It is the world of those who believe that man is slave of circumstances. It is the world of strife and conflict, the world of personal separateness, the world of "every man for himself, and the devil take the hindmost."

This false world simply is *not*, nor has it ever been. It has no real existence. It is as fabulous as those regions peopled with strange monsters, to be seen on old maps. It is a lying image held in the race consciousness. What we are to renounce is this lie, so that the image of truth may take its place.

The *real* world is a thing of joy, a dance of life. It is a world in which no one finds it difficult to be a means of bringing happiness to others. It is a world of abundance, a world of health and prosperity; and one of the means to knowing it is to awaken in ourselves full functioning of the Intelligence of Desirous Quest.

The practical secret of this twenty-first path is to be found in the final clauses of the quotation that begins this section. In the real world there is no place for partiality and favoritism, no room for sectionalism, no reason for that false patriotism that has been called the last refuge of scoundrels.

Those who would ascend to the highest pinnacles of human attainment must learn that the way to them is one that enables a man to become an instrument of blessing for all mankind. It is a way that levels all barriers of race, caste, or creed. He who follows this way blesses those who suppose themselves to be his enemies just as heartily as he blesses those who recognize him as a friend.

This does by no means make him a namby-pamby "yes-man," always turning his coat to suit the company in which he finds himself. On the contrary, such a man is free from all tendency toward hypocrisy. He has no need to resort to blandishments. He will combat evil as vigorously as anyone, but his heart holds no trace of rancor toward evil-doers.

This path is that of the letter Kaph and of Key 10, The Wheel of Fortune. The fundamental nature of this path is related astrologically to the planet Jupiter, and this planet has its sphere of manifestation through the fourth circle of the Tree of Life, which corresponds to the Grade of Exempt Adept. In the human body this is an influence working through the abdominal "brain," or solar plexus.

The solar plexus is the organ of our psychological rapport with other human beings. It is, furthermore, the occult center of our contact with the memory of nature. Much nonsense has been written concerning it and a good deal of rather dangerous nonsense. To concentrate on the solar plexus in order to "awaken" it (whatever that may mean) to the end that one shall be successful and opulent, in the ordinary meaning of those terms, is to expose oneself to the risk of serious consequences.

The Wheel of Fortune indicates the present stage of development of the mass of humanity by the symbol of the ascending Hermanubis, a human figure with a dog's or jackal's head. These are the "dogs" to whom holy things are not to be given. They are human beings in whom the functions of the brain beyond mere intellection have not yet awakened.

Thus, the figure of Hermanubis is colored red, the color of Mars and physical activity, to show that at this stage of unfoldment man is yet more animal than spiritual and thoroughly tinged with the emotional qualities of his animal nature.

Above Hermanubis, at the top of the wheel, is a sphinx. This is the same creature that represents sensation in Key 7, The Chariot. But there is only one sphinx in Key 10, and its predominant color is blue. This is also the predominant color in Key 2, The High Priestess. Furthermore, the sphinx is a combination of woman and lion, as if the two figures in Key 8 were united in a single symbol. Again, this sphinx has a sword, like that carried by Justice in Key 11.

The sphinx is the propounder of the eternal riddle, the answer to which is "Man." It represents the supreme attainment in practical occultism, the indentification of the inner Self of human personality with the cosmic Self, *Yekhidah*, seated in *Kether*. In that identification all the errors of personality are destroyed with the sword of truth. Furthermore, that identification is a personal expression of a state of consciousness that persists eternally in the cosmic Self-consciousness. For us, however, it seems to be a recollection. When we remember what we really are we are freed from all delusion.

This right recollection, however, is not to be confounded with the silly self-assertion of those who take the mighty name, I AM, in vain. Insofar as popular interest in the I AM has a tendency to eliminate the attachment of false and negative predicates to this name, such instruction is commendable. To say "I am sick" is false, and so is every other like statement. But it is equally false to say "I am success" or "I am health," if one simply parrots the words, or any other kind of affirmations, without having some true *recollection* of what is meant by I AM.

Even *The Pattern on the Trestleboard,* used by those who have received instruction from the sources represented by this book, does more harm than good if it is regarded as a set of statements applicable to human personality that has advanced no farther on the Way of Return than the stage represented by Hermanubis on Key 10. Let it then be stated, and this is an acid test, that the use of these or any other "I am" statements to establish *personal* poise, or gain *personal* advantages of any sort whatever, is a grave misuse of what is known in occultism as the "Power of the Word."

What the Greater Adept seeks, as he traverses the twenty-first path, is a realization of what is symbolized by Key 10. This is the truth that even the least manifestation of the Life Power, anywhere and at any time, is related to every other manifestation. Nothing happens by itself. All that has gone before is focused in the event of this moment, and that event has its share in all that is to come. There is not the least break in the continuity of the Life Power's expression of its potencies.

Thus, the Life Power never forgets anything. We seem to forget, but this is because our lives are part of a process of unfoldment. The record is by no means lost, even though we are not yet at the stage of development that enables us to recall some of the details, nor yet at the stage where we are vividly aware of events outside the narrow limits of our present field of sensation. As we do advance nearer the goal of human evolution, that field of awareness expands, and the senses, which now respond to nothing but the grosser forms of stimuli, begin to record the *metaphysical* counterparts of ordinary seeing, hearing, etc.

In this respect occult metaphysics differs from academic metaphysics. It differs also from the various insane systems of mere rationalization that in these days have the temerity to call themselves metaphysical. Occult metaphysics is grounded on *direct sensory experience*, transcending the limitations of physical sensation. Nor must that "beyond physical" experience be confused with any form of negative psychism. The person who enjoys such experience retains the full measure of his ordinary self-consciousness, *but the range of his awareness is increased.* Essentially, he senses those states of the Life Power's self-manifestation that are beyond the physical plane. Hence, in Key 10 a sphinx, symbolizing sensation, typifies the attainment of the adept. And here it should be noted that just as physical sensation merely supplies the materials for higher forms of mental activity, so does metaphysical sensation bring us materials that must be worked on by reason and intuition. Some of the appearances on planes beyond the physical are just as fruitful sources of delusion, if they are accepted at face value, as are the experiences we get through physical sensation. It is a great mistake to suppose that the awakening of the metaphysical senses gives us immediate access to unadulterated truth.

For example, if the metaphysical sense of hearing is awakened, one is just as likely to hear the "voices" as the "Voice." In fact, one does hear the "voices" and must learn to distinguish them from the "Voice." The "voices" are auditory perceptions of the thoughts in the minds of personalized centers of the Life Power. The "Voice" is the auditory perception of the thought in the mind of the One Self.

Not all the voices are false. Some of them bring us the thoughts of very advanced and wise personalities. Some of them reveal to us the wisdom of that order of nonhuman personalities that are often termed angels. But all we receive from any of these voices has to be tested most critically.

The same principle holds good of other forms of metaphysical sensation. Just because we begin to see beyond the limits of the physical plane is no guarantee that we have any better apprehension of truth. On the contrary, truth—essential truth—may be discerned by persons who have had no metaphysical experience whatever. And unless one does apprehend essential truth before the inner sensorium begins to be active, one is more likely to go astray if he becomes, say, clairvoyant, than if his higher vision never manifested itself.

A Greater Adept, of course, has had long training in the use of reason and intuition. Hence, the expansion of his field of sensation is attended by none of the dangers exposed in the foregoing paragraphs.

Furthermore, he develops his metaphysical senses for a specific purpose. It is necessary for him to be able to come into rapport with persons whose location in space may be far distant from the place occupied by his own physical body. In order to act as a conscious channel for distributing the divine influence, he must be able to direct that influence toward others. His help must be specific as well as general. Thus, he develops the occult powers of his Jupiter center, so that he becomes one of those described in the *Fama* as cognizant of the secrets of persons living in distant places.

A Greater Adept, as he advances toward the Grade of Exempt Adept, is careful never to become an occult Paul Pry. Nor does he ever interfere with the freedom of others. But he becomes aware of those who need his aid and is able to help them, pouring out the force he derives from higher levels to those with whom he is connected by occult ties that his work as a Greater Adept has enabled him to recognize.

THE TWENTIETH PATH

The twentieth path is called the Intelligence of Will. It is so called because it forms the patterns of all creatures; and by this intelligence, when it is perceived, the pre-existent Wisdom is discovered.
Book of Formation

The Hebrew noun translated "will" is RTzVN, *rawtsone*, signifying grace, favor, delight, acceptance, satisfaction, graciousness, and good will. The number of the word is 346, equivalent to MQVR, *mawkore*, literally, something dug, and thus a spring, a well. Another word having the number 346 is TzNVR, *tsinnoor*, from a root meaning to be hollow, and signifying a water pipe, a canal, or a channel. Both of these words have to do with the ideas of the finding of water and its transmission. Thus, they are connected with the occult theory of will power, which has much to do with the discovery and transmission of the "watery" aspect of the One Energy.

The letters of RTzVN (and of TzNVR) also relate to a Qabalistic formula for the four elements. R is the alphabetical symbol for the fire of the sun; Tz stands for Aquarius, the fixed air sign; V for Taurus, an earth sign; and N for Scorpio, a water sign. Three of the letters in the word thus relate to fixed signs of the zodiac, represented by the mystical animals of Ezekiel, shown in the corners of Tarot Keys 10 and 21. The other letter, R, may be taken as corresponding to Leo, since that sign is the zodiacal house of the sun, and the sun is attributed to R.

The idea intended is that what Qabalists call Will is a synthesis of the elemental powers. These powers also are represented by the word IHVH, a verbal symbol of the One Reality, which was, is, and will be. This synthesis is referred to in Key 9, The Hermit, where it is represented by the six-rayed star in the lantern. This star is a key to the alchemical symbolism of the four elements, and it also suggests (as do the correspondences of the letters in RTzVN and TzNVR) that the cosmic Will-force is manifested in the radiant energy of the heavenly bodies.

We are told that the Intelligence of Will forms the patterns of all creatures. The purposes of the One Life are worked out by the synthesis of elemental forces. The forms taken by these forces are determined by mental patterns that subsist in mental space during the entire cycle of cosmic expression. They subside during the period of rest which Hindus call "the Night of Brahma," but they come into manifestation again when a new cycle begins.

Thus, the twentieth path logically connects *Tiphareth*, the seat of imagination, with *Chesed*, the seat of memory and the sphere that represents the outpouring of the divine influence. As it descends on the Tree of Life, this influence flowing from *Chesed* takes form in the images formulated in *Tiphareth*; but on the Way of Return, which is also the Way of Advancement through the Rosicrucian Grades, the twentieth path begins in *Tiphareth* and ends in *Chesed*. That is to say, he who seeks to reach the Grade of Exempt Adept will utilize the power of mental imagery developed in his Lesser Adeptship. But now he proceeds from images to the discovery of the power behind them. Students of Patanjali's *Yoga Sutras* will see here something corresponding to the third aphorism in Book III: "When the perceiving consciousness in this meditation is wholly given to illuminating the essential meaning of the object contemplated, and is freed from the sense of separateness and personality, this is contemplation *(samadhi)*."[2]

One attends first to some thing, event, or object. Apparently the thing is outside oneself, but discriminating study leads to the discovery that the real object of attention is always a mental image within the mental space of the person engaged in concentration. Practice enables us to keep this mental image at the center of the field of attention for a long time. Gradually, this exercise frees us from the delusion of separateness, and the inner essence of the image contemplated is revealed to us. That inner essence is always the divine influence from above that is focused in the Receiving Intelligence of *Chesed*.

He who is advancing into the Grade of Exempt Adept must identify himself with the One Will represented in Key 9 by The Hermit. He then sees that the only Willpower is the Divine Willpower. Thereafter logic forces him to say, as did Jesus, "I seek not mine own will but the will of the One sending me." Note that the Authorized Version interpolates the word *Father* in this verse. The literal translation of the original Greek is "the will of the One sending me."

---

[2]Patanjali, *Yoga Sutras*, translated by Charles Johnston (New York: The Quarterly Book Department, 1922), 95.

In this surrender of personal will there is nothing of the dramatic sacrifice imagined by persons who are yet under the delusion that there is any such thing. One simply sees the truth of the matter, and that is all there is to it. There is nothing emotional about it. One might as well be excited about giving up the delusion that telegraph poles are rushing past the window of a train.

On the other hand, it must not be supposed that as one reaches adeptship one becomes colder and colder. Tarot Key 9, to be sure, shows The Hermit standing on an icy peak, but it should be noted that he is warmly and comfortably clad. The abstractions by which intellect is forced to express what little it can of this high order of knowing are certainly cold enough. The experience thus feebly set forth in words is anything but cold. One does not get dramatically wrought up over the giving up of personal will; but the depth of emotion stirred by the perception of the true nature of the One Will is indicated by the Oriental name for that perception—"Bliss Absolute." Think of the most blissful moment in all of your experience and multiply that by infinity. Even then you will fall short of the bliss of this direct knowledge of the One Will.

The perception of the real nature of Will identifies it with the Original Energy from which all things proceed. What we feel in ourselves as volition is the movement of that Energy. The importance of perceiving this (at first intellectually and later in another order of experience) is that the perception brings about an entirely new understanding of the nature and potency of will.

Eliphas Levi says truly that all magic is in the will, but neither Levi nor any other adept has ever supposed will power to be something merely personal. As a magician identifies his volition with the Cosmic Will, his words become "Words of Power," his thoughts work subtly to achieve extraordinary results, and his deeds take on the appearance of miracles.

The keynote of this magical attunement to reality is to be found in the original meanings of the noun *rawstone*—"delight, acceptance." A magician does not attempt to coerce life. He has nothing to do with the nonsensical endeavors of some modern movements, which provide their dupes with affirmations guaranteed to make the Life Power assume any particular form that happens to strike the fancy of the seeker of personal benefits. A real magician has learned to accept life, not at its face value, but as it really is. He works with formulas, to be sure. There are genuine words of power, genuine magical invocations, genuine and specific methods for making manifest the hidden potencies of the Life Power. Without exception, however, they are methods whose efficacy is to be found in the fact that they express the magician's total and delighted *obedience* to the real nature behind the veil of appearances.

The two words, *mawkore* and *tsinnoor*, which are connected by number with *rawtsone,* and signifying, respectively, a "well" and a "water-course," show the nature of true magical practice. A magician digs down deep into the recesses of his own innermost nature. There he finds an unfailing source of the Water of Life, the fluidic energy that can mold itself through mental imagery into any conceivable form. The adept then looks upon himself as being merely a channel through which this energy is carried out into external expression.

He himself does nothing, for there is actually nothing for him to do. He is a practical Qabalist in the strict sense of the word. He practices reception. He opens himself without reserve to the flow of the One Life through the channel of his personality. He sees that he has no will other than the Will of the One Reality. It is not that he sets aside his own will in order that a higher will may take its place. It is rather that he perceives the absolute nonexistence of any will but that of the Original Energy.

He is like a person who is offered a sum of money on condition that he empty his pockets of counterfeits. The counterfeits are not money at all. There is no loss in throwing them away. They were never what they seemed to be. Neither is the false sense of personal will anything but a counterfeit. It is no sacrifice to dispense with it. There is none of the false humility so often expressed by the phrase "Thy Will be done." As most persons use these words, they are nothing but a defense for lazy ineffectiveness, a cowardly expression of the will to fail. A true magician takes delight in things as they really are. He accepts the universe joyously, not in a spirit of martyrdom and false resignation. He knows that the One Will is done, eternally, and that nothing else is volition at all.

THE NINETEENTH PATH

The nineteenth path is called the Intelligence of the Secret of all Spiritual Activities. It is so called because of the influence spread by it from the most high benediction and the most high glory.
Book of Formation

The original meaning of the word SVD, *Sod,* translated "secret" in this quotation, is "seat." Thus, the title of this path might be rendered as "Intelligence of the Seat of all Spiritual Activities." The suggestion is that in this path there is revealed the basis or foundation of all manifestations of the cosmic Life-breath.

In the Bible, the word translated "influence" occurs but once and is rendered "abundance." "They shall suck the abundance of the seas" (Deut. 33.19). We shall find the same word again in connection with the eighteenth path. It will then be seen that this influence flows down from the highest and innermost sources of being.

Those innermost sources are represented by the word *benediction* (or *blessing*) and *glory*. These are technical terms of the Qabalah. The first refers particularly to *Chokmah*, the second aspect of Reality. The second, from one point of view, refers to the whole system of thirty-two paths, and from another is a reference to the "heart," or "innermost."

The great secret of the nineteenth path is that of the combination of the occult elements fire and water. For the path connects *Chesed*, said to be watery in nature and ruled by rain-giving Jupiter, to *Geburah*, said to be fiery and ruled by Mars, a fiery planet. The word SVD, *Sod*, also gives a similar intimation, for its first letter, Samekh, corresponds to the fiery sign Sagittarius; its second letter, Vav, is the Hebrew conjunction "and"; and its third letter, Daleth, represents Venus, born from the foam of the sea. In the symbolism of Key 8, Strength, the woman is a symbol for water, and the lion is a symbol for fire.

It is hardly necessary to say that neither the water nor the fire are the ordinary physical elements bearing those names. Occult use of these terms is based always on similarity of qualities.

Occult water is something characterized by fluidity, by wavelike motion, by the formation of currents, tides, and whirlpools, and by its tendency to run downhill, that is, from higher to lower levels of expression. It is sometimes called "astral fluid," and sometimes "first matter." Its first representation in Tarot is the flowing robe of The High Priestess, but it is also suggested by the icy mountain peaks in the background of Key 0, and its presence is implied by the rich fertility of the garden in Key 1. Similarly, such rich verdure as is to be seen in the valley pictured in Key 8 could not exist without abundance of water.

Occult fire, on the other hand, is that aspect of the One Cosmic energy that has qualities similar to fire, of which the chief is its power of disintegrating and consuming physical forms. The quality of radiation is also another characteristic of occult fire, as of physical heat.

In the nineteenth path, as illustrated by Key 8, we see the occult fire in its animal aspects under the control of occult water in its human aspects. Thus, this path is said to spread the influence represented by Key 7 and the eighteenth path of *Cheth*. What is represented by Key 8 is the means by which the descent of power from above down to the human level is continued and spread by its further descent through the human level into the animal, vegetable, and mineral worlds.

It is an ancient Qabalistic doctrine that the archetypal Adam was created before the universe was formed. This means that the human level of consciousness, or of the manifestation of the Life Power, was an actuality before human beings were brought into manifestation on the upward arc of evolution. It is not that the characteristically human level of consciousness began to exist only when the first human beings were differentiated from lower types of organisms; rather is it true that the human level of consciousness began then to find expression through physical organisms. Similarly, the levels of consciousness beyond our present human average of expression *already are realities*, but they cannot be manifested through human beings unless those human beings transform their physical bodies into vehicles capable of integrating these higher orders of life activity.

To this transformation of man by himself is addressed what is called the Great Work. It is accomplished by the recognition of the law typified in Key 8. That law is also symbolized by the Hebrew letter Teth, whose shape suggests what its name signifies—a serpent. The law in question is the law of vibration and transformation, which the ancients represented by the serpent symbol. In the use of that law we apply the power they called the "serpent power," known in Tibetan occultism as *Fohat*, which has been described as "vital electricity."

This *Fohat* is a power like water in that it moves in currents and like fire in that it has a tendency to disintegrate and consume physical form. It is that to which alchemists refer when they assert, "We burn with water." It is by the control and regulation of this power that all works of practical occultism are accomplished. Such control depends primarily on grasp of the law symbolized by Key 8. In the description of the nineteenth path this is said to be the secret of *all* spiritual activities or works. To understand this correctly we must remember that occultism recognizes no activities but those of the One Spirit. Therefore, the secret applies to all activities whatsoever.

Briefly and in the most general terms, it is the law that in its self-expression through action and form the energy of the Life Power always descends from higher potentials to lower ones. The practical application to human life is that the normal and natural order of the operation of this power brings about the control of all modes of activity below the human level through the agency of human subconsciousness, when that is under the direction of human self-consciousness. For this reason there is placed over the head of the woman in Key 8 the same symbol that is over the head of the man in Key 1. It is as if his power and royalty had been transferred to her.

It may seem that no very startling truth has been advanced in these last few paragraphs. Yet it is really the one truth which, when it is *lived*, constitutes the difference between an adept and the average human being. It is even literally true in the terms presented by the symbolism of Key 8. He who understands that the human level of consciousness is naturally and rightfully master of all lower levels is soon able to subdue the most savage wild animals, and without cowing them by cruelty.

It is a commonplace of occult knowledge that no wild animal will harm an adept. Thus, we have the story of Daniel in the lion's den. Note that this story is closely related to the story of the three youths in the fiery furnace, another example of control of the power of fire.

He who has trained his subconsciousness so that it holds no tinge of fear of any form of animal life and no fear of anything in the subhuman levels of his environment becomes master of all things whatsoever. The elimination of fear is achieved by the culture of courage, which must have a rational basis if it is to meet all tests. That basis is afforded by calm, earnest and often-repeated meditation on the abundant evidence that the higher, intenser levels of life activity have power to impose their qualities and characteristics on the lower, less intense levels. The Bible sums up the matter when it says that man was made to have dominion over all things. Between reading or hearing this declaration, however, and *realizing* it so as to put it into practice, there intervenes a period of training.

This training is not devoted to making man's power to control his environment a fact. It is already a fact and has been so always. The training is aimed at developing adequate recognition of this power and then devising practical, constructive methods for making use of it so as to bring about results favorable to man's welfare and happiness.

The occult teaching is that wild beasts attack, injure, and kill man because he exercises his control over them negatively. Recently it has been ascertained that fear releases adrenalin into the bloodstream and that this substance gives off an odor, imperceptible to the human sense of smell, that infuriates the lower animals. Thus, man's fear actually incites the animal impulse to attack. If he is fearless, they will not harm him. And it should be remembered that the adrenalin odor is not the only product of fear. Subtler impulses pass from human to subhuman levels and condition subhuman responses.

Man is always superior to the forces below him, but by inverting the mental states by which he controls these forces, he produces the appearance that he is subject to what he really rules. Even these negative conditions are evidences of his rulership. Occult training, therefore, consists largely in man's own reeducation with respect to the nature and scope of his powers. It does not aim at the acquisition of these powers but rather at their intelligently directed use.

DOCTRINES OF THE GRADE

The title of this Grade, Exempt Adept, indicates that he who has reached this stage of advance through the Grades of the Order is freed from certain necessities that fall to the lot of those in lower Grades. He who has reached this point of occult development no longer has to struggle to maintain consciousness of identity with the One Reality. He is freed also from the need for certain kinds of practice.

In other words, he is exempt from the delusion that he does anything of himself, exempt from the error that he ever acts from his "own" initiative. This does not mean that he is inactive—far from it. He may be and usually is a very active human being, engaged in many great enterprises. Yet he is free from all personal concern as to the outcome of these enterprises, because it has become second nature for him to regard even those activities in which the functions of his personality are most closely involved as being in reality expressions of the cosmic life to which the word *own* can never be correctly applied.

The doctrines of the Grade all emphasize this, even the fact that the fourth circle on the Tree of Life is called the Sphere of Jupiter, because Jupiter in Tarot is associated with Key 10, The Wheel of Fortune, symbol of the wheels within wheels of interlocking activity from which the motive power for all human actions proceeds. The doctrines of the Grade are derived from the letters and Tarot Keys spelling the words *Chesed* and *Qavuah*, or "Mercy" and "Receiving." The seven doctrines are as follows:

1. THE CHARIOT
Key 7 (Ch)

The I AM does nothing, for the I AM is the One Identity called "God," and God is changeless. That One Identity is the witness of activity, but is not itself modified or altered by the transformations that go on around it. All change, all modification, is in the field of energy that revolves around the I AM. The Self does nothing. It never has done anything. It is simply the witness of the panorama of transformations proceeding from its own mysterious power.

2. TEMPERANCE
Key 14 (S)

All circumstances are gifts from the Almighty. Personality is the instrument of the One Self. Every detail of our daily experience is a good gift from the One Source. There can be no evil gift from the One Giver of All Good.

3. THE EMPRESS
Key 3 (D)

To know that all circumstances are gifts from the One Identity is to free subconsciousness from every erroneous image of terror, lack, hatred, sorrow, or mistrust. Whatever external appearances may be, they are invariably veils of manifestation for the Divine Beneficence. Hope, courage, happiness, and joy are fruits of the spirit, the expressions of accurate measurement of the facts of experience.

4. THE MOON
Key 18 (Q)

The Self never changes. Personality undergoes continual transformations. The changeless perfection of the I AM is manifested as organic perfection in the body of an Exempt Adept. Such a one is a New Creature, offering the Life Power an adequate vehicle for its beneficence.

5. THE MAGICIAN
Key 1 (B)

These organic changes are the result of conscious intention and long practice. They do not come about as the outcome of the general averages of evolution. They are acquired characteristics, not transmissible by heredity. "Flesh and blood cannot inherit the Kingdom of God."

6. THE HIEROPHANT
Key 5 (V)

The personal effort involved in the intention and practice that bring about these changes requires the supervision of the Superconscious Self. "No man comes to the Father save through the Son" means just this. Unless we hear the Word and obey it, we cannot live the life that will transform us by the renewing of our minds.

7. THE DEVIL
Key 15 (O)

The Exempt Adept fears no appearance of evil. He has reached the point where it is safe for him to look evil in the face. No appearance of evil arouses in him the least trace of antagonism. He regards every semblance of evil as an opportunity for the demonstration of good. He by no means passively accepts evil conditions, nor does he deny the relative reality of any evil appearance. He knows all appearances of evil as unfinished expressions of good, and thus he transforms evil by discovering in it the good toward which it is moving.

To this last doctrine it may be objected that we have high scriptural authority for occupying our minds with thoughts of things pure, holy, and of good report. Yet it must be remembered that here we are speaking of an adept of high Grade. He never refuses to examine appearances of evil, for he has power to see through them. The scriptural admonition is for beginners. Advice intended for tyros is not necessarily good advice for experts. Beginners are not strong enough to look on the face of evil. They are frightened by it. They are aroused to antagonism by it. Thus, they must occupy themselves with thoughts that will bring out constructive reactions.

The consideration of seeming evils does bring out constructive reactions from an Exempt Adept's subconsciousness. In consequence of his perfect freedom from the erroneous interpretations that give most of the world so much trouble, an Exempt Adept enjoys an extraordinary degree of subconscious creative power. This is in accordance with what is said in the third doctrine of this Grade. An Exempt Adept's subconsciousness presents him with nothing but constructive, courageous, happy, and *accurate* imagery, for he now reaps the fruits of work done in lower Grades. In those Grades he planted the seed. Now he has the harvest.

An Exempt Adept is strong. He welcomes the consideration of problems that would terrify weaker and less experienced men. Indeed, he is always on the lookout for them. Yet you will never find an Exempt Adept playing the censor or holding up his hands in holy horror. He is utterly free from that ignorant and destructive emotion. This does not mean that he passively accepts evil conditions. It does mean that his mind is so habituated to constructive imagery that he finds in every appearance of evil an immediate stimulus to the mental creation of its opposite. He is therefore really more *against* evil than any other type of human being. The difference is that he is *scientifically* against it, and he applies the only remedy that will get rid of evil appearances. He does not make the mistake of denying the actuality of the evil appearance itself. He knows perfectly well that it looks as it does and wastes none of his time in the silly "denials" affected by some schools of pseudometaphysicians. He goes to the root of the matter, not for a moment judging by appearance, and thus really overcomes evil by good.

Further comment on the doctrines of this Grade seems both unwise and unnecessary. They are here set forth as they were received, but it should be understood that they are doctrines *received* and by no means represent the level of conscious realization attained by the writer of this book. It would take an Exempt Adept to write accurate comment, and such comment would be sure to be misunderstood by any but others who had reached the same Grade.

That these doctrines have been put into words at all is due to the "unlooked-for graciousness," as the *Confessio* puts it, of one who knows them and understands their many implications. It is for us to take what advantage we can of this example of the quality of beneficence that is the special characteristic of this Grade.

CHAPTER XIX

THE GRADE OF MAGISTER TEMPLI, 8 = 3

OW WE COME TO THE THREE Grades composing the Third (innermost) Order of the Rosicrucian Fraternity. If it has been difficult to write adequately concerning the Grades of the Second Order, how much harder must be an endeavor to expound the august mysteries of the Third! Let it be understood then that what is given here is only what has been received. There is no claim to the revelation of inner secrets.

The Grade of Magister Templi, 8 = 3, corresponds to the Qabalistic meanings of the number 3, represented on the Tree of Life by the third circle, named BINH, *Binah*, Understanding. This Sephirah is known also as the Sphere of Saturn, or field for the manifestation of Saturn; and it is likewise known as the Root of Water. In the alchemical symbolism of *The Book of Purifying Fire*, it is associated with the principle Salt and the alchemical "metal" Tin.

This last attribution appears to contradict the attribution of the third circle to the Sphere of Saturn, but the reader will be well-advised to pause before coming to the conclusion that such a contradiction really exists. It may well be that there is a sense in which alchemical Tin *is* the field of manifestation, or sphere, of the Saturnine influence. But here it is best to be content with this warning against hasty conclusions.

The Grade of Magister Templi is reached by two paths, the eighteenth, corresponding to the letter Cheth and the Key 7, The Chariot, and the seventeenth, which is assigned to the letter Zain, symbolized in Tarot by Key 6, The Lovers.

THE EIGHTEENTH PATH

This path is not open to the aspirant until he has become an Exempt Adept, though it leads from the circle corresponding to the Grade of

Greater Adept. He who goes this way that leads to Understanding must first have overcome all sense of "my-ness." The conception of unchanging law, unless it is tempered by the realization of beneficence, will not carry him through the eighteenth path. Great as the powers are of one who has attained the Grade corresponding to the fifth sphere, he must be rounded out by the beneficence characteristic of the Exempt Adept before proceeding to become a Master of the Temple. One must be truly exempt from the delusions of *personal* will and *personal* action before one may traverse the eighteenth path.

The Hebrew text of the eighteenth path is very obscure, but the following rendering is a carefully considered translation: "The eighteenth path is called the Intelligence of the House of Influence. From the center of its inmost perfections the arcana spring forth, with the hidden things in its shadow, and the commixture of this inmost reality with the Primordial of the Primordials" (*Book of Formation*).

This path is represented in Tarot by Key 7, The Chariot. In Waite's version, and in that used by the Builders of the Adytum, a city, or collection of houses, is shown in the background, and in the middle distance flows a river. In the eighteenth-century exoteric pack and in Oswald Wirth's designs (reproduced in Papus' *Tarot of the Bohemians*) these details are not introduced; but all four versions show lunar crescents on the shoulders of the charioteer, thus emphasizing the lunar rulership of the sign Cancer, to which the letter Cheth is attributed.

The arcana that spring forth into manifestation in this path come from "the center of inmost perfections." In Tarot that center is symbolized by Key 2, The High Priestess, and this Key corresponds also to the moon, ruler of Cancer. The robe of The High Priestess is the source of the river shown in Key 7. Key 2 represents the inner Holy of Holies, which has been called "the adytum of god-nourished silence." From this source are derived the deepest and most recondite secrets of practical Qabalah. These secrets are never written. Neither are they communicated in the words of any human tongue. Yet the eighteenth path, through its connection with the letter Cheth, is related to speech, the function assigned by Qabalists to this letter. What is meant is occult speech. It is the Word of the Voice of the Silence.

In Tarot the word *Shefah* (ShPO) (Influence), is represented by Keys 20, 16, and 15. Key 20 is a symbol of the fourth dimension, of the plane of being that is above, yet within, all other planes. This Key shows the coffins of personal consciousness floating on the Great Sea of *Binah*, Understanding. The eighteenth path proceeds from *Binah* as we go down the Tree of Life, and the same path leads to *Binah* on the Way of Return. Key 16, corresponding to the second letter of ShPO, shows the Holy Influence as a lightning flash, which destroys the tower of false knowledge. Key 15, corresponding to the third letter of ShPO, shows how man interprets the operation of this same Holy Influence when he knows nothing about it except the superficial appearances reported by the physical senses.

Under this last aspect the Holy Influence propounds riddles to us and presents us with problems. Thus, the sphinxes of Key 7 and the Devil of Key 15 are related symbols. Both represent incongruous combinations of human and animal elements. They are types of the Great Magical Agent, the force employed in all works of practical occultism.

Numerically ShPO is 450, or 10 × 45, representing the multiplication of the powers of the Sephiroth (10) by Man (Adam, *ADM*, 45). The number 450 is also the number of LVChVTh, *looakhuth,* "the tables of the Law." The Law is the *Tora* written on the scroll of The High Priestess. The manifestation of the Law is the result of reactions among the ten Sephiroth composing the Tree of Life. Thus, 450 also corresponds to the words PRI OTz, *peree etz,* "The Fruit of the Tree." Finally, 450 is the number of PShO, *peshah* "rebellion, sin, transgression." In this word the letter P is put before Sh, instead of after it, as in ShPO. That is, the tower of personality represented by Key 16 is put before the liberty of spiritual reality represented by Key 20.

This is the essence of transgression. It creeps into and poisons much of what is offered as occult teaching. It signifies the attempt to determine the action of superconscious power by imposing on it forms built up by the delusive "personal" will. To attempt this is to set about building a Tower of Babel. This is the real black magic—the attempt to force the Universal Life to assume forms dictated by personal minds.

White magic, the practical side of Rosicrucianism and Qabalah, is just the reverse. It makes our world what we want it to be by giving us power to see that the *real* world is already more beautiful, more wonderful, more harmonious than we can possibly imagine.

Reality is beyond all that we can ask or think. It is the satisfaction of every desire, the *actual* satisfaction. The perception of reality is no mental narcotic, wafting us into a dream world where we forget what some call the "harsh actualities." To know truth is to become wide awake. It is to enter into a state of consciousness wherein no good or perfect thing, small or great, is ever withheld from us. This realization brings us into the *real* world—the world of health and of beautiful human relationships, where work is joy, and no means are wanting to its completion. In this real world every moment is an experience of victory, a phase of that eternal success that for ages has been symbolized in numbers by 7.

Key 7 shows the essence of this realization. It is the perception that the Self of all selves is the actual rider in the chariot of personality. This personal existence of ours is but the vehicle for the One Life. To know it as such is to have the consciousness named the Intelligence of the House of Influence.

This knowledge cannot be assumed, and it cannot be counterfeited. We cannot pretend to it, in the hope that by so doing we may reap the benefits pertaining to it. We must make ourselves wholly receptive to the One Will, and this receptivity cannot be simulated. A person may talk about it fluently and even convincingly. His words, indeed, may even lead another to the direct perception itself. Yet he himself cannot become truly receptive *so long as there remains in him any trace of the fallacy of working to satisfy his personal wants.*

The Kingdom of Spirit must be sought for its own sake. They who really put the quest for it before all else actually have added to their lives all things needful. So long as one seeks the kingdom in order to get things, his real objectives are the things, not the kingdom. Thus, he misses both.

In Key 7, therefore, the chariot is shown standing still. Not until one really sees that all seeming activity of the personality results from the outward and downward flow of the Holy Influence of the One Self can liberation come.

The eighteenth path is the channel of the abundant overflow of the activity of the Life Power, taking form as objects. The Life Power takes these forms through the operation of its quality of self-limitation, directed by the rational self-consciousness depicted in Tarot as The Magician. The objects into which it enters are both things and creatures.

To traverse the eighteenth path on the Way of Return, therefore, is to overcome the illusive power of these limitations by learning how to use it. By the work of this path the advancing aspirant masters the destructive force of the Mars vibration, awakens in himself the regenerative potency of the flame of the cosmic Life-breath, and as *The Book of Formation* puts it, "restores the Creator to His throne."

In Tarot Key 7, corresponding to this path, the chariot represents the living temple of the Life Power. The driver is the I AM. He is master of the positive and negative expressions of the Astral Light. The positive manifestation is symbolized by the white sphinx, the negative manifestation by the black one.

The field of his mastery is that of speech. In the occult sense, speech signifies thought as well as articulate sound. A Master of the Temple is one who has learned the secrets of magical speech. He builds by ideas. Furthermore, he knows the vibratory values of certain combinations of sound and the ideas corresponding to them. By his use of the subtle forces of sound combined with thought, he builds himself a body that resists every hostile external force.

A Master of the Temple realizes to the full the meaning of the statement, "Filled with understanding of its perfect law, I am guided, moment by moment, along the path of liberation." He feels within him the urge of that resistless Will that others, of less understanding, mistake for something of their own. He *makes* no plans, but carefully follows the Great Plan, step by step, as it is unfolded to him. He is certain of success. From his earlier experiences in the Grade of Philosophus, he knows that every stage in the cosmic undertaking is a step toward perfect fulfillment of the law of freedom.

THE SEVENTEENTH PATH

The seventeenth path is called the Disposing Intelligence (or Intelligence of Sensation). It disposes the righteous to faithfulness, and clothes them with the Holy Life-Breath; and it is called the Foundation of Beauty in the place of the Supernals.

Book of Formation

This is the path that links *Tiphareth* to *Binah*, and it is to be remembered that in Qabalistic psychology *Tiphareth* is the seat of the personalized Ego, as *Kether*, the Crown, is the seat of *Yekhidah*, the Universal Self.

In the diagram of the Tree of Life, *Tiphareth* is midway between the circle numbered 1 and that numbered 10. It is also the center of the group of circles numbered from 4 to 9 inclusive. This group of Sephiroth, with *Tiphareth* at its center, constitutes in man the apparatus of personality, with the personalized Ego at the center.

In the planetary attributions of these circles on the Tree of Life, *Tiphareth* is the Sphere of the Sun, and the circles from 4 to 9 that surround it are the spheres of various planets. What is meant by this imagery is that the Ego is as the Sun in the midst of the planets. Remember, too, that the ancients knew as well as modern astronomers that the light of the planets is only reflected sunlight.

"As above, so below"—the microcosmic correspondences of the planets borrow their light from the central Self. It is the power of that Self we see reflected in the interlocking cycles of the world system represented by Key 10 and associated in the Rosicrucian and Qabalistic systems with Jupiter, whose field of influence is the fourth circle of the Tree. The activity of the Self is the form-destroying power of Mars, shown in Key 16 and operative within the field represented by the fifth circle of the Tree. To the unenlightened, desires appear to have a life and independence of their own, but the forms taken by desire are really objectifications of the creative essence of the Self. The working of that creative essence is associated with Venus, pictured in Tarot as The Empress and operative in the sphere represented by the seventh circle of the Tree. The consciousness of the Self, knowing itself to be the witness of the drama of manifestation, is the source of all our intellectual activity. It is personified as Hermes, or Mercury, and has its representation in Tarot as The Magician, whose field of operation is the eighth circle of the Tree. And the light of the One Self also is reflected by that mysterious automatic consciousness personified by The High Priestess, symbol of the Moon, whose field of manifestation is in the ninth circle of the Tree.

Remember, though, that they are in error who suppose the Ego in *Tiphareth* (the selfhood that we intuitively locate within us, near the heart) to be something independent, something separate from the Great and Indivisible Self seated in *Kether*. Just as it is beginning to be dimly apprehended by astronomers that the physical sun of our world system is a center for the concentration of energy that must be focused within it before it may be radiated to the planets of that system, so has it been known, but more clearly, by the sages that every personal center of selfhood is a point at which the power of the single, universal Self is concentrated.

Thus, the path of Zain leads upward from the Sphere of the Sun to the Sphere of Saturn, because in traversing this path we depart from the illusion of separate selfhood, which still persists while we are still Lesser Adepts, and arrive at the realization that the semblance of separate individuality is but the effect produced by the One Self's power of *concentrating its limitless energy at any particular point in time and space*. Read and reread this paragraph until you grasp its inner meaning. Here is something that leads the mind beyond the limits of words, and if you will follow the clue, you will discover the secret.

Note that the path of Zain is called "The Foundation of Beauty in the place of the Supernals." The Foundation is *Yesod*, the ninth Sephirah, seat of the automatic consciousness. Beauty is *Tiphareth*, the seat of the Ego-consciousness. The place of the Supernals is the archetypal world of the Qabalists, which includes the three Supernal Sephiroth, *Kether, Chokmah*, and *Binah*, corresponding to the three highest Grades of the Order. It is because the path of Zain leads to *Binah* that its influence is said to be in the "Place of the Supernals."

Its function is to combine the powers of the automatic consciousness (subconsciousness) and the Ego-consciousness (self-consciousness) in perfect equilibrium. All the practical work of a true Rosicrucian has to do with this. The essence of the technique is developed from the theory taught in the Grade of Theoricus, namely, that subconsciousness is always amenable to control by suggestion. By putting this to the test of practical application, we gradually divest subconsciousness of her various disguises (and in the process also divest self-consciousness of its disguises) until the two modes of personal consciousness are in the purified state represented by the two human figures in Key 6, The Lovers, which corresponds to the path of Zain.

This, as the text says, "disposes the righteous to faithfulness," for the righteous are those who have brought their thought, feeling, and action into harmony with the universal order. And the faithfulness to which they are disposed is represented by Key 11 in Tarot. It is serene confidence that *even now, despite all appearances to the contrary,* perfect Justice is manifested in all the complex operations of the Great Work of the Life Power's self-manifestation. The wise do not look forward to a day when Justice will rule the universe. They perceive intuitively that Justice *does* rule and they school themselves to discern its operation, even though that operation may be thickly veiled by appearances.

Men and women who are so disposed to faithfulness are said to be "clothed with the Holy Life-Breath," and this is another reason for the nudity of the human figures in Key 6. They are clothed with Spirit, and the word for *Spirit*, in all tongues, is synonymous with *Air*. They have nothing to hide. In yet a deeper sense such persons are clothed with the Life-Breath, for they are invested with powers unknown to ordinary human beings.

In traversing the seventeenth path on the Way of Return, the advancing adept goes through a series of tests that correspond to the letters of the word *Zain*, ZIN, taken in reverse order. First he must prove conclusively that he has overcome death, and these tests correspond to the letter Nun and Key 13. He then demonstrates his mastery of the powers that enable him to identify himself with the One Will represented in the Hebrew alphabet by the letter Yod and in Tarot by The Hermit. Finally, he passes the tests that show that he knows how to wield the "sword of discrimination." In those tests he is able to show that in his personality exists the condition pictured in Key 6. The perfectly harmonious relationship between the conscious, subconscious, and superconscious aspects of the Life Power, as symbolized by that picture, is an actual state of being for the adept who is about to complete his advancement to the Grade of Magister Templi.

This is necessary, because the "mastery of the Temple" is more than control of the physical body. It is control of every vehicle of the Self, from the innermost to the outermost. From the causal body down to the conditions of what is commonly understood as environment, a Master of the Temple is able to determine every form taken by the Life Power.

You are not to understand from this that he is a "miracle-worker" in the commonly accepted sense. But he has completely identified his personal consciousness with that abstract mind that has its seat in *Binah* and that Oriental teachers usually describe as the Higher Manas and Qabalists call *Neshamah* (NShMH). By identity of numeration, this word *Neshamah* corresponds to *Ha-Shayaim*, (HShMIM), "the Heavens," a noun technically representing the archetypal plane of causes. A Magister Templi has so completely identified his inner life with this causal plane of consciousness that he knows himself to be at all times the channel of the power that does actually control the forms of all things.

All of the forces known to science are perceived by him as flowing outward into manifestation through his personality. All laws perceived by scientists are recognized by him as being in actual operation through his daily life. He goes even further than this. He knows himself to be a channel of forces that no exoteric scientist has ever recognized, and an administrator of laws that exoteric science may never discover. Please consider carefully what has just been said. Persons who are far below the Grade of Magister Templi may *believe* themselves to be vehicles of such forces and admini-

strators of such laws, and their belief is correct. A Master of the Temple
knows what others merely believe, and his knowledge is based on experience.

He has learned the secret of directing the creative forces that are
called "Elohim" in the Bible. These are the seven phases of the One Life-
breath, symbolized by the seven sides of the Rosicrucian Vault. A Magister
Templi understands this sevenfold power and can control the forms taken
by its self-expression. Thus, he is in the position described by Swami
Vivekananda, who uses Hindu terminology and calls the Holy Life-Breath
by its Sanskrit name, *Prana*. Speaking of the adept who can direct the *Prana*
perfectly, Vivekananda says:

> What power on earth could there be that would not be
> his? He would be able to move the suns and stars out of
> their places, to control everything in the universe, from
> the atoms to the biggest suns....When the Yogi becomes
> perfect there will be nothing in nature not under his
> control. If he orders the gods to come, they will come at
> his bidding; if he asks the departed to come, they will
> come at his bidding. All the forces of nature will obey
> him as his slaves, and when the ignorant see these
> powers of the Yogi they call them miracles.[1]

Such is the power of a Master of the Temple, and its roots are in
the states of consciousness represented by the letters of the word *Binah*,
BINH. First of all, he is an absolutely transparent medium for the outflow of
the resistless energy of the Originating Principle. All of his magic is in his
total obedience to the One Law. He is like The Magician in Tarot, who
corresponds to the letter B. Second, he enjoys conscious awareness that his
innermost I AM is identical with the Ancient of Days. Like Jesus, he can say,
"Before Abraham was, I am"; and his power over the forms of nature is the
direct consequence of his inner identification with That which determines
these forms. This is represented by the second letter of BINH, corresponding in Tarot to The Hermit. Third, he has really overcome death,
and perceives nothing in the universe but the perpetual renewal of life
through changes of form. Because he has identified himself with the Cause
of all change, his mental imagery enables him to determine what forms shall
be taken by the forces that flow through him. This is what is meant by the
letter N, and Tarot Key 13. Finally, by the mental states already indicated, a
Master of the Temple is able to identify his inner life with the Constituting

---

[1]Swami Vivekananda, *Raja Yoga* (New York: The Baker & Taylor Co., 1899), 31.

Intelligence represented by the letter *H* and The Emperor in Tarot. He is one with that power in the universe that makes, frames, composes, and defines all forms.

All this is summed up in the attribution of this Grade to the Sphere of Saturn. In ancient mythology, Saturn is the father of all the gods, and in astrology the influence of Saturn is said to be binding, limiting, and productive of form. The Mastery of the Temple is therefore attributed to this sphere, because the adept's control of the condition of his own body and his power over the forms of his environment are all the result of perfect concentration. Concentration is essentially the *limitation* of the flow of the currents of the Life Power, the establishment of specific boundaries, the carving out or separation of form from form.

DOCTRINES OF THE GRADE

The four doctrines of the Grade of Magister Templi are derived from the name BINH, *Binah,* Understanding. They are as follows:

1. THE MAGICIAN
Key 1 (B)

Human personality is a medium for the transmission of the high potentials of the Life Power, working at superconscious levels, to the lower potentials of embodiment in the field of existence below the level of human self-consciousness. A Master of the Temple never for a moment loses his awareness of his relationship to that which is above, nor his awareness of innate power to control that which is below. No appearance ever frightens him. He never makes the mistake of supposing that he, personally, performs any action, or that he, personally, is responsible for any result. He is the witness of the mighty works of the One Identity. Watching the phenomena of his world, he sees everything working out for the inevitable freedom that is the necessary consequence of the Life Power's self-expression.

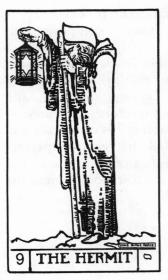

2. THE HERMIT
Key 9 (I)

A Master of the Temple has fully identified himself as being none other than the Silent Watcher on the heights of being. He perceives, with that Watcher, that all activity is a series of transformations of the energy of subconsciousness. He knows that the Self moves not, nor enters into any action. He knows it as the eternal witness of the activities of its own power.

3. DEATH
Key 13 (N)

A Master of the Temple perceives the necessity and the beneficence of the continual transformation of physical vehicles. He sees that this principle of endless change in the world of form brings about the appearance of death. He does more than see. He has grasped the affirmative factor in the phenomena of death. He has "borrowed strength from the eagle" by using nerve currents that in ordinary men have no outlet save through the sex function. A Master of the Temple employs these currents to stimulate certain parts of his brain. Through their functions he gains the knowledge that delivers him from "the body of this death" and gives him joyous freedom from the limitations of three-dimensional existence.

4. THE EMPEROR
Key 4 (H)

Perfectly identified with the One Will, a Master of the Temple shares with that One its power as the Constituting Intelligence that makes, frames, and composes the world. He has taken the full measure of his humanity in its relation to the Life Power. He sees himself as he really is. In that unwavering vision of truth there is no place for any faulty adjustment, either of his personal vehicles or of that larger vehicle of life, his environment.

Thus, this Grade is said to correspond also to the mode of consciousness named "Sanctifying Intelligence." To sanctify is to make perfect. A saint is a man or woman who measures up to the God idea of humanity. God's image of man is free from every flaw existing in the opinions of man held by mortals. Thus, the Hebrew word for "Sanctifying" is MQVDSh, and its numeral value, 450, is the same as that of the word *Shefah*, "influence," explained above. If we examine MQVDSh, letter by letter, with the aid of the Tarot Keys, we discover that the Sanctifying Intelligence, which is the same as the consciousness of a Master of the Temple, consists of the following:

> M: Key 12 (The Hanged Man): A consciousness of perfect dependence on the Life Power.
>
> Q: Key 18 (The Moon): A consciousness resulting from perfect organization of all cell groups in the physical body.
>
> V: Key 5 (The Hierophant): A consciousness of perfect communion with the Inner Teacher and of unquestioning obedience to the directions of the Inner Voice.
>
> D: Key 3 (The Empress): A consciousness fertile in imagery, filled with clear, definite pictures of beautiful consequences flowing from the recognition of the true nature of the Life Power.

> Sh: Key 20 (Judgement): A vivid consciousness of im-
> mortality, and of the state of being we vaguely designate
> as the Fourth Dimension.

It should be noted also that since BINH, *Binah,* includes the letters of BN, *Ben* (the Son), and IH, *Yah* (the Father), this intimates that the Sanctifying Intelligence, which *is Binah,* is a state of consciousness in which the Master of the Temple is able to say, with Jesus, "I and the Father are One."

CHAPTER XX

THE GRADE OF MAGUS, 9 = 2

HE GRADE OF Magus corresponds to the meanings of the number 2 and to the various ideas associated with *Chokmah*, ChKMH, Wisdom, the second circle of the Tree of Life, corresponding to the sentence in the *Pattern*: "Through me its unfailing Wisdom takes form in thought and word." The human vehicle owes its importance to the fact that it permits the flow of the Life Power through it. The Life-force in man is identical with the second Sephirah. It is not a separate force distinct from the other forces in nature. The radiant energy of which the suns are centers, and our bodies transformers, is the *Chokmah* force. It is not only a mechanical light but a living light and a vehicle of consciousness. Hence, life comes from light. Stones are as certainly alive as men, though not obviously so. Our bodies are part and parcel of our earthly environment. Life on our plane is carried on under mechanical and chemical laws, but the substance of things is energy, and all energy is living energy.

Chokmah is called the sphere of the zodiac or the sphere of the "Highway of the Stars," the latter because it includes the relations in the cosmic order established by the Life Power itself. Our way of life is not, however, in the stars but in tune with the stars.

The color of this second circle is gray, the equal mixture of white, the color of *Kether*, and black, the color of *Binah*. This color also results from the balanced mixture of any two complementary colors, such as red and green, blue and orange, yellow and violet. You will notice that the pairs of colors just mentioned are those attributed to *Geburah* and *Netzach, Chesed* and *Hod*, and *Tiphareth* and *Yesod*, on the Tree of Life.

The Magus is one who has succeeded in overcoming the influence of these and all other pairs of opposites. He has perfectly equilibrated all the powers of the lower Grades and is himself perfectly equilibrated between the first and third Grades. He is Wisdom incarnate, and his consciousness goes a stage beyond that represented by the Master of the Temple.

In the Third Grade, the work of the adept has to do with the control of the power called *Prana* by Hindus. It is a control exerted on the form side of life, even though its range extends to the vehicles of the Life Power that are invisible to the physical eye and imperceptible to any physical sense. But in the Grade of Magus the advancing adept is no longer concerned with form. He has arrived at the stage of perfect identification with the Life-force itself.

To describe such a degree of advancement in words that are built up from physical experience is manifestly impossible. Even were I actually a Magus, I could not make this state intelligible to anyone but another Magus. And since I am not anywhere near that degree of advancement, I can only report what I have been taught.

What a Magus really is may be better understood by reference to the words of Eliphas Levi:

> Magic is the divinity of man achieved in union with faith; the true Magi are Men-Gods, in virtue of their intimate union with the divine principle. They are without fears and without desires, dominated by no falsehood, sharing no error, loving without illusion, suffering without impatience, reposing in the quietude of eternal thought. A Magus cannot be ignorant, for magic implies superiority, mastership, majority, and majority signifies emancipation by knowledge. The Man-God has neither rights nor duties, he has science, will, and power. He is more than free, he is master; he does not command, he creates; he does not obey, because nobody can possibly command him. What others term duty, he names his good pleasure; he does good because he wishes to, and never wills anything else; he co-operates freely in everything that forwards the cause of Justice, and for him sacrifice is the luxury of the moral life and the magnificence of the heart. He is implacable toward evil because he is without a trace of hatred for the wicked. He regards reparatory chastisement as a benefit and does not comprehend the meaning of vengeance.[1]

That such a person is truly "more than man," a Rosicrucian phrase, must be conceded. And we must admit that none of us can form more than

---

[1]Eliphas Levi, *The Mysteries of Magic* (London: Kegan, Paul, Trench, Trubner & Co., 1897), 49, 50.

a vague conception of such a character. Yet we altogether miss the point of the Wisdom Teaching unless we perceive that this is no ideal picture of what we may some day become. On the contrary, it is the barest outline of what the real Man in every human being is, now and always.

That Man is the true Magus. He lives this moment in you and me. To reach the Grade of Magus in the True and Invisible Order is to become aware of His real presence in our lives.

Three paths on the Tree of Life lead to the Grade of Magus. They are (1) the path of Triumphant and Eternal Intelligence, corresponding to the letter Vav and the zodiacal sign Taurus; (2) the path of the Constituting Intelligence, corresponding to the letter Heh and the sign Aries; and (3) the path of Luminous Intelligence, corresponding to the letter Daleth and the planet Venus.

THE SIXTEENTH PATH

The first of the three paths leading to the Grade of Magus begins in *Chesed,* the Sephirah to which is assigned the Grade of Exempt Adept. This path remains closed until the aspirant has attained to the Grade of Magister Templi. One cannot enter into the state of consciousness that Qabalists call the "Triumphant and Eternal Intelligence" until all the vehicles of personality have been cleansed and mastered. Indeed, only a Master of the Temple can experience this degree of consciousness.

In Hebrew, "triumphant" is NTzChI (158), formed from the noun NTzCh, *Netzach,* with the letter Yod added as a suffix. *Netzach* is the name of the Sephirah to which the Grade of Philosophus is assigned. Qabalistically, the addition of the letter Yod to this noun is the addition of the *hand,* suggesting the practical application of a ripened philosophy. To make this practical application, one must be master of his own personal instrument. To be serviceable, in order to perform service—that is the idea. A hard lesson this, but one we all must learn thoroughly, sooner or later.

The Qabalistic dictionary says that 158 is represented by the words ChITzIM, *chitzaim* (arrows); ChNQ, *cheneq* (to strangle); MAZNIN (Aramaic), *mozenin* (balances). We find little difficulty with "arrows," because an arrow suggests the penetrating directness of the concentrated magical will; nor with the word "balances," since we know by this time that equilibrium is the basis of the Great Work. But at first glance, "to strangle" has little connection with the idea of the state of consciousness described as triumphant. Yet further consideration will remind us that in every ancient symbolic initiation the candidate had to simulate death. More than this, strangulation is death by constriction of the throat, and this path that we are studying is connected with the letter Vav and with the sign Taurus, which rules the throat. What is really meant is the total eradication of the sense of separate personality. The false belief in "self" must be strangled before the true Self can be made manifest.

Consider, now, the word ChNQ, *cheneq*, in connection with Tarot Keys. Ch is represented by The Chariot, N by Death, and Q by The Moon. Add the numbers of the Keys together and you have 38; by reduction, 11, the number of Justice. The Chariot represents mastery of the vehicle of personality. Death indicates the transforming agency by which that mastery is made effective. The Moon is a picture of the slow process of unfoldment. Justice sums up the whole matter. The equilibrium of the balances is unattainable if the bias of false personality tips the scales. To direct the arrows of volition to their mark is impossible when the aim is spoiled by personal considerations. While yet we speak of rights and duties something of the old error of separateness remains to be killed, and there is something yet of the lie of division to be strangled.

This is the first step toward the Grade of Magus. Until it is taken, the Eternal Intelligence cannot be known. To be conscious of eternity instead of time is to leave behind every vestige of the old, false "self." It is to effect the great conjunction indicated by the grammatical use in Hebrew of the letter Vav ("and").

The picture of The Hierophant sums up the meaning of the sixteenth path. He is the One Teacher of the aspirant who seeks truth. His voice is a silent voice and cannot be heard while the insistent demands of the false personality are clamoring for recognition. The Exempt Adept who has become a Master of the Temple has so perfected the organization of his vehicles of consciousness that there is no obstruction between him and his communication with that One Teacher. He hears the truth that can set him free. Liberation is the result of knowing and remembering the truth.

THE FIFTEENTH PATH

This path begins in the sixth sphere of the Tree of Life, in the Grade of Lesser Adept, for the Magus must be perfected in imagination, and must be able to make definite mental patterns. Yet when he does so, it is not of himself, as in the case of the Lesser Adept. The Magus' vision is the creative sight attributed to the letter Heh and The Emperor. He sees the world with God's eyes, and sees it always, therefore, as proceeding in orderly sequence from that center that is within himself.

This path of the letter Heh is said by Qabalists to be that of the Constituting Intelligence, "because it constitutes creation in the darkness of the world." Qabalists also say that creation took place with the letter Heh. On this point some light may be shed by the "Meditation on Heh" in the *Book of Tokens*.

The Secret Wisdom of Israel says that the fifteenth path bears the name MOMID, *Ma'amiyd* (Constituting), because it constitutes the substance of creation in pure darkness. A hint of similar import is in the Gospel of St. John: "That which hath been made was life in Him [the Logos], and the life was the light of men. And the light shineth in the darkness, and the darkness overcame it not." (John 1:4,5)

The same L.V.X. (i.e., light) appears in Bible symbology under the figure of the Lamb, borrowed from the Hindu symbol of Agni, god of fire. The Lamb refers to the mystery of the cosmic sacrifice. In one sense the wise have always regarded creation as a self-sacrifice of the Life Power.

The first letter of MOMID, *Ma'amiyd*, is that which Tarot pictures as The Hanged Man. Creation is the self-limitation of that which is really limitless. It is the assumption of the illusions of time and space, the apparent differentiation between "I, the Maker" and "That, the Made." But that which has been made, we are told, was life in the Maker. By reason of its own nature the Life Power is creative, yet creation involves the appearance of the Not I. The limitless takes on the form of the limited. The eternal expresses itself in time. The boundless establishes boundaries. The universal enters into existence as the particular. The absolute enters into the conditions of the relative.

Thus, we see that limitation, or definition, is the basis of the Constituting Intelligence, and this is plainly indicated by the grammatical meaning of Heh, the Hebrew definite article, corresponding to the English "the." With the idea of limitation enters the idea of something opposed to the creative power, something external that is the object of that power's mental contemplation. Thus, the second letter of MOMID, *ayin* (the eye), is connected with the restrictive, materialistic influence that astrology assigns to Saturn, and this latter is represented in Tarot by The Devil. We point out these correspondences to assist you in your meditation, but the mere numeration is by no means sufficient. If you hope to penetrate into the profounder mysteries of the occult gnosis, you must ponder these details, earnestly desiring further illumination.

By traversing this fifteenth path, the aspirant to the Grade of Magus associates himself mentally with the cosmic sacrifice. Thus, he unifies his being with the current of the cosmic creative impulse. Levi says, you recall, that he who can master the currents of the Astral Light becomes the depository even of the power of God.

The origin of the fifteenth path is in *Tiphareth*, so that one must go back to the state of the Lesser Adept to traverse it. That is, he must identify himself with the Son, the Solar Logos. In other words, at this stage of initiation the aspirant so identifies himself with the Solar Logos that no shadow even of the sense of separateness sullies his consciousness. This is why he must first pass through the sixteenth path, where the last vestige of personality is eradicated. The least tinge of personal motive vitiates the seeker's endeavor to utilize the cosmic creative energy. To do nothing for self, but all for the Self, is here the test. It involves what the world misinterprets as sacrifice. Thus, the third letter of MOMID is, like the first, explained by the Tarot picture of The Hanged Man.

Again, to be a conscious channel of the cosmic creative impulse is to know the state that Hindus call *Kaivalya* (isolation), for he who would really be a conscious creator must stand alone. Creation begins at a point where there is nothing other than the Creator. All this is set forth in the symbolism of The Hermit (the fourth letter of MOMID).

The last letter of MOMID looks ahead to the path we have yet to consider in this Grade. But let us now consider the MOMID, *Ma'amiyd* (Constituting), as a whole, from the point of view afforded by Gematria. Its numeration, 164, corresponds to ChDBQIM, *chadbaquim*, "ye shall cleave"; ChITzVN, *chitzon*, "external"; and OMDIM, *omdim* (or *ammudim*), "the Pillars" (Jachin and Boaz). The suggestion is that the Constituting Intelligence is one of close union with the Life Power, in which the manifested cosmos is seen as external to the Self, and as proceeding from that Self at the heart of all being. Again, it is a state of perfect equilibrium, understood as the support (pillars) of existence.

To put the matter more explicitly, the aspirant to the Grade of Magus, passing through the fifteenth path, vividly identifies himself with the Great Heart of Life, knows himself to be one with the Great Within from which all that is manifested and external proceeds, and realizes in himself the union of positive and negative, of Mercy and Severity, the pillars of the Tree of Life. We who know only a little about this stage of unfoldment can but faintly imagine what the actual experience is like; but even that dim image will prepare us for the time when, instead of knowing about it, we shall truly know it.

Moreover, two Hebrew words are concealed in MOMID—*Mem*, "waters," and *Od*, "eternity." He who has reached the height of the fifteenth path sees himself alone at the center of the Great Sea of Eternal Subsistence. For him there is naught but the true Self, the Self which is *All*. One of the commonest symbols of this state is that of a great ocean. Boundless it extends on every hand, its circumference nowhere, its center everywhere. These words correspond to no actuality of our sense experience and are meaningless unless one has known the Presence beyond personality. Yet we believe that to most readers of this text they will convey a great deal of significance.

The Fourteenth Path

We come now to the last of the three paths leading to the Grade of Magus. In Hebrew its title is MAIR,*Meyir*, an adjective derived from *Aur*, "Light" and meaning "Luminous."

This path joins *Binah* to *Chokmah*, the Mother to the Father, the root of Water to the Root of Fire. It is the only path connecting the Grade of Master of the Temple with the Grade of Magus and is attributed to the planet Venus.

You are familiar with the astrological meaning of Venus, having learned that it governs the generation of mental images by subconsciousness in response to impulses and suggestions originating in the self-conscious field. Its activity is summed up in the one word, *Imagination*.

Here we may again refer to Eliphas Levi. He says:

> Imagination is actually as the eye of the soul, and it is therein that forms are delineated and preserved; by its means we behold the reflections of the indivisible world; it is the mirror of visions and the apparatus of magical life. Thereby we cure diseases, modify the seasons, ward off death from the living, and resuscitate those who are dead, because this faculty exalts the will and gives it power over the universal agent.
>
> Imagination is the instrument of the adaptation of the Logos. In its application to reason it is genius, for reason, like genius, is one amidst the complexity of operations. Demons, souls, and the rest, can therefore be really and truly beheld by means of the imagination; but the imagination of the adept is diaphanous, whilst that of the uninitiated is opaque. The light of truth traverses the one as through a crystal window, and is refracted in the other as in a vitreous mass full of scoriae and foreign matter.
>
> The things which contribute most to the errors of the vulgar and the extravagances of the insane are the reflections of depraved imaginations in one another. But the seer knows with an absolute knowledge that the things he imagines are true, and experience invariably confirms his visions.[2]

Eugenius Philalethes (Thomas Vaughan) says that he regards the cosmic imagination as being the cause of the great ocean of primordial substance, the chaos from which all forms proceed. "If it [the chaos] be created," he writes, "I conceive it the effect of the Divine Imagination, acting beyond itself in contemplation of that which was to come, and producing this passive darkness for a subject to work upon in the circumferences."

---

[2]Levi, *The Mysteries of Magic*, 66ff.

The adept learns to utilize the cosmic imagination by means of his passage through the fourteenth path. It may be employed safely by none who has not surrendered himself to the direction of the Higher Self. The Tarot hints at this, for 3, the number of The Empress, is the reduction of 12, the number of The Hanged Man. Hence, too, the first letter of MAIR is that to which The Hanged Man is attributed.

What does this mean? Primarily that the only way in which to be sure of using the cosmic imagination in its purity is to silence the waves of personal consciousness, to hold the personal mind in suspension. Thus, we find the books on Yoga defining that art as the subduing of the modifications or waves in the mind-stuff, which they compare to a lake. When the surface is still it gives a clear reflection. Likewise, when we have silenced the tumult of self-consciousness, the Luminous Intelligence of the cosmic mind can be reflected by and through our personal lives. He who succeeds in this undertaking does so by prolonged practice in concentration and meditation. When he succeeds, he appears to have miraculous powers and is able to manipulate the chaos, or root matter, in ways that dumbfound all beholders. Yet such an adept always says, as Jesus said, "Of myself I can do nothing." By stopping the modifications of the personal mind-stuff he lets the light of the Divine Imagination shine through, unobstructed.

The second letter of MAIR brings out another phase of the state of mind called Luminous. Aleph is the Ox, and its primary significance is derived from the fact that oxen are beasts of burden, symbols of patience. The aspirant for the post of Magus must be more than Master of the Temple. He must be ready consciously to assume his share of the burden of creation. To utilize the Luminous Intelligence, one must become a partner with the Cosmic Life.

The third letter of MAIR, Yod, indicates, as shown in Key 9 of Tarot, that detachment is necessary. Seeking for results, indentification with the illusions of appearance—all that partakes of these must be extirpated from the consciousness of the Magus. Yet this detachment is unselfish. The Hermit, although he stands alone far above the others who toil upward, is really actively cooperating with them. He holds up a light for their guidance, and he is concerned only with their progress, as one may see from the earnestness of his downward gaze.

The last letter of MAIR sums up all these that have gone before and is the key to the Luminous Intelligence. It is Resh, letter of the Sun, represented in Tarot by Key 19. "Whosoever shall not receive the kingdom of God as a little child, he shall in nowise enter therein," said Jesus. Childlikeness is the test of mastership. The intensity of the initiate's consciousness that he is truly the Eternal Child of the Eternal Father is the measure of his Understanding and the root of his Wisdom.

We have heard a great deal about the Masters of the Wisdom, about their wonderful knowledge and powers, about the molding of the affairs of nations. From all this we are often led to the conclusion that they must be men of great foresight, in the human sense, great schemers and planners. This conclusion, however, is not according to the teaching of the Ageless Wisdom. All that a Master of the Wisdom practices in his long training has the one object of enabling him to lead a planless life. He is unconcerned about results; he is so perfectly concentrated that neither past nor future enters into his calm consideration of the thing to be done now.

Let none misunderstand us. We do not mean to say that the Masters may not see far into the future, may not be prophets among prophets, knowing the outcome of many currents of activity whose end is not perceived by ordinary human beings. What we mean is that they do not make personal plans, that they have no need for plotting out a scheme of future action, because their whole training has made them so exquisitely responsive to the direction of the cosmic superconsciousness that every moment of their lives is a perfect obedience to spiritual law. Obeying perfectly, they achieve perfect results. This, of course, is true of none but Masters in the highest Grades. Many adepts who are comparatively well known to occultists are, by their own statements, far below this exalted height of attainment, though they are far ahead of us beginners on the Way.

The correspondences to MAIR by Gematria are ARN, *oren*, the noun for a sort of slender fir or cedar from which masts were made, carrying the suggestion of uprightness; and VRIHL, one spelling of *Uriel*. (Compare VRIHL with the *Vril* of Lytton's *Coming Race*[3]). Qabalists call Uriel the archangel of the North, and of the element of Earth, but his name is commonly spelled Auriel.

DOCTRINES OF THE GRADE

This Grade is attributed to the second circle on the Tree of Life. It is named *Masloth* in Hebrew, meaning literally, "the highway of the stars." It is also known as the Illuminating Intelligence (Hebrew, ZHIR, *Zohir*); and to it is likewise attributed ChIH, *Chaiah*, the Life-force.

As an aspect of the Life Power this circle is named *Chokmah*, spelled ChKMH, "Wisdom," and the letters of this word, represented by Keys 7, 10, 12, and 4, indicate four doctrines in this Grade as follows:

---

[3]Sir Edward Bulwer Lytton, *Vril: The Power of the Coming Race* (Blauvelt, N.Y.: Rudolf Steiner Publications, 1972).

1. THE CHARIOT
Key 7 (Ch)

The Magic of Light is the practical application of the science of Reality. A Magus is not a mountebank, nor a producer of illusions, nor a caster of glamour. He has mastered the sphinxes of sensation by the invisible reins of his mind. He has perfected himself in the art of occult speech, so that he transmits, from higher planes to lower, the creative Word of the One Identity. His path of life is one with the highway of the stars. His thought and word embody the truth of Reality as opposed to the lie of appearances.

2. THE WHEEL OF FORTUNE
Key 10 (K)

Popular opinion conceives Magic to be a method of circumventing the law, of going against Nature. The contrary is true. Many works of Magic are exceptions to the law of averages that dominates the average man and the kingdoms of life below him, but these works are exceptions only in the sense that they go beyond the usual phenomena of common experience. A Magus completes the circle of life expression and ascends to the position of unity with the One Reality. His works never contradict the Law, nor do they destroy it. Always they are fulfillments.

Thus, it is that all perfect Magi say with Jesus: "I am come, not to destroy, but to fulfill the Law"; and the Bible story that Magi came to the child of Bethlehem is witness that, guided by their knowledge of times and cycles, these adepts of the Law were glad to pay homage to one whom they recognized as an Avatar, destined to bring to fruition certain long-expected consummations of their ancient Gnosis.

3. THE HANGED MAN
Key 12 (M)

The Magic of Light correctly estimates the place of human personality in the Cosmic order and thus reverses the opinions of the mass of humanity. The Magus is not driven by the false will to power, which is really a feeling of lack of power. He is animated by the will to serve, based on his immediate perception of all power. His one concern is the wise distribution of the limitless riches at his disposal. To the world of ignorant men he seems to sacrifice himself, because he strives for none of the baubles they hold dear. To himself nothing that he does wears the aspect of sacrifice. All of his acts are works of purest joy.

4. THE EMPEROR
Key 4 (H)

A Magus sees eye to eye with the Ancient of the Ancient Ones. He has "restored the Creator to his throne." The Magic of Light is the exercise of the Constituting Intelligence, which frames the universe.

That "throne" to which the Creator is restored is at the heart of human personality, not where error puts it, in some inaccessible remoteness of the skies. He who is a transparent vehicle for the transmission of the Constituting Intelligence through thought and word into the world of action is a true Magus, and all his mighty works are really deeds of perfect submission to the One Identity.

At this point in his progress the body of a Magus is perfectly organized, and thus the great store of Ageless Wisdom preserved in the subconscious level of the Life Power's activity is always at his command. And the marvelous generative and regenerative powers of subconsciousness, which extend, remember, throughout the whole field of this plane of physical forms, are also under his control. With the Magus, the formation of mental pictures is followed instantly by their materialization. He sees water as wine, and wine it is. He sees a sick body whole, and every cell is restored to normal function. Yet he does nothing of himself. He acts merely as the vehicle of the Universal Life.

Such are the first four doctrines of the Grade of Magus. There are also four others derived from the letters of the word ZHIR, "Illuminating."

5. THE LOVERS
Key 6 (Z)

A Magus is a man of discrimination. He is free from the influence of the pairs of opposites, because he has sharply distinguished between these positives and negatives. By keen discrimination between the various polarities of differentiation, a Magus is able to combine them, neutralize them, and transcend them. His liberation comes through knowledge, not through ignorance.

In the consciousness of a Magus, free from the influence of the pairs of opposites, there is perfect balance between self-consciousness and subconsciousness; and these two aspects of human personality are harmoniously related to the superconsciousness, which is above them. The difference between the functions of self-consciousness and subconsciousness must be known, so that there may be no confusion in their proper exercise. Not until these differences are clearly perceived may we avail ourselves of the full power of either level of human mentality. Not until this discrimination is made can subconsciousness become the perfect mirror of superconsciousness pictured in Key 6. The illumination that characterizes a Magus thus begins with acts of keen discrimination.

6. THE EMPEROR
Key 4 (H)

In consequence of this accurate discrimination, which is largely an exercise of perceptive power, a Magus gains the ability to measure all experience correctly. Thus, the Illuminating Intelligence is largely mercurial, or discriminative. One must watch before he can reason. A Magus takes correct measures because he has watched; and because he has watched, he has learned to see.

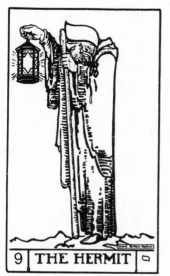

7. THE HERMIT
Key 9 (I)

Illumination, of which the Magic of Light is at once the consequence and the expression, comes about through subtle chemical and psychical tranformations. A Magus does nothing of himself. He is an embodiment of the Will of God. Thus, nothing can withstand him. All things obey him.

In his own consciousness a Magus is one with the witness of all activity. It is not that he exerts himself with great effort to produce this or that result. He is simply the calm, untroubled observer of the play of events that work together to bring about the inevitable success of the Operation of the Sun, or Magnum Opus.

8. THE SUN
Key 19 (R)

There is no self-importance in a Magus. He has become the "Little Child." Free from care, free from the burden of false responsibilities, free from the limitations of human conventions and opinions, he extracts the nectar of wisdom from the experience of the Eternal Now. Thus, it is written that he "has access to the fruition of all desire whatever, at one sweep, being one with the All-seeing Self."

It is noteworthy that this word ZHIR is one of the many multiples of the number 37 that we encounter throughout the literature of Ageless Wisdom. Its numeral value is 222, or 6 × 37. Since 6 is the number of Beauty and represents also the perfection of the cosmic order, and 37 is the number of a word that means "Breath" or "Spirit" and is also, in the Pythagorean Triangle, the value of the angle that expresses the relation of the ascending hypotenuse to the base, we see that ZHIR, or 6 × 37, intimates that the Illuminating Intelligence is the result of the perfect relationship of the personal organism of the Magus to the fundamental laws of life. All of his thoughts are beautiful, all of his words are beautiful; and because action and environment are reflections of thought and word, he is continually surrounded by beauty, and that beauty is contagious. That is the reason why Magi are always healers and teachers. They heal by their presence. They teach without speech. In their circle of influence, ignorance is dispelled, as darkness flees before the sun, and with the cessation of ignorance vanish also all the evil consequences thereof.

What I have said concerning this Grade must suffice for this book, meager as is the instruction I feel able to give. Neither writer nor readers are near enough to the Third Order to make any other course anything but arrant presumption. I have transmitted to you what I have received. When your time for greater knowledge comes, you will find it waiting for you.

CHAPTER XXI

THE GRADE OF IPSISSIMUS, 10 = 1

HE GRADE OF IPSISSIMUS corresponds to the first sphere, *Kether*, the Primal Will, the Crown. Its color is pure white brilliance, the synthesis of all colors. The divine name attributed to it is AHIH, *Eheyeh*, which means "Existence."

Only one path leads to this Grade, that of the letter Gimel. The reason is that *Kether* is the goal of the initiatory journey, and when that goal has been reached, there is nothing more to be done. Thus, the eleventh path of Aleph and The Fool, which leads from the first sphere to the second, always leads downward, and the same is true of the twelfth path of Beth and The Magician, which connects *Kether* with the third sphere.

Ipsissimus, the title of the Grade, means "He who is most himself" and connects with the Qabalistic attribution of IChIDH, *Yekhidah* (pronounced *ya-kee-dah*) to the first Sephirah. *Yekhidah* means "the Indivisible" and is the Hebrew technical term for "Self," practically equivalent to the Sanskrit *Atman.* It designates the cosmic Self, the One I AM that is manifested through innumerable personalities, on this earth and elsewhere.

The Grade of Ipsissimus is that of the Head of the Invisible Order. After our cursory review of the stages of attainment, it should be apparent that the self-appointed "Heads" of the various pseudo-Rosicrucian societies are, to say the least, absurd in their pretensions. For the Supreme Head of the Order is none other than the Christos, the universal Logos. Below Him are the Logoi, or spirits of the separate planets. Among incarnate beings on any planet, the post of "Head" is occupied by that one among the Magi who has attained to the most perfect unification with the Primal Will. No man is appointed to this post, nor elected to it. The degree of attainment is the only deciding factor in his selection. And this degree is judged by no man. It simply *is.*

Perhaps an illustration will help. In any circle of human beings, the dominant center is that person who has the highest degree of self-realization. That person's thought dominates the minds of the other members of the group, even though he may never say a word. Close observation will show you how true this is, even among small companies of people. He who is most truly self-possessed, i.e., "possessed by the Self," is the ruler of the rest; for in his thought there is a strength, a positiveness, and a clarity that impose themselves by induction on the minds of all the others in the company.

THE THIRTEENTH PATH

The letter name Gimel, GML, is the number 73, and this is the numeration of the word *Chokmah*, ChKMH, the name of the second Sephirah, to which is attributed the Grade of Magus. Thus, there is intimated an identity between the Uniting Intelligence of the thirteenth path and the Life Power's perfect self-knowledge, which is *Chokmah*.

In Tarot, too, this is subtly hinted at, because the number of The High Priestess (2) is also the number of *Chokmah* on the Tree of Life. The *Lesser Holy Assembly*, one of the books of the *Zohar*, also speaks of the lesser *Chokmah*, which it says is feminine. In the Proverbs of Solomon too, *Chokmah* is frequently spoken of in the feminine gender, as in Prov. 7:4, "Say unto wisdom, Thou art my sister." To this feminine aspect of wisdom, says the *Lesser Holy Assembly*, that riddle alludes that is given in the Song of Solomon, 8:8; "We have a little sister, and she hath no breasts; what shall we do for our sister in the day when she shall be spoken for?"

Thus, although *Chokmah* is usually described as masculine and has attributed to it the name AB, *Ab* (the Father), it is also, when considered as receptive to the influence of *Kether*, described as feminine. And even when it is called AB, *Ab* (the Father), the numeration of that word shows a correspondence to the letter Gimel, because AB is the number 3, and this is the number of Gimel, considered as a single letter.

The thirteenth path, moreover, conveys to every Qabalist the combined ideas of Unity and Love associated with the number 13, and as all love is typified by the Woman who is the object of love, there is a profound connection between the thirteenth path and the various feminine aspects of the Life Power.

The beginning of the thirteenth path is *Tiphareth*, and the work that is performed by the Magus as he advances through it is symbolized by the scroll of The High Priestess. We draw nigh to the Self by recollection, by unrolling the scroll of memory. Thus, we unite ourselves with the One. In short, as I have intimated throughout this book, the "attainment" of an adept is not the gaining of something that he does not possess. It is the recollection of what he really is, the perpetual remembrance that "the Lord *is* in his holy temple."

The name usually given to the thirteenth path is MNHIG, *Menahig,* "Conductive"; 108. One of the words corresponding by Gematria to this number is ChTzI, *chatziy,* "middle." It refers, in part, to the position of the thirteenth path on the Tree of Life. Through its letters, ChTzI says that control of speech (Ch) through meditation (Tz) leads to the perfect marriage (I) of Consciousness and Subconsciousness, a uniting of subject and object that results in the experience of Superconsciousness. This hints at the secret of equilibrium utilized by the adept during his journey up this path to *Kether.*

Another correspondence to 108 is ChNN, *chanan,* "to favor, to bestow." It suggests an idea often mentioned by the sages, that the supreme attainment is rather by the grace or favor of God than as the result of the aspirant's personal efforts. Yet it must be clearly understood that the grace or favor is not capriciously extended. God does not grant it to some and withhold it from others. It should be realized that this grace inheres in the inmost nature of the Life Power. What is here intended to be conveyed is that this particular aspect of the Life Power, rather than personal endeavors of the aspirant, is what brings about the final attainment of the Crown.

Finally there is ChQ, *chaq* (or *choq*), "a conclusion, an enactment, a decree." It suggests the fulfillment of the Divine Intention by the final stage of the aspirant's journey on the Way of Return to the Supreme Goal.

The full name of the thirteenth path is MNHIG HAChDVTh, *Menahig Ha-Acheduth,* "Conductive Intelligence of Unity." In Hebrew, "Unity" is AChDVTh, *Acheduth,* 419, which is also the number for TITh, *Teth,* "Serpent," the name of the ninth letter, represented in Tarot by Strength. The unity here designated is by no means a colorless abstraction. It is the One Thing "whence all proceed by adaptation, for the performance of the miracles of the One." By letter it is symbolized as the serpent power, by the symbolism of Tarot, as a lion, and it is the *Fohat* of Theosophical writers.

MNHIG HAChDVTh is the number 532, which may be represented by the following words: ABN HChKMVTh, *Ehben Ha-Chokmath* (Stone of the Wise); ABN HDOTh, *Ehben Ha-Da'ath* (Stone of Knowledge); ChMH HChKMVTh, *Khammaw Ha-Chokmath* (Sun of Wisdom); ChMH HDOTh, *Khammaw Ha-Da'ath* (Sun of Knowledge). (*N.B.:* As a clue to the meaning of alchemy—i.e., ALChMH—observe that ChMH, a poetical name for the sun, and ABN, "Stone," are identical by Gematria.)

If you will give a little time to considering the meaning of these four names, you will perceive that the work of the thirteenth path must be closely related to the alchemical operation called "sublimation." The completion of that work is the confection of that which may be called either ABN HChKMVTh, "Stone of the Wise" (i.e., Philosophers' Stone), or ABN HDOTh, "Stone of Knowledge." In connection with the latter name note that the place of DOTh, *Da'ath* (Knowledge), on the Tree of Life is on the thirteenth path, at the point where the fourteenth path crosses it—midway between *Chokmah* and *Binah.*

The "Short Lexicon of Alchemy" appended to A.E. Waite's translation of the *Hermetic Writings of Paracelsus* gives this definition of sublimation:

"Sublimation is purification of the Matter by means of dissolution and reduction of the same into its constituents. It is not the forcing of the Matter to the top of the vessel, and then maintaining it separate from its *caput mortuum*, but its subtilization and purifaction from all earthly and heterogeneous parts, imparting to it a degree of perfection not previously possessed, or more correctly, its deliverance from the bounds which bind it, and hinder its operation."

The Matter is the Astral Light of Eliphas Levi. Yogis call it *Kundalini*. It is the serpent power represented by the letter Teth. Observe that it is not *forced* to rise, for in this statement is to be found an important key to the whole work. The Matter is simply purified from the adulterations of heterogeneity, from the semblance of diversity that it presents to us in its ordinary manifestations. In simple truth this means that the Magus performs the Great Work by divesting the serpent power of all appearances of "Many-ness." Because of this, the thirteenth path is said to be the Conductive Intelligence of Unity. When the work of this path is completed, the One Energy, which presents itself to our senses in the innumerable forms we call "objects," is directly experienced as One, One and Alone.

As we know it here on earth, the Matter is solar force. The Stone and the sun are two aspects of one reality. Therefore, ABN = ChMH. Alchemists agree that the Great Work that results in the perfection of the Stone is an operation of the sun and moon. To this idea the thirteenth path relates, especially as part of the Way of Return. As we climb the Tree of Life, this path begins in *Tiphareth*, sphere of the sun, and is itself, through its correspondence to Gimel, the path of the moon.

To traverse it, one must be a Magus, having full comprehension of the principles of cyclic motion, which are exemplifed in astronomy. Hence, the Grade of Magus corresponds to *Chokmah*, "highway of the stars."

The principle of cyclic motion is fundamental in the cosmos. To understand it correctly is to possess true wisdom. The Ageless Wisdom, applying to the Hermetic axiom, "That which is below is as that which is above," teaches that the same law that keeps the stars in place is manifest in all activity everywhere. The discoveries of modern science confirm the ancient doctrine—particularly those discoveries, so often referred to in these pages, that have to do with the constitution of atoms.

The true magician and alchemist knows how to apply these laws of cyclic motion. Indeed, many of the seeming marvels accomplished by adepts are based on control of interatomic energy, in accordance with these laws. The principles of this control, we may say (although it would be extremely unwise to give specific information even if we dared claim that we possess it), are principles identical with those revealed in the science of astronomy.

To make the Stone of the Wise, so that we may change base metal into gold, we therefore apply the knowledge that Qabalists attribute to *Chokmah*. And when we speak of this transmutation, we are by no means using purely figurative expressions. True as it is that the Stone of the Wise effects a transmutation of consciousness, so that the base metal of sense illusion is transformed into the pure gold of spiritual knowing, it is also true that one who has that consciousness gets along with it a command of physical forces that enables him to alter the structure of atoms. Such a man can make gold, if he needs to, and the ancient Rosicrucian declaration that the Brothers of the Order have at their disposal "more gold than both the Indies bring to the King of Spain" is far from being an exaggeration. The knowledge by which this is brought about is represented by the first two letters of ABN (Stone), because AB (Father) is a Qabalistic title of *Chokmah*.

To make use of these principles of cyclic motion, we must have some specific object. Furthermore, this object must aim at some realization of beauty. So the Qabalists teach, and this they indicate by the last two letters of ABN, which form the word BN, *Ben* (Son), a title of *Tiphareth*. This title, BN, is by Gematria equal to AIMA, *Aima* (Mother), a name of *Binah*. *Aima*, the Sphere of Saturn, represents concrete, definite applications of the principles of *Chokmah*, the Father. *Ben*, Sphere of the Sun, alludes to the idea of beauty, which must qualify these separate aims.

In brief, then, the Great Work makes the Sun of Wisdom rise and perfects the Stone of the Wise. It is a work in which *Chokmah* (AB) supplies the mathematical knowledge of principles, *Binah* (AIMA) provides the specific understanding of concrete application, and *Tiphareth* (BN) contributes the motive of beauty. Thus, the powers of a Magus *(Chokmah)* and a Master of the Temple *(Binah)* are conjoined in an operation that begins at the level of the seemingly inferior Grade of Lesser Adept *(Tiphareth)*. The operator must be a Magus, because one who has not attained to that Grade does not know the secret of True Will, nor does he possess a sufficient command of the Life-force. For True Will and ChIH, *Chaiah* (the Life-force), are both realized in *Chokmah*.

Jesus expressed the mystery of True Will when he said, "My meat is to do the will of him that sent me, and to finish his work." The Will expressed in the thought, word, and action of a Magus is not personal. It is the resistless impulse of the eternal universal vital energy. In truth, the Life-force in every human being is identical with the energy of the One Life. This is the cosmic Life-force, which Jesus personified as "Father," using the very name *Ab*—which Qabalists attribute to *Chokmah*—and following the Secret Wisdom also in this saying: "The Father [*Ab*] hath life [*Chaiah*] in himself." He openly declared that what is hinted at time and again in occult writings, viz., that when we are actually doing the Will of the Father, by letting the universal life energy flow freely through a personality cleansed from all sense of separateness, our work is not labor. We are not fatigued by our endeavors, no matter how strenuous they may seem to other people. On the contrary, work that is an expression of True Will vitalizes us, fills us to overflowing with an abundance of power, really feeds us. Hence, we find Jesus saying, "I have meat to eat ye know not of."

A Magus does not infer this. He does not believe it. He does not hold to it as a conviction, as we do. He *knows* it. His personal consciousness is lost, swallowed up, in complete identification with the One Life. He does nothing of himself. His personality is an unobstructed vehicle for the perfectly regulated operation of the Life Power. His least action, therefore, is a conscious expression of the inexhaustible power of the All. To human eyes he seems to perform miracles. He seems to have developed a tremendous personal will. He seems to have powers not possessed by other men. To himself it is quite otherwise. He knows that the mightiest of his works are simply demonstrations of unchanging law. He knows that he wills nothing but what the Father wills. He knows that he has not a jot or tittle or power peculiar to himself. The difference between a Magus and other men is that the All Power flows through his life into external expression, unchecked by the illusions and ignorance of personal consciousness.

Such a man is Master of the Temple of Spirit—that sevenfold body symbolized in ancient architecture by Babylonian temples of seven stories, by the Great Pyramid, which has a vertical axis of seven units, and also by the seven-sided vault described in the *Fama Fraternitatis.*

As Master of the Temple, he is guided moment by moment by the clear direction of true Intuition. Not merely in times of stress and trial is he aware of the Inner Voice. Whether his physical body wakes or sleeps, he hears always, and always obeys.To other men he seems to have extraordinary foresight. When they do not call him a prophet, they imagine that he is a most careful planner. As a matter of fact, he lives a planless life, and his one rule of action is that of Jesus, "As I hear, I judge."

Therefore, having identified himself with the Pure Source of all life and having so harmonized his least actions that whatever he does, he says, "I am doing nothing," because he lives only to express the perfect rhythms of the All—guided by an understanding that foresees and forewarns and keeps his feet on the true path—the Magus is duly and truly prepared to essay the last stage of the Great Work.

Yet he begins this final operation by placing himself in the Grade of Lesser Adept. The initial processes of this undertaking depend on mental powers peculiar to that Grade. In beginning his last advance along the Way of Return, he proceeds not from the point of view of a Magus nor from the vantage ground of a Master of the Temple but from the relatively simple realization of Sonship.

His starting point is the mode of consciousness called "Intelligence of Mediating Influence." The Hebrew is ShPO NBDL, *Shepa Neobedal.* ShPO is 450, the same number as PRI OTz, *Peree Etz,* "Fruit of the Tree." NBDL is 86, the same number as ALHIM, *Elohim.* The Fruit of the Tree is *Ben,* the Son. Its number, 450, is 10 × 45, suggesting the tenfold expression of ADM, *Adam* (45), Man. NBDL is a formula for the powers of the Elohim. Thus, the title of the sixth path hints Qabalistically that the Sonship of Man makes him heir to the powers of the Elohim. The idea is similar to that suggested by the symbols of The Hanged Man.

Bear in mind also that the letter name, GML, *Gimel,* is by Gematria equivalent to *Chokmah.* This indicates that the thirteenth path has a close correspondence to the specific powers developed in the consciousness of the aspirant by attaining the Grade of Magus.

Corresponding to The High Priestess, the path of Gimel is predominantly a path of recollection and of the equilibration of the Life Power represented by the twin pillars depicted in that Key. To traverse the thirteenth path is to read the scroll of cosmic memory. As the scroll must be read by unrolling it in reverse order, so do the letters of GML, read in reverse, indicate the steps of the Magus' progress upward along this path:

L (Lamed): His faith in his Sonship must be firmly established. He must not only believe himself to be a veritable Son of the Elohim but must also have established that faith by works. These are the works by which the power of *Ruach* (here understood as imagination) has been controlled and directed. All of these practices are aimed at the equilibration of the conflicting elements of personal consciousness, together with the elimination of everything superfluous.

M (Mem): The aspirant also must eliminate all sense of personal action. He must be fixed in union with the One Life. High as are his attainments in comparison with ours, no slightest trace of pride of power can be mixed with his realization that his personality is absolutely and unconditionally dependent on the All.

G (Gimel): In this condition of self-surrender, the Magus begins his journey upward. In no other way can perfect mastery of the power of the cosmic subconsciousness be developed. What this mastery really is cannot be put into intelligible language. Even if this were possible, adequate description would be impossible here, because neither the writer of these pages nor those who read them has reached the Grade of Magus. We can only do our best to pass on what reports have reached us from Those who have made the journey, knowing full well that what we write will fall far short of the truth.

The goal of the thirteenth path is *Kether,* the Crown, The corresponding Rosicrucian Grade is called Ipsissimus, which means "I my very Self." Thus, the Grade title agrees with the Qabalists' attribution of IChIDH, *Yekhidah* (the Self), to *Kether.* The Latin word *Ipsissimus* indicates by its form what we might call the superlative degree of selfhood. It represents the highest possible realization of the meaning of I AM. Qabalists indicate this realization by IChIDH, the feminine form of IChID, "unity." The feminine construction shows that although the I AM is one and alone, it is also conceived in the Ageless Wisdom as the vehicle for AIN SVP AUR, *Ain Soph Aur*, "The Limitless Light." As a vehicle or receptacle, it is therefore feminine.

It is said that there are ten degrees of this Grade in each of the four worlds, that is: *Kether of Kether, Kether of Chokmah, Kether of Binah, Kether of Chesed, Kether of Geburah, Kether of Tiphareth, Kether of Netzach, Kether of Hod, Kether of Yesod,* and *Kether of Malkuth*—all in *Atziluth;* and a like tenfold expression in *Briah, Yetzirah,* and *Assiah.*

Thus, we may reckon forty degrees of this one realization that Rosicrucians call Ipsissimus. It is also said that here on the physical plane (in *Assiah,* that is) there are at any one time just ten human beings in whom this realization of *Kether* is perfected. One has the perfect realization of *Kether* in *Malkuth,* another the realization of *Kether* in *Yesod,* and so on, up to *Kether* in *Kether.*

These ten human beings are said to be the Secret Chiefs of the ten sections of the True and Invisible Rosicrucian Order on the physical plane. Each section of the Order corresponds to a Sephirah, and consists of persons whose basic development corresponds to that Sephirah.

This statement, however, should not be interpreted as meaning that only ten persons now incarnate have attained to the Grade of Ipsissimus in the world of *Assiah.* What has been said is that there are but ten in whom this realization is perfected. These ten are the Heads of the Outer Hierarchy of the Order.

This information, however, can be of little more than academic interest to readers of these pages. It is mentioned merely to give some idea of the constitution of the occult hierarchy. The terms here used differ superficially from those familiar to readers of Theosophical literature, but there is no real difference in the teaching itself.

After all, what is important is that you yourself may gain a flash of this high perception. For from that august Being Whose consciousness is the IChIDH, *Yekhidah,* of *Kether* of *Kether* in *Atziluth,* down through the hierarchy, vibrates the "wavelength," so to speak, of this supreme realization. If you tune in, you will receive as much as you can respond to.

At the center of being of each human is IChIDH, *Yekhidah,* "the Self," the Eternal Center of Creative Activity. It is a center of expression from which all things proceed. It is ThTh ZL, *Tayth Zal,* "the Profuse Giver," the original Source from which every supply comes. In pondering these high ideas, the more we keep in mind that we ourselves are centers of expression for some phase of the activity of the All, the more we shall find ourselves actually able to draw on the illimitable resources of this inexhaustible treasure.

DOCTRINES OF THE GRADE

This Grade corresponds to the uppermost circle of the Tree of Life, named *Kether* (KThR), the Crown, or Primal Will. In Qabalistic psychology, *Kether* is the seat of *Yekhidah* (IChIDH), the Self, identical with the *Atman* of Hindu philosophy. *Kether* is also called the Admirable, or Mystical, Intelligence. The Hebrew is *Pehleh*, PLA, said to be the "light which imparts understanding of the beginning which is without beginning." Observe that *Yekhidah*, IChIDH, adds up to 37, and PLA, *Pehleh*, is a reversal of ALP, Aleph, and adds up to 111, 3 × 37.

The doctrines of the Grade are derived from the letters of KThR, *Kether*, and PLA, *Pehleh*, as follows:

1. THE WHEEL OF FORTUNE
Key 10, (K)

All activity is spiritual activity, and the center of all spiritual activity is the One Self. The Limitless Light, condensing itself in a single point, begins a whirling motion. The Small Point is within. It is the point of consciousness, the center of expression for the One Identity. It is for every human being the point of contact with Absolute First Cause. This Indivisible One depends on nothing whatever. It itself does not act, but from it all action proceeds. There is no limitation to its power to initiate cycles of expression. Precedent does not restrict it. Conditions do not affect it. Contingencies do not modify it.

In reference to this condensation of the energy of the Limitless Light, *Kether* is sometimes called *Nequdah Rashunah*, NQDH RAShVNH, "the Primordial Point." And it is also called *Rashith Ha-Galgalim*, RAShITh HGLGLIM, "the Beginning of the Whirlings," in allusion to the movement set up by this condensation of energy. This "Small Point" is the One Self, or Atman, which natural men erroneously suppose to be isolated within their personal organisms. He who truly knows the Self knows that at this "Small Point" he is one with All Power.

The Ipsissimus ("He who is most himself") is that person in any circle of human society who best realizes the presence of this One Identity, as Absolute First Cause, at the heart of his personality. In any group of persons, the master mind is he who best understands the Self.

2. THE WORLD
Key 21 (Th)

The world for any human being is really the projection on the screen of space and time of mental imagery. This projection is from within outward. Self-consciousness is the lens through which Absolute Reality is projected as relative imagery. Happiness and freedom are ours to the extent that our personal world, or the projection of our personal interpretation of experience, coincides with the real world, which is the expression of the One Identity.

As Van der Leeuw says, in his most illuminating work:

When I take up a book and drop it on the ground only one event takes place and that is the event as it is in the world of the Real. There is nothing unreal about that event, it is entirely, wholly and thoroughly real. But my awareness of that event, the way in which it presents itself in my world-image, is my interpretation of the real event, and that interpretation is only relatively real, real for me, not in itself. When then, in my world-image, I am aware of my hand grasping the book and dropping it on the ground, what really happens is that in the world of the Real an interaction takes place. What appears in my world-image is my version of it, in which version the unity of the event is broken up in measure of time and space and in a multitude of qualities. Then I externalize my awareness of the event itself and *that externalized image becomes for me the event itself.* Unreality or illusion never resides in the event, or thing itself, nor even in my interpretation of it, which is true enough *for me,* but in the fact that I take my interpretation to be the thing in itself, exalting it to the stature of an absolute and independent reality.[1]

Hence, if we remember that the letter Tav represents "Administrative Intelligence," we shall see that to the degree that we succeed in our efforts toward making our personal thought, speech, and action adequate and unobstructed channels for the Life and Wisdom of the One Identity, to that degree will we share in the government of the world.

---

[1]J.J. Van der Leeuw, *The Conquest of Illusion* (New York and London: Alfred A. Knopf, 1928), 31.

3. THE SUN
Key 19 (R)

When the conscious and subconscious phases of mentality are regenerated, or born anew, a human personality becomes a radiant center through which the Life Power manifests itself. The Ipsissimus knows that circumstances are the projections of his interpretations of Reality. He has made this knowledge deep-rooted and permanent. Therefore, his mode of life is incomprehensible to the merely natural man. He is a free channel for the expression of Omnipotent Spirit.

Appearances are against this doctrine. The mass of human beings believe themselves to be the creatures of circumstances. Thus, we have among us all varieties of this ignorant superstition, from the beliefs of primitive peoples who suppose themselves to be at the mercy of malignant spirits of the elements to the equally superstitious notions of the modern materialists who talk learnedly about "heredity," "environment," and the like.

Here it may be well to say that the knowledge that appearances are so largely illusive does nothing whatever to remove the illusion itself. To an astronomer the sun *seems* to rise in the East, just as to a person who believes that it actually does so rise; but the astronomer knows better. To the Ipsissimus, human personality *seems* to be conditioned by environment and seems to be hedged about with various limitations, but the Ipsissimus *knows* better.

4. THE TOWER
Key 16 (P)

The extraordinary works of a "Knower of the Self" are largely applications of the Mars force. Essentially like electricity and governed by similar laws, this force is inimical to man only so long as he misunderstands and misuses it. Rightly understood, it breaks down all structures of error, overthrows the false knowledge of separateness, and rids the personal mind of all delusion.

A ganglion in the sympathetic nervous system, at about the height in the body represented by the navel, is the great center of this power. By various practices devised at various times, such as those found in Yoga teaching and in the ceremonial magic of the Western occult school, this Mars force is brought under control. Used with understanding, its action in the brain awakens the Constituting Intelligence represented in Tarot by The Emperor. But ordinarily it is destructive; it is the force that brings about the physiological changes that result in physical death. An Ipsissimus has mastered this force. He has overcome the false knowledge of separateness, rooted in error and illusion. He is consciously immortal. He has identified the "I" in his own personality with the Universal Self. He no longer acts as a separate being. All that he thinks, all that he says, all that he does is understood by him as being the activity of the Universal Self.

5. JUSTICE
Key 11 (L)

An Ipsissimus is a perfectly poised personality. He has transmuted ambition entirely but works as do those who are ambitious. He has transmuted desire of life but respects life as do those who desire it. He has transmuted desire for comfort but is happier than those who live for happiness. His will is one with the Originating Will of the universe, and he shares the mastery of that Will over all things.

The Ipsissimus leads a life of perfect faith, in which belief and action are perfectly balanced. Subconsciously, he is one with the Law, and whatsoever he does is therefore a perfect expression of that Law.

6. THE FOOL
Key 0 (A)

The "Knower of Self" is the Mystical Fool of all sacred allegories. Nothing binds him. He is beyond every limitation of "this world." His motives and his actions are incomprehensible to the masses of merely natural men. Sometimes they worship him. Oftener they deride him. Always they fear him. His instruction they may grasp, so far as he makes it comprehensible to intellect, but the essence of the man eludes them. They who have attained to the highest Grade of the Invisible Order have few companions in the world, yet they are never lonely. They live in silent but vivid communication with each other, and they share in the bliss of the Heavenly vision. Their light shines in the darkness of the "false world," but that darkness cannot swallow it up.

AFTERWORD

CHAPTER XXII

THE INNER SCHOOL

SUBJECT HAVING SO MANY ramifications as this one could be expanded into a whole library of volumes the size of this, but I trust I have done what I set out to do, namely, to demonstrate that the original Rosicrucian documents are allegories of the unfoldment of the inner life of man, based on the Secret Wisdom of Israel, to which certain Hermetic elements have been added.

It is my hope that this book will serve still another purpose. During many years of occult research, I have often met men and women who were fully persuaded that they belonged to the "only true" Rosicrucian Order. Again and again I have seen them suffer bitter disillusionment, as they came to learn that what seemed to them to be the gold of pure truth was, at best, only the "fool's gold" of well-meant ignorance or, at worst, a gold brick of lying imposture.

I have long since given up any attempt to persuade such persons of their errors while they remain believers. But I have hopes that this book will do something to bring aid and comfort to the disillusioned, so that they may learn that after all there *is* a real Rosicrucian Fraternity, although it has never been organized as, for instance, the Masons are.

I have been careful to refrain from any direct attack on any specific Rosicrucian imposture, although there are in this present day a number of glaring instances that certainly tempt me. But I believe that even this mere outline of Rosicrucian teaching, based on indubitable sources, will do more to protect seekers for light against imposture than a whole series of exposures.

There is a Rosicrucian Order. And there are Rosicrucian societies that are undoubtedly in touch with that invisible Inner School. None of these societies, however, claims to be the Order itself, and none makes any particular pretension to antiquity, although some have been working for a relatively long period.

These organizations of occult students quietly carry on the work of initiation and instruction in various parts of the world. If you are duly and truly prepared, you will undoubtedly make contact with such schools in due season. Such contact, however, is invariably made through personal channels and not through advertising in the public press. If you meet a member of such a body of students, he will recognize your readiness for further instruction, and will make tests of your knowledge and understanding.

But if somebody all dressed up in gaudy regalia, publicly or semipublicly announcing himself to be the "Head" of the Rosicrucians, makes a bid for your allegiance or financial support, on your own head be it if you afterward go through a period of cruel disillusion, should you accept him as such.

I do not condemn such pretenders. They condemn themselves. Besides, I think I know why they are permitted to carry on their impostures. Above all, the practical occultist must develop the quality of discrimination, and they who lack it have to learn some bitter lessons. So also do those who, themselves disbelieving in spiritual verities, pretend to such belief in order to gain control of the lives and purses of their fellowmen. Their own want of discrimination is as great as that of those who are led astray by their claptrap. Sooner or later the frauds and their dupes will learn better. Meanwhile, be on your guard.

Seek only the highest. Remember the words of the original texts, quoted on page 23: "To the false and to imposters, and to those who seek other things than wisdom, we cannot be betrayed to our hurt." Here the word "wisdom" refers to the Qabalistic ChKMH, *Chokmah*, to which the Grade of Magus is attributed.

That Wisdom recognizes human personality as the vehicle of the real Self, a recognition that finds expression in the most careful direction of thought and speech (Ch, The Chariot). It is the grasp of the truth that all the details of personal action are really manifestations of the "wheels within wheels" of the cosmic cycles (K, The Wheel of Fortune). It is the reversal of most people's attitude toward life, expressed in a total self-surrender resulting in the perfect concentration and meditation, which Hindus term *Samadhi* (M, The Hanged Man).

Finally, it is the clear vision gained by union with the real Self, who is the ruler and Lord of all things (H, The Emperor). If this is what you seek, and you keep the flame of aspiration burning bright, doing all that you know how to perfect yourself in concentration and meditation, to the end that your personality may be unified with the cosmic life, you will progress steadily toward adeptship.

Of all descriptions of the Inner School that is the True and Invisible Rosicrucian Order, none better has been written than that contained in Karl von Eckhartshausen's *The Cloud Upon the Sanctuary*, from which I have condensed the following paragraphs.[1]

---

[1]Karl von Eckhartshausen, *The Cloud Upon the Santuary* (London: George Redway, 1896).

Sons of truth, there is but one Order, but one Brotherhood, but one association of men who are agreed in the sole object of acquiring light. From this center misunderstanding has brought forth innumerable orders, but all will return, from the multiplicity of opinions, to the only truth and to the true Order—the association of those who are able to receive the light, the Community of the Elect....

This community of light has existed since the first days of the world's creation, and its duration will be to the end of time. It is the society of those elect who know the Light in the Darkness and separate what is pure therein.

This community possesses a School, in which all who thirst for knowledge are instructed by the Spirit of Wisdom itself; and all the mysteries of God and of nature are preserved therein for the children of light. Perfect knowledge of God, of nature and of humanity are the objects of instruction in this school. It is thence that all truths penetrate into the world; herein is the School of the Prophets and of all who search for wisdom; it is in this community alone that truth and the explanation of all mystery is to be found. It is the most hidden of communities, yet it possesses members gathered from many orders; of such is this School....

This Sanctuary, composed of scattered members, but knit by the bonds of perfect unity and love [N.B. Eckhartshausen here gives a Qabalistic clue, for "unity" and "love" are AChD, *achad,* and AHBH, *ahebah,* and both are 13, or 5 plus 8], has been occupied from the earliest ages in building the grand Temple to the regeneration of humanity, by which the reign of God will be manifest. This society is in the communion of those who have the most capacity for light, i.e., the Elect....

It was formed immediately after the fall of man, and received from God at first-hand the revelation of those means by which fallen humanity could be again raised to its rights and delivered from the misery.[2]

But, when men multiplied, the frailty of man and his weakness necessitated an exterior society which veiled the interior one, and concealed the spirit and the truth in

[2]Compare this with the traditional account of the origin of the Qabalah and remember that a true Qabalist is one who is *receptive* to Light: "It received the key of true science, both divine and natural."

the latter. The people at large were not capable of compre-
hending high interior truth, and the danger would have
been too great in confiding that which was of all most
holy to incapable people. Therefore, inward truths were
wrapped in external and visible ceremonies, so that men,
by the perception of the outer, which is the symbol of
the interior, might by degrees be enabled to safely
approach the interior spiritual truths.

But the secret depository has always been confided
to him who in his day had the most capacity for
illumination, and he became the sole guardian of the
original Trust, as High Priest of the Sanctuary....

This interior community of light is the reunion of all
those capable of receiving light, the elect thereto; it is
known as the *Communion of Saints*. The primitive deposit of
all power and truth has been confided to it from all
time—it alone, says St. Paul, is the possession of the
science of the Saints. By it the agents of God were
formed in every age, passing from interior to the
exterior, and communicating spirit and life to the dead
letter—as already said.

This illuminated community has been through time
the true school of God's spirit, and considered as school,
it has its Chair, its Doctor, it possesses a rule for
students, it has forms and objects for study, and, in
short, a method by which they study. It has, also, its
degrees for successive development to higher altitudes....

This school of wisdom has been for ever most secretly
hidden from the world, because it is invisible and
submissive solely to Divine Government.

It has never been exposed to the accidents of time
and to the weakness of man, because only the most
capable were chosen for it, and the spirit which selected
could suffer no deception.

By this school were developed the germs of all the
sublime sciences, which were next received by external
schools, were then clothed in other forms, and in time
sometimes degenerated therein.

This society of sages communicated, according to
time and circumstances, unto the exterior societies their
symbolic hieroglyphs, in order to attract external man to
the great truths of the interior.

But all exterior societies subsist only in proportion
as this society communicates its spirit thereto. As soon
as external societies wish to be independent of the

interior one, and to transform a temple of wisdom into a political edifice, the interior retires and leaves only the letter without the spirit. It is thus that the secret external societies of wisdom were nothing but hieroglyphic screens, the truth remaining invariably without the sanctuary so that it might never be profaned.

In this interior society man finds wisdom and therewith the All—not the wisdom of this world, which is but scientific knowledge, which revolves round the outside but never touches the center (wherein is contained all power), but true wisdom and men obedient thereto.

All disputes, all controversies, all the things belonging to the false prudence of this world, fruitless discussions, useless germs of opinion which spread the weeds of disunion, all error, schisms and systems are banished therefrom. Neither calumny nor scandal are known. Every man is honored. Satire, that spirit which seeks diversion to the disadvantage of its neighbor, is unknown. Love alone reigns. Never does the monster of calumny rear among the sons of wisdom its serpent head; estimation in common prevails, and this only; the faults of a friend are passed over; there are no bitter reproaches heaped on imperfection. Generously and lovingly, the seeker is placed upon the way of truth. It is sought to persuade and touch the hearts of those who err, leaving the punishment of sin to the Lords of Light.

Want and feebleness are protected; rejoicings are made at the elevation and dignity which man acquires. No one is raised above another by the fortune which is the gift of chance; he only counts himself most happy who has the opportunity to benefit his brethren; and all such men, united in the spirit of love and truth, constitute the Invisible Church, the society of the Kingdom within, under that one Chief who is God.

We must not, however, imagine that this society resembles any secret order, meeting at certain times, choosing its leaders and members, united by special objects. All associations, be these what they may, can but come after this interior illuminated circle, which society knows none of the formalities belonging to the outer rings, the work of man. In this kingdom of power the outward forms cease.

God Himself is the Power always present. The best man of his times, the chief himself, does not invariably know all the members, but the moment when it is the Will of God that they should be brought into communication he finds them unfailingly in the world and ready to work for the end in view.

This community has no outside barriers. He who may be chosen by God is as the first; he presents himself among the others without presumption, and he is received by them without jealousy.

If it be necessary that true members should meet together, they find and recognize each other with perfect certainty. No disguise can be used, neither hypocrisy nor dissimulation could hide the characteristic qualities of this society, because they are too genuine. All illusion is gone, and things appear in their true form.

No one member can choose another, unanimous choice is required. All men are called, the called may be chosen, if they become ripe for entrance.

Any one can look for entrance, and any man who is within can teach another to seek for it; but only he who is ripe can arrive inside. Unprepared men occasion disorder in a community, and disorder is not compatible with the Sanctuary. This thrusts out all who are not homogeneous. Worldly intelligence seeks this Sanctuary in vain; in vain also do the efforts of malice strive to penetrate these great mysteries; all is undecipherable to him who is not prepared; he can see nothing, read nothing in the interior.

He who is ripe is joined to the chain, perhaps often where he thought least likely, and at a point of which he knew nothing himself. Seeking to become ripe should be the effort of him who loves wisdom.

But there are methods by which ripeness is attained, for in this holy communion is the primitive storehouse of the most ancient and original science of the human race, with the primitive mysteries also of all science. It is the unique and really illuminated community which is in possession of the key to all mystery, which knows the centre and source of nature and creation. It is a society which unites superior power to its own, and includes members from more than one world. It is the society whose members form a theocratic republic, which one day will be the Regent Mother of the whole World.

May this outline of its constitution and degrees, and this explanation of the Way of Return, which leads at length to illumination, be the means of encouraging you to persevere in the Great Work whose fruit is the "ripeness" of which Eckhartshausen speaks. This book has come to you because you are already among those who are called. My best wish for you is that as a result of reading it, you may come to be numbered among the chosen.

INDEX

Luke, St., 56, 59
Lully, Raymond, 30, 112
Lumen de Lumine, 108, 109n.1
Luminous Intelligence, 109, 285, 288, 290; *see also* Daleth
Luther, Martin, 58
Lutheranism, 43, 110, 143, 144, 147
Lytton, Sir Edward Bulwer, 291n.3

M

M.P., Brother, 16
Mackey, Albert G., 47n.4
macrocosm, 80, 121, 132, 140, 183, 184, 201
Macroprosopus, 213; *see also* Greater Countenance
Magi, 284, 296, 297; *see also* Magus
Magic, 8, 9, 83, 84, 129, 140, 198, 224, 261, 273, 278, 284, 292, 293, 295, 307
Magical Language, 11, 24, 32, 90; *see also* Gematria
Magician, The, 94, 170, 171, 187, 188, 233, 247, 267, 274, 275, 278, 279, 297; *see also* Beth; Mercury
Magister Templi, 156 tab.4, 157 fig.7, 271, 277, 278, 279, 283
Magnum Opus, 112, 137, 295; *see also* Great Work
Magus, 156 tab.4, 283, 284, 285, 286, 287, 288, 289, 292, 293, 294, 295, 296, 298, 300, 301, 302, 303, 312
Mahatma Letters to A.P. Sinnet, The, 92, 146, 146n.3
Maier, Michael, 36
male, 49, 51, 80, 245
Malkuth, 127, 159, 162, 165, 213, 304; *see also* Kingdom
Man, 285
manifestoes, 41, 45, 58, 64, 65, 69, 74, 86, 88, 110, 111, 128, 142, 143, 145, 147, 150, 155, 159, 165, 206, 223, 244, 247; *see also* Fama; Confessio
Mark, St., 56
Mars, 42, 127, 128 tab.3, 172, 244, 257, 263, 274, 275, 307, 308; *see also* Peh; Tower
Mary, 57
Masonic, 29, 30, 47, 58, 61, 63, 70, 88, 94, 118, 124, 133, 141, 214, 225, 311; *see also* Freemasonry
Master of the Temple, 251, 272, 274, 277, 278, 279, 280, 281, 282, 284, 285, 286, 289, 290, 301, 302; *see also* Magister Templi
Master of the Wisdom, 291
Masters, 60, 75, 76, 77, 82, 90, 99, 193, 239, 290, 291
materialism, 84, 89, 120, 147, 149, 235, 307
Mathematics, 7, 8, 10, 66, 75, 78, 83, 90, 110, 162, 215
Mathers, S.L. MacGregor, 79n.7
Matthew, St., 56, 57, 249
Maya-shakti, 115
Measuring Intelligence, 221, 253; *see also* Chesed; Receptacular Intelligence
Mediating Influence, Intelligence of, 213, 218, 228, 302; *see also* Tiphareth; Beauty
Medicine, 7, 8, 20, 25, 31, 38, 58, 71, 75, 83, 151

Meditation, 199, 207, 211, 260, 290, 299, 312
Mediterranean Sea, 8, 69, 70, 83
medulla oblongata, 198
Melchizedek, 141
Melek, 107, 213; *see also* Tiphareth
Mem, 49, 193, 237, 238, 239, 240, 241, 303; *see also* Water; Hanged Man
Memorial Table, 13, 107, 109
Mercury, 38, 40, 41, 48, 49, 71, 83, 94, 108, 127, 128 tab.3, 172, 187, 190, 275; *see also* Sulphur; Salt; Alchemy; Beth
Mercy, 116, 156 tab.4, 157 fig.7, 188, 221, 253, 266, 288; *see also* Chesed
Messiah, 39, 148, 173, 215; *see also* Christ
metals, 17, 25, 29, 70, 95, 127, 128, 172
metaphysical, 120, 121, 258, 259
metaphysics, 258
Meung, Jean de, 106
Mezla, 85; *see also* Holy Influence
microcosm, 32, 70, 83, 120, 121, 132, 140, 183, 184, 185, 201, 227
Microcosmus, 7, 20, 31, 32, 108
Microprosopus, 107, 108, 117, 140, 213
Middle Pillar, 46
mind-stuff, 290
mineral, 52
Minitum Mundum, 16, 132
Mirandola, John Picus de, 30
Modern Reader's Bible, 56, 56n.8
Mohammed, 11, 20, 71, 146
money, 73
Moon, 48, 49, 70, 71, 79, 94, 107, 108, 119, 127, 128 tab.3, 172, 183, 184, 245, 272, 275, 300; *see also* Gimel; High Priestess; Silver
Moon, The, 92, 93, 281, 286; *see also* Qoph; Pisces
Moses, 17, 31, 41, 44, 49, 50, 51, 52, 110, 111, 117, 124, 125, 130, 215
Mother, 46, 47, 49, 52, 57, 62, 79, 115, 213, 243, 289, 301, 316; *see also* Aima; Binah
Moulton, Richard Green, 56, 56n.8
mountain, 55, 108, 177, 263
multiplication, 108, 223, 241
Myer, Isaac, 112, 112n.2
Mysteries of Magic, The, 112n.3, 140n.7, 192n.1-2, 284n.1, 289n.2
mystery, 32, 41, 42, 45, 53, 69, 108, 119, 120, 123, 130, 132, 140, 144, 145, 148, 162, 163, 167, 168, 174, 211, 224, 225, 287, 313, 316
Mystical Intelligence, 305; *see also* Kether; Crown

N

N.N., Brother, 13, 105, 106, 107, 113
Nachash, 173, 215; *see also* Serpent
Nail, 13, 107, 108, 109, 110, 149; *see also* Vav
Name of Names, 45, 51, 92, 107
Natural Intelligence, 199; *see also* Tzaddi; Star; Aquarius

ABOUT THE AUTHOR

To portray Paul Foster Case is to attempt to describe the great spiritual teachers and messengers who have from time to time walked the earth throughout recorded history. A vast and eternal Being looked out from behind his eyes, bringing gifts which neither moths nor rust can corrupt. His erudite scholarship, piercing and discriminating mentality, and direct spiritual perception were a rare combination. Yet his humanness expressed itself in wit, humor and complete compatibility with people of all social classes, races and creeds.

As a precocious child, he was an avid reader, had unusual musical talent, discovered he could consciously manipulate his dream states, and experienced supersensory states of consciousness. At nine, he carried on a correspondence with Rudyard Kipling who assured him of the reality of these inner awarenesses. As a result of his contact with Claude Bragdon at age sixteen, he discovered that playing cards were descendants of Tarot, originally called the Game of Man. Thenceforward, he collected every book about Tarot and set of Keys available. Year after year, he poured over these Archetypal Images of Power, researching, delving, studying, meditating. He began to hear a Voice guiding him in his researches. The stimulus of Tarot had opened up his Inner Hearing to the highest spiritual levels, for the Voice never interfered with his personal life, never flattered, never gave orders.

His research inevitably led him also to Qabalah, the "Secret Wisdom of Israel," which he found he "already knew." He did not have to study the Hebrew-Chaldean Script, for he "remembered" it. Immersing himself in Tarot and Qabalah was really like a review, preliminary to some greater Work.

Eventually he was given a choice between a relatively easy incarnation and successful musical career, and the harder way of full dedication to the service of humanity. His decision is apparent, and let it be known that all the difficulties of which he had been forewarned did become a part of the sacrifice he willingly made. Through personal contact, the Master whose Voice had become familiar to him years before suggested he form a new outer vehicle for the dissemination of the Mystery Teachings. Builders of the Adytum was established, making available in written form teachings which in the past had been, for the most part, an oral tradition. He became a prolific writer and enthralling speaker, able to draw from the riches of the Higher Self because he shared them so generously.

He more than fulfilled his mission to translate the techniques of Tarot and Qabalah into terms understandable to the modern mind, and to extend the teachings of Ageless Wisdom. Because of his dedication, aspirants will have available a thoroughly tested and true method for travelling the Path of Spiritual Return to the Most High.